The Black Resource Guide

10th Edition

70463

Published by

R. Benjamin and Jacqueline L. Johnson

Washington, D.C.

Copyright ©

All Rights Reserved

BLACK RESOURCE GUIDE
1993-94
Tenth Edition

No part of this book may be reproduced in any form, by photostat, microfilm, xerography or any other means, or incorporated into any information retrieval system, electronic or mechanical, without the written permission of the copyright owner.

Library of Congress Catalog Card No. 85-91077
ISBN 0-9608374-8-5

Price $69.95

Preface

The Black Resource Guide is the leading national black directory in America. It was designed to inform the networking public of key African American individuals and organizations in the United States. This important reference book was first published in 1981 to fill a need between cheaply produced black directories on the one hand, and unworkable compilations on the other. The Black Resource Guide is a very attractive directory, with a modest layout and an easy-to-use style.

This edition features several important new categories, including sections on African-American sports agents, union officials, and sources of scholarship assistance to needy students. Our subscribers have found previous editions to be enormously valuable in wide ranging African American applications.

The Black Resource Guide gives subscribers immediate access to African-American power centers in the United States. With just a flip of a page, this much sought after reference book allows you to network with thousands of key African-Americans nationwide. Regardless of who they are, if they are important African Americans . . . most are likely to be listed in this national directory.

Finally, this important directory is not meant to collect dust on your book shelf. Networking in the national black community always leads to positive results. We hope that our subscribers will continue using The Black Resource Guide to fulfill their networking needs.

R. Benjamin and Jacqueline Johnson
Publishers

Table of Contents

Accounting Firms

This section contains a partial listing of accounting firms with roots in black and minority communities across the U.S.

ALABAMA

SMITH & ASSOCIATES
1167 Old Montgomery Road
Tuskegee, AL 36088
Harvey L. Smith, President
(205) 727-6130

JENKINS & JENKINS
529 South Perry Street, Suite 16
Montgomery, AL 36104
Frank A. Jenkins, Managing Partner
(205) 834-6086

CALIFORNIA

COLEMAN & COLEMAN, CPA'S
1000 Corporate Pointe
Suite 103
Culver City, CA 90230
Kevin M. Coleman, Contact
(213) 215-3500

GRANT & SMITH
1535 East Oliver, Suite A
Fresno, CA 93728
Ralph Grant, Contact
(209) 266-6738

GRANT & SMITH, CPA'S
505 14th Street
Suite 950
Oakland, CA 94612
Ralph Grant, Contact
(510) 832-0257

**CLINTON, PEER ACCOUN-
TANCY CORP.**
Certified Public Accountants
Koll Center One, Suite 450
226 Airport Parkway
San Jose, CA 95110
Carver L. Clinton, President
(408) 453-2525

WILLIAM D. COLLINS, CPA
3741 Stocker, Suite 105
Los Angeles, CA 90008
(213) 295-4405

MORRIS, DAVIS & COMPANY
7700 Edgewater Drive, Suite 320
Oakland, CA 94621
Herman Morris, Contact
(510) 430-3077

GWENDOLYN D. SKILLERN, CPA
1611 Telegraph Avenue, Suite 1030
Oakland, CA 94612
(510) 763-6985

DONALD R. WHITE, CPA
505 Fourteenth Street, Suite 950
Oakland, CA 94612
(510) 832-2008

WILLIAMS, ADLEY & COMPANY
1330 Broadway
Suite 1825
Oakland, CA 94612
Tom W. Williams, Jr., Contact
(510) 893-8114

TEMPLE & TEMPLE, CPA'S
9465 Wilshire Boulevard
Suite 844
Beverly Hills, CA 90212
John Temple, Owner
(213) 278-4051

Accounting Firms

DISTRICT OF COLUMBIA

F.S. TAYLOR & ASSOCIATES, P.C.
801 Pennsylvania Ave., S.E., Suite 250
Washington, D.C. 20003
Frank S. Taylor, President
(202) 547-4700

JACK MARTIN & COMPANY, P.C.
One Thomas Circle, N.W.
Suite 1150
Washington, D.C. 20005
Jack Martin, President
(202) 371-8270

LUCAS, TUCKER & COMPANY, CPA'S
733 15th Street, N.W.
Suite 1150
Washington, D.C. 20005
Olive Walcott, Contact
(202) 371-8270

MITCHELL, TITUS & COMPANY
1825 K Street, N.W., Suite 115
Washington, D.C. 20006
Robert P. Titus, Contact
(202) 293-7500

BERT W. SMITH, JR. COMPANY, CHARTERED
201 Kennedy Street, N.W.
Washington, D.C. 20011
George Willie, Contact
(202) 291-6661

THOMPSON, CURTIS, BAZILIO ASSOCIATES, P.C.
1010 Vermont Avenue, N.W.
Suite 300
Washington, D.C. 20005
Jeff Thompson, Contact
(202) 737-3300

DAVIS, GRAVES, LIVINGSTON, CPA'S
1511 K Street, N.W.
Suite 740
Washington, D.C. 20005
Walter Davis, Contact
(202) 347-9244

THE MC MILLIAN GROUP
1225 Eye Street, N.W.
Suite 850
Washington, D.C. 20085
Jimmy McMillian, Contact
(202) 371-1133

WALKER & COMPANY, CPA'S
1800 K Street, N.W.
Suite 801
Washington, D.C. 20006
Jacqueline G. Walker, Contact
(202) 429-4568

WATSON, RICE & COMPANY
1110 Vermont Avenue, N.W.
Washington, D.C. 20005
Carmen Jones, Contact
(202) 628-0833

WILLIAMS, ADLEY & COMPANY
1000 Vermont Avenue, N.W.
Suite 610
Washington, D.C. 20005
Henry Adley, Contact
(202) 371-1397

FLORIDA

SHAUN M. DAVIS, CPA
5042 Pembroke Road
Hollywood, FL 33021
Shaun M. Davis, Contact
(305) 966-1328

Accounting Firms

W.B. KOON & COMPANY
540 N.W. 165th Street Road
Room 209
North Miami Beach, FL 33169
W. B. Koon, Owner
(305) 948-6201

GEORGIA

**BANKS, FINLEY, WHITE &
  COMPANY**
3504 East Main Street
College Pard, GA 30337
Gregory Ellison, Contact
(404) 659-7470

**W. E. RICHARDSON &
  ASSOCIATES**
46 Jeptha Street, S.W.
Atlanta, GA 30314
Dr. W.E. Richardson, Jr., Owner
(404) 755-2552

ILLINOIS

BOLLING & HILL, CPA'S
8527 Stoney Island
Chicago, IL 60617
Howard Hill, Contact
(312) 734-7133

CECIL B. LUCY
555 West Jackson Blvd., Suite 300
Chicago, IL 60606
(312) 922-2079

JONES, ANDERSON & ROGERS
471 East 31st Street
Chicago, IL 60616
Clifton Rogers, Managing Partner
(312) 842-2900

**WASHINGTON, PITTMAN &
  MCKEEVER**
819 South Wabash Ave., Suite 600
Chicago, IL 60605
Lester McKeever, Managing Partner
(312) 786-0330

JAMES WILLIAMS & COMPANY
8 South Michigan Avenue, Suite 1520
Chicago, IL 60603
John Williams, Owner
(312) 346-8883

KANSAS

**RALPH C. JOHNSON &
  COMPANY**
825 North 7th Street, Suite 500
Kansas City, KS 66101-3040
Ralph C. Johnson, Contact
(913) 281-4466

LOUISIANA

BRUNO, TERVALON, CPAS
650 South Pierce, Suite 203
New Orleans, LA 70119
Michael Bruno, Managing Partner
(504) 482-8733

RABB & MICHEL
1683 North Claborne Avenue
New Orleans, LA 70116
George Rabb, Managing Partner
(504) 943-0675

The listings in this directory are available as Mailing Labels. See last page for details.

Accounting Firms

MARYLAND

ABRAMS, FOSTER, NOTE & WILLIAMS, CPAS
The Village of Cross Keys
The Quadrangle, Suite 272B
Baltimore, MD 21210
Gerald Abrams, Contact
(410) 433-6830

ANDERSON & ASSOCIATES
7203 C Hanover Parkway
Greenbelt, MD 20770-2000
Lloyd G. Anderson, Contact
(301) 220-3086

BENNETT, HUFF & COMPANY
10408 Little Patuxent Pkwy., Suite 300
Columbia, MD 21044
Charles Bennett, Contact
(301) 730-1429

COWAN & ASSOCIATES
3306 Shortridge Road
Mitchellville, MD 20721
Ernest E. Cowan, President
(301) 390-4437

DEATRICE RUSSELL & ASSOCIATES
12621 MacDuff Drive
Fort Washington, MD 20744
Deatrice D. Russell, Contact
(410) 292-0500

TAYLOR & JENNINGS
11 East Mt. Royal Avenue
Baltimore, MD 21202
LeRoy C. Taylor, President
(301) 685-4210

BENJAMIN L. KING, CPA
4804 York Road
Baltimore, MD 21212
(410) 685-4210

BRUCE D. ROYSTER, CPA
2901 Druid Park Dr., Suite 303 B & C
Baltimore, MD 21215
Bruce D. Royster, Contact
(410) 669-6033

MASSACHUSETTS

DANIEL DENNIS & COMPANY
100 Huntington Avenue
Copley Place, Suite 37
Boston, MA 02116
Daniel Dennis, Contact
(617) 262-9898

MICHIGAN

MARIO J. DANIELS & ASSOCIATES, P.C.
432 North Saginaw, Suite 404
Flint, MI 48502
Mario J. Daniels, Contact
(313) 232-1551

BARROW, ALDRIDGE & COMPANY
719 Griswold, Suite 1700
Detroit, MI 48226
Thomas J. Barrow, Managing Partner
(313) 963-3300

DAVIS, MONJOY & COMPANY
20131 James Couzens Drive, Suite 12
Detroit, MI 48235
Milton Monjoy, President

JACK MARTIN & COMPANY, P.C.
30150 Telegraph Road
Suite 155
Birmingham, MI 48010
Jack Martin, Managing Partner
(313) 645-5370

Accounting Firms

JACK MARTIN & COMPANY, P.C.
2080 Penobscot Building
Detroit, MI 48226.
Jack Martin, Managing Partner
(313) 964-1370

MINNESOTA

ROGERS, HAYES & COMPANY, CPA'S
1421 Park Avenue
Suite 204
.Minneapolis, MN 55404
O. Barry Rogers, Contact
(612) 332-1906

MISSOURI

RAY, JACKSON AND ASSOCIATES
1734 East 63rd Street
Kansas City, MO 64110
Linda Jackson, Managing Partner
(816) 363-2020

SELLERS & COMPANY, CPA'S
2300 Main, Suite 790
Kansas City, MO 64108
Wayne Sellers, Managing Partner
(816) 842-6190

CHARLES A. STEWART, JR., CPA
1010 Market Street
Suite 1710
St. Louis, MO 63101
Charles A. Stewart, Contact
(314) 444-6750

NEW JERSEY

FRYE, WILLIAM & COMPANY, PA, CPA
43 Halsey Street
Newark, NJ 07102-3030
Walter K. Frye, Contact
(201) 643-3236

YOUR ACCOUNTANT OF NEW JERSEY, INC.
255 Route 3 East
Suite 201
Secaucus, NJ 07094
Brenda Weathers, President
(201) 866-5122

NEW YORK

MICHAEL LEE & COMPANY, CPA
60 East 86th Street
New York, NY 10028
Michael Lee, Managing Partner
(212) 879-7500

STARNES & TANKSLEY, CPA'S
98 Fort Greene Place
Brooklyn, NY 11217
Kenneth Starnes, Contact
(718) 852-0707

WATSON, RICE & COMPANY
246 Fifth Avenue
New York, NY 10001
Bennie L. Hadnott, Contact
(212) 447-7300

HERMAN JOHNSON, CPA
1210 Fulton Street
Brooklyn, NY 11216
Herman Johnson, Owner
(718) 622-6876

Accounting Firms

LUCAS, TUCKER & COMPANY
26 Broadway, Suite 524
New York, NY 10004
Oliver Walcott, Managing Partner
(212) 425-9000

MITCHELL, TITUS & COMPANY
One Battery Park Plaza
New York, NY 10004
Bert Mitchell, Contact
(212) 709-4500

NORTH CAROLINA

**DAVIS MANAGEMENT
SERVICES**
1334 North Patterson Avenue
Winston-Salem, NC 27105
Richard N. Davis, Contact
(919) 723-2015

OLIVER W. BOWIE, CPA
1020 East Wendover Ave., Suite 104
Greensboro, NC 27405
Oliver Bowie, Owner
(919) 273-9461

**GARRETT AND DAVENPORT,
CPA, PC**
5 West Hargett St., Suite 401
P.O. Box 989
Raleigh, NC 27602
Walter Davenport, CPA, President

BOBBY MARTIN, CPA
700 East Stonewall St., Suite 665
Charlotte, NC 28202
Bobby Martin, CPA, Owner
(704) 375-7361

OHIO

**DAVIS L. JONES & COMPANY,
INC.**
1342 West Third Street
Dayton, OH 45407
(513) 222-4352

PHILLIPS, HARRIS & COMPANY
17 South High Street, Suite 1060
Columbus, OH 43215
C. Michael Harris and Robert Phillips
  Principals
(614) 464-2727

**WRIGHT, RICHARDSON &
COMPANY, INC.**
13855 Superior Road, Suite 1901
East Cleveland, OH 44118
John R. Wright, Contact
(216) 397-0099

PENNSYLVANIA

TERRY & STEPHENSON, P.C.
Allegheny Building
Suite 1600
429 Forbes Avenue
Pittsburgh, PA 15219
Samuel J. Stephenson, Contact

SOUTH CAROLINA

T.R. MCCONNELL & COMPANY
1545 Sumter Street
Suite 200
Columbia, SC 29201
Virgil Reginald McConnell, Contact
(803) 799-1929

Accounting Firms

TENNESSEE

BANKS, FINLEY, WHITE & CO., P.C. OF TENNESSEE
346 South Main
Memphis, TN 38103
Stanley B. Sawyer, President
(901) 526-1327

BRANDON, SMITH & JONES, CPAS
100 North Main Building
Suite 1210
Memphis, TN 38103
Ernest Jones, Jr., Managing Partner
(901) 526-5956

HOSKINS-VANCE & COMPANY
1314 Fifth Avenue, North
Suite 100
Nashville, TN 37208
Harvey E. Hoskins, Contact
(615) 244-2727

FLOYD E. MILLER
508 Franklin Street
Clarksville, TN 37040
Floyd E. Miller, Contact
(615) 552-0166

BOBBIE O. RANCHER, CPA
9040 Executive Park Drive, Suite 370
Knoxville, TN 37923
Bobbie O. Rancher, Contact
(615) 531-0090

TATE & JENKINS, CPAS
233 Martin Luther King, Jr. Blvd.
Suite 100
Chattanooga, TN 37401
David A. Jenkins, Contact
(615) 756-4724

TEXAS

J. L. JOVIET & COMPANY
2626 South Loop West, Suite 270
Houston, TX 77054
A. R. Morrison, CPA, Contact
(713) 666-0609

J. L. JOVIET & COMPANY
3300 Eastex Freeway
P.O. Box 21264
Houston, TX 77226
J. L. Joviet, Sr., Contact
(713) 222-8660

DAVIS, GRAVES, LIVINGTON, CPAS
4500 Bissonnet at Newcastle
Suite 340
P.O. Box 270985
Houston, TX 77277-9998
Walter D. Davis, Contact
(713) 667-8600

JOHN L. GREEN, CPA
4848 Loop Central Drive, Suite 960
Houston, TX 77801
John Green, Contact
(713) 660-7400

CALVIN E. PERSON & ASSOCIATES
6200 North Central Expressway
Suite 222
Dallas, TX 75206
Calvin Person, Contact
(214) 739-3996

EMMA S. WALKER, CPA
600 Texas Street
Fort Worth, TX 76102
(817) 332-3049

Accounting Firms

VIRGINIA

A. G. REESE & ASSOCIATES, P.C.
515 North Third Street
Richmond, VA 23219
Alan Reese, Contact
(804) 649-3300

WASHINGTON

BRANCH, RICHARDS, ANDERSON & COMPANY, P.S.
2201 Sixth Avenue, Suite 1009
Seattle, WA 98121-1899
Andrew L. Branch, Contact
(206) 624-4723

FRANCIS & COMPANY
701 Dexter Avenue, North, Suite 404
Seattle, WA 98109
Horace C. Francis, Contact
(206) 282-3949

PEOPLES & ASSOCIATES
2301 South Jackson, Suite 104
Seattle, WA 98144
Reed Peoples, Contact
(206) 325-8007

GEORGE A. STEWART, CPA
1120 East Terrace
Suite 300
Seattle, WA 982122
George Stewart, Contact
(206) 328-8554

WISCONSIN

COLEMAN & WILLIAMS, LTD.
316 North Milwaukee Street
Suite 350
Milwaukee, WI 53202
William B. Coleman, Contact
(414) 278-0170

M. L. THARPES & ASSOCIATES
1845 Farwell Avenue
Suite 310-A
Milwaukee, WI 53202
M. L. Tharpes, Contact
(414) 278-8532

The listings in this directory are available as Mailing Labels. See last page for details.

Adoption Agencies and Services

The organizations listed in this section are directly involved in adoption assistance aimed at black youth. Because of their efforts, barriers that previously discouraged potential adopters are being removed.

ALABAMA

ONE CHURCH ONE CHILD PROGRAM
Old Ship of Zion, A.M.E.
483 Holcombe Street
Montgomery, AL 36104
Rev. Curtis Walker
(205) 262-3922

ARKANSAS

BLACK FAMILY OUTREACH ADOPTION UNIT
Central Baptist Professional Building
1700 West 13th Street, Sixth Floor
Little Rock, AR 72202
Gloria Aboagye, Director
(501) 371-5526

CALIFORNIA

BLACK ADOPTION PLACEMENT & RESEARCH CENTER
505 15th Street, Suite 200
Oakland, CA 94612
Pat Reynolds, Director
(415) 839-3678

INSTITUTE FOR BLACK PARENTING
7100 South Western Avenue
Los Angeles, CA 90047
Zena F. Oglesby, Jr., Director
(213) 752-0223

OPEN ARMS ADOPTION PROJECT
P.O. Box 15254
San Francisco, CA 94115

COLORADO

PEOPLE OF COLOR LEADER-SHIP INSTITUTE
American Association for Protecting Children
63 Inverness Drive, East
Englewood, CO 80112-5117
(303) 792-9900

CONNECTICUT

HIGHLAND HEIGHTS
St. Francis Home for Children, Inc.
651 Prospect Street, Box 1224
New Haven, CT 06505
Sister Mary Frances McMahon, Director
(203) 777-5513

HALL NEIGHBORHOOD HOUSE
52 Green Street
Bridgeport, CT 06608
Marilyn Lewis, Director
(203) 334-3900

Adoption Agencies and Services

SMALL BLACK FAMILY ADOPTION PROGRAM

Highland Heights - P.O. Box 1224
New Haven, CT 06450
(203) 777-5513

DELAWARE

ADOPTIVE FAMILIES WITH INFORMATION & SUPPORT

2610 Northgate Road
Wilmington, DE 19810
Mary Lou Edgar, Contact
(302) 475-1027

BLACK ADOPTIVE RECRUITERS

1825 Faulkland Road
Wilmington, DE 19805
Jane Hovington, Contact
(302) 856-6534

DISTRICT OF COLUMBIA

NATIONAL ADOPTION INFORMATION CLEARINGHOUSE

1400 Eye Street, N.W., Suite 600
Washington, D.C. 20005
Ruth Hubbell, Director
(301) 231-7541

ASSOCIATED CATHOLIC CHARITIES, INC.

1438 Rhode Island Avenue, N.E.
Washington, D.C. 20018
Rev. Msgr. James F. Montgomery
(202) 526-4100

THE BARKER FOUNDATION, INC.

4114 River Road, N.W.
Washington, D.C. 20015
Robin Allen, Director
(202) 363-7751

FAMILY AND CHILD SERVICES, INC.

Homes for Black Children
929 L Street, N.W.
Washington, D.C. 20001
Mae Best, Director
(202) 289-1510

CHILDREN'S ADOPTION RESOURCE EXCHANGE

1039 Evarts Street, N.E.
Washington, D.C. 20017
Gloria Swieringa, Director
(202) 526-5200

BLACK ADOPTIVE PARENTS SUPPORT INFORMATION GROUP

1353 H Street, N.E.
Washington, D.C. 20002
Pat Jacobs, Contact
(202) 399-9266

GEORGIA

FAMILIES FIRST

1105 West Peachtree Street, N.E.
Atlanta, GA 30309
(404) 853-2800

The listings in this directory are available as Mailing Labels. See last page.

Adoption Agencies and Services

ILLINOIS

CHILDREN'S HOME AND AID SOCIETY
1122 North Dearborn
Chicago, IL 60610
(312) 238-3203

BENSENVILLE HOME SOCIETY
331 South York Road
Bensenville, IL 60106

CATHOLIC CHARITIES
126 North Desplaines
Chicago, IL 60606
(312) 236-5162

CENTRAL BAPTIST FAMILY SERVICES
201 North Wells
Chicago, IL 60606
(312) 782-0874

CHICAGO CHILD CARE SOCIETY
5467 University Avenue
Chicago, IL 60615
(312) 643-0452

CHILDREN'S HOME AND AID SOCIETY OF ILLINOIS
2151 West 95th Street
Chicago, IL 60643
Edwin Millard, President

EVANGELICAL CHILD AND FAMILY AGENCY
1530 North Main
Wheaton, IL 60187
(312) 653-6400

ADOPTION FAMILY DEVELOP-MENT UNIT
950 East 61st Street
Chicago, IL 60637
(312) 947-3528

LUTHERAN CHILD AND FAMILY SERVICES
7620 Madison Street
P.O. Box 78
River Forest, IL 60305
(312) 771-7180

ILLINOIS PARENTS FOR BLACK ADOPTIONS
7930 Drucilla Fair
Chicago, IL 60617
(312) 734-2305

INDIANA

HOMES FOR BLACK CHILDREN
3131 East 38th Street
Indianapolis, IN 46218
(317) 875-7066

BLACK ADOPTION COMMITTEE
1631 Kessler Boulevard
Indianapolis, IN 46208

AMERICANS FOR AFRICAN ADOPTIONS
8910 Timberwood Drive
Indianapolis, IN 46234
(314) 271-4567

KANSAS

ADOPTION FOR BLACK CHILDREN
1855 North Hillside
Wichita, KS 67214
(316) 776-4622

BLACK ADOPTION PROGRAM & SERVICES
Gateway Centre II, Suite 729
Fourth & State Avenue
P.O. Box 17-1273
Kansas City, KS 66117

Adoption Agencies and Services

LUTHERAN SOCIAL SERVICES
1855 North Hillside
Wichita, KS 67214
(316) 686-664

MARYLAND

CONCERNED CITIZENS FOR BLACK ADOPTIONS
1009 Reddick Drive
Silver Spring, MD 20901

NATIONAL ADOPTION INFORMATION CLEARINGHOUSE
11426 Rockville Pike
Suite 410
Rockville, MD 20852
Debrah Smith, Director
(301) 231-6512

MICHIGAN

ALTERNATIVES FOR CHILDREN AND FAMILIES
644 Harison
Flint, MI 48502
(313) 235-0638

BETHAN CHRISTIAN SERVICES
905 Eastern, N.E.
Grand Rapids, MI 49503
(616) 459-6273

BLACK FAMILY REGISTRY
17390 West Eight Mile Road
Southfield, MI 48075
Nadirah Abdul, Registry Coordinator
(313) 443-0300

D.A. BLODGETT SERVICES FOR CHILDREN & FAMILIES
805 Leonard, N.E.
Grand Rapids, MI 49503
George Washburn, Executive Director
(616) 451-2021

CATHOLIC SOCIAL SERVICES - WAYNE COUNTY
9751 Hamilton
Detroit, MI 48202
(313) 883-2100

CHILDREN'S AID SOCIETY
7700 Second
Detroit, MI 48202
(313) 874-9495

EVERGREEN CHILDREN'S SERVICES
21500 Greenfield
Oak Park, MI 48237
(313) 968-1416

ENNIS AND ASSOCIATES
20100 Greenfield
Detroit, MI 48235
Robert E. Ennis, Executive Director
(313) 342-2699

HOMES FOR BLACK CHILDREN
2340 Clavert
Detroit, MI 48202
(303) 869-2316

MACOMB DEPARTMENT OF SOCIAL SERVICES
21885 Dunham
Mt. Clemens, MI 48043
(313) 469-6759

Adoption Agencies and Services

METHODIST CHILDREN'S HOME
26645 West Six Mile Road
Detroit, MI 48240
(313) 531-4060

MICHIGAN HUMAN SERVICES
15160 West Eight Mile Rd., Suite 200
Detroit, MI 48237

**ORCHARDS CHILDREN'S
SERVICES**
30215 Southfield
Southfield, MI 48076
Gerald Levine, Chief Executive
(313) 433-8600

SPAULDING FOR CHILDREN
800 Livernois
Ferndale, MI 48220
(313) 544-0850

YOUTH LIVING CENTER
715 South Inkster
Inkster, MI 48141

MINNESOTA

**COALITION ON PERMANENTS
FOR CHILDREN**
P.O. Box 35722
Minneapolis, MN 55435
Judith Anderson
(612) 941-5146

*The listings in this directory
are available as Mailing Labels.
See last page for details.*

MISSOURI

**FAMILY AND CHILDREN
SERVICES**
2650 Olive Street
St. Louis, MO 63103
(314) 371-6500

NEBRASKA

**BLACK HOMES FOR BLACK
CHILDREN**
115 South 46th Street
Omaha, NE 68132
(405) 592-2912

NEW JERSEY

**BLACK ADOPTION CONSOR-
TIUM**
5090 Central Highway
Suite 6
Pennsauken, NJ 08109
(800) 552-0222

SPAULDING FOR CHILDEN
36 Prospect Street
Westfield, NJ 07090
(201) 233-2282

NEW YORK

**NATIONAL ASSOCIATION OF
BLACK SOCIAL WORKERS
CHILD ADOPTION**
271 West 125th Street
New York, NY 13205
(212) 222-5200

Adoption Agencies and Services

COMMITTED PARENT FOR BLACK ADOPTION
c/o ABSW
271 West 125th Street, Suite 414
New York, NY 10027
(212) 222-5200

BLACK HOMES FOR BLACK CHILDREN
Main Post Office Box 2193
Niagara Falls, New York, 14302
(716) 282-4471

NEW LIFE FOR BLACK CHILDREN
P.O. Box 11164
Rochester, NY 14611
(716) 436-6075

NORTH CAROLINA

CHILDRENS HOME SOCIETY OF NORTH CAROLINA, INC.
P.O. Box 14608
Greensboro, NC 27415
(919) 274-1538

NORTH CAROLINA FRIENDS OF BLACK CHILDREN
620 West Humber Street
Sanford, NC 27330
Ruth Amerson, Contact
(919) 774-4880

STATE CONSULTANT TO FRIEND OF BLACK CHILDREN
325 N. Salisbury Street
Raleigh, NC 27603
Amelia Lance, Contact
(919) 733-3801

OHIO

HARAMBEE, SERVICES TO BLACK FAMILIES
1466-68 East 55th Street
Cleveland, OH 44013
(216) 391-7044

BLACK ADOPTIVE PARENT OUTREACH
1565 Thurston Street
Akron, OH 44320
Carolyn Rucker, Contact

GROUP OF BLACK ADOPTIVE PARENTS
1055 Grayview Court
Cincinnati, OH 45224
Bob Simpson, Contact
(513) 541-4166

BLACK ADOPTION RECRUITMENT COMMITTEE
440 South 22nd Street
Columbus, OH 43205
Aisha Saunders, Contact
(614)-644-2576

PENNSYLVANIA

NATIONAL ADOPTION EXCHANGE CENTER
1218 Chestnut Street, 2nd Floor
Philadelphia, PA 19102
Carolyn Johnson, Executive Director
(800) TO-ADOPT

Adoption Agencies and Services

BLACK ADOPTION SERVICES
Three Rivers Adoption Council
307 Fourth Avenue, Suite 710
Pittsburgh, PA 15222
Bev Schultz, Contact
(412) 471-8722

RHODE ISLAND

**MINORITY RECRUITMENT
AND CHILD PLACEMENT
PROGRAM**
246 Prairie Avenue
Providence, RI 02905
(401) 351-5000

SOUTH CAROLINA

**MINORITY PLACEMENT
PROJECT**
Division of Adoption and Birth Parent
Services
P.O. Box 1520
Columbia, SC 29202
(803) 734-6095

CHILDREN'S UNLIMITED
P.O. Box 11463
Columbia, SC 29211
(803) 799-8311

TEXAS

**THE MINORITY ADOPTION
COUNCIL**
P.O. Box 760605
Dallas, TX 75376-0605
(214) 320-6097

UTAH

FOCUS ON BLACK ADOPTION
1366 VanBuren Avenue
Salt Lake City, UT 8404
(801) 533-5657

VIRGINIA

**VIRGINIA'S ONE CHURCH, ONE
CHILD PROGRAM**
10250 Glendye Road
Richmond, VA 23235

WASHINGTON

**ADOPTION OF BLACK CHIL-
DREN COMMITTEE**
Post Office Box 22831
Seattle, WA 98122
(206) 723-6224

**GOOD NEWS FOR BLACK
CHILDREN**
P.O. Box 22638
Seattle, WA 98122
(206) 723-2513

WISCONSIN

BLACK ADOPTIVE FAMILIES
3267 North 47th Street
Milwaukee, WI 53216
Marie Granberry, Contact

Advertising Agencies and Marketing Research Companies

This is a partial listing of major Black Firms involved in advertising and marketing products in America.

ALABAMA

JESSE J. LEWIS & ASSOCIATES
115 Third Avenue West
Birmingham, AL 35204
Jesse L. Lewis, Owner
(205) 251-5158

CALIFORNIA

AUSTIN, MC CLAIN ASSOCIATES
4655 Ruffner Street, Suite 180
San Diego, CA 92111
Arlene Lowenthal, Owner
(619) 268-4803

ROBERT CARLISLE ADVERTISING, INC.
P.O. Box 480159
Los Angeles, CA 90048
Robert Carlisle, President
(213) 299-4800

FINANCIAL COMMUNICATIONS CLEARING HOUSE, INC.
3691 Bandini Boulevard
Los Angeles, CA 90023
Eduardo Manon, President
(213) 263-9054

CHARLES GIBBS PROMOTIONS
3007 Royce Lane
Costa Mesa, CA 92626
Charles Gibbs, President
(714) 545-5888

NAOMI GRAY ASSOCIATES, INC.
385 Ivey Street
San Francisco, CA 94105
Naomi Gray, President
(415) 441-8554

XODEX ENTERPRISES, LIMITED
494 Ninth Street
Oakland, CA 94607
Samual Wallace, President
(415) 763-3420

COLORADO

HAMILTON TILTON ADVERTISING, INC.
707 Sherman St.
Denver, CO 80203
Sherman Hamilton, President
(303) 837-0505

MEDIA MANAGEMENT GROUP
1380 Lawrence, Suite 1101
Denver, CO 80204
Susan Burks, Partner
(303) 893-8011

CONNECTICUT

J C BROWN ASSOCIATES
17 Ben Merrill Road
Clinton, CT 06416
James Brown, Owner
(203) 669-8757

Advertising Agencies and Marketing Research Companies

DISTRICT OF COLUMBIA

ASSOCIATED COUNSELORS INTERNATIONAL
1101 Pennsylvania Avenue, S.E.
Washington, D.C. 20003
Dolphin Thompson, President
(202) 547-2636

CONCEPTS INCORPORATED
4626 Wisconsin Ave., N.W.
Suite 102
Washington, D.C. 20016
Dianne Gayle-Dory, President
(202) 364-8266

FLORIDA

GLOVER SIGNS
3466 Washington Street
Orlando, FL 32805
Walter Glover, President
(407) 290-9075

J. D. RUFFIN ASSOCIATES, INC.
P.O. Box 14634
Fort Lauderdale, FL 33301
John Ruffin, Jr., President
(305) 731-4800

GEORGIA

ACT 1 COMPOSITION, INC.
575 Courtland Street, N.E.
Atlanta, GA 30308
Margo Woods, President
(404) 875-1091

ANDERSON COMMUNICATIONS
2245 Godby Road
Atlanta, GA 30349
Al Anderson, President
(404) 766-8000

FIRST CLASS, INC.
1422 West Peachtree Street, N.W.
Suite 500
Atlanta, GA 30309
Bunnie Jackson-Ransom, President
(404) 892-1434

MEDIA CONNECTIONS, INC.
7 Piedmont Center, Suite 500
Atlanta, GA 30305
Cie Meadows, President
(404) 261-5144

REFLECTO GRAPHICS
15 Perry Street
Newnan, GA 30263
Dan Moten, Owner
(404) 251-5108

ILLINOIS

BROWN & BROWN ADVERTISING & PUBLIC RELATIONS
28 North Grove Ave., Suite 203
Elgin, IL 60120
Floyd A. Brown, President
(312) 888-0737

BURRELL ADVERTISING, INC.
20 North Michigan Avenue
Suite 300
Chicago, IL 60602
Thomas A. Burrell, Chairman
(312) 443-8600

Advertising Agencies and Marketing Research Companies

CENTRAL CITY PRODUCTIONS
435 North Michigan Avenue
Suite 1120
Chicago, IL 60611
Don Jackson, President
(312) 222-9012

VINCE CULLERS ADVERTISING, INC.
676 North St. Clair
Suite 2222
Chicago, IL 60611
Vince Cullers, President
(312) 321-9296

CHARLES A. DAVIS & ASSOCIATES
2400 South Michigan Avenue
Chicago, IL 60616
Charles Davis, President
(312) 326-4140

EDWARD H. PATE & ASSOCIATES
520 North Michigan Avenue
Chicago, IL 60611
Edward Pate, President
(312) 787-8848

PROCTOR & GARDNER ADVERTISING, INC.
111 East Wacker Drive
Suite 321
Chicago, IL 60601
Barbara Proctor, President
(312) 565-5400

R. J. DALE ADVERTISING, INC.
500 North Michigan Avenue
Suite 2204
Chicago, IL 60611
Will Stewart, Senior Vice President
(312) 644-2316

INDIANA

WILLIAM G. RYDER GRAPHICS ARTS, INC.
3417 Clifton
Indianapolis, IN 46208
William Ryder, III, President
(317) 924-6168

KENTUCKY

NICHE MARKETING, INC.
P.O. Box 2883
Louisville, KY 40201
Rohena Miller, Contact
(502) 581-9365

MARYLAND

PRISM-DAE CORPORATION
2 Wisconsin Circle, Suite 300
Chevy Chase, MD 20815
Don A. Grigg, Chairman & CEO

STAR STEP, INC.
304 Meadow Way
Landover, MD 20785
Stephanie Colbert Hopkins, President

TERRY MANGUM/NEAL, INC.
10908 Breewood Road
Silver Spring, MD 20901
Henryette A. Neal, Secretary/Treasurer
(301) 593-9180

VANITA ENTERPRISES, INC.
2901 Druid Park Drive, Suite A201
Baltimore, MD 21215
Wanda Persons Wickham, Business
    Development Manager

Advertising Agencies and Marketing Research Companies

MASSACHUSETTS

BOSTON ADVERTISING & ASSOCIATES, INC.
763 Massachusetts Avenue
Cambridge, MA 02139
William D. Venter, President
(617) 661-3674

FACILITIES DATA, INC.
721 Main Street
Waltham, MA 02154
Michael Benn, President
(617) 899-4411

MICHIGAN

ALTERNATIVE DESIGN
P.O. Box 13158
Detroit, MI 48213
Desmond Jones, Production Manager
(313) 922-5289

BBA GRAPHIC DESIGN
1014 Woodlawn
Ann Arbor, MI 48104
Beverly Hunter, Co-Owner
(313) 769-0826

BADGETT INDUSTRIES, INC.
715 E. Milwaukee Avenue
Detroit, MI 48202
Maurice L. Badgett, Sr., President
(313) 873-2372

CLIFTON ASSOCIATES
65 Cadillac Square
 Suite 3200
Detroit, MI 48226
Edith Clifton, President

THE CREATIVE COMMUNICATIONS CENTRE
6475 28th Street, S.E., Suite 126
Grand Rapids, MI 49506
Argie N. Holliman, President

MINNESOTA

QUALITY HOUSE DIRECT MAIL SERVICES
2288 University Avenue, West
St. Paul, MN 55114
James A. Cook, CEO
(612) 646-2885

MISSOURI

GODBOLD GRAPHICS, INC.
3200 Gilham Road
Kansas City, MO 64109
Dell Godbold, President

JOE GRAY GRAPHIC DESIGN & ILLUSTRATION
8367 Olive Street Road
University City, MO 63132
Joseph Gray, President
(314) 991-0507

HARRIS GRAPHIC DESIGN
7309 Natural Bridge Road
St. Louis, MO 63121
Lee Harris, Owner
(314) 389-2636

M.T. PRODUCTIONS
301 East Amour,
Suite 201
Kansas City, MO 64111
Rodney Thompson, Partner

Advertising Agencies and Marketing Research Companies

PROUD INCORPORATED
625 North Euclid Avenue
St. Louis, MO 63108
Ernie McMillan, President
(314) 361-7877

NEW JERSEY

THE GRAPHIC SIGN COMPANY
48 West Palisade Avenue
Englewood, NJ 07631
Ralph Johnson, Owner

MANN-HORTON & ASSOCIATES, INC.
82 Grand Avenue
Englewood, NJ 07631
George Horton, President

NEW YORK

AD-CENTIVE IDEAS, INC.
35-01 Twenty-fourth Street
Long Island City, NY 11106
Kenneth Graham, President
(718) 786-2277

BLACK RESOURCES, INC.
231 West 29th Street
Suite 1205
New York, NY 10001
Carolyn Smith, Vice President
(212) 897-4000

LOCKHART & PETTUS, INC.
212 Fifth Avenue
20th Floor
New York, NY 10010
Keith E. Lockhart, President
(212) 725-2828

LOUIS-ROWE ENTERPRISES
455 Main Street
Suite 99
New Rochelle, NY 10801
William Rowe, President
(914) 636-1131

CRYSTAL MC KENZIE, INC.
30 East 20th Street
New York, NY 10003
Crystal McKenzie, President
(212) 598-4567

THE MINGO GROUP, INC.
228 East 45th Street, 2nd Floor
New York, NY 10017
Samuel J. Chisholm, President
(212) 697-4515

JERRY PINKNEY STUDIO
41 Furnace Dock Road
Croton-On-Hudson, NY 10520
Jerry Pinkney, Owner

JASPER SAMUEL PRINTING COMPANY
406 West 31st Street
New York, NY 10001
Jasper Samuel, Pesident
(212) 239-9544

SEGMENTED ACCESS MARKETING, INC. (S.A.M.)
1841 Broadway
New York, NY 10023
Jon Carlton, Vice President

UNIWORLD GROUP, INC.
100 Avenue of the Americas
New York, NY 10013
Byron Lewis, Chairman & CEO
(212) 219-1600

Advertising Agencies and Marketing Research Companies

NORTH CAROLINA

B&C ASSOCIATES, INC.
808 Greenboro Rd.
P.O. Box 2636
High Point, NC 27261
Robert Brown, President
(919) 884-0744

S B R & ASSOCIATES, INC.
P.O. Box 3162
Winston-Salem, NC 27102
W. Larry Shirley, Creative Director
(919) 748-9399

OHIO

THE ADVERTISING CONNEC- TION
222 Leader Building
Cleveland, OH 44114
Hilton P. Murray, Exec. Vice President
(216) 861-6146

BURNS PUBLIC RELATIONS SERVICES, INC.
668 Euculid Avenue, Suite 516
Cleveland, OH 44114
Dargan J. Burns, President
(216) 621-5950

COMMUNIPLEX SERVICES, INC.
2081 Seymour Avenue, Building B
Cincinnati, OH 45237
Steven Reece, President
(513) 731-6300

GAP PRODUCTIONS, INC.
5000 Euclid Avenue, Suite 210
Cleveland, OH 44103
Alexandria Boone, President

MULTI-WESTERN PUBLIC RELATIONS/ADVERTISING COMPANY
7 East Fourth Street, Suite 612
Dayton, OH 45402
Don Black, President
(513) 223-8060

THE PIPKINS GROUP, INC.
994 Dana Avenue
Cincinnati, OH 45229
Morris Pipkins, Jr., Owner
(513) 281-0564

PRIME OUTDOOR ADVERTIS- ING
1367 East Sixth Street, Suite 314
Cleveland, OH 44114
Alan Shatten, President
(216) 696-1951

PENNSYLVANIA

GEORGE BEACH, INC.
225 South 15th Street
Philadelphia, PA 19102
George Beach, President
(215) 735-7121

MARK HYMAN ASSOCIATES, INC.
5070 Parkside, Suite 1122
Philadelphia, PA 19131
Mark Hyman, President
(215) 473-0050

NOEL MAYO ASSOCIATES, INC.
1523 Walnut Street
Philadelphia, PA 19102
Noel Mayo, President
(215) 563-8555

Advertising Agencies and Marketing Research Companies

R L & A ASSOCIATES ADVERTISING
437 Chestnut Street
Suite 1017
Philadelphia, PA 19106
Ronald W. Lucas, President

URBAN MARKET DEVELOPERS, INC.
4627 Spruce Street
Philadelphia, PA 19139
Napoleon Vaughn, President
(215) 472-3333

TENNESSEE

THE FELIX WAY ADVERTISING
937 Peabody Avenue
Memphis, TN 38104
Linda A. R. Walker, Owner
(901) 529-9987

TEXAS

DAVIS & ASSOCIATES, INC.
802 Lingco Drive
Richardson, TX 75081
Dave Davis, President
(214) 234-5422

FOCUS COMMUNICATIONS GROUP
350 West St. Paul, Suite 1500
Dallas, TX 75201-4215
Ken Carter, President
(214) 954-0939

METRO MEDIA BUYERS
736 Havenwood,
P.O. Box 210647
Dallas, TX 75211
Elaine Thornton, Partner
(214) 224-0513

VIRGINIA

ADJ ENTERPRISES
7 Wirt Street, S.W., Suite 103
Leesburg, VA 22075
Gladys Pinckney-Burke, President
(703) 777-3480

WISCONSIN

BLACK MEDIA ADVERTISING
238 West Wisconsin Avenue
Milwaukee, WI 53203
Victor L. Welch, President
(414) 271-5683

The listings in this directory are available as Mail Labels. See last page for details.

Architectural Firms

These firms represent a partial listing of companies involved in the field of Architecture. They also serve as a point of contact for the National Organization of Minority Architects.

ALLAINE & ASSOCIATES
120 Ralph McGill Blvd., N.E., #835
Atlanta, GA 30308
Leon Allain

BAKER-COOPER & ASSOCI-ATES, P.C.
2000 Florida Ave., N.W., Suite 100
Washington, D.C. 20009
Isham O. Baker, FAIA

EDWARD C. BARKER & ASSO-CIATES ARCHITECTS, AIA
306 South Union Place
Los Angeles, CA 90017
Edward C. Barker

BELL & ASSOCIATES
1409 28th Street
Sacramento, CA 95816
Willie Alexander Bell

BROWN & HALE, ARCHITECTS
60 Pomona Avenue
Newark, NJ 07112
William M. Brown

BETRAM A. BRUTON, AIA
2001 York Street
Denver, CO 80205

BRYANT & BRYANT ASSOCIATES
4301 Connecticut Avenue, N.W.
Washington, D.C. 20008
Charles E. Bryant

THE CADD GROUP, INC.
P.O. Box 6235
Silver Spring, MD 20906
William L. Holloway, III, President
(301) 598-0503

WENDELL CAMPBELL ASSOCIATES, INC.
1326 South Michigan Avenue
Chicago, IL 60605
Wendell Campbell

JOHN S. CHASE FAIA ARCHI-TECT, INC.
1201 Southmore Street
Houston, TX 77004
John S. Chase, FAIA

E. HEDRIC CLAY AND ASSOCIATES
P.O. Box 362
Champaign, IL 61820
E. Hedric Clay

ROBERT TRAYHAM COLES ARCHITECT
730 Ellicott Square
Buffalo, NY 14203
Robert T. Coles, FAIA

DEVROUAX & PURNELL AR-CHITECTS PLANNERS, P.C.
717 D Street, N.W.
Washington, D.C. 20004
Paul S. Devrouax

Architectural Firms

**JOHN C. DODD AND
ASSOCIATES, INC.**
2710 X Street, Suite 2
Sacramento, CA 95818
John C. Dodd President

**RONALD E. FRAZIER &
ASSOCIATES, P.A.**
5800 N.W. Seventh Avenue
Suite 206
Miami, FL 33127
Ronald E. Frazier, AIA

**FRY & WELCH ASSOCIATES,
P.C.**
7600 Georgia Avenue, N.W.
Washington, D.C. 20012
Louis E. Fry, Jr., President

**JOHN L. GRAY ASSOCIATES,
ARCHITECTS**
7603 Georgia Avenue, N.W.
Washington, D.C. 20012
John L. Gray, President

**JAMES R. GUTIERRES ARCHI-
TECT & PLANNER**
P.O. Box 7564
Metrairie, LA 70011

**NELSON A. HARRIS & ASSOCI-
ATES**
2003 McGuffey Road
Youngstown, OH 44505
Nelson O. Harris

HEARD & ASSOCIATES, LTD.
332 South Michigan Avenue
Suite 1610
Chicago, IL 60604
Andrew Heard, FAIA, President

**MAJOR L. HOLLAND, ARCHI-
TECT AND ASSOCIATES, P.C.**
111-B South Main Street
P.O. Box 547
Tuskegee, AL 36083
Major L. Holland, Owner

JEH VINCENT JOHNSON, FAIA
14 Edgehill Road
Wappingers Falls, NY 12590
Jeh Vincent Johnson FAIA

KENNARD DESIGN GROUP
3600 Wilshire Blvd., Suite 1820
Los Angeles, CA 90010
Robert Kennard

CARL M. KINSEY & ASSOCIATES
347 South Ogden Drive
Los Angeles, CA 90036
Carl M. Kinsey, AIA

**MADISON, MADISON
INTERNATIONAL**
2930 Euclid Avenue
Cleveland, OH 44115
Robert Madison

MARGERUM ARCHITECTS
2111 Woodward Avenue, Suite 607
Detroit, MI 48201
Roger Margerum, President

THE MARSHALL GROUP, LTD.
590 Herndon Parkway, Suite 130
Herndon, VA 22070
Mortimer Marshall, Jr.

JOSEPH MASK ARCHITECTS
508 East 78th Street, Suite 2C
New York, NY 10021
Joseph C. Mask, Jr.

CHARLES F. MC AFEE, FAIA, NOMA
Architects and Planners
2600 North Grove
Wichita, KS 67219
Charles F. McAfee, President

MC DONALD WILLIAMS BANKS CORNEILLE, P.C. ARCHI-TECTS AND PLANNERS
7705 Georgia Avenue, N.W.
Washington, D.C. 20012
Andrei T. Banks, President

JOSEPH MIDDLEBROOKS & ASSOCIATES, INC.
640 South West 62nd Avenue
South Miami, FL 33143
Joseph Middlebrooks, President

MILLER & ASSOCIATES
9842 Stearns Avenue
Oakland, CA 94605
Terry Miller, AIA

MIRALLES ASSOCIATES, INC.
729 West Woodbury Road
Altadena, CA 91001
Adolfo E. Mirales

ROBERT J. NASH, FAIA & ASSOCIATES, P.C.
5113 Georgia Avenue, N.W.
Washington, D.C. 20012
Robert J. Nash

The listing in this directory are available as Mailing Labels. See last page for details.

THE OWENS & WOODS PARTNERSHIP
214 North 24th Street
Birmingham, AL 35203
Kenneth Owens

J. W. ROBINSON & ASSOCIATES, INC.
1020 Gordon Street, S.W.
Atlanta, GA 30310
Joseph W. Robinson

E. M. ROSE & ASSOCIATES, AICP
Urban Design & Environmental Planning
435 Bryant Street, Suite 2/F
San Francisco, CA 94017

SIMS-VARNER & ASSOCIATES
1101 Washington Boulevard
Detroit, MI 48226
Howard F. Sims

BENJAMIN A. SKYLES, SR. & ASSOCIATES
7603 Georgia Avenue, N.W.
Washington, D.C. 20012
Benjamin a. Skyles, Sr.

SPENCER & SPENCER, INC.
33 North High Street, Suite 901
Columbus, OH 43215
John Spencer, AIA, President

AUSTIN L. SPRIGGS ASSOCIATES
433 Massachusetts Avenue, N.W.
Washington, D.C. 20001
Austin L. Spriggs

STANLEY ARCHITECTS
48 Cambridge Place
Brooklyn, NY 11238
T. Barrett Stanley, AIA

Architectural Firms

STANLEY, LOVE & STANLEY, P.C.
120 Ralph McGill Blvd., Suite 815
Atlanta, GA 30308
William J. Stanley, III AIA, NOMA

**SULTON, CAMPBELL, BRITT,
  OWENS & ASSOCIATES**
6031 Kansas Avenue, N.W.
Washington, D.C. 20011
John D. Sulton, Owner

KARLE THORNE ASSOCIATES, INC.
1216 N.W. Ninth Avenue
Gainesville, FL 32604
Karl Thorne

**CARL TRIMBLE ARCHITECTS/
  DEVELOPERS**
360 Westview Avenue, S.W.
Atlanta, GA 30310
Carl Trimble

TURNER ASSOCIATES
111 Massachusetts Avenue, N.W.
Suite 540
Washington, D.C. 20001
Larry Turner

**VICTOR H. WILBURN &
  ASSOCIATES**
4301 Connecticut Avenue, N.W.
Washington, D.C. 20008
Victor H. Wilburn

**HAROLD WILLIAMS
  ASSOCIATES**
1052 West Sixth Street
Suite 320
Los Angeles, CA 90017
Harold Williams, AIA

Bar Associations

The organizations highlighted in this section represent a key element in the legal profession. Their membership is made up of some of the best legal minds in America.

ALABAMA

ALABAMA LAYWERS ASSOCIATION
Madison County Courthouse
Huntsville, AL 35801
Lynn M. Sherrod, President
(205) 532-3470

ARIZONA

ARIZONA BLACK LAWYERS ASSOCIATION
3875 North 44th Street, Suite 102
Phoenix, AZ 85018
Penny Ladell Willrich, President
(602) 258-3434

ARKANSAS

W. HAROLD FLOWERS LAW SOCIETY
124 West Capitol Avenue
Suite 990
Little Rock, AR 72201-3742
Sheila Campbell, President
(501) 372-4623

CALIFORNIA

BERNARD S. JEFFERSON LAW SOCIETY
2122 North Broadway, Suite 200
Santa Ana, CA 92706-2614
Charlotte Adams, President
(714) 558-1059

CALIFORNIA ASSOCIATION OF BLACK LAWYERS
Crosby Heafey Roach & May
1999 Harrison
Oakland, CA 94612
Valerie Lewis, president
(415) 763-2000

JOHN LANGSTON BAR ASSOCIATION
Warner Brothers
400 Warner Boulevard, Building 154
Burbank, CA 91522
Rachel D. Young, President
(818) 954-6670

CHARLES HOUSTON BAR ASSOCIATION
1970 Broadway, Suite 820
Oakland, CA 94612
Lloyd Johnson, President
(510) 839-1966

EARL B. GILLIAM BAR ASSOCIATION OF SAN DIEGO COUNTY
220 Euclid Avenue, Suite 110
San Diego, CA 92119
Douglas A. Oden, President
(619) 266-8006

Bar Associations

SOUTH BAY BLACK LAWYERS ASSOCIATION

Moore Law Firm, APC
55 South Market Street
Suite 1020
San Jose, CA 95110
Rodney G. Moore, President

WILEY M. MANUEL BAR ASSOCIATION

State Bar of California
Office Of Government Affairs
915 L Street, Suite 1260
Sacramento, CA 95814
Mark T. Harris, President
(916) 444-2762

WILLIAM H. HASTIE LAWYERS ASSOCIATION

James & Jeffers
870 Market Street, Suite 1200
San Francisco, CA 94102
Clifton R. Jeffers, President
(415) 557-1600

BLACK WOMEN LAWYERS ASSOCIATION OF NORTHERN CALIFORNIA

State Bar of California
555 Franklin Street
San Francisco, CA 94102
Phyllis Culp, President
(415) 561-8200

BLACK WOMEN LAWYERS ASSOCIATION OF LOS ANGELES

Gronemeier & Barker
301 North Lake Avenue
Suite 800
Pasadena, CA 91101
Brenda Johns Perry, President
(213) 681-0702

COLORADO

SAM CARY BAR ASSOCIATION

15400 East 14th Place
Aurora, CO 80011
Hon. Robert Russell, President
(303) 363-7005

CONNECTICUT

GEORGE W. CRAWFORD LAW ASSOCIATION

P.O. Box 3291
Hartford, CT 06103
Kimberly Graham, President
(203) 566-5996

SOUTHERN CONNECTICUT LAWYERS ASSOCIATION

106 Ledgebrook Drive
Norwalk, CT 06854
Gary White, President
(203) 846-9519

DISTRICT OF COLUMBIA

CHAPTER, NATIONAL CONFERENCE OF BLACK LAWYERS

P.O. Box 1760
Washington, D.C. 20013
Alake Johnson-Ford, Co-Chairperson
(202) 797-9880

WASHINGTON BAR ASSOCIATON

7406 Ninth Street, N.W.
Washington, D.C. 20012
Belva D. Newsome, President
(202) 626-5114

Bar Associations

FLORIDA

FLORIDA CHAPTER, NATIONAL BAR ASSOCIATION
4770 Biscayne Boulevard, Suite 1130
Miami, FL 33137
Larry R. Handfield, President
(305) 576-1011

GEORGIA

GATE CITY BAR ASSOCIATION
141 Pryor Street, S.W.
Atlanta, GA 30303
Avarita L. Hanson, President
(404) 730-8232

DEKALB LAWYERS ASSOCIATION
P.O. Box 2403
Decatur, GA 30031-2403
Bobby simmons, President
(404) 366-2123

ILLINOIS

COOK COUNTY BAR ASSOCIATION
3 First National Plaza
Chicago, IL 60602
Larry Rogers, President
(312) 236-9381

INDIANA

JAMES KIMBROUGH LAW ASSOCIATION
1001 North Shelby
Gary, IN 46403
Karen Trueblood, President

MARION COUNTY BAR ASSOCIATION
1515 N. Delaware Street, 18th Floor
Indianapolis, IN 46204
Lisa R. Hayes, President
(317) 631-1395

IOWA

IOWA NATIONAL BAR ASSOCIATON
Attorney General's Office
Hoover State Office Building
Des Moines, IA 50319
Robin Humphrey, President

KANSAS

KANSAS CITY BAR ASSOCIATION
103 Cross Lines Towers
1021 North Seventh Street
Kansas City, KS 66101-2823
Hosea Ellis Sowell, President

KENTUCKY

KENTUCKY CHAPTER, NATIONAL BAR ASSOCIATION
934 South Sixth Street
Louisville, KY 40203-3318
Rhonda Richardson, President
(502) 582-1942

JOHN W. ROWE CHAPTER, NATIONAL BAR ASSOCIATION
106 West Vine Street
Lexington, KY 40507
John McNeill, President

Bar Associations

LOUISIANA

SOUTHWEST LOUISIANA LAW ASSOCIATION
619 Surrey Street
Lafayette, LA 70501
Connie Welcome-Sadler, President
(318) 235-2093

LOUIS A. MARTINET LEGAL SOCIETY
P.O. Box 57317
New Orleans, LA 70157
Angelique A. Reed, President
(504) 525-2256

LOUIS A. MARTINET LEGAL SOCIETY
Baton Rouge Chapter
328 Government Street
Baton Rouge, LA 70802
Luke A. La Vergne, President

BLACK LAWYERS ASSOCIATON OF SHREVE-PORT BOSSIER
2419 Kings Highway
P.O. Box 1788
Shreveport, LA 71166-1788
Sam L. Jenkins, Jr., President
(318) 636-4266

MARYLAND

J. FRANKLIN BOURNE BAR ASSOCIATION
9200 Basil Court, Suite 300
Landover, MD 20785
Toni E. Clarke, President
(301) 952-4501

MONUMENTAL CITY BAR ASSOCIATION
P.O. Box 2195
Baltimore, MD 21203-2195
Marcella A. Holland, President
(410) 396-4996

WARING MITCHELL LAW SOCIETY OF HOWARD COUNTY
P.O. Box 651
Columbia, MD 21045
John L. Clark, President
(301) 9964-0181

ALLIANCE OF BLACK WOMEN ATTORNEYS
P.O. Box 13460
Baltimore, MD 21203
Zakia Mahasa, President
(410) 539-5340

MASSACHUSETTS

MASSACHUSETS BLACK LAWYERS ASSOCIATION
P.O. Box 2411
Boston, MA 02208
Michael Brown, President
(617) 298-4269

MICHIGAN

FLOYD SKINNER BAR ASSOCIATION
934 Scribner Avenue, N.W.
Grand Rapids, MI 48226
Stephen R. Drew, President
(616) 774-0003

LANSING BLACK LAWYERS ASSOCIATION
City Hall, Fifth Floor
Lansing, MI 48933
Melvin C. McWilliams, President
(517) 483-4320

WOLVERINE BAR ASSOCIATION
645 Giswold
Suite 1312
Detroit, MI 48226
Camille Stearns Miller, President
(313) 961-2550

MALLORY, VAN-DYNE & SCOTT BAR ASSOCIATION
432 North Saginaw, Suite 810
Flint, MI 48502
Archie Hayman, President
(313) 239-2323

MINNESOTA

MINNESOTA MINORITY LAW-YERS ASSOCIATION
Loop Station
P.O. Box 2754
Minneapolis, MN 55402
Jarvis Jones, President

MISSISSIPPI

MAGNOLIA BAR ASSOCIATION
P.O. Box 648
Jackson, MS 39225-2849
John L. Walker, President
(601) 948-4589

MISSOURI

MOUND CITY BAR ASSOCIATION
200 North Broadway
Suite 700
St. Louis, MO 63102
Thomas Carter, II, President
(314) 421-5364

NEBRASKA

MIDLANDS BAR ASSOCIATON
216 Aquila Court
1615 Howard Street
Omaha, NE 68102
Frederick D. Franklin, President
(402) 341-8500

NEVADA

LAS VEGAS CHAPTER, NA-TIONAL BAR ASSOCIATION
302 East Carson
Suite 903
Las Vegas, NV 89101
Lizzie R. Hatcher, President
(702) 386-2988

NEW JERSEY

GARDEN STATE BAR ASSOCIATON
c/o Robinson, St. John & Wayne
Gateway One
Newark, NJ 07102
Karol Corbin Walker, President

Bar Associations

NEW MEXICO

NEW MEXICO BLACK LAW-YERS ASSOCIATION
1003 Luna Circle, N.W.
Albuquerque, NM 87102
Hanna B. Best, President
(505) 247-2727

NEW YORK

THE MINORITY BAR ASSOCIA-TION OF WESTERN NEW YORK
1800 One MNT Plaza
Buffalo, NY 14203
Edward Peace, President
(716) 856-4000

METROPOLITAN BLACK BAR ASSOCIATION
352 Seventh Avenue
Suite 1500
New York, NY 10001
Le'Roi L. Gill, President
(212) 563-1971

ASSOCIATION OF BLACK LAWYERS OF WESTCHESTER COUNTY, INC.
19 Chestnut Hill Avenue
White Plains, NY 10606
Eric Lamar Harris, President
(914) 347-2244

BRONX COUNTY BLACK BAR ASSOCIATION
19828 Pompeii Avenue
Queens, NY 11423
Teresa Mason, President
(212) 804-1512

ASSOCIATION OF BLACK WOMEN ATTORNEYS
134 West 32nd Street, Suite 602
New York, NY 10001
Diane Ridley Gatewood, President
(212) 244-4270

MACON B. ALLEN BAR ASSO-CIATION
110-11 225th Street
Queens Village
New York, NY 11429
Mortimer Lawrence, President
(516) 829-3190

NORTH CAROLINA

NORTH CAROLINA ASSOCIA-TION OF BLACK LAWYERS
700 E. Stonewall Street, Suite 730
Charlotte, NC 28202
Geraldine Sumser, President
(704) 375-8461

OHIO

NORMAN S. MINOR BAR ASSOCIATION
P.O. Box 99823
Cleveland, OH 44199
Allison Nelson, President
(216) 443-2061

The listings in this directory are available as Mailing Labels. See last page for details.

ROBERT B. ELLIOT LAW CLUB
P.O. Box 15235
Columbus, OH 43215
Shirley Mays, President
(614) 445-8836

**BLACK LAWYERS ASSOCIA-
TION OF CINCINNATI**
230 East Ninth Street, Suite 200
Cincinnati, OH 45202
Ernest F. McAdams, President

AKRON BARRISTERS CLUB
75 East Market Street
Akron, OH 44308
Orlando Williams, President
(419) 867-9028

**THURGOOD MARSHALL LAW
ASSOCIATION**
Board of Community Relations
One Government Center
Toledo, OH 42604
Keith Mitchell, President

**THURGOOD MARSHALL LAW
SOCIETY**
2115 North Main Street
Dayton, OH 45402-3526
Nicholas L. Garren, Jr., President
(513) 276-6115

OKLAHOMA

**NORTHEAST OKLAHOMA
BLACK LAWYERS
ASSOCIATION**
2400 First National Tower
Tulsa, OK 74103
Hannibal B. Johnson, President
(918) 586-8562

PENNSYLVANIA

**HARRISBURG BLACK
ATTORNEY'S ASSOCIATION**
Department of State - Room 302
North Office Building
Harrisburg, PA 17120
Pamella Raisson, President
(717) 787-7630

**THE BARRISTERS ASSOCIA-
TION OF PHILADELPHIA**
Eighteenth and Arch
2 Logan Square Number 3000
Philadelphia, PA 19103
A. Michael Pratt, President

**HOMER S. BROWN LAW
ASSOCIATION**
Office of University Counsel
University of Pittsburgh
3200 Cathedral of Learning
Pittsburgh, PA 15280
Andrew Hughey, President
(412) 624-5674

**ERIE CHAPTER, NATIONAL
BAR ASSOCIATION**
925 French Street, Suite 3
Erie, PA 16501
Melvin T. Toran, President
(814) 454-2139

SOUTH CAROLINA

**SOUTH CAROLINA BLACK
LAWYERS ASSOCIATION**
P.O. Box 1431
Columbia, SC 29202
Ann McCrowly Mickle, President
(803) 252-9700

Bar Associations

TENNESSEE

**BEN F. JONES CHAPTER,
NATIONAL BAR ASSOCIATION**
130 North Court Street
Memphis, TN 38103
Ricky E. Watkins, President

**NAPIER-LOOBY CHAPTER,
NATIONAL BAR ASSOCIATION**
1502 Parkway Towers
Nashville, TN 37219
Monte Watkins, President

**TENNESEE ASSOCIATION FOR
BLACK LAWYERS**
203 Second Avenue, North
Nashville, TN 37208
Richard Dinkins, President
(615) 244-3988

TEXAS

J. L. TURNER LEGAL ASSOCIATION
6500 Greenville, Suite 610
Dallas, TX 75206
Rhonda Hunter, President
(214) 361-7971

**AUSTIN BLACK LAWYERS
ASSOCIATION**
P.O. Box 13181
Austin, TX 78711
Gary Cobb, President
(512) 473-9400

**HOUSTON LAWYERS
ASSOCIATION**
P.O. Box 300009
Houston, TX 77230-0009
Renee Y. Smith, President
(713) 527-7950

**SAN ANTONIO BLACK LAW-
YERS ASSOCIATION**
257 East Hildebrand
San Antonio, TX 78212
John Wilkerson, President
(512) 826-6618

**TARRANT COUNTY BLACK BAR
ASSOCIATION**
2100 First Republic Bank Tower
801 Cherry Street
Fort Worth, TX 76102
Winfred T. Colbert, President
(817) 877-2802

**TEXAS ASSOCIATION OF
AFRICAN AMERICAN
LAWYERS**
2208 Blodgett
Houston, TX 77004
U. Lawrence Boze, President
(713) 520-0260

VIRGINIA

**OLD DOMINION BAR
ASSOCIATION**
2509 East Broad Street
Richmond, VA 23223
Roger Gregory, President
(804) 643-8401

WASHINGTON

**LOREN MILLER BAR
ASSOCIATION**
P.O. Box 4233
Seattle, WA 98104
Leah Cattrell, President
(206) 722-4061

WEST VIRGINIA

MOUNTAIN STATE BAR ASSOCIATION

P.O. Box 20017
Charleston, WV 25302
Sharon Mullens, President
(304) 348-0546

WISCONSIN

WISCONSIN ASSOCIATION OF MINORITY ATTORNEYS, INC.

8500 West Capital Drive
Milwaukee, WI 53222
Celia M. Jackson, President
(414) 536-8300

Black Pages

The following entries represent the nation's local black business directories.

ALABAMA

THE BLACK BUSINESS NET-WORK
P.O. Box 11332
Birmingham, AL 35302
Adrienne Royster, Publisher

ALASKA

BLACK ENTREPRENEUR BUSINESS DIRECTORY
Post Office Box 103291 DT
Anchorage, AK 99510-3291
Larry Morrow, Publisher

ARIZONA

THE BLACK COMMERCE DIRECTORY
P.O. Box 63701
Phoenix, AZ 85082
Tony Brown, Publisher

ARKANSAS

LITTLE ROCK BLACK PAGES
2420 South Broadway Street
Little Rock, AR 72206
Simon S. Smith, Publisher

CALIFORNIA

SOUTHERN CALIFORNIA BLACK PAGES
1888 West Sixth Street, Suite G
Corona, CA 94107
Colin Heron, Publisher

LOS ANGELES BLACK PAGES
12333 1/2 A Washington Boulevard
Los Angeles, CA 90066
Stephon Buckley, Publisher

TRI-COUNTY MINORITY PRO-FESSIONAL DIRECTORY
1l9649 Kauri Avenue
Rialto, CA 92376
Wilmer Carter, Publisher

MINORITY BUSINESS DIREC-TORY
P.O. Box 77227
San Francisco, CA 94107
Harold Mullins, Publisher

COLORADO

COLORADO BLACK PAGES
2413 Washington Street
Suite 210
Denver, CO 80205
Toni Ingram, Publisher

MINORITY BUSINESS AND PROFESSIONAL DIRECTORY
P.O. Box 22747
Denver, CO 80222
Marcellus Jackson, Publisher

DISTRICT OF COLUMBIA

MINORITY BUSINESS AND PROFESSIONAL DIRECTORY
1901 Eleventh Street, N.W.
Washington, D.C. 22001
Audrey Cain, Publisher

FLORIDA

BLACK PAGES OF THE PALM BEACHES
1337 West 28th Street
Riviera Beach, FL 33404
Ray Nelson, Publisher

FLORIDA MINORITY BUSINESS DIRECTORY
P.O. Box 4734
Jacksonville, FL 33201-4734
Cleveland Washington, Publisher

GREATER MIAMI BLACK PAGES
3510 Biscayne Boulevard
Suite 303
Miami, Fl 33137
Alvino Monk, Publisher
(305) 571-9505

NORTH FLORIDA BLACK PAGES
Post Office Box 3636
Tallahassee, FL 32315
Al Lawson, Publisher

TAMPA BLACK PAGES
1405 Tampa Park Plaza
Tampa, FL 33605
Derrick DeVerger, Publisher
(803) 221-6204

GEORGIA

ATLANTA BLACK PAGES
3711 College Street, Suite 201
College Park, GA 30337
Ken Reid, Publisher

COLUMBUS/PHOENIX BLACK PAGES
2900 B Manchester Expressway
Columbus, GA 31903
Ken Reid, Publisher

MACON/MIDDLE GEORGIA BLACK PAGES
761 Poplar Street, Suite B-12
Macon, GA 31201
Ken Reid, Publisher

SAVANNAH/AUGUSTA AREA BLACK PAGES, INC.
1810 Avercorn Street
Savannah, GA 31401
Mance Mullino, Publisher
(912) 234-5731

HAWAII

HAWAII BLACK PAGES
99 Aypuni Street, Suite 116-813
Honolulu, HI 96720
Paula Harris-White, Publisher
(808) 966-8511

ILLINOIS

CHICAGO BLACK PAGES
407 East 25th Street, Suite 100
Chicago, IL 60616
Arnette French, Publisher

Black Pages

KANSAS

TOPEKA BLACK PAGES
1800 Harrison, Suite 1
Topeka, KS 66612
Vernon E. Davis, Publisher

KENTUCKY

LOUISVILLE BLACK PAGES
1156 South Brook Street, Suite 3
Louisville, KY 40203
Rohena Miller, Publisher
(502) 581-9365

LOUISIANA

BATON ROUGE BLACK PAGES
1926 Woodale Boulevard, Suite 101B
Baton Rouge, LA 70806
Bonnie Jackson, Publisher

NEW ORLEANS METRO BLACK PAGES
650 South Pierce Street, Suite 350
New Orleans, LA 71109
David Walton, Publisher

MARYLAND

BALTIMORE METRO BLACK PAGES
2901 Druid Park Drive, Suite 202A
Baltimore, MD 21215
David Walton, Publisher

MINORITY BUSINESS DIRECTORY
P.O. Box 13513
Baltimore, MD 21203
Cleveland Washington, Publisher

WASHINGTON METRO BLACK PAGES
6192 Oxon Hill Road, Suite 402
Oxon Hill, MD 20745
David Walton, Publisher

MASSACHUSETTS

GREATER BOSTON BUSINESS DIRECTORY
Post Office Box 166
Boston, MA 02121
Leon Nelson, Publisher

MASSACHUSETTS BLACK BUSINESS DIRECTORY
P.O. Box 1848
Brockton, MA 02403
Thelma Sullivan, Publisher

MINNESOTA

TWIN CITIES BLACK PAGES
3540 Hennepin Ave., S., Suite 104
Minneapolis, MN 55408
Lennie Chisholm, Publisher

MISSISSIPPI

GULF PORT BLACK PAGES
4707 15th Street
Gulf Port, MS 39501
LaBot Parker, Publisher

The listings in this directory are available as Mailing Labels. See last page for details.

MISSOURI

BLACK PAGES, USA
9811 West Florissant Avenue
Suite 207
St. Louis, MO 63136
Arnette D. French, Sr., Publisher
(314) 521-0800

KANSAS CITY BLACK PAGES
1601 East 18th Street
Suite 315
Kansas City, MO 64108
Kenneth Stone, Manager
(816) 421-0400

ST. LOUIS BLACK PAGES
951 Jeanerete Drive
St. Louis, MO 63130
Howard D. Denson, Publisher
(314) 862-2555

NEVADA

LAS VEGAS BLACK PAGES DIRECTORY
6333 Stonegate Way
Las Vegas, NV 89102
Dr. Porter Troutman, Publisher

NEW JERSEY

NORTH & CENTRAL NEW JERSEY RARE PAGES
Post Office Box 5756
Somerset, NJ 08873
George Davis, Publisher

NEW JERSEY STATE MINORITY BUSINESS DIRECTORY
144 N Avenue
Plainsfield, NJ 07060
Henry C. Johnson, Publisher

NEW YORK

THE BIG BLACK BOOK
Post Office Box 400476
Brooklyn, NY 11240-0476
Celeste Morris, Publisher

WESTCHESTER BLACK BUSINESS DIRECTORY
Post Office Box 1020
Yonkers, NY 10703-1020
Phyllis M. Kelly, Publisher

NORTH CAROLINA

ASHEVILLE BLACK PAGES
7 Biltmore Avenue
Asheville, NC 28801
Derrick DeVerger, Publisher
(704) 253-2019

CHARLOTTE METRO BLACK PAGES
700 East Stonewall, Suite 350
Charlotte, NC 28202
Rod Terry, Publisher

OHIO

CLEVELAND BLACK PAGES
3030 Euclid Avenue, Suite 31
Cleveland, OH 44115
Bob LeNeir, Publisher

PENNSYLVANIA

BLACK DIRECTORY OF GREATER PITTSBURGH
1516 Fifth Avenue
Pittsburgh, PA 15219
Connie Portis, Publisher

Black Pages

SOUTH CAROLINA

CHARLESTON TRIDENT BLACK PAGES
701 East Bay Street
BTC 1113
Charleston, SC 29403
Darrin Thomas, Publisher

COLUMBIA MIDLAND BLACK PAGES
2401 Main Street
Columbia, SC 29201
Darrin Thomas, Publisher

TENNESSEE

BLACK YELLOW PAGES
Post Office Box 252
Antioch, TN 37011
Doris Black-Kennedy, Publisher
(615) 731-2144

MEMPHIS BLACK PAGES
1117 Madison, Suite 402
Memphis, TN 38104
Melvin Jones, Publisher

TEXAS

DALLAS FT. WORTH BLACK PAGES
3606 Marvin D. Love Freeway
Suite 130
Dallas, TX 75224
Alicia Hicks, Manager
(214) 315-5200

FORT WORTH BLACK PAGES
2914 East Rosedale, Suite 105
Fort Worth, TX 76105
Arnette D. French, Publisher

HOUSTON BLACK PAGES
Post Office Box 4032
Houston, TX 77210
Joseph Amenkara Head, Publisher

TEXARKANA BLACK PAGES
Post Office Box 5823
Texarkana, TX 77505
Sandra Cherry, Publisher

VIRGINIA

HAMPTON ROAD BLACK PAGES
605 Green Street, Suite 204
Portsmouth, VA 23704
David Walton, Publisher

RICHMOND BLACK PAGES
101 North Sixth Street
Richmond, VA 23219
David Walton, Publisher

WISCONSIN

MILWAUKEE BLACK PAGES
2821 North Fourth Street
Milwaukee, WI 53212
Kathy Bailey, Publisher
(414) 562-5225

Book Publishers & Book Stores

This is a partial listing of Book Publishers and Book Stores. They specialize in publications related to African Americans and people of African descent from other parts of the world.

BOOK PUBLISHERS

AFRICANA PUBLISHING
30 Irving Place
New York, NY 10003
Miriam J. Holmes, Managing Director
(212) 254-4100

AFRICA WORLD PRESS
P.O. Box 1892
Trenton, NJ 08607
Kassahun Checole, Director
(609) 771-1666

AFRO-AM PUBLISHING COMPANY, INC.
407 East 25th Street, Suite 600
Chicago, IL 60616
Eugene Winslow, President
(312) 791-1611

ASHLEY PUBLISHING COMPANY, INC.
4600 West Commercial Boulevard
Fort Lauderdale, FL 33319
Billie Young, President
(305) 739-2221

BAYSIDE TO-GO
401 Biscayne Boulevard, Suite P107
Miami, FL 33132
Carole Ann Taylor, Owner
(305) 374-5935

BLACK REGISTRY PUBLISHING COMPANY
1223 Rosewood Avenue
Austin, TX 78702
T. L. Wyatt, Publisher
(512) 476-0082

BLIND BEGGAR PRESS/ LAMPLIGHT EDITIONS
P.O. Box 437
Bronx, NY 10467
C.D. Grant and Gary Johnston, Publishers
(914) 683-6792

BROADSIDE PRESS
P.O. Box 04257
Detroit, MI 48204
Hilda Freeman Vest, Publisher
(313) 934-1231

CAAS PUBLICATIONS
Center for Afro-American Studies Publications
160 Haines Hall
405 Hilgard Avenue
Los Angeles, CA 90024-1545
Toyomi Igus, Managing Editor
(310) 825-3528

GRINNELL FINE ART COLLECTIONS
800 Riverside Drive, Suite 5E
New York, NY 10032
Ademola Olugebefola, Co-Director
(212) 927-7941

HOWARD UNIVERSITY PRESS
1240 Randolph Street, N.E.
Washington, D.C. 20008
Rudolph Aggrey, Director
(202) 806-4935

Book Publishers & Book Stores

JOHNSON PUBLISHING COMPANY, INC.
1820 South Michigan Avenue
Chicago, IL 60605
John H. Johnson, Publisher

JUJU PUBLISHING COMPANY, INC.
1310 Harden Street
Columbia, SC 22902
Isaac Washington, Publisher
(803) 799-5252

LOTUS PRESS
P.O. Box 21607
Detroit, MI 48221
Naomi Madgett, Executive Director Officer
(313) 861-1280

THE MAJORITY PRESS
P.O. Box 538
Dover, MA 02030
Anthony Martin, Chief Executive
(508) 655-5636

NEW BEACON BOOKS. LTD.
76 Strong Green Road
Finsbury Park, London N.4

TECHNIPLUS PUBLISHING COMPANY
887 South Lucerne Blvd.
Suite 4
Los Angeles, CA 90005
Aaron Jones, III, Marketing/Publicist
(213) 934-3001

THIRD WORLD PRESS
7524 South Cottage Grove
Chicago, IL 60619
Haki Madhubuti, Publisher
(312) 651-0700

VINCOM, INC.
P.O. Box 702400
Tulsa, OK 74170
George Vinnett, President
(918) 254-1276

BOOK STORES

AFRO-AMERICAN BOOK SOURCE
Your Black Bookstore by Mail
P.O. Box 851
Boston, MA 02120
Charles Pinderhughes, President
(617) 445-9209

AFRO IN BOOKS 'N THINGS
5675 N.W. 7th Avenue
Miami, FL 33127
Eursla A. Wells, Owner

AMISTAD BOOKPLACE
1413 Holman Street
Houston, TX 77004
(713) 528-3561

AQUARIAN BOOKSHOP
3995 South Western Avenue
Los Angeles, CA 90062
Bernice Ligon, Owner
(213) 296-1633

AUTHENTIC BOOK DISTRIBUTORS
P.O. Box 52916
Baton Rouge, LA 70892
Kwaku O Kushindana, Bus. Manager
(504) 356-0076

BLACK IMAGES BOOK BAZAAR
142 Wynnewood Village
Dallas, TX 75224
Emma Rodger, President
(214) 943-0142

Book Publishers & Book Stores

DUSABLE MUSEUM GIFT SHOP/ BOOKSTORE
740 East 56th Place
Chicago, IL 60637
Useni Eugene Perkins, Executive Director
(312) 947-0600

HAKIM'S BOOKSTORE
210 South 52nd Street
Philadelphia, PA 19139
Dawud Hakim, Owner
(215) 474-9495

HUE-MAN EXPERIENCE BOOK-STORE
911 23rd Street
Denver, CO 80205
Clara C. Villarosa, President
(303) 293-2665

LIBERATION BOOKSTORE
421 Lenox Avenue
New York, NY 10037
Una G. Mulzac, Manager
(212) 281-4615

MARCUS BOOKS
1712 Fillmore Street
San Francisco, CA 94115
Julian Richardson, President
(415) 346-4222

POSITIVE IMAGES UNLIMITED BOOKSTORE
137-07 Bedell Street
Rochdale Village, NY 11434
Brad McLeod, Manager
(718) 949-2535

PROGRESSIVE BOOKS
6265 Delmar Blvd.
St. Louis, MO 63130
Johnson Lancaster, Manager
(314) 721-1344

PYRAMID BOOKSTORE
2849 Georgia Avenue, N.W.
Washington, D.C. 20001
Hodari Ali, Owner
(202) 328-0191

PYRAMID BOOKSTORE
3500 East-West Highway
Hyattsville, MD 20782
Hodari Ali, Owner
(301) 559-5200

SAVANNA BOOKS
858 Massachusetts Avenue
Cambridge, MA 02139
Gail Pettiford Willett, Director
(617) 868-3423

SHRINE OF THE BLACK MADONNA BOOKSTORE
13535 Livernois Avenue
Detroit, MI 48238
Barbara Martin, Director
(313) 491-0777

SHRINE OF THE BLACK MADONNA
5309 Martin Luther King, Jr., Blvd.
Houston, TX 77021
Barbara Martin, Director
(713) 645-1071

SHRINE OF THE BLACK MADONNA CULTURE CENTER AND BOOKSTORE
946 Gordon Street, S.W.
Atlanta, GA 30310
Barbara Martin, Director

UNIVERSAL BOOKS & RELI-GIOUS ARTICLES
51 Court Street
White Plains, NY 10601
Carrie Coard, President
(914) 681-0484

Business Associations

These organizations are the primary advocates for business development in black America. They are central to the success of blacks gaining a foothold in the American Marketplace.

ALABAMA

METROPOLITAN BUSINESS LEAGUE
60 Seventeenth Court, South
Birmingham, AL 35205
Leola Early, President

ARIZONA

ARIZONA BLACK CHAMBER OF COMMERCE
P.O. Box 20191
Phoenix, AZ 85036
Deborah L. Ellison, Executive Director
(602) 243-1857

CALIFORNIA

GOLDEN STATE BUSINESS LEAGUE
117 Broadway
Oakland, CA 94607
C. J. Patterson, President
(510) 835-4900

THE AFRICAN AMERICAN CHAMBER OF COMMERCE OF CENTRAL CALIFORNIA
P.O. Box 12144
Fresno, CA 93776
Dorothy J. Smith, President
(209) 266-1432

DISTRICT OF COLUMBIA

D.C. CHAMBER OF COMMERCE
1411 K Street, N.W., Suite 603
Washington, D.C. 20005
Gregory Davis, President
(202) 347-7202

FLORIDA

FLORIDA FIRST COAST CHAPTER
8905 Castle Boulevard
Jacksonville, FL 32209
Isiah J. Williams, III, President
(904) 764-4740

SOUTH FLORIDA BUSINESS LEAGUE
555 North East Fifteenth Street
Suite 31A
Miami, FL 33132
Alexis Snyder, President
(305) 375-5318

TRI-COUNTY CHAPTER, NATIONAL BUSINESS LEAGUE
771 N.W. 22nd Road
Fort Lauderdale, FL 33311
Luther Jackson, President
(305) 581-2916

GEORGIA

ATLANTA BUSINESS LEAGUE
818 Washington Street, S.W.
Atlanta, GA 30315
Valerie H. Montague, President
(404) 584-8126

CSRA BUSINESS LEAGUE
P.O. Box 1283
Augusta, GA 30903
Dr. Faye Hargrove, President
(404) 722-0994

COLUMBUS BUSINESS LEAGUE
P.O. Box 431
Columbus, GA 31902
Leonard L. Leavell, President
(404) 649-3635

ILLINOIS

COSMOPOLITAN CHAMBER OF COMMERCE
1326 South Michigan Ave., Suite 100
Chicago, IL 60605
Consuelo M. Pope, President
(312) 786-0212

KANSAS

WICHITA CHAPTER, NATIONAL BUSINESS LEAGUE
1125 East Thirteenth Street
Wichita, KS 67214
Anderson Jackson, President
(316) 262-5431

LOUISIANA

NEW ORLEANS BUSINESS LEAGUE
107 Harbour Circle
New Orleans, LA 70126
Sherman N. Copelin, Jr., President
(504) 264-1166

MARYLAND

BUSINESS LEAGUE OF BALTIMORE
1831 West North Avenue
Baltimore, MD 21217
Ms. Frankie Taylor, President
(301) 728-1234

DELMARVA CHAPTER, NATIONAL BUSINESS LEAGUE
106 West Circle Avenue
Suite 208
Salisbury, MD 21801
Karl V. Binns, President
(410) 860-2640

MINORITY ALLIANCE NATIONAL BUSINESS LEAGUE
P.O. Box 542
Lexington, MD 20653
Eddie Williams, President

NATIONAL BUSINESS LEAGUE OF MONTGOMERY COUNTY, MARYLAND, INC.
8720 Georgia Avenue
Suite 301
Silver Spring, MD 20910
Michele Dyson, President
(301) 588-2977

NATIONAL BUSINESS LEAGUE OF SOUTHERN MARYLAND, INC.
9200 Basil Court
Suite 210
Landover, MD 20785
Weldon Howard, President
(301) 772-3683

Business Associations

MASSACHUSETTS

BOSTON CHAPTER, NATIONAL BUSINESS LEAGUE
500-502A Harrison Avenue
Boston, MA 02118
Bob Winstead, President
(617) 267-5800

MICHIGAN

BTW BUSINESS ASSOCIATION
2990 West Grand Blvd.
Suite 310
Detroit, MI 48202
Alan C. Young, President
(313) 873-7500

MINNESOTA

MINNESOTA BUSINESS LEAGUE
900 Eighth Avenue, North
Minneapolis, MN 55411
(612) 342-1523

MISSISSIPI

NATCHEZ BUSINESS & CIVIC LEAGUE
1044 Pine Street
Natchez, MS 39120
Harden Wallace, President
(816) 442-6644

MISSOURI

MOUND CITY BUSINESS LEAGUE
10345 Nashua
Dellwood, MO 63136
Marvin Batey, President
(314) 361-2613

NEW JERSEY

SOUTH JERSEY CHAPTER, NATIONAL BUSINESS LEAGUE
P.O. Box 807
Brigantine, NJ 08203-0807
Fred Porter, President
(609) 344-3449

NEW YORK

AFRICAN MINERALS AND RESOURCES EXCHANGE
4 Park Avenue, Floor 16-R
New York, NY
Frank Weston, President
(212) 532-5449

GREATER NEW YORK BUSI- NESS LEAGUE
P.O. Box 181, Adelphi Station
Brooklyn, NY 11238
Byron A. Lee, President
(718) 622-3888

NORTH CAROLINA

DURHAM BUSINESS & PROFES-
SIONAL CHAIN
P.O. Box 1088
Durham, NC 27702
Larry Hester, President

FAYETTEVILLE BUSINESS AND
PROFESSIONAL CHAIN
P.O. Box 1387
Fayetteville, NC 28301
Luther Jerold, President
(919) 483-6252

OHIO

CLEVELAND BUSINESS
LEAGUE
P.O. Box 99556
Cleveland, OH 44199
R. Turner-Hickson, President
(614) 755-2755

DAYTON CHAPTER, NATIONAL
BUSINESS LEAGUE
323 Salem Avenue
Dayton, OH 45406
Bill Littlejohn, President
(513) 222-2889

EL-JABE & COMPANY
28 West Third Street
Dayton, OH, 45402
Eleanore Stocks, President
(513) 461-7005

STARK COUNTY CHAPTER,
NATIONAL BUSINESS
LEAGUE
1514 Maple Avenue, N.E.
Canton, OH 44705
Will Dent, President
(216) 454-8081

OKLAHOMA

NATIONAL BUSINESS LEAGUE
OF OKLAHOMA CITY
P.O. Box 11221
Oklahoma City, OK 73136
Anita Arnold, President

OREGON

OREGON CHAPTER, NATIONAL
BUSINESS LEAGUE
3802 Union Avenue, N.E., Suite 303
Portland, OR 97212
Chad Debnam, President
(503) 249-0711

PENNSYLVANIA

BUSINESS & PROFESSIONAL
ASSOCIATION OF PITTS-
BURGH
4909 Pennsylvania Avenue
Pittsburgh, PA 15224
Lewis Goodman, President
(412) 362-5702

Business Associations

TENNESSEE

MID SOUTH CHAPTER, NA-TIONAL BUSINESS LEAGUE
918 South Parkway, East
Memphis, TN 38106
M. LaTroy Williams, President
(901) 774-8576

TEXAS

AUSTIN CEN-TEX CHAPTER, NATIONAL BUSINESS LEAGUE
1223A Rosewood Avenue
Austin, TX 78702
T. L. Wyatt, President
(512) 476-0179

PYLON SALESMANSHIP CLUB, INC.
P.O. Box 151211
Dallas, TX 75215
Emerson Emory, M.D., President
(214) 421-8333

VIRGINIA

METROPOLITAN BUSINESS LEAGUE
121 East Marshall Street
Richmond, VA 23261
Gladys Jackson-Weston, President
(804) 649-7473

WASHINGTON

TAKOMA-PIERCE COUNTY BUSINESS LEAGUE
1321 South K Street
P.O. Box 5076
Takoma, WA 98405
Frank J. Russell, President
(206) 272-7498

WASHINGTON STATE BUSINESS LEAGUE
P.O. Box 18528
Seattle, WA 98118
James L. McGhee, President
(206) 856-8284

Businesses

The firms listed on these pages represent a partial listing of the top black businesses in the United States. Together they have a combined sales total of over 4 billion dollars.

ALL-STAINLESS, INC.
75 Research Road
Bingham, MA 02143
Eugene Roundtree, Chief Executive
(617) 749-7100

AMERICAN STITCHING & BOX, INC.
P.O. Box 2133
Fairfield, CA 94533
Charles, A. Bell, Chief Executive

ALEXANDER & OLIVER
795 Lake Avenue, N.E.
Atlanta, GA 30307
Josie A. Alexander, Managing Partner
(404) 524-8276

ATLANTIC PACIFIC TECH-NOLOGIES, INC.
450 East Tenth Street
Tracy, CA 95376
Roy Austin, Chief Executive

BARANCO PONTIAC, INC.
4299 Covington Highway
Post Office Box 36237
Decatur, GA 30032
Gregory T. Branco, Chief Executive
(404) 284-4400

THE ATLANTA ECONOMIC DEVELOPMENT CORPORA-TION
230 Peachtree Street, N.W., Suite 1650
Atlanta, GA 30303
Walter R. Huntley, President

THE BARFIELD COMPANIES
800 Lowell Street
Ypsilanti, Mi 48197
John W. Barfield, Chief Executive
(313) 483-5070

BATTEAST CONSTRUCTION COMPANY, INC.
430 LaSalle Avenue
South Bend, IN 46617
Robert Batteast, Chief Executive
(219) 234-3539

BAYSIDE TO-GO
401 Biscayne Boulevard
Suite P107
Miami, FL 33132
Carole Ann Taylor, Owner
(305) 374-5935

BEST FOAM FABRICATORS, INC.
9633 South Cottage Grove
Chicago, IL 60628
Ed Clark, Chief Executive

BLANKINSHIP DISTRIBUTORS
1927 Vine Street
Kansas City, MO
G. L. Blankinship, President
(816) 842-6825

Businesses

BLUNT ENTERPRISES
2018 Fifth Street, N.E.
Washington, D.C. 20018
Roger Blunt, Sr., President
(202) 832-4789

E. G. BOWMAN COMPANY, INC.
97 Wall Street
New York, NY 10005
Ernesta G. Procope, President
(212) 425-8150

BROADCAST ENTERPRISES NATIONAL, INC.
1422 Chestnut Street
8th Floor
Philadelphia, PA 19102
Ragan Henry, Chief Executive
(215) 563-2910

BURNETT'S PACKAGE EX-PRESS
7425 Marilyn Lane
Houston, TX 77016
Burnett Davis Jackson, President
(713) 631-5547

THE CADD GROUP, INC.
P.O. Box 6235
Silver Spring, MD 20916
William Holloway

CAMBRI ENTERPRISES
P.O. Box 24426
Richmond, VA 23224
Stephanie Wingate, Manager
(804) 643-8503

CAM PRI COMMUNICATIONS
500 North Capitol Street, N.W.
Eighth Floor
Washington, D.C. 20001
Lynette Y. Alexander, President
(202) 783-8350

WILLIAM CARGILE CONTRAC-TOR, INC.
2008 Freeman Avenue
Cincinnati, OH 45214
William Cargile, III, Chief Executive

THE CERTIFIED GROUP
517 East 16th Avenue
Denver, CO 80203
Neel Levy, Chief Executive

CENTURY CHEVROLET, INC.
6501 Market Street
Upper Darby, PA 19082
Robert L. Myers, Jr., President
(215) 734-1750

CHAMBERS-THOMPSON MOV-ING AND STORAGE, INC.
P.O. Box 201
Windsor, CT 06095
Emma Scruse, President
(203) 278-5845

COCOLINE CHOCOLATE COMPANY, INC.
689 Myrtle Avenue
Brooklyn, NY 11205
Thomas Bourelly, President
(718) 522-4500

COMMERCIAL MAINTENANCE SERVICES, INC.
P.O. Box 580625
Houston, TX 77258
John W. Rickett, Chief Executive

COMMUNICATIONS INNOVA-TIONS NETWORK, INC.
P.O. Box 67584
Baltimore, MD 21215
Edward Ross Brunson, Chief Exec.
(310) 764-0876

CONYERS FORD, INC.
2475 West Grand Boulevard
Detroit, MI 48208
Nathan G. Conyers, Chief Executive
(313) 894-5704

D&H TIRE SERVICE COMPANY
919 Troup
Kansas City, MO 66104
Luther D. White, Chief Executive
(816) 621-1155

DANNY DUKES MACHINERY-CONVEYORS, INC.
14600 Stansbury
Detroit, MI 48227
Danny Dukes, Preident
(313) 272-0598

DATA COMMUNICATIONS EQUIPMENT, INC.
3492 Souffer Road
Suite 100
Columbus, OH 43225

DAVENPORT'S COMPANY
449 Fifteenth Street
Suite 303
Oakland, CA 94612
Dwight Davenport, President

DISTRICT HEALTHCARE & JANTORIAL SUPPLY
726 Seventh Street, S.E.
Washington, D.C. 20003
Pernell J. William, Chief Executive
(202) 546-0022

EBONY OIL CORPORATION
107-35 Merrick Boulevard
Jamaica, NY 11443
Lawrence J. Cormier, President
(212) 657-2544

ENCORE TEMPORARY, INC.
1012 14th Street, N.W., Suite 904
Washington, D.C. 20005
Teresa Brown, Chief Executive

ENDECON, INC.
P.O. Box 9543
Wilmington, DE 19809
Desmond Baker, President
(302) 764-1991

ENGLISH ENTERPRISES
248 Forest Avenue
Englewood, NJ 07631
Whittie English, Chief Executive
(201) 568-6897

E.P.C. INTERNATIONAL, INC.
141 South Harrison Street
P.O. Box 880
East Orange, NJ 07018
(201) 678-6500

ESSENCE COMMUNICATIONS
1500 Broadway
New York, NY 10036
Edward Lewis, Chief Executive
(212) 730-4260

EXCLUSIVE TEMPORARIES OF VIRGINIA, INC.
100 North Franklin Avenue
Richmond, VA 23219
LaVerne King, Vice President, Personnel
(804) 644-1808

MEL FARR FORD, INC.
24750 Greenfield Road
Oak Park, MI 48237
Mel Farr, Chief Executive

Businesses

FCS COMPUTING SERVICES
601 West Randolph Street
Chicago, IL 60661
John Finch, Chief Executive

FLORIDA REGIONAL REPORT-ING SERVICE
Jefferson Square Building
99 Northwest 183rd Street
Suite 203
Miami, FL 33169
Georgia Foster, President/Court
  Reporter
(303) 653-6164

FULLER OIL COMPANY, INC.
867 Amye Street
Fayetteville, NC 28301
Charles Fuller, Chief Executive
(919) 488-2815

GEMINI SERVICES, INC.
4005 Stearn Mill Raod
Columbus, GA 31907
Sidney G. Ragland, Chief Executive
(404) 687-1207

DICK GIDRON CADILLAC, INC.
696 East Fordham Road
Bronx, NY 10459
Richard Gidron, Chief Executive
(212) 295-3000

GILLESPIE FORD, INC.
3333 Grant Street, Box M-89
Gary, IN 46408
Tom P. Gillespie, Sr., President
(219) 887-6442

GOLD MEDAL HAIR PROD-UCTS, INC.
1 Bennington Avenue
Freeport, NY 11520
Phil Laban, President
(516) 378-6900

GORDON BUICK CADILLAC OLDSMOBILE, INC.
1016 South Delsea Drive
Vineland, NJ 08360
Darrell R. Gordon, President
(609) 794-8600

GORDON BUICK - GMAC TRUCKS, INC.
4211 North Broad Street
Philadelphia, PA 19140
Darrell R. Gordon, President
(215) 457-3900

GOURMET SERVICES, INC.
1100 Spring Street, Suite 450
Atlanta, GA 30367
Nathaniel R. Goldston, III, President
(404) 876-5700

EARL G. GRAVES, LTD
130 Fifth Avenue
New York, NY 10011
Earl G. Graves, Chief Executive
(212) 242-8000

J. S. GRIFFIN & ASSOCIATES, INC.
761 Kenilworth Avenue
Dayton, OH 45405
Joseph S. Griffin, II, President
(513) 275-5761

GRIMES OIL COMPANY
165 Norfolk Street
Boston, MA 02124
Calvin M. Grimes., Jr., President
(617) 825-1200

HEMPSTEAD LIMOUSINE SERVICE CORPORATION
266 Main Street
Hempstead, NY 11550
Henry Holley, President

H. F. HENDERSON INDUSTRIES
45 Fairfield Place
West Caldwell, NJ 07006
Henry F. Henderson, Jr.
(201) 227-9250

HIGH TECHNOLOGY SERVICES, INC.
250 Jordan Road, Suite 210
Troy, NY 12180
Milton L. Evans, President
(518) 283-8072

GEORGE HUGHES CHEVROLET GEO
Route 9, Box 6697
Freehold, NJ 07728
George Hughes, President
(908) 462-1324

IDEAL ELECTRONIC SECURITY COMPANY
1106 Bladensburg Road., N.E.
Washington, D.C. 20002
Cora H. Williams, Chief Executive

INNER CITY BROADCASTING CORPORATION
801 Second Avenue
New York, NY 10017
Percy Sutton, Chief Executive
(212) 953-0300

INNER CITY FOODS, INC.
2412 South Michigan Avenue
Chicago, IL 60616
Garland C. Guide, Chief Executive
(312) 225-8295

INTEGRITY LIMOUSINE SERVICE, INC.
P.O. Box 383
Fair Lawn, NJ 07410
Frank Gonzalez, President
(201) 427-6996

INTERNATIONAL & DOMESTIC DEVELOPMENT CORPORA-TION
4511 Bragg Boulevard
Fayetteville, NC 28303
Marion "Rex" Harris, Chairman
(919) 864-5515

INTERNATIONAL SCIENCE AND TECHNOLOGY INSTITUTE, INC.
2033 M Street, N.W.
Suite 300
Washington, D.C. 20036
B. K. Wesley Copeland, President
(202) 466-7290

INVESTORS EDGE, INC.
1779 Elton Road
Silver Spring, MD 20903
Clinton E. Scott, Jr., President
(301) 445-1228

JAMES W. COLLINS & ASSOCI-ATES, INC.
2070 Chain Bridge Road
Suite 320
Vienna, VA 22182
Paul Smith, Chief Executive

THE JAMES CORPORATION
Lock Box 10170
Station C
Charleston, WV 25357-0170
Charles H. James, II, President
(304) 744-1531

JASPER SAMUEL PRINTING COMPANY
406 West 31st Street
New York, NY 10001
Jasper Samuel, President
(212) 239-9544

Businesses

JEWEL ELEVATOR SERVICES, INC.
1601 South Gayoso Street
New Orleans, LA 70125
Alvin L. Carthon, Sr., Chief Executive

AL JOHNSON CADILLAC-SAAB, INC.
8425 West 159th Street
Tinley Park, IL 60477
Albert Johnson, Sr., President
(312) 429-6600

SAM JOHNSON LINCOLN & MERCURY, INC.
5201 East Independence
Charlotte, NC 28121
Sam Johnson, Chief Executive
(704) 535-7810

JOHNSON PRODUCTS COMPANY, INC.
8522 South Lafayette Avenue
Chicago, IL 60620
George E. Johnson, Chief Executive
(312) 483-4100

JOHNSON PUBLISHING COMPANY, INC.
820 South Michigan Avenue
Chicago, IL 60605
John H. Johnson, Chief Executive
(312) 322-9200

LANDMARK FORD SALES, INC.
P.O. Box 9010
Fairfield, OH 45014
Kenneth C. Younger, Chief Executive
(513) 874-3300

LISMARK DISTRIBUTING COMPANY
1350 South Kings Highway
St. Louis, MO 63110
C.W. Gates, Chief Executive
(314) 534-8000

MC ANARY FORD, INC.
333 Grant Street
Box M89
Gary, IN 46401
Tom Gillespie, Sr., Chief Executive
(219) 887-6442

MC LAUGHLIN OLDSMOBILE
8621 Central Avenue
Capitol Heights, MD 20027
K. McLaughlin, President
(301) 350-1700

METTERS INDUSTRIES, INC.
8200 Greensboro Drive
Suite 500
McLean, VA 22102
Leon Armour, Chief Executive

MISSO SERVICES CORPORATION
5201 Leesburg Pike
Suite 1200
Falls Church, VA 22041
Shelby Coates, Chief Executive
(703) 671-8580

MOORE LAW FIRM, APC
Market Post Tower
55 South Market Street
Suite 1020
San Jose, CA 95113
Rodney G. Moore, Esquire, President
(408) 286-6431

MOTOWN INDUSTRIES
6255 West Sunset Boulevard
Los Angeles, CA
Jheryl Busby, Chief Executive
(213) 468-3500

ON LINE/OFF LINE
5002 Doppler Street
Capitol Heights, MD 20743
Maxwell R. Michell, President
(301) 735-5176

BILL NELSON CHEVROLET, INC.
3233 Auto Plaza
Richmond, CA
William W. Nelson, Sr., Chief
  Executive
(415) 529-0355

NU-DIMENSION FINANCIAL SERVICES
1516 East Princess Anne Road
Suite 205
Norfolk, VA 23504
Bernard L. Scott, Jr. President
(804) 627-2140

PARKER HOUSE SAUSAGE COMPANY
4605 South State Street
Chicago, IL 60609
Daryl F. Grisham, Chief Executive
(312) 538-1112

PARK SAUSAGE COMPANY
501 West Hamburg Street
Baltimore, MD 21230
Raymond V. Haysbert, Sr., President
(301) 727-2212

C. J. PATTERSON COMPANY
117 Broadway
Oakland, CA 94607-3715
Clarence J. Patterson, President
(510) 835-4900

PEYTON OLDSMOBILE-CADILLAC
3550 Homer Adams Parkway
Alton, IL 62002
Henry E. Peyton, President
(618) 465-3550

PHILADELPHIA INTERNATIONAL RECORDS
309 South Broad Street
Philadelphia, PA 19107
Kenneth Gamble, Chief Executive
(215) 985-0900

POLYTECH, INC.
1744 Payne Avenue
Cleveland, OH 44114
Norman R. Bliss, President
(216) 696-3141

PRO-LINE CORPORATION
2121 Panoramic Circle
Dallas, TX 75212
Comer J. Cottrell, President
(214) 631-Hair

PULSAR DATA SYSTEMS, INC.
5000 Philadelphia Way, Suite H
Lanham, MD 20706
William W. Davis, President
Edward G. Viltz, Vice President and
  Chief Operating Officer
(301) 459-2650

Businesses

RAN-DER INDUSTRIES, INC.
P.O. Box 683
Morgan City, LA 70381
Allison B. Randolph, President
(504) 384-1341

R P EXHIBIT SERVICE, INC.
1761 Olive Street
Capitol Heights, MD 20743
Rodney K. West

REALTY WORLD/ENGLISH REALTY
248 Forest Avenue
Englewood, NJ 07631
Whittie English, Chief Executive
(201) 568-6897

BOB ROSS BUICK, INC.
85 Loop Road
Centerville, OH 45459
Robert Ross, Chief Executive
(513) 433-0990

SEIDEL CHEVROLET, INC.
7610 Central Avenue
Landover, MD 20786
John S. Seidel, Chief Executive
(301) 350-4100

SENTRY BUICK, INC.
11522 West Dodge Road
Omaha, NE 68154
Gregory Williams, Chief Executive
(402) 333-8000

L. H. SMITH OIL CORPORATION
P.O. Box 88157
Indianapolis, IN 46208
Lannie H. Smith, Jr., Chief Executive
(317) 637-2999

S.T.R. CORPORATION
17315 Miles Avenue
Cleveland, OH 44128
Steve Rogers, Chief Executive
(216) 233-5550

SYSTEMS MANAGEMENT AMERICA (SMA) CORPORA-TION
254 Monticello Avenue
Norfolk, VA 23510
Herman E. Valentine, President
(804) 627-9331

SYMBIONT, INC.
901 Fifteenth Street, N.W., Suite 310
Washington, D.C. 20005
James Bud Ward, Chief Executive

TECHNOLOGY APPLICATIONS, INC.
6101 Stevenson Avenue
Alexandria, VA 22304
James I. Chatman, Chief Executive
(703) 461-2000

TELECOMMUNICATIONS SERVICES COMPANY, INC.
1807 Brightseat Road
Landover, MD 20785
Dennis Harris, Chief Executive

THE TRIAD GROUP
1625 K Street, N.W., Suite 1210
Washington, D.C. 20006
Kent Amos, Contact
(202) 775-3500

ULTIMATE MARKETING, INC.
713 Westbank Expressway
Gretna, LA 70053
David St. Etienne, Chief Executive

UNIFIED INDUSTRIES, INC.
6551 Loisdale Court
Suite 400
Springfield, VA 22150
Theodore A. Adams, Jr., President
(703) 922-9800

VITA-ERB LIMITED
1359 North Stewart
Springfield, JO 65802
Mary Barnes, Chief Executive

VIDEO DIMENSIONS, INC.
330 Washington Blvd.
Suite 510
Marina Del Rey, CA 90292
Dwight Blackshear, Chief Executive

WALLACE & WALLACE ENTERPRISES, INC.
200-33 Linden Boulevard
St. Albans, NY 11412
Charles Wallace, Chief Executive
(212) 528-6000

WALTON BUICK-OPEL, INC.
4100 Mystic Valley Parkway
Medford, MA 02155
Roland Walton, Chief Executive
(617) 395-6400

PAYTON WELLS FORD, INC.
1510 North Meridian Street
Indianapolis, IN 46202
Payton R. Wells, Chief Executive
(317) 638-4838

Church Denominations & Organizations

Black churches play a crucial role in black America. Numbering approximately 65,000, they represent the most independent black institutions in the United States. Whether it's supporting black colleges or registering people to vote, they are a power to be reckoned with.

© **Robert Sengstacke**

AFRICAN METHODIST EPISCO-PAL CHURCH
1134 Eleventh Street, N.W.
Washington, D.C. 20001
Bishop Vernon R. Byrd, President,
   Council of Bishops
(203) 371-8700

AFRICAN METHODIST EPISCO-PAL CHURCH FINANCE DEPARTMENT
1134 Eleventh Street, N.W.
Washington, D.C. 20001
Dr. Joseph C. McKinney, Treasurer
(202) 371-8700

AFRICAN METHODIST EPISCO-PAL ZION CHURCH
P.O. Box 32843
Charlotte, NC 28232
William M. Smith, Senior Bishop
(704) 598-7419

AMERICAN MUSLIM MISSION
7330 South Stoney Island
Chicago, IL 60649
Warith Dean Muhammad, Iman
(312) 667-7220

BIBLE WAY TEMPLE
1100 New Jersey Avenue, N.W.
Washington, D.C. 20001
Elder James Silver
(202) 789-0700

BLACK WOMEN IN CHURCH & SOCIETY
c/o Interdenominational Church &
   Society
671 Beckwith Street, S.W.
Atlanta, GA 30314
Jacquelyn Grant, Director
(404) 527-7740

CHURCH OF GOD IN CHRIST
272 South Main Street
Memphis, TN 38101
Bishop J.P. Patterson
(901) 527-1422

Church Denominations & Organizations

CONGRESS OF NATIONAL BLACK CHURCHES
1225 Eye Street, N.W., Suite 750
Washington, D.C. 20005
Rev. H. Michael Lemmons, Executive
    Director
(202) 371-1091

GOSPEL MUSIC WORKSHOP OF AMERICA, INC.
P.O. Box 4632
Detroit, MI 48234
Edward D. Smith, Executive Secretary
(313) 989-2340

KNIGHTS AND LADIES OF ST. PETER CLAVER
1825 Orleans Avenue
New Orleans, LA 70116
Chester J. Jones, Supreme Knight
(504) 821-4225

NATIONAL ASSOCIATION OF BLACK CATHOLIC ADMINIS-TRATORS
50 North Park Avenue
Rockville Centre, NY 11570
Barbara Horsham-Brathwaite
(516) 678-5800

NATIONAL BAPTIST CONVEN-TION OF AMERICA, INC.
1327 Pierre Avenue
Shreveport, LA 71103
Dr. E. Edward Jones, President
(318) 221-3701

NATIONAL BAPTIST CONVEN-TION USA, INC.
1700 Baptist World Center
Nashville, TN 37207
T. J. Jemison, D.D., President
(615) 228-6292

NATIONAL BLACK CATHOLIC CONGRESS
320 Cathedral Street
Baltimore, MD 21202
Leodia Gooch, Executive Director
(301) 547-5330

NATIONAL BLACK CATHOLIC SEMINARIAN ASSOCIATION
1818 W. 71st Street
Chicago, IL 60636
Dr. Robert Smith, President
(312) 994-7468

NATIONAL BLACK SISTERS' CONFERENCE
7871 Hillside Street
Oakland, CA 94605-3242
Sister Marie de Porres Taylor, SNJM,
    Executive Director
(415) 891-9292

NATIONAL CATHOLIC CONFERENCE FOR INTERRACIAL JUSTICE
3033 Fourth Street, N.E.
Washington, D.C. 20017
Jerome Ernst, Executive Director
(202) 529-6480

NATIONAL OFFICE OF BLACK CATHOLICS
5005 Eastern Avenue
P.O. Box 29260
Washington, D.C. 20017
(202) 635-1778

NATIONAL UNITED CHURCH USHERS ASSOCIATION OF AMERICA, INC.
1431 Shepard Street, N.W.
Washington, D.C. 20011
Paul L. Finch, President
(202) 722-1192

Church Denominations & Organizations

PROGRESSIVE NATIONAL BAPTIST CONVENTION, INC.
601 50th Street, N.E.
Rev. Charles Adams, President
(202) 356-0558

SOCIETY OF AFRICAN MISSIONS
23 Bliss Avenue
Tenafly, NJ 07670
Father Thomas Conlon, Director
(201) 567-0450

THE AFRICAN PEOPLE'S CHRISTIAN ORGANIZATION
415 Atlantic Avenue
Brooklyn, NY 11217
Rev. Herbert Daughtry, President
(212) 596-1991

THE NATION OF ISLAM
4855 South Woodlawn
Chicago, IL 60615
Honorable Louis Farrakhan,
   Chief Executive
(312) 324-6000

THE PAN AFRICAN ORTHODOX CHRISTIAN CHURCH
13535 Livernois Avenue
Detroit, MI 48238
Rev. Albert Cleage, Jr., President
(313) 491-0777

UNION OF BLACK EPISCOPALIANS
26 Leyland Street
Dorchester, MA 02125
Edrick Bain, President
(617) 442-5495

UNITED BLACK CHURCH APPEAL
860 Forrest Avenue
Bronx, NY 10456
Honorable Wendell Foster, President
(212) 992-5315

UNITED CHURCH OF CHRIST COMMISSION FOR RACIAL JUSTICE
700 Prospect Avenue
Cleveland, OH 44115-1100
Dr. Benjamin F. Chavis, Jr.,
   Executive Director
(216) 736-2168

WOMEN MINISTERS OF GREATER WASHINGTON
624 17th Street, N.E.
Washington, D.C. 20002
Rev. Mozelle J. Fuller, President
(212) 683-5656

Civil Rights Organizations

© Robert Sengstacke

Despite setbacks in the civil rights arena, these organizations stand poised to oppose injustice wherever it is found. Their hard work has made a difference in the lives of millions of Americans.

A. PHILLIP RANDOLPH INSTITUTE
260 Park Avenue, South
New York, NY 10010
Norman Hill, President
(212) 533-8000

CENTER FOR DEMOCRATIC RENEWAL
P.O. Box 50469
Atlanta, Ga 30302
Rev. C.T. Vivian, Chairman
(404) 221-0025

CONGRESS OF RACIAL EQUALITY (CORE)
30 Cooper Square, 9th Floor
New York, NY 10003
Roy Innis, National Chairman
(212) 598-4000

LAWYERS' COMMITTEE FOR CIVIL RIGHTS UNDER LAW
1400 Eye Street, N.W., Suite 400
Washington, D.C. 20005
Barbara Arnwine, Executive Director
(202) 371-1212

LEADERSHIP CONFERENCE ON CIVIL RIGHTS
2027 Massachusetts Avenue, N.W.
Washington, D.C. 20036
Benjamin Hooks, Chairman
(202) 667-1780

MARTIN LUTHER KING CENTER FOR NONVIOLENT SOCIAL CHANGE, INC.
449 Auburn Avenue, N.E.
Atlanta, GA 30312
Coretta S. King, President
(404) 524-1956

NATIONAL ASSOCIATION FOR THE ADVANCEMENT OF COLORED PEOPLE
4805 Mt. Hope Drive
Baltimore, MD 21215
(301) 358-8900

Civil Rights Organizations

**NAACP LEGAL DEFENSE AND
  EDUCATIONAL FUND, INC.**
99 Hudson Street, 16th Floor
New York, NY 10013
Julius L. Chambers, Director-Counsel
(212) 219-1900

OPERATION PUSH, INC.
930 East 50th Street
Chicago, IL 6015
(312) 373-3366

NATIONAL URBAN LEAGUE
500 East 62nd Street
New York, NY 10021
John E. Jacobs, President
(212) 310-9000

**SOUTHERN CHRISTIAN LEAD-
  ERSHIP CONFERENCE**
334 Auburn Avenue, N.E.
Atlanta, GA 30312
Rev. Dr. Joseph Lowery, President
(404) 522-1420

**UNITED CHURCH OF CHRIST
  COMMISSION FOR RACIAL
  JUSTICE**
700 Prospect Avenue
Cleveland, OH 44115-1100
Rev. Dr. Benjamin F. Chavis, Jr.,
Executive Director
(216) 241-5400

Consultants

Many of the organizations listed in this section are national in scope and provide valuable services to our nation.

ALABAMA

AMERICAN TECHNICAL SERVICE
3822 Timbrcrest Drive, N.W.
Huntsville, AL 35801
Charles Brandon, President
(205) 859-3198

FOUR J ASSOCIATES
616 Treehaven Drive
Birmingham, AL 35214
W. J. Tigner, President
(205) 798-4642

CALIFORNIA

ADMINISTRATIVE PLANNING & SUPPORT
11917 Ainsworth
Los Angeles, CA 90044
Barbara D. Moore, Director of
  Projects
(213) 755-2054

THE DENVER GROUP
6222 Wilshire Blvd.
Suite 400
Los Angeles, CA 90048
Bridget Hally Graves, Vice President
(213) 936-9200

THE IRVING HAMPTON COMPANY
8150 Beverly Blvd., Suite 302
Los Angeles, CA 90048
Lawrence K. Irvin, President
(213) 653-6571

JEFFERSON ASSOCIATES, INC.
683 McAllister Street
San Francisco, CA 94102
James D. Jefferson, President
(415) 931-3001

REYNAUD E. MOORE & ASSOCIATES
3711 West Jefferson Blvd.
Los Angeles, CA 90016
Rey Moore, President
(213) 735-2203

PERCY E. BOLTON ASSOCIATES, INC.
2121 Ave. Of The Stars., Suite 600
Los Angeles, CA 90067
Percy E. Bolton, Managing Director
(310) 551-6563

P.O.S. ASSOCIATES
P.O. Box 10728
Santa Ana, CA 92711
Ken Caines, Director
(714) 835-3163

SLAUGHTER & ASSOCIATES
5819 Manton Avenue
Woodland Hills, CA 91367
Leonard S. Slaugter, Jr., Managing
  Partner
(818) 888-1730

Consultants

E. H. WHITE & COMPANY
245 Clement Street
San Francisco, CA 94118
Earl H. White, President
(415) 668-0076

COLORADO

PEOPLE SKILLS INSTITUTE
244 South Oman Road
Castle Rock, CO 80104
Bob Cornell, President
(303) 688-2152

PLANNERS, ETC.
1722 Lafayette
Denver, CO 80218
Glenda Swanson Lyle, Owner

JAMES F. POOLE ASSOCIATES, INC.
201 West Eighth
Pueblo, CO 81003
James Poole, President
(719) 542-3313

CONNECTICUT

BREWSTER ASSOCIATES
40 West High Street
East Hampton, CT 06424
William S. Brewster, President
(203) 267-2973

DISTRICT OF COLUMBIA

A. M. HERMAN & ASSOCIATES, INC.
1050 17th Street, N.W.,Suite 560
Washington, D.C. 20036
Alexis Herman, President
(202) 797-7206

ASSOCIATES CONSULTANTS, INC.
1726 M Street, N.W., Suite 600
Washington, D.C. 20036
Lawrence A. Landry, President
(202) 737-8062

CONSULTING ASSOCIATES
1420 Sixteenth Street, N. W.
Washington, D.C. 20036
Cherie D. Jones, President
(202) 234-7333

CREATIVE UNIVERSAL PROD-UCTS, INC.
2025 I Street, N.W. , Suite 605
Washington, D.C. 20006
Gary T. Williams, President
(202) 347-2534

D R & ASSOCIATES
1776 K Street, N.W., Suite 607
Washington, D.C. 20006
DeVera Redmond, President
(202) 966-6791

EBON RESEARCH SYSTEMS
820 Quincy Street, N.W.
Washington, D.C. 20011
Florence Alexander, President
(202) 722-5242

ENTERPRISES FOR NEW DIRECTION, INC.
7315 Wisconsin Avenue, Suite 1125N
Washington, D.C. 20814
Charles L. Wilson, President

WILSON HILL ASSOCIATES, INC.
1220 L Street, N.W., Suite 200
Washington, D.C. 20005
Alan B. Tolk, Director Corporate
  Development
(202) 842-7700

KOBA ASSOCIATES, INC.
1156 Fifteenth Street, N.W.
Washington, D.C. 20005
Ford Johnson, President
(202) 328-5700

**ROY LITTLEJOHN ASSOCI-
ATES, INC.**
1101 Fourteenth Street, N.W.
Washington, D.C. 20005
Roy Littlejohn, President
(202) 842-0002

**MCCLURE-LUNDBERG ASSOCI-
ATES, INC.**
1515 U Street, N.W.
Washington, D.C. 20009
James W. Lundberg, Vice President
(202) 483-4107

METRO STUDY CORPORATION
1347 South Capital Street, S.W.
Washington, D.C. 20024
Albert L. Beverly, President
(202) 488-0556

METROTEC, INC.
1623 Connecticut Avenue, N.W.
Washington, D.C. 20009
Jack E. Nelson, President
(202) 232-8484

**A. L. NELLUM & ASSOCIATES,
INC.**
1900 L Street, N.W., Suite 405
Washington, D.C. 20036
Sharlynn E. Bobo, Vice President
(202) 466-4920

THE PATA GROUP
617 K Street, N.W.
Washington, D.C. 20001
Patricia A. Toney, President
(202) 789-1330

**TRUST INTERNATIONAL
SERVICES COMPANY, INC.**
1511 K Street, N.W., Suite 1100
Washington, D.C. 20005
Donnie M. Vinson, President
(202) 737-3568

**WILLIAMS & COMPANY,
INTERNATIONAL**
2016 O Street, N.W.
Washington, D.C. 20036
Walker A. Williams, President
(202) 296-1936

FLORIDA

AAA RESOURCES, INC.
P.O. Box 13143
Bradenton, FL 33505
Charles J. Benton, President
(813) 753-9133

**CAREER CONSULTANTS OF
MELBOURNE, INC.**
1900 S. Harbor City Blvd., Suite 124
Melbourne, FL 32901
Ted Lane, President
(407) 725-4903

GEORGIA

**ADMILL CONSULTING AND
ASSOCIATES**
2550 Sandy Plains Road, Suite 30191
Marietta, GA 30066
Richard L. Admill, President
(404) 578-0774

**ATLANTA INTERNATIONAL
CONSULTING GROUP, INC.**
664 Queens Street
Atlanta, GA 30310
Clayvon Croom, President

Consultants

BOTTOMLINE PERFORMANCE INTERVENTIONS CORPORATION
100 Galleria Parkway, Suite 400
Atlanta, GA 30339
David Hector, President
(404) 951-4888

WILLIAM CAMERON & ASSOCIATES, INC.
6100 Lake Forest Drive, Suite 550
Atlanta, GA 30328
Harold Armstrong, Marketing Director
(800) 334-6014

COLEMAN MANAGEMENT CONSULTANTS, INC.
11 Piedmont Center, Suite 200
Atlanta, GA 30305
Harvey J. Coleman, President
(404) 266-2991

"DIGGING IT UP"
Research & Consultants
546 Blake Avenue, S.E.
Atlanta, GA 30313
Herman Mason, Jr. President
(404) 627-7799

DIVERSIFIED PROJECT MANAGEMENT, INC.
500 Fair Street, S.W.
Atlanta, GA 30313
Arthur J. Clement, President
(404) 522-6573

GOLDEN EAGLE BUSINESS SERVICES, INC.
1401 Peachtree Street, N.E., Suite 101
Atlanta, GA 30309
Ivory J. Dorsey, President
(404) 881-6777

JOHN GRISSOM & ASSOCIATES
2189 Cascade Road, S.W.
Atlanta, GA 30311
(404) 755-4542

HUMAN RESOURCES MANAGEMENT CORPORATION
111 Petrol Point, Suite 204
Peachtree City, GA 30269
Reginald Williams, Executive Vice
President
(404) 631-3633

ROGER SMITH & ASSOCIATES
P.O. Box 50207
Atlanta, GA 30302
Roger Smith, President
(404) 752-6099

ILLINOIS

ASSOCIATED PSYCHOLOGICAL SERVICES
53 West Jackson Blvd., Suite 1621
Chicago, IL 60604
Theophilus E. Green, Director
(312) 922-2165

JOHN BELL & ASSOCIATES, INC.
300 West Washington
Suite 706
Chicago, IL 60606
J. H. Bell, President
(312) 346-7677

CALMAR COMMUNICATIONS
500 North Dearborn, Suite 1118
Chicago, IL 60610
Lilliam Calhoun, Co-Owner
(312) 670-3540

Consultants

HUMAN RESOURCE DEVELOPERS, INC.
112 West Oak
Chicago, IL 60610
Dr. D.C. Dauw, President
(312) 644-1920

JAMES H. LOWRY & ASSOCIATES
218 North Jefferson Street
Fourth Floor
Chicago, IL 60661
James H. Lowry, President
(312) 930-0930

MARTIN, BOONE ASSOCIATES
1829 Bissell, Suite 3
Chicago, IL 60614
William A. Boone, Owner
(312) 266-8867

MC CLINTON MANAGEMENT SERVICES, INC.
407 South Dearborn
Suite 1150
Chicago, IL 60605
Suzzanne, McClinton, President
(312) 922-3194

RALPH G. MOORE & ASSOCIATES
35 East Wacker Drive
Suite 1990
Chicago, IL 60601
Ralph G. Moore, President
(312) 222-9011

NIX & ASSOCIATES
1700 East 73rd Street
Chicago, IL 60649
Sylvia Nix, Owner
(312) 955-2807

STRATEGIC BUSINESS SERVICES, INC.
19710 South Governors Highway, Suite 1
Flossmoor, IL 60430
Lorine S. Samuels, President
(708) 957-0022

TARIFERO & TAZEWELL, INC.
211 South Clark
P.O. Box 2130
Chicago, IL 60690-2130
Richard Biggles, Vice President
(312) 721-2191

TURNBULL ENTERPRISES, INC.
333 North Michigan Avenue, Suite 532
Chicago, IL 60601
Arthur Turnbull, President
(312) 726-5252

INDIANA

DEVELOPMENT PLUS
3008 North Capital
Indianapolis, IN 46208
Jesse L. Carter, Sr., President
(317) 924-6381

MALICHI, INC.
Capital Center North Tower
Box 44165
Indianapolis, IN 46244
T. R. Malichi, President
(317) 637-3944

SHERMAN ROBINSON, INC.
708 Bungalow Court
Indianapolis, IN 46220
Sherman Robinson, President
(317) 257-4485

Consultants

IOWA

SPENCE, EWING & ASSOCIATES
420 Fleming Boulevard
Des Moines, IA 50309
Silas S. Ewing, President
(515) 283-2473

LOUISIANA

TUCKER & ASSOCIATES, INC.
616 Girod Street
New Orleans, LA 70130
Janee M. Tucker, President
(504) 522-4627

MARYLAND

ASSOCIATED ENTERPRISES, INC.
120 Admiral Cochrane Drive
Annapolis, MD 21401
Leonard A. Blackshear, President
(301) 841-6920

BIRCH & DAVIS ASSOCIATES, INC.
8905 Fairview Road, Suite 300
Silver Spring, MD 20910
Willie H. Davis, President
(301) 589-6760

CHILDREN FIRST, INC. (CFI)
3514 Bank Street
Baltimore, MD 21224
Thomas C. Taylor, President

CITIMEDIA, INC.
Communications Consultants
6821 Reistertown Road, Suite 205
Baltimore, MD 21215
(410) 764-0876

JAMES V. CLARK, & ASSOCIATES, INC.
10680 Rain Dream Hill
Columbia, MD 21044
James V. Clark, President
(301) 596-6609

CREATIVE COMMUNICATIONS ASSOCIATES
3603 Tyrol Drive
Landover, MD 20785
Robert W. Maddox, Director
(301) 772-5839

DICOMM.
4 West 26th Street
Baltimore, MD 21218
Brenda Goburn Smith, President

EXPAND ENTERPRISES, INC.
1400 Spring Street, Suite 300
Silver Spring, MD 20910
Reid E. Jackson, II, President
(301) 585-7400

MABARNES CONSULTANT ASSOCIATES, INC.
9470 Annapolis Road, Suite 224
Lanham, MD 20706
Dr. Margaret A. Barnes, Ph.D.,
  Managing Officer
(301) 459-4990

THE MAXIMA CORPORATION
4200 Parliment, Suite 300
Lanham, MD 20706-1849
Joshua Smith, President
(301) 230-2000

MORGAN MANAGEMENT SYSTEMS, INC.
5401 White Mane
Columbia, MD 21045
Walter E. Morgan, Owner
(301) 997-4060

NICHOLSONNE & ASSOCIATES
2211 Maryland Avenue
Baltimore, MD 21218
W. Nicholsonne, President
(301) 235-3500

PROFESSIONAL TRAINING SYSTEMS, INC.
7272 Cradlerock Way
Columbia, MD 21045
Wesley Harvey, President
(301) 381-4233

MASSACHUSETTS

BELL ASSOCIATES, INC.
17 Story Street
Cambridge, MA 02138
Alan Bell, President
(617) 876-2933

SMITH/GILL ASSOCIATES
10 White Pine Lane
Lexington, MA 02173
Geraldine G. Smith, President
(617) 861-1726

MICHIGAN

B & F MARKETING/PIONEER'S CO-OP
182 West Manchester Avenue
Battle Creek, MI 49016
Felton E. Lewis, III, Owner
(616) 968-6989

BADGETT ELECTRONICS CONSULTING
P.O. Box 20098
Detroit, MI 48220
Maurice Badgett, Jr., Operations
  Manager
(313) 893-9807

BURDETTE AND DOSS ASSOCIATES
17368 West 12 Mile Road, Suite 101
Southfield, MI 48076
LaVere E. Burdette, Partner
(313) 569-0344

CAREERWORKS, INC.
1200 East McNicholas
Hamtramick, MI 48202
Rick Drabant, Vice President
(313) 873-0700

HOLLAND CONSULTING, INC.
17177 North Laurel Park Drive
Livonia, MI 48152
Elliott Holland, President
(313) 591-0666

MARKET RESEARCH GROUP
910 East Second Street
Flint, MI 48503
Ed J. Selby, Vice President
(313) 234-3371

RONNOC, INC.
2712 North Saginaw Street
Flint, MI 48505
Venetia Chaney, Accounts Executive
(313) 234-3408

MINNESOTA

P.E.C.
Professional EEO Consultants, Inc.
6103 Creekview Trail
Minnetonka, MN 55345
Wil Ternoir, President
(612) 934-1376

J. TABORN ASSOCIATES
1614 Harmon Place, Suite 300
Minneapolis, MN 55403
Joyce Taborn Jackson, Secretary
(612) 338-9012

Consultants

MISSISSIPPI

SYSTEMS CONSULTANT ASSOCIATES, INC.
510 George Street, Suite 230
Jackson, MS 39202
William M. Cooley, President
(601) 353-6862

MISSOURI

BRISCOE-CARR CONSULTANTS, INC.
3519 Walnut
Kansas City, MO 64111
James Briscoe, President
(816) 931-5626

DYNAMIC SYSTEMS INTERNATIONAL LIMITED
6468 Fairford Court
Florissant, MO 63033
Gerald Carson, Vice President

REFLECTIONS AND ASSOCIATES
P.O. Box 4889
St. Louis, MO 63108
Delores Merritts, Vice President
(314) 361-1991

The listings in this directory are available as Mailing Labels. See last page for details.

URBAN BEHAVIORAL RESEARCH ASSOCIATES, INC.
1204 Washington Avenue
St. Louis, MO 63103
Dr. Miller Boyd, President
(314) 421-4470

NEBRASKA

CHANDLER & ASSOCIATES, LTD.
4220 Pratt Street
Omaha, NE 68111
Virgil R. Chandler, President
(402) 453-4560

NEW JERSEY

BOONE, YOUNG & ASSOCIATES, INC.
270 Sylvan Avenue
Englewood Cliffs, NJ 07632
M. David Boone, President
(201) 871-3900

NATURAL RESOURCE DYNAMICS, INC.
P.O. Box 333
Newton, NJ 07860
Sylvester Fletcher, President
(201) 383-6111

NEW YORK

CAISSE CAPITAL LIMITED
234 Fifth Avenue
New York, NY 10001
Colin Mukete, President
(212) 696-1310

JOSEPH A. DAVIS CONSULTANTS, INC.
104 East 40th Street
New York, NY 10016
Joseph A. Davis, President
(212) 682-4006

DIMPEX ASSOCIATES, INC.
79 Madison Avenue
New York, Ny 10016
V.R. Hazlewood, Vice Pesident
(212) 679-1977

INTERCONTINENTAL SYSTEMS
3537 Grace Avenue
Bronx, NY 10466
Vernon Byron, President
(212) 652-8597

ONYX MANAGEMENT & TRAINING, INC.
35 Leaf Road
Delmar NY 12054
Annette De Lavallade, President
(518) 439-0310

JOHN T. PATTERSON & ASSOCIATES
90 Riverside Drive
New York, NY 10024
John Patterson, President
(212) 292-3113

BRUCE ROBINSON ASSOCIATES
250 West 57th Street, Suite 417
New York, NY 10107
Bruce Robinson, President
(212) 541-4140

SANDS ASSOCIATES
16 Ross Lane
Middletown, NY 10940
George Sands, President
(914) 692-6296

NORTH CAROLINA

DAVIS MANAGEMENT SERVICES
1334 North Patterson Avenue
Winston-Salem, NC 27105
Richard Davis, Owner
(919) 723-2015

MANAGEMENT MANPOWER ASSOCIATES, INC.
1409 East Boulevard
Charlotte, NC 28203
James K. Polk, President
(704) 334-3007

NATIONAL FINANCIAL BUSINESS CONSULTANTS, INC.
P.O. Box 1333
High Point, NC 27261
S. N. Gnato Waden Jr., President
(919) 841-3491

SOUTHEASTERN INTERNATIONAL
2120 California Drive
Lumberton, NC 28358
Mildred Lohr, President
(919) 738-9546

OHIO

BURNS PUBLIC RELATIONS SERVICES, INC.
668 Euclid Avenue, Suite 516
Cleveland, OH 44114
Dargan J. Burns, President
(216) 621-5950

TOM DAVIS AGENCY
1501 Euclid Avenue, Suite 712
Cleveland, OH 44115
Thomas J. Davis, President
(216) 621-6093

Consultants

**DAVID GORDON HILL &
   ASSOCIATES**
1228 Euclid Avenue, Suite 900
Halle Building
Cleveland, OH 44115
David G. Hill, President

POPE AND ASSOCIATES, INC.
1313 East Kemper Road
Suite 171
Cincinnati, OH 45246
Patricia C. Pope, Vice President
(513) 671-1277

THE RESEARCH GROUP
P.O. Box 17639
Dayton, OH 45417-0639
Phyllis J. Wiley, Owner
(513) 268-4245

**ERNEST J. WAITS &
   ASSOCIATES**
The Human Resource Laboratory
35 East Seventh Street
Suite 605
Cincinnati, OH 45202
Ernest J. Waits, President
(513) 721-1383

OKLAHOMA

**BERN L. GENTRY &
   ASSOCIATES**
P.O. Box 52528
Tulsa, OK 74152
Bern L. Gentry, President
(918) 745-2120

OREGON

NERO & ASSOCIATES, INC.
520 S.W. Sixth Avenue, Suite 1250
Portland, OR 97204-1510
David M. Nero., Jr., CEO
(503) 223-4150

PENNSYLVANIA

GOULD ASSOCIATES
160 North Gulph Road
NBS, Suite 201
King of Prussia, PA 19406
Marie Gould, President
(800) 829-1728

PORTIS CONSULTING, INC.
900 Wood Street
Pittsburgh, PA 15221
Charles Portis, President
(412) 731-8005

**PROGRAM RESEARCH AND
   DEVELOPMENT, INC.**
6025 Broad Street
Pittsburgh, PA 15206
John C. Mosely, Ph.D., President
(412) 441-6657

TEXAS

APROPOS BUSINESS SYSTEMS
6363 Beverly Hills, Suite 9
Houston, TX 77057
Gwen Davis, President
(713) 965-9966

ENTERPRISE ADVISORY SERVICES, INC.
6671 Southwest Freeway
Houston, TX 77074
Robert E. Carter, President
(713) 270-7177

VIRGINIA

CAPITOL POLICY & RESOURCE GROUP
P.O. Box 16336
Alexandria, VA 22302
John Singleton, Partner
(703) 683-4868

THE PRAGMA GROUP
116 East Broad Street
Falls Church, VA 22046-4501
Jacques Defay, President
(703) 237-9303

UNIFIED INDUSTRIES, INC.
6551 Loisdale
Springfield, VA 22150
James B. Lee, Vice President
(703) 922-9800

WASHINGTON

NAT JACKSON & ASSOCIATES, INC.
208 West Bay Drive
Olympia, WA 98502
Nat Jackson, President
(206) 943-6000

WISCONSIN

NEW DIRECTIONS MANAGE-MENT SERVICES, INC.
419 Pleasant Street, Suite 204
Beloit, WI 53511
Regina M. Prude, President
(608) 362-8183

The listings in this directory are available as Mailing Labels. See last page for details.

Detective Agencies

The following is a partial listing of African American detective agencies in America.

ARIZONA

UNITED GUARD SECURITY
4220 South Sixteenth Street
Phoenix, Az 85040
Lonnie Gray, President
(602) 268-3403

DISTRICT OF COLUMBIA

COLORADO SECURITY AGENCY, INC.
5521 Colorado Avenue, N.W.
Washington, D.C. 20011
John Payne, President
(202) 829-9233

FLORIDA

JOEY CLEMENTS INVESTIGA-TIVE & DETECTIVE AGENCY, INC.
P.O. Box 471102
Miami, FL 33147
Joey Clements, President
(305) 358-4518

ILLINOIS

STAR DETECTIVE & SECURITY AGENCY, INC.
813 East 75th Street
Chicago, IL 60619
Vivian V. Wilson, President
(312) 874-1900

INDIANA

DILWORTH'S DETECTIVE AGENCY
553 Taney Place
Gary, IN 46404
Fred Dilworth, Owner
(219) 949-4224

MARYLAND

SECURITY AMERICA SERVICES, INC.
8850 Stanford Boulevard, Suite 2800
Columbia, MD 21045
Melvin Bilal, President
(301) 740-2111

NEW JERSEY

UNIQUE SECURITY SERVICES
7 Watchung Avenue
Plainfield, NJ 07060
John S. LaGoff, President
(201) 756-5650

NEW YORK

LANCE INVESTIGATION SERVICE, INC.
1438 Boston Road
Bronx, NY 10460
John Bullard, Sales Manager
(212) 893-1400

MILLS PATROL SERVICE, INC.
1 West 125th Street
New York, NY 10027
Curtis L. Mills, President
(212) 369-6066

OHIO

MID-AMERICAN SECURITY SERVICE, INC.
2641 South Arlington Road
Akron, OH 44319
William G. McGarvey, President
(216) 644-0655

PENNSYLVANIA

J. TURNERS DETECTIVE AND SECURITY AGENCY
3408 Pennsylvania Avenue
Pittsburgh, PA 15201
J. Turner, Owner & Director
(412) 687-6884

Education

African American Studies Programs

The entries in this section are key to the study of African and African-American history.

ABILENE CHRISTIAN UNIVERSITY
Box 8245
Abilene, TX 79601
Professor B. F. Speck

ALBANY STATE COLLEGE
Black Studies Program
Albany, GA 31705
Professor Lois Hollis
(912) 439-4381

AMHERST COLLEGE
Black Studies Department
17 Chapin Hall
Amherst, MA 01002
Andrea Benton Rushing, Chairperson
(413) 542-2300

ANDERSON COLLEGE
Anderson, In 46012
James C. Hendrix, Minority Student
   Advisor
(317) 649-9071

ATLANTA UNIVERSITY
Afro-American Studies
Atlanta, GA 30314
(404) 681-0251

AUGSBURG COLLEGE
Women & Minority Studies Department
731 - 21st Avenue South
Minneapolis, MN 55454
Professor Winston Minor
(612) 330-1022

BAKER UNIVERSITY
Minority Studies
Baldwin City, KS 66006
Professor Claude Walker

BALL STATE UNIVERSITY
Afro-American Studies
Special Program House
Muncie, IN 47306
Professor Hal Chase

BARD COLLEGE
Higher Education Program
Annondale-on-the-Hudson, NY 12504
Dr. Maurice Lee

BENNETT COLLEGE
Afro-American Studies
Greensboro, NC 27420
Professor P.E. Adotey

BEREA COLLEGE
Black Cultural Center & Interracial
   Education Program
CPO 134
Berea, KY 40404
Andrew Baskin, Director
(606) 986-9341

BOSTON COLLEGE
Black Studies Program
Lyons Hall 301
Chestnut Hill, MA 02167
Professor Amanda Houston

BOSTON UNIVERSITY
Afro-American Studies Center
138 Mountfort Street
Brookline, MA 02146
Dr. Wilson J. Moses, Director
(617) 353-2795

Education

African-American Studies (Cont.)

BOWDOIN COLLEGE
Afro-American Studies Program
Brunswick, ME 04011
Professor Randolph Stakeman, Director
(207) 725-8731

BOWLING GREEN STATE UNIVERSITY
Ethnic Studies Department
117 Shalzell Hall
Bowling Green, OH 43403
Dr. Robert Perry, Chairperson
(419) 536-2503

BRADLEY UNIVERSITY
Black Studies
Peoria, IL 61606
Dr. Norris B. Clark
(309) 676-7611

BRANDEIS UNIVERSITY
Department of African & Afro-American
   Studies
Waltham, MA 021554
Professor Wellington Nyangoni

BRIDGEWATER STATE COLLEGE
Afro-American Society
Cultural Center
Bridgewater, MA 02324
Professor Paul Gray

BRONX COMMUNITY COLLEGE-CUNY
Cultural Affairs
University Avenue & West 181st Street
Bronx, NY 10453
Professor Glen Ray

BROWN UNIVERSITY
Afro-American Studies Program
Box 1904
Providence, RI 02912
Dr. Wilson J. Moses, Chairman
(401) 863-3137

CALIFORNIA STATE UNIVERSITY-FRESNO
Black Studies Department
Fresno, CA 93740
Professor Franklin Ng

CALIFORNIA STATE UNIVERSITY-FULLERTON
Department of Afro-Ethnic Studies
800 North Sate College Boulevard
Fullerton, CA 92637
Professor Carl Jackson

CALIFORNIA STATE UNIVERSITY-HAYWARD
Afro-American Studies Program
Hayward, CA 94542
Professor Barbara Poindexter

CALIFORNIA STATE UNIVERSITY-LONG BEACH
African American Studies
1250 Bellflower Boulevard
Long Beach, CA 90840
Dr. Maulana Karenga, Chairperson

CALIFORNIA STATE UNIVERSITY-LOS ANGELES
Department of Pan-African Studies
Los Angeles, CA 90032
Dr. Michael Martin

CALIFORNIA STATE UNIVERSITY-SACRAMENTO
Pan-African Studies Program
6000 J Street
Sacramento, CA 95819
David Covin, Program Director

Education

African-American Studies (Cont.)

CARLETON COLLEGE
African-Afro American Studies
Program
Northfield, MN 55057
Professor Ray Kea, Director

CENTRAL STATE UNIVERSITY
Wilberforce, OH 45384
Dr. Arthur E. Thomas, President
(513) 376-6332

CHATHAM COLLEGE
Black Studies Program
Woodland Road
Pittsburgh, PA 15232
Dr. Emma T. Lucas, Assistant Vice
   President for Academic Affairs

CITY COLLEGE OF NEW YORK
Department of African & Afro-American
   Studies
New York, NY 10031
Professor Leonard Jeffries

CLAREMONT COLLEGE
Department of Black Studies
240 East 11th Street
Claremont, CA 91711

CLEMSON UNIVERSITY
Afro-American Studies
105 Hardin Hall
Clemson, SC 29631
Professor Allan Schaffer

CLEVELAND STATE UNIVERSITY
Black Studies Program
University Center
Room 103
Cleveland, OH 44115
Howard A. Mims, Ph.D., Director

COE COLLEGE
Afro-American Studies
Cedar Rapids, IA 52402
Professor James Randall

COLBY COLLEGE
Black Studies Department
Waterville, ME 04901
Jonas O. Rosenthal, Program Director

CONNECTICUT COLLEGE
Student Special Programs
Box 1453
New London, CT 06320
Professor Ernestine Brown

CORNELL UNIVERSITY
African Studies & Research Center
310 Triphammer Road
Ithaca, NY 14853
Assoc. Professor James Turner, Director
(607) 256-5218

CREIGHTON UNIVERSITY
Black Studies
Omaha, NE 68108
Professor A. W. Welch

CUYAHOGA COUNTY COMMUNITY COLLEGE
Department of Black Affairs
Cleveland, OH 44101
Professor Brooker Tall

DARTMOUTH COLLEGE
African & Afro-American Studies Program
6134 Silsby Hall
Hanover, NH 03755
Keith L. Walker, Chairperson

DENISON UNIVERSITY
Center for Black Studies
Granville, Oh 43023
Rev. John H. Jackson, Director
(614) 587-0810

African-American Studies (Cont.)

DEPAUW UNIVERSITY
Black Studies
609 South Locust Street
Greencastle, IN 46135
Professor Stanley Warren

DILLARD UNIVERSITY
Afro-American Studies
Cross Hall, 2601 Gentilly Blvd.
New Orleans, LA 70122
Professor Earl Smith

DUKE UNIVERSITY
Black Studies
Durham, NC 27701
Professor William Turner

EASTERN ILLINOIS UNIVERSITY
Afro-American Studies
Coleman Hall
Charleston, Il 61922
Professor Johnetta Jones

EASTERN MICHIGAN UNIVERSITY
Afro-American Studies Program
304 Goodison Hall
Ypsilanti, MI 48197
Ronald Woods, Director
(313) 487-3460

EASTERN NEW MEXICO UNIVERSITY
Black Studies Program
Portales, NM 88130

EASTERN WASHINGTON UNIVERSITY
Black Education Program
MS-164
Cheyney, WA 99004
Dr. Felix Boatend, Director/Professor
(509) 359-2205

EMORY UNIVERSITY
African American & African Studies
    Program
Chandler Library - Building 201B
Atlanta, GA 30322
Dr. Delores P. Aldridge, Chairperson
(404) 329-6847

FAYETTEVILLE STATE UNIVERSITY
Black Studies
Fayetteville, NC 28301
Professor Shia-ling Lio

FLORIDA STATE UNIVERSITY
Afro-American Studies Program
172 Bellamy Building
Tallahassee, FL 32306-4028
Professor William R. Jones, Director
(904) 644-5512

GETTYSBURG COLLEGE
Intercultural Advancement
239 North Washington Street
Gettysburg, PA 17325
Harry B. Matthews, Dean
(717) 337-6311

GOSHEN COLLEGE
Department of Urban & Afro-American
    Affairs
Goshen, IN 46526
Dr. Wilma Bailey

GOVENOR STATE UNIVERSITY
Pan-African Studies
Park Forest, IL 60466
Dr. Roger Oden

HAMPDEN-SYDNEY COLLEGE
Afro-American Studies Program
P.O. Box 26
Hampden-Sydney, VA 23943
Professor George Bagsby, Chairperson
(804) 223-4381

Education

African-American Studies (Cont.)

HAMPSHIRE COLLEGE
Black Studies
Amherst, MA 01003
Professor E. Francis White

HAMPTON INSTITUTE
Ethnic Studies
Box 6271
Hampton, VA 23668
Professor Patrick Lewis

HARVARD UNIVERSITY
Afro-American Studies Department
77 Dunster Street
Cambridge, MA 02138
Professor Werner Sollors, Chairman
(617) 495-4113

HEIDELBERG COLLEGE
Tiffin, OH 44883
Professor Leslie Fishel

HIGHLAND PARK COMMUNITY COLLEGE
Afro-American Studies
160 Glendale
Highland Park, MI 48203
Professor Howard Lindsey

HOWARD UNIVERSITY
African-American Resource Center
P.O. Box 746
Washington, D.C. 20059
E. Ethelbert Miller, Director

ILLINOIS WESLEYAN UNIVERSITY
Department of History
Bloomington, IL 61701
Professor Paul Bushnell

INDIANA CENTRAL
Minority Affairs
Indianapolis, IN 46237
Dr. Fred Hill

INDIANA STATE UNIVERSITY
Center for Afro-American Studies
Stalker Hall, Room 203
Terre Haute, IN 47809
Dr. Warren Swindell, Director
(812) 237-2550

INDIANA UNIVERSITY-BLOOMINGTON
Afro-American Studies Department
Memorial Hall, East
Bloomington, IN 47408
Mellonee Burnim, Ph.D., Chairperson
(812) 855-3874

INDIANA UNIVERSITY-NORTHWEST
Department of Minority Studies
3400 Broadway, Raintree Hall
Gary, IN 46408
Dr. Robert Catlin

INDIANA UNIVERSITY-PURDUE UNIVERSITY-INDIANAPOIS
Afro-American Studies Program
CA504L
425 Agnes Street
Indianapolis, IN 46202
Monroe H. Little, Jr., Director

JACKSON STATE UNIVERSITY
Institute for the Study of History, Life
and Culture of Black People
P.O. Box 17008
Jackson, MS 39217
Dr. Alferdteen Harrison, Director
(601) 968-2055

African-American Studies (Cont.)

JERSEY CITY STATE COLLEGE
African-Afro American Studies Center
96 Audubon Avenue
Jersey City, NJ 07305
Dr. Lee Hagan, Coordinator
(201) 547-3153

KANSAS STATE UNIVERSITY
Department of History
Manhattan, KS 66502
Professor Joseph Hawes

KENT STATE UNIVERSITY
Department of Pan-African Studies
18 Ritchie Hall
Kent, OH 44240
Professor Dr. Edward W. Crosby,
   Chairman
(216) 672-2300

LANEY COLLEGE
Ethnic Studies Department
Oakland, CA 94607
Professor Carole Ward-Allen

LEHMAN COLLEGE
Department of Black Studies
Bronx, NY 10451
Professor James Jarvis

LINCOLN UNIVERSITY
Lincoln University, PA 19352
Dr. Clara Brock

LINFIELD COLLEGE
Minority Students
McMinnville, OR 91728
Professor Bobby James

LOYOLA MARYMOUNT UNIVERSITY
Department of Afro-American Studies
7101 West 80th Street
Los Angeles, CA 90045
Professor John Davis

LOYOLA UNIVERSITY OF CHICAGO
Afro-American Studies
6225 North Sheridan Road
Chicago, IL 60626
Professor Carol Adams

LUTHER COLLEGE
African-American Studies
Decorah, IA 52101
Professor Tiffany Patterson

MANCHESTER COLLEGE
Afro-American Studies
North Manchester, In 46962
Dr. David Waas

MEDGAR EVERS COLLEGE
Department of Humanities
1150 Carroll Street
Brooklyn, NY 11225
Dr. Dominic Nwasike

METROPOLITAN STATE COLLEGE OF DENVER
Institute for Intercultural Studies and
   Services
P.O. Box 173362, Campus Box 36
Denver, CO 80217
Dr. Akbarali Thobhani
(303) 556-4004

MIAMI UNIVERSITY
Afro-American Studies
Oxford, OH 45056
Professor W. Sherman Jackson

Education

African-American Studies (Cont.)

MICHIGAN STATE UNIVERSITY
College of Urban Development
East Lansing, MI 48823

MISSISSIPPI STATE UNIVERSITY
Department of History
Post Office Drawer H
Starkville, MS 39762
Dr. William Parish

MOREHOUSE COLLEGE
Afro-American/African Studies
Atlanta, GA 30314
Professor W. P. Smith

MORGAN STATE UNIVERSITY
Department of History
Holnes 103
Baltimore, MD 21239
Dr. J. Carleton Hayden

MORNINGSIDE COLLEGE
Minorities Counselor
Sioux City, IA 51106
Professor George Boykin

MOUNT HOLYOKE COLLEGE
Black Studies Department
South Hadley, MA 01075
Professor Monica Gorden

MUSKINGUM COLLEGE
Afro-American Studies
New Concord, OH 43762
Professor Dorothy Delenga

NASSAU COMMUNITY COLLEGE
Stewart Avenue
Garden City, NY 11520
Professor Jewelle Greshen

NEW JERSEY INSTITUTE OF TECHNOLOGY
Educational Opportunity Program
323 Dr. Martin Luther King Boulevard
Newark, NJ 07102
Saul K. Kenster, President
(201) 596-3684

NEW MEXICO STATE UNIVERSITY
Black Programs
P.O. Box 4188
Las Cruces, NM 88003
Professor Andrew Wall, Driector
(505) 646-4208

NEW YORK CITY TECHNICAL COLLEGE-CUNY
African American Studies Department
300 Jay Street
Atrium Building Number 643
Brooklyn, NY 11201
Professor Mark Duodu, Chairperson
(718) 643-5594

NORTHEASTERN UNIVERSITY
Department of African & Afro-Amrican Studies
426 Ruggles Building
Boston, MA 02115

NORTHERN ILLINOIS UNIVERSITY
Center for Black Studies
620 West Locust Street
DeKalb, IL 60115
Dr. Admasu Zike, Director
(815) 753-1423

NORTHWESTERN UNIVERSITY
African American Studies Department
Anderson Hall
Room 2-134
2003 Sheridan
Evanston, IL 60201
William Exum, Chairman

African-American Studies (Cont.)

OAKLAND UNIVERSITY
Department of History
Rochester, MI 48063
Professor Dewitt Dykes

OBERLIN COLLEGE
Black Studies Department
210 Rice Hall
Oberlin, OH 44074
Dr. Yakubu Saaka, Chairperson
(216) 775-8591

OHIO STATE UNIVERSITY
Department of Black Studies
P486 University Hall
230 North Oval Mall
Columbus, OH 43210
Professor William E. Nelson

OHIO UNIVERSITY
Afro-American Studies
312 Lindley Hall
Athens, OH 45701
Professor Vattel Rose

OTTAWA UNIVERSITY
Department of History
Ottawa, KS 66067
Dr. Donald Averyt

PARK COLLEGE
Black Studies
Kansas City, MO 64152
Professor Edythe Grant

PASADENA CITY COLLEGE
Pan-African Affairs
1570 East Colorado Boulevard
Pasadena, CA 91106
Professor Jarvis Johnson

PENNSLYVANIA STATE UNIVERSITY
Black Studies Program
236 Grange Building
University Park, PA 16802
Dr. James Stewart, Program Director
(814) 863-4243

PENNSYLVANIA COLLEGE OF OPTOMETRY
Minority Student Affairs
1200 W. Godfrey
Philadelphia, PA 19141
Professor Robert Horne

PHILANDER SMITH COLLEGE
Freshman Studies
Little Rock, AR 72203
Professor Rapheal Lewis

PORTLAND STATE UNIVERSITY
Black Studies Center
P.O. Box 751
Portland, OR 97027
Professor Darrell Millner

PRINCETON UNIVERSITY
Afro-American Studies Program
70 Washington Road
Princeton, NJ 08544

PURDUE UNIVERSITY
Afro-American Studies Center
110 Matthews Hall
West Lafayette, IN 47907
Ceola Ross Baber, Ph.D., Director
(317) 494-5680

QUEENS COLLEGE
Africana Institute
6530 Kissena Boulevard
Flushing, NY 11367
Dr. W. Ofuatey Kodjoe

Education

African-American Studies (Cont.)

REED COLLEGE
Black Studies
Portland, OR 97202
Professor W. H. McClendon

RHODE ISLAND COLLEGE
African/Afro-American Studies
  Program
Providence, RI 02908
Dr. Richard Lobban, Director
(401) 456-8784

ROLLINS COLLEGE
Afro-American Studies
Winter Park, FL 32789
Professor Alzo Reddick

ROOSEVELT UNIVERSITY
African, Afro-American & Black Studies
430 South Michigan Avenue
Chicago, IL 60605
Professor S. Miles Woods

**RUTGERS UNIVERSITY-
  NEWARK**
Afro-American & African Studies
  Department
Conklin Hall, Room 418
Newark, NJ 07102
Dr. Wendell A. Jean Pierre
(201) 648-5496

**RUTGERS UNIVERSITY-NEW
  BRUNSWICK**
Department of African Studies
Beck Hall 112
New Brunswick, NJ 08903
Dr. Leonard Bethel, Chairperson
(201) 932-3335

SAINT LOUIS UNIVERSITY
Afro-American Studies Institute
221 North Grand Boulevard
St. Louis, MO 63103
Barbara M. Woods, Director
(314) 658-2242

SALEM STATE COLLEGE
African American Studies Program
352 Lafayette Street
Salem, MA 01970
Dr. Gerdes Fleurant, Coordinator
(617) 745-0556

SAN DIEGO STATE UNIVERSITY
Department of Afro-American Studies
San Diego, CA 92182
Dr. Shirley N. Weber, Chairperson
(619) 265-6531

SAN FRANCISCO STATE
Black Studies
1600 Holloway
San Francisco, CA 94132
Dr. Syed Khatib

SAN JOSE CITY COLLEGE
Black Studies
San Jose, CA 95192
Professor Leonard Washington

SAN JOSE STATE UNIVERSITY
Afro-American Studies Department
San Jose, CA 95192
Professor Carlene Young

SANTA CLARA UNIVERSITY
Ethnic Studies Program
Santa Clar, CA 95053
Gary Y. Okihiro, Program Director

SEATTLE PACIFIC COLLEGE
Minority Affairs
Peterson Hall
Seattle, WA 98199

African-American Studies (Cont.)

SETON HALL UNIVERSITY
African American Studies
400 South Orange Avenue
South Orange, NJ 07079
Dr. Julia Miller
(201) 761-9415

SHAW UNIVERSITY
Afro-American Studies
Raleigh, NC 27602
Professor John Fleming

SHELBY STATE COMMUNITY COLLEGE
Afro-American Studies
Memphis, TN 38104
Professor Jerome Jamerson

SIMMONS COLLEGE
Afro-American Studies Program
300 The Fenway
Boston, MA 02115
Professor Marcia Halford

SOUTHERN ARKANSAS UNIVERSITY
Black Studies Office, Box 1369
Magnolia, AR 71753
Professor David Sixbey

SOUTHERN CONNECTICUT STATE COLLEGE
Department of History
Ceasbury Hall 400
New Haven, CT 06520
Professor William Wright

SOUTHERN ILLINOIS UNIVERSITY
Black American Studies Program
Southern Illinois University
Carbondale, IL 62901
Luke Tripp, Ph.D., Coordinator

SPRINGFIELD COLLEGE
Black Culture Center
Post Office Box 1713/Alden
Springfield, MA 01109
Mr. Bob Albert

SPRINGFIELD TECHNICAL COMMUNITY COLLEGE
Afro-American Resource Center
Post Office Box 402
Highland Station
Springfield, MA 01109
Mr. Al Carter

STANFORD UNIVERSITY
African & Afro-American Studies
Stanford, CA 95305
Dr. Kennel Jackson, Chairperson
(415) 497-3781

SUNY-ALBANY
African & Afro-American Studies
1400 Washington Avenue
Albany, NY 12222
Dr. Joseph A. Sarfoh, Chairman
(518) 442-4730

SUNY-BINGHAMTON
Afro-American & African Studies
 Department
Binghamton, NY 13901
Dr. Akbar Muhammed
 Chairperson
(607) 777-2635

Education

African-American Studies (Cont.)

SUNY-BROCKPORT
Department of African & Afro-American Studies
Brockport, NY 14220
Ena L. Farley, Chairperson
(716) 395-2470

SUNY-BUFFALO
Afro-American Studies
533 Baldy Hall
Buffalo, NY 14260
Professor James Pappas

SUNY-CORTLAND
African-American Studies Program
P.O. Box 2000
Cortland, NY 10345
Dr. Samuel L. Kelley, Director
(607) 753-2226

SUNY-NEW PALTZ
Black Studies Department
New Paltz, NY 12561
Professor A. Williams-Myers

SUNY-ONEONTA
Department of Black & Hispanic Studies
Oneonta, NY 13820
Dr. Rashid Hamid

SUNY-STONY BROOK
Africana Studies Program
Stony Brook, NY 11794-4340
Amiri Baraka, Program Director
(516) 632-7470

SWARTHMORE COLLEGE
Black Cultural Center
Swarthmore, PA 19081
Professor Leandre Jackson

SYRACUSE UNIVERSITY
Afro-American Studies Department
200 Sims Hall V
Syracuse, NY 13244-1230
Dr. Bruce R. Hare, Chairperson
(315) 443-4302

TAYLOR UNIVERSITY
Special Services Program
Upland, IN 46989
Professor Nellie McGee

TEMPLE UNIVERSITY
Department of African-American Studies
12th & Berks, Gladfelter Hall
Philadelphia, PA 19122
Dr. Molefi K. Asante, Chairperson
(215) 787-3451

TRENTON STATE COLLEGE
African American Studies
Hillwood Lakes, CN 4700
Trenton, NJ 08650
Dr. Gloria Harper Dickinson,
Department Chairperson

TRINITY COLLEGE
Intercultural Center
70 Vermont Street
Hartford,CT 06106
Professor Johnetta Richards

TUFTS UNIVERSITY
African and the New World Program
316 East Hall
Medford, MA 02155
Ms. Veve A. Clark, Coordinator
(617) 628-5000

UNIVERSITY OF AKRON
The Black Cultural Center
Akron, OH 44325-1801
William Lewis, III, Director
(216) 972-7030

African-American Studies (Cont.)

UNIVERSITY OF ARKANSAS-LITTLE ROCK
Black Studies Department
Little Rock, AR 72205
Professor Patricia McGraw

UNIVERSITY OF CALIFORNIA-BERKELEY
Afro-American Studies Department
Berkeley, CA 94720
Professor Barbara Christenson

UNIVERSITY OF CALIFORNIA-DAVIS
Afro-American Studies Program
460 Kerr Hall
Davis, CA 95616
Professor Jacquelyn Mitchell, Director
(916) 752-1548

UNIVERSITY OF CALIFORNIA-LOS ANGELES
Center for Afro-American Studies
3105 Campbell Hall
Los Angeles, CA 90024
Dr. Claudia Mitchell Kernan

UNIVERSITY OF CALIFORNIA-RIVERSIDE
Afro-American Studies
Watkins Hall 1141
Riverside, CA 92521
Dr. Jacquelyn Haywood

UNIVERSITY OF CALIFORNIA-SANTA BARBARA
Department of Black Studies
Santa Barbara, A 93106
Douglas H. Daniels, Chairperson
(805) 961-3847

UNIVERSITY OF CINCINNATI
Department of Afro-American Studies
Cincinnati, OH 45221
(513) 556-0350

UNIVERSITY OF COLORADO-BOULDER
Black Studies Program
Campus Box 294
Boulder, CO 80302
Dr. Charles Nilon

UNIVERSITY OF CONNECTICUT-STORRS
Center for Black Studies, U-162
Storrs, CT 06268
Professor Floyd Bass

UNIVERSITY OF DELAWARE
Center for Black Culture
192 South College Avenue
Newark, DE 19716
Vernese E. Edghill, Assistant Dean
(302) 831-2991

UNIVERSITY OF DETROIT
Center for Black Studies
Detroit, MI 48221
Professor Roger Buckley

UNIVERSITY OF HOUSTON
African American Studies Program
4800 Calhoun
Houston, TX 77204-3784
Dr. Linda Reed, Director
(713) 743-2811

UNIVERSITY OF ILLINOIS AT CHICAGO
Black Studies Program
Box 4348, M/C 069
Chicago, IL 60680
Dr. Lansine Kaba, Director
(312) 996-2950

Education

African-American Studies (Cont.)

UNIVERSITY OF ILLINOIS-URBANA
Afro-American Studies & Research Center
1204 West Oregon
Urbana, IL 61801
Dianne M. Pinderhughes, Associate Professor
(217) 333-7781

UNIVERSITY OF IOWA
African-American World Studies Program
303 English-Philosophy Building
Iowa City, IA 52242
Dr. Darwin Turner, Chairman

UNIVERSITY OF KENTUCKY
Afro-American Studies
335 Dickey Hall
Lexington, KY 40506
Professor Earnest Middleton

UNIVERSITY OF LOUISVILLE
Department of Pan-African Studies
Louisville, KY 40292
Professor Yvonne Jones

UNIVERSITY OF MARYLAND-COLLEGE PARK
Afro-American Studies
College Park, MD 20742

UNIVERSITY OF MARYLAND-BALTIMORE COUNTY (UMBC)
African-American Studies Department
5401 Wilkins Avenue
Baltimore, MD 21228
Dr. Daphne D. Harrison, Chairperson
(301) 455-2158

UNIVERSITY OF MASSACHUSETTS-AMHERST
W.E.B. DuBois Department of Afro-American Studies
325 New Africa House
Amherst, MA 01003
Professor Chestor Davis
Department Chairperson
(413) 545-2751

UNIVERSITY OF MASSACHUSETTS-BOSTON
Black Studies
Boston, MA 02125
Dr. Robert Moore

UNIVERSITY OF MIAMI
Caribbean, African & Afro-American Studies
P.O. Box 248231
Coral Gables, FL 33124
Professor O.R. Dathorne, Chairperson
(305) 284-6340

UNIVERSITY OF MICHIGAN-ANN ARBOR
Center for Afro-American & African Studies
550 East University Street
200 West Eng. Building
Ann Arbor, MI 48109-1092
Professor Earl Lewis, Director
(313) 764-5513

UNIVERSITY OF MICHIGAN-FLINT
African, Afro-American Studies Program
Room 364 CROB
Flint, MI 48502-2186
Clinton B. Jones, Director
(313) 762-3353

Education

African-American Studies (Cont.)

UNIVERSITY OF MINNESOTA
Department of Afro-American and
  African Studies
808 Social Science Building
267-19th Avenue South
Minneapolis, MN 55455
Professor John S. Wright, Chairperson
(612) 624-9847

UNIVERSITY OF MINNESOTA
Black Learning Resource Center
117 Pleasant Street, S.E.
Minneapolis, MN 55455
Sue W. Hancock, Director
(612) 373-7947

UNIVERSITY OF MISSOURI-
  COLUMBIA
Black Studies Program
207 Hill Hall
Columbia, MO 65211
Marvin A. Lewis, Director
(314) 882-6229

UNIVERSITY OF NEBRASKA-
  OMAHA
Black Studies Department
Arts & Sciences Hall, 60th Dodge
Omaha, NE 68182
Dr. Julien J. Lafontant
(402) 554-2414

UNIVERSITY OF NEW HAVEN
Minority Student Affairs
300 Orange Avenue
West Haven, CT 06516
H. Richard Dozier, Assistant Dean of
  Students
(203) 932-7178

UNIVERSITY OF NEW MEXICO
African-American Studies
1816 Las Lomas, N.E.
Albuquerque, NM 87131-1581
Dr. Shiame Okunor, Director
(505) 277-5644

UNIVERSITY OF NORTH CAROLINA
  CHAPEL HILL
Afro-American Studies
401 Alumni 004A
UNC-CH
Chapel Hill, NC 27514
Dr. Colin A. Palmer, Chairman
(919) 966-5496

UNIVERSITY OF NORTH CAROLINA
  CHARLOTTE
Afro-American & African Studies
UNCC
MACY 203
Charlotte, NC 28223
Dr. Bertha L. Maxwell, Chairperson
(704) 597-2371

UNIVERSITY OF NORTHERN
  COLORADO
Afro-American Studies
Greeley, CO 80639
Dr. Robert Dillingham

UNIVERSITY OF NOTRE DAME
Black Studies Program
345 O'Shaugnessy Hall
Notre Dame, IN 46556
Frederick D. Wright, Director
(219) 239-5628

UNIVERSITY OF THE PACIFIC
Department of Black Studies
Stockton, CA 95211
Professor Mark Ealey

Education

African-American Studies (Cont.)

UNIVERSITY OF PENNSYLVANIA
Afro-American Studies Program
204 Bennett Hall, 3340 Walnut Street
Philadelphia, PA 19104
Dr. Jacqueline E. Wade,
  Administrative Director
(215) 898-4965

UNIVERSITY OF PITTSBURGH
Department of Black Studies
Forbes Quad.
Pittsburgh, PA 15260
Benda F. Berrian, Chairperson
(412) 648-7452

UNIVERSITY OF RHODE ISLAND
The African and Afro-American Studies
  Program
Davis Hall, Room 11
Kingston, RI 02881
Professor Melvin K. Hendrix, Director

UNIVERSITY OF SANTA CLARA
Ethnic Studies Program
Santa Clara, CA 95053
Dr. Gary Y. Okihiro, Director
(408) 554-4472

UNIVERSITY OF SOUTH CAROLINA
Afro-American Studies
1621 College
Columbia, SC 29208
Professor Willie Harriford, Jr., Director
(803) 777-3264

UNIVERSITY OF SOUTH FLORIDA
Department of African & Afro-American
  Studies
Soc. 107/4202 Fowler Avenue
Tampa, FL 33620
Dr. Kosi Glover

UNIVERSITY OF TENNESSEE
Afro-American Studies Program
Alumni Hall, Suite 416C
802 Volunteer Boulevard
Knoxville, TN 37916
Professor Marvin Peek, Director
(615) 974-5052

UNIVERSITY OF TEXAS-ARLINGTON
Minority and Foreign Studies Affairs
UTA Box 19337
Arlington, TX 76019

UNIVERSITY OF TEXAS-AUSTIN
African & Afro-American Studies
  Research Center
Jester Center, A231A
Austin, TX 78712
Professor John Warfield

UNIVERSITY OF TOLEDO
Minority Affairs
2801 Bancroft Street
Toledo, OH 43606
Professor Leon Carter

UNIVERSITY OF UTAH
Afro-American Studies
205 Carlson Hall
Salt Lake City, UT 84112
Professor Ronald Coleman

UNIVERSITY OF VIRGINIA
Carter G. Woodson Institute
1512 Jefferson Park Avenue
Charlottesville, VA 22903
Armstead Robinson, Director
(804) 924-3109

UNIVERSITY OF WASHINGTON-SEATTLE
Afro-American Studies Prog., GN-107
Seattle, WA 98195
(206) 543-7410

African-American Studies (Cont.)

UNIVERSITY OF WISCONSIN-MADISON
Afro-American Studies Department
4231 Humanities Bulding
455 N. Park Street
Madison, WI 53706
Freida High W. Tesfagiorgis
(608) 263-1642

UNIVERSITY OF WISCONSIN-MILWAUKEE
Afro-American Studies Department
Milwaukee, WI 53201
Professor Winston Van Horne

UPSALA COLLEGE
Black Studies
East Orange, NJ 07109
Professor Carolyn Thorburn

VASSAR COLLEGE
Africana Studies Program
Box 517
Poughkeepsie, NY 12601
Joyce Bickerstaff, Director
(914) 452-7000

VIRGINIA COMMONWEALTH UNIVERSITY
Afro-American Studies Program
312 North Shafer Street
Richmond, VA 23284
Dr. Richard K. Priebe, Acting Coordinator
(804) 257-1384

WABASH COLLEGE
Black Culture Center
Crawfordsville, IN 47933
Professor Horace Turner

WASHBURN UNIVERSITY
Afro-American Studies
Topeka, KS 66621
Professor Roderick McDonald

WASHINGTON STATE UNIVERSITY
Heritage House
Pullman, WA 99164
Dr. Talmadge Anderson, Coordinator
(509) 335-8681

WASHINGTON UNIVERSITY
Black Studies
334 McMillan Hall
St. Louis, MO 63130
Dr. Gerald Patton

WAYNE STATE UNIVERSITY
Center for Black Studies
586 Student Center Building
Detroit, MI 48202
Dr. Perry A. Hall, Acting Director
(313) 577-2321

WELLESLEY COLLEGE
Black Studies Department
Wellesley, MA 02181
Professor Tony Martin, Chairman
(617) 235-0320

WESLEYAN UNIVERSITY
Center for Afro-American Studies
Middletown, CT 06457
Marshall Hyatt, Director
(203) 344-7943

WEST VIRGINIA UNIVERSITY
Center for Black Culture
G-11 East Moore Hall
Morgantown, WV 26506
Dr. Frederick L. Hord, Director
(304) 293-7029

Education

African-American Studies (Cont.)

WICHITA STATE UNIVERSITY
Student Affairs
Box 81
Wichita, KS 67208
Professor R. W. Blake, Jr.

WICHITA STATE UNIVERSITY
Department of Minority Studies
Box 66
Wichita, KS 67208
Dr. John Gaston, Chairperson
(316) 689-3380

WILLIAM PATTERSON COLLEGE
Faculty of Black Studies
Wayne, NJ 07470
Professor Muruku Walguchu

WILLIAMS COLLEGE
Afro-American Studies Program
Stetson Hall
Williamstown, MA 02167
David L. Smith

COLLEGE OF WOOSTER
Black Studies Program
Wooster, OH 44691
Josephine Wright, Chairperson
(216) 263-2044

WRIGHT STATE UNIVERSITY
Bolinga Cultural Resources Center
129 Millett Hall
Dayton, OH 45424
Lillian M. Jackson, Director

YALE UNIVERSITY
Afro-American Studies Department
3388 Yale Station
New Haven, CT 06520
Professor John Blassingame

YORK COLLEGE-CUNY
Afro-American Studies
94-20 Guy R. Brewer Boulevard
Jamaica, NY 11451
Dr. Celestine Anderson, Coordinator

YOUNGSTOWN STATE UNIVERSITY
Black Studies Program
410 Wick Avenue
Youngstown, OH 44555
Professor L. Alfred Bright, Director
(216) 742-3097

The listings in this directory are available as Mailing Labels. See last page for details.

Black Colleges and Universities

In their more than 100 years of experience, historically black colleges have often accomplished much with little. They have proven through dedication and perserverance that they are great resources.

ALABAMA AGRICULTURAL AND MECHANICAL UNIVERSITY
P.O. Box 285
Normal, AL 35762
Dr. David B. Henson, President
(205) 851-5200

ALABAMA STATE UNIVERSITY
P.O. Box 271
Montgomery, AL 36101-0271
Dr. C. C. Baker, President
(205) 293-4100

ALBANY STATE COLLEGE
504 College Drive
Albany, GA 31705-2794
Dr. Billy C. Black, President
(912) 430-4604

ALCORN STATE UNIVERSITY
Box 359
Lorman, MS 39096
Dr. Walter Washington, President
(601) 877-6100

ALLEN UNIVERSITY
1530 Harden Street
Columbia, SC 29204
Dr. Collie Coleman, President
(803) 254-4165

ARKANSAS BAPTIST COLLEGE
1600 High Street
Little Rock, AR 72202
Dr. William Keaton, President
(501) 374-7856

ATLANTA METROPOLITAN COLLEGE
1630 Stewart Avenue, S.W.
Atlanta, GA 30310
Dr. Edwin Thompson, President
(404) 756-4000

BARBER-SCOTIA COLLEGE
145 Cabarrus Avenue, West
Concord, NC 28025
Dr. Joel O. Nwagbaraocha, President
(704) 786-5171

BENEDICT COLLEGE
Harden and Blanding Streets
Columbia, SC 29204
Dr. Marshall C. Grigsby, President
(803) 256-4220

BENNETT COLLEGE
900 East Washington Street
Greensboro, NC 27402
Dr. Gloria Scott, President
(919) 273-4431

BETHUNE-COOKMAN COLLEGE
640 Second Avenue
Daytona Beach, FL 32114
Dr. Oswald P. Bronson, Sr., President
(904) 253-5172

BISHOP STATE COMMUNITY COLLEGE
351 North Broad Street
Mobile, AL 36690
Dr. Yvonne Kennedy, President
(205) 690-6416

Education

Colleges and Universities (cont.)

BLUEFIELD STATE COLLEGE
Bluefield, WV 24701
Dr. Gregory D. Adkins, President
(304) 327-4000

BOWIE STATE COLLEGE
Bowie, MD 20715
Dr. James E. Lyons, Chancellor
(301) 464-3000

CENTRAL STATE UNIVERSITY
1400 Brush Row Road
Wilberforce, OH 45384
Dr. Arthur E. Thomas, President
(513) 376-6332

CHEYNEY UNIVERSITY
Cheyney, PA 19319
Dr. Valarie Swain Cade, Interim
  President
(215) 399-2000

CHICAGO STATE UNIVERSITY
95th Street at King Drive
Chicago, IL 60628
Dr. Delores Cross, President
(312) 995-2000

CLAFLIN COLLEGE
College Avenue
Orangeburg, SC 29115
Dr. Oscar A. Rogers, Jr., President
(803) 534-2710

CLARK ATLANTA UNIVERSITY
James Brawley Drive at Fair St., S.W.
Atlanta, GA 30314
Thomas W. Cole, Jr., President
(404) 880-8000

CLINTON JUNIOR COLLEGE
Rock Hill, SC 29732
Dr. Sallie Moreland, President
(803) 327-7402

COAHOMA COMMUNITY COLLEGE
Clarksdale, MS 38614
Dr. Vivian M. Presley,
  Interim President
(601) 627-2571

COMPTON COMMUNITY COLLEGE
1111 East Artesia Boulevard
Compton, CA 90221
Dr. Warren A. Washington, President
(213) 637-2660

CONCORDIA COLLEGE
1804 Green Street
Selma, AL 36701
Dr. Julius Jenkins, President
(205) 874-5700

COPPIN STATE COLLEGE
Baltimore, MD 21216
Dr. Calvin Burnett, President
(410) 383-5400

CUYAHOGA COMMUNITY COLLEGE
700 Carnegie Avenue
Cleveland, OH 44115
Dr. Jerry Sue Owens, President
(216) 987-6000

DELAWARE STATE COLLEGE
1200 North Dupont Highway
Dover, DE 19901
Dr. William B. DeLauder, President
(302) 739-4901

Colleges and Universities (cont.)

DENMARK TECHNICAL COLLEGE
P.O. Box 327
Denmark, SC 29042
Dr. Douglas W. Brister, Interim
  President
(803) 793-3301

DILLARD UNIVERSITY
New Orleans, LA 70122
Dr. Samuel Cooke, President
(504) 286-4640

CHARLES R. DREW UNIVERSITY OF MEDICINE AND SCIENCE
1621 East 120th Street
Los Angeles, CA 90059
Dr. Reed V. Tuckson, President
(213) 563-4987

EDWARD WATERS COLLEGE
Jacksonville, FL 32209
Dr. Richard L. Mitchell, President
(904) 366-2500

ELIZABETH CITY STATE UNIVERSITY
Campus Box 790
1704 Weesville Road
Administration Building
Elizabeth City, NC 27909
Dr. Jimmy R. Jenkins, Chancellor
(919) 335-3400

FAYETTEVILLE STATE UNIVERSITY
Fayetteville, NC 28301
Dr. Lloyd V. Hackley, Chancellor
(919) 486-1111

FISK UNIVERSITY
17th Avenue North
Nashville, TN 37203
Dr. Henry Ponder, President
(615) 329-8555

FLORIDA AGRICULTURAL AND MECHANICAL UNIVERSITY
Foote-Hilyer Administration, Room 301
Tallahassee, FL 32307
Dr. Frederick S. Humphries, President
(904) 599-3225

FLORIDA MEMORIAL COLLEGE
15800 N.W. 42nd Avenue
Miami, FL 33054
Dr. Bennie L. Reeves, Acting President
(305) 625-4141

FORT VALLEY STATE COLLEGE
805 State College Drive
Fort Valley, GA 31030
Dr. Oscar L. Prater, President
(912) 825-6315

GRAMBLING STATE UNIVERSITY
P.O. Drawer 607
Grambling, LA 71245
Dr. Harold W. Lundy, President
(318)274-2211

HAMPTON UNIVERSITY
Hampton, VA 23668
William R. Harvey, President
(804) 727-5231

HARRIS STOWE STATE COLLEGE
St. Louis, MO 63103
Dr. Henry Givens, Jr., President
(314) 533-3366

Education

Colleges and Universities (cont.)

HIGHLAND PARK COMMUNITY COLLEGE
Glendale at Third
Highland Park, MI 48203
Dr. Comer Heath, III, President
(313) 252-0436

HINDS JUNIOR COLLEGE
Utica, MS 39175
Dr. George E. Barnes, President
(601) 885-6062

HOWARD UNIVERSITY
2400 Sixth Street, N.W.
Washington, D.C. 20059
Franklyn G. Jenifer, President
(202) 806-6100

HUSTON-TILLOTSON COLLEGE
900 Chicon Street
Austin, TX 78702-2793
Dr. Joseph T. McMillan, Jr., President
(512) 476-7421

J. F. DRAKE STATE TECHNICAL COLLEGE
Huntsville, AL 35811
Dr. Johnny L. Harris, President
(205) 539-8161

JACKSON STATE UNIVERSITY
1400 J.R. Lynch Street
Jackson, MS 39217
Dr. Herman B. Smith, Jr., Interim President
(601) 968-2121

JARVIS CHRISTIAN COLLEGE
Post Office Drawer G
Hawkins, TX 75765
Dr. Sebetha Jenkins, President
(903) 769-2174

JOHNSON C. SMITH UNIVERSITY
100 Beatties Ford Road
Charlotte, NC 28216
Dr. Robert L. Albright, President
(704) 378-1000

KENNEDY-KING COLLEGE
6800 South Wentworth Avenue
Chicago, IL 60621
Dr. Harold Pates, President
(312) 962-3701

KENTUCKY STATE UNIVERSITY
East Main Street
Frankfort, KY 40601
Dr. Mary L. Smith, President

KNOXVILLE COLLEGE
901 College Street
Knoxville, TN 37921
Dr. John B. Turner, President
(615) 524-6511

LA GUARDIA COMMUNITY COLLEGE
Long Island City, NY 11101
Dr. Raymond C. Bowen, President
(718) 482-5050

LANE COLLEGE
545 Lane Avenue
Jackson, TN 38301
Dr. Alex A. Chambers, President
(901) 426-7500

Colleges and Universities (cont.)

LANGSTON UNIVERSITY
P.O. Box 907
Langston, OK 73050
Dr. Ernest L. Holloway, President
(405) 466-3201

LAWSON STATE COMMUNITY COLLEGE
3060 Wilson Road, S.W.
Birmingham, AL 35221
Dr. Perry W. Ward, President
(205) 925-2515

LE MOYNE-OWEN COLLEGE
807 Walker Avenue
Memphis, TN 38126
Dr. Burnett Joiner, President
(901) 774-9090

LEWIS COLLEGE OF BUSINESS
17370 Meyer Road
Detroit, MI 48235
Dr. Majorie Harris, President
(313) 862-6300

LINCOLN UNIVERSITY OF PENNSYLVANIA
Lincoln University, PA 19352
Dr. Niara Sudarkasa, President
(215) 932-8300

LINCOLN UNIVERSITY OF MISSOURI
Post Office Box 29
Jefferson City, MO 65102-0029
Wendell G. Rayburn, Sr., President
(314) 681-5000

LIVINGSTON COLLEGE
701 West Monroe Street
Salisbury, NC 28144
Dr. Bernard W. Franklin, President
(704) 638-5500

MARTIN UNIVERSITY
2171 Avondale Place
Post Office Box 18567
Indianapolis, IN 46218
Rev. Boniface Hardin, President
(317) 543-3235

MARY HOLMES COLLEGE
West Point, MS 39773
Dr. Sammie Potts, President
(601) 494-6820

MEDGAR EVERS COLLEGE-CUNY
1650 Bedford Avenue
Brooklyn, NY 11225
Dr. Edison O. Jackson, President
(718) 270-4900

MEHARRY MEDICAL COLLEGE
1005 18th Avenue North
Nashville, TN 37208
Dr. David Satcher, M.D., Ph.D., President
(615) 327-6111

MILES COLLEGE
P.O. Box 3800
Birmingham, AL 35208
Dr. Albert J. H. Sloan, II, President
(205) 923-2771

MISSISSIPPI VALLEY STATE UNIVERSITY
Itta Bena, MS 38941
Dr. William W. Sutton, President
(601) 254-9041

Education

Colleges and Universities (cont.)

MOREHOUSE COLLEGE
830 Westview Drive, S.W.
Atlanta, GA 30314
Dr. Leroy Keith, Jr., President
(404) 681-2800

MOREHOUSE SCHOOL OF MEDICINE
720 Westview Drive., S.W.
Atlanta, GA 30310
Dr. James A. Goodman, President
(404) 752-1740

MORGAN STATE UNIVERSITY
Cold Spring Lane and Hillen Road
Baltimore, MD 21239
Dr. Earl S. Richardson, President
(410) 444-3333

MORRIS BROWN COLLEGE
643 Martin Luther King Drive, N.W.
Atlanta, GA 30314
Dr. Calvert H. Smith, President
(404) 220-0270

MORRIS COLLEGE
North Main Street
Sumter, SC 29150
Dr. Luns C. Richardson, President
(803) 775-9371

NATCHEZ JUNIOR COLLEGE
1010 North Union Street
Natchez, MS 39120
Dr. James E. Gray, President
(601) 445-9702

NORFOLK STATE UNIVERSITY
Norfolk, VA 23504
Dr. Harrison Wilson, President
(804) 683-8600

NORTH CAROLINA AGRICUL- TURAL AND TECHNICAL STATE UNIVERSITY
312 North Dudley Street
Greensboro, NC 27411
Dr. Edward B. Fort, Chancellor
(919) 334-7940

NORTH CAROLINA CENTRAL UNIVERSITY
1801 Fayetteville Street
Durham, NC 27707
Dr. Donna J. Benson, Interim President
(919) 560-6100

OAKWOOD COLLEGE
Post Office Box 107
Huntsville, AL 35896
Dr. Benjamin F. Reaves, President
(205) 726-7000

PAINE COLLEGE
1235 Fifteenth Street
Augusta, GA 30901-3182
Dr. Julius S. Scott, Jr., President
(706) 821-8200

PAUL QUINN COLLEGE
Dallas, TX 75241
Dr. Warren Morgan, President
(214) 371-1015

PHILANDER-SMITH COLLEGE
812 West 13th Street
Little Rock, AR 72202
Dr. Myer L. Titus, President
(501) 375-9845

PRAIRIE VIEW AGRICULTURAL AND MECHANICAL UNIVERSITY
Post Office Box 2670
Prairie View, TX 77446
Dr. Julius Becton, Jr., President
(409) 857-3311

Colleges and Universities (cont.)

RUST COLLEGE
One Rust Avenue
Holly Springs, MS 38635
Dr. William A. McMillan, Sr., President
(601) 252-4661

SAINT AUGUSTINE'S COLLEGE
1315 Oakwood Avenue
Raleigh, NC 27610
Dr. Prezell R. Robinson, President
(919) 828-4451

SAINT PAUL'S COLLEGE
406 Winsor Avenue
Lawrenceville, VA 23668
Dr. Thomas M. Law, President
(804) 848-3111

SAVANNAH STATE COLLEGE
P.O. Box 20427
Savannah, GA 31404
Dr. Annette K. Brock, Acting President
(912) 356-2240

SELMA UNIVERSITY
1501 Lapsley
Selma, AL 36701
Dr. B. W Dawson, President
(205) 872-2533

SHAW UNIVERSITY
Raleigh, NC 27611
Dr. Talbert O. Shaw, President
(919) 546-8300

SHORTER COLLEGE
604 Locust Street
North Little Rock, AR 72114
Dr. Katherine Mitchell, President
(501) 374-6305

SIMMONS UNIVERSITY BIBLE COLLEGE
1811 Dumesnell Street
Louisville, KY 40210
Dr. W. J. Hodge, President
(502) 776-1443

SOJOURNER-DOUGLASS COLLEGE
500 North Caroline Street
Baltimore, MD 21205
Dr. Charles Simmons, President
(410) 276-0306

SOUTH CAROLINA STATE COLLEGE
Box 1628
Orangeburg, SC 29117
Dr. Carl A. Carpenter, Interim President
(803) 536-7013

SOUTHERN UNIVERSITY SYSTEMS
Southern University Branch Post
Office
Baton Rouge, LA 70813
Dr. Dolores R. Spikes, President
(504) 771-4600

SOUTHERN UNIVERSITY AT BATON ROUGE
Post Office Box 9614
Baton Rouge, LA 70813-9614
Dr. Marvin L. Yates, President
(504) 771-5020

SOUTHERN UNIVERSITY AT NEW ORLEANS
6400 Press Drive
New Orleans, LA 70126
Dr. Robert B. Gex, Chancellor
(504) 286-5000

Education

Colleges and Universities (cont.)

SOUTHERN UNIVERSITY AT SHREVEPORT
3050 Martin Luther King Drive
Shreveport, LA 71107
Dr. Robert H. Smith, President
(318) 674-3300

SOUTHWESTERN CHRISTIAN COLLEGE
P.O. Box 10
Terrell, TX 75160
Dr. Jack Evans, President

SPELMAN COLLEGE
350 Spelman Lane, S.W.
Atlanta, GA 30314
Dr. Johnetta B. Cole, President
(404) 681-3643

STILLMAN COLLEGE
Post Office Box Drawer 1430
Tuscaloosa, AL 35403
Dr. Cordell Wynn, President

TALLADEGA COLLEGE
627 West Battle Street
Talladega, AL 35160
Dr. Joseph B. Johnson, President
(205) 362-2752

TENNESSEE STATE UNIVERSITY
Nashville, TN 37203
Dr. James A. Hefner, President
(615) 320-3432

TEXAS COLLEGE
2404 North Grand Avenue
Tyler, TX 75703
Dr. A. C. Mitchell Patton, Acting
President
(903) 593-8311

TEXAS SOUTHERN UNIVERSITY
3100 Cleburne Avenue
Houston, TX 77004
Dr. William Harris, President
(713) 527-7011

TOUGALOO COLLEGE
The President's Office
500 County Line Road
Tougaloo, MS 39174
Dr. Adib A. Shakir, President
(601) 977-7700

TRENHOLM STATE TECHNICAL COLLEGE
1225 Air Base Boulevard
Montgomery, AL 36108
Dr. Thad McClammy, President

TUSKEGEE UNIVERSITY
317 Kresge Center
Tuskegee, AL 36088
Dr. Benjamin F. Payton, President
(205) 727-8501

UNIVERSITY OF ARKANSAS-PINE BLUFF
Pine Bluff, AR 72114
Dr. Lawrence A. Davis, Jr., President
(501) 541-6500

UNIVERSITY OF THE DISTRICT OF COLUMBIA
4200 Connecticut Avenue, N.W.
Washington, D.C. 20008
Dr. Tilden J. LeMelle, President
(202) 282-7550

UNIVERSITY OF MARYLAND-EASTERN SHORE
Princess Anne, MD 21853
Dr. William P. Hytche, Chancellor
(410) 651-2200

Colleges and Universities (cont.)

UNIVERSITY OF THE VIRGIN ISLANDS
St. Thomas, US VI 00802
Dr. Orville E. Kean, President
(809) 776-9200

VIRGINIA SEMINARY AND COLLEGE
Garfield & Dewitt Street
Lynchburg, VA 24501
Dr. Ada M. Palmer, President
(804) 528-5276

VIRGINIA STATE UNIVERSITY
Petersburg, VA 23803
Dr. Wesley C. McClure, President
(804) 524-5070

VIRGINIA UNION UNIVERSITY
1500 North Lombardy Street
Richmond, VA 23220
Dr. S. Dallas Simmons, President
(804) 257-5600

VOORHEES COLLEGE
1411 Voorhees Road
Denmark, SC 29042
Dr. Leonard E. Dawson, President
(803) 793-3351

WAYNE COUNTY COMMUNITY COLLEGE
Detroit, MI 48226
Dr. Raphael Cortada, President
(313) 496-2500

WILBERFORCE UNIVERSITY
1055 North Bickett Road
Wilberforce, OH 45384
Dr. John L. Henderson, President
(513) 376-2911

WILEY COLLEGE
711 Wiley Avenue
Marshall, TX 75671
Dr. David L. Beckley, President
(903) 927-3200

WINSTON-SALEM STATE UNIVERSITY
601 Martin Luther King, Jr. Drive
Winston-Salem, NC 27110
Dr. Cleon F. Thompson, Jr., Chancellor
(919) 750-2000

WEST VIRGINIA STATE COLLEGE
P.O. Box 336
Institute, WV 25112
Dr. Hazo Carter, President
(304) 766-3000

XAVIER UNIVERSITY
New Orleans, LA 70125
Dr. Norman Francis, President
(504) 486-7411

The listings in this directory are available as Mailing Labels. See last page for details.

Education

Scholarship Assistance Organizations

The following entries represent a partial listing of organizations that offer scholarship assistance to African -American Students

---

ALPHA KAPPA ALPHA EDU-CATIONAL ADVANCEMENT FOUNDATION
5656 South Stony Island Avenue
Chicago, IL 60637
Doris Parker, Executive Secretary
(312) 684-1282

ALPHA PHI ALPHA FRATER-NITY SCHOLARSHIP FUND
P.O. Box 92576
Atlanta, GA 30314

AME ZION SCHOLARSHIP PROGRAM
1200 Windemere Drive
Pittsburgh, PA 15218

AMERICAN FUND FOR DEN-TAL HEALTH FELLOWSHIP
211 East Chicago Avenue
Chicago, IL 60611

AMERICAN INSTITUTE OF ARCHITECTURE
1735 New York Avenue
Washington, D. C. 20006

AMERICAN INSTITUTE OF CERTIFIED PUBLIC ACCOUNTANTS SCHOLAR-SHIP PROGRAM
1211 Avenue of the Americas
New York, NY 10036

AMERICAN NURSES ASSOCIATION SCHOLARSHIP PROGRAM
1030 15th Street, N.W., Suite 716
Washington, D.C. 20005

AMERICAN SOCIETY OF WOMEN ACCOUNTANTS SCHOLARSHIP PROGRAM
1135 Stillwood Drive, N.E.
Atlanta, GA 30306

ARBY'S HANK AARON SCHOLARSHIP
Arby's Foundation
10 Piedmont Center
3495 Piedmont Road, Suite 700
Atlanta, GA 30305

ATLANTA ASSOCIATION OF BLACK JOURNALIST SCHOL-ARSHIP PROGRAM
Post Office Box 54128
Atlanta, GA 30308

CARNEGIE-MELLON UNIVERSITY SCHOLARSHIP PROGRAM
5000 Forbes Avenue
Pittsburgh, PA 15213

CATHOLIC NEGRO SCHOLAR-SHIP FUND
Post Office Box 1730
Springfield, MA 01101-1730

Scholarship Assistance Organizations (cont.)

COCA-COLA SCHOLARS FOUNDATION, INC.
One Buckhead Plaza
3060 Peachtree Rd, N.W., Suite 1000
Atlanta, GA 30305
Mebane M. Pritchett, Chief Executive
(404) 237-1300

COLLEGE & SCHOLARSHIP HELP
1401 Johnson Ferry Road.
Suite 328-A9
Marietta, GA 30062

CONGRESSIONAL BLACK CAUCUS SPOUSES' SCHOLARSHIP FUND
1004 Pennsylvania Avenue, S.E.
Washington, D.C. 20003

C-SPAN SCHOLARSHIP PROGRAM
400 N. Capitol St., N.W., Suite 650
Washington, D.C. 20001

KODAK MINORITY ACADEMIC AWARDS PROGRAM
Eastman Kodak Company
343 State Street
Rochester, NY 14658

THE EPISCOPAL CHURCH CENTER SCHOLARSHIP FUND
815 Second Avenue
New York, NY 10017

GEORGIA INSTITUTE OF TECHNOLOGY
School of Aerospace Engineering
Scholarship Program
Atlanta, GA 30332-0150

GEORGIA STATE FOUNDATION SCHOLARSHIP PROGRAM
4200 Northside Parkway
Building 9, Suite 100
Atlanta, GA 30327

GEORGETOWN UNIVERSITY LAW CENTER SCHOLARSHIP PROGRAM
37th & O Streets, N.W.
Washington, D.C. 20057

GULF OIL SCHOLARSHIP PROGRAM
Gulf Oil Corporation Foundation
Durham, NC 27706

MARTIN LUTHER KING CENTERS SCHOLARS INTERNSHIP PROGRAM
The King Center
449 Auburn Avenue, N.E.
Atlanta, GA 30312

KROGER/MARTIN LUTHER KING, JR., SCHOLARSHIP PROGRAM
2175 Parklake Drive
Atlanta, GA 30345

LUTHERAN AMERICAN MINORITY SCHOLARSHIPS
4321 North Ballard Road
Appleton, WI 54919-1001

Education

Scholarship Assistance Organizations (cont.)

DELTA SIGMA THETA SOROR-ITY SCHOLARSHIP PROGRAM
Marietta-Roswell Alumnae Chapter
P.O. Box 70786
Marietta, GA 30007-0786

MARTIN LUTHER KING., JR., SCHOLARSHIP
Emory University
Boisteuillet Jones Center
Atlanta, GA 30322

MICHAEL JACKSON SCHOLARSHIP
United Negro College Fund
500 East 62nd Street
New York, NY 10021

THURGOOD MARSHALL SCHOLARSHIP PROGRAM
Miller Brewing Company
One DuPont Circle
Suite 710
Washington, D.C. 20036

MCDONALD'S BLACK MAKERS OF TOMORROW
Paragon Public Relations
3951 Snapfinger Parkway
Suite 345
Decatur, GA 30035

MCDONALDS CREW COLLEGE EDUCATION PROGRAM
Paragon Public Relations
3951 Snapfinger Parkway
Suite 345
Decatur, GA 30035

MOREHOUSE SCHOOL OF MEDICINE SCHOLARSHIP PROGRAMS
720 Westview Drive, S.W.
Atlanta, GA 30310-1492

NATIONAL ACHIEVEMENT SCHOLARSHIP PROGRAM
One American Plaza
Evanston, IL 60201

NATIONAL MERIT SCHOLAR-SHIP
One Rotary Center
Evanston, IL 60201

NATIONAL NEWSPAPER FOUN-DATION SCHOLARSHIP PROGRAM
1627 K Street, N.W., Suite 400
Washington, D.C. 20006-1790

NATIONAL NEWSPAPER PUB-LISHERS ASSOCIATION SCHOLARSHIP PROGRAMS
National Press Building, Room 948
Washington, D.C. 20245

NEW YORK PHILHARMONIC ORCHESTRA SCHOLARSHIP PROGRAMS
Avery Fisher Hall
Broadway at 65th Street
New York, NY 10023

NATIONAL PRESS PHOTOGRA-PHERS ASSOCIATION SCHOLARSHIP PROGRAMS
P.O. Box 1146
Durham, NC 27702

Scholarship Assistance Organizations (cont.)

NATIONAL SCHOLARSHIP RESOURCES
1401 Johnson Ferry Road
Suite 328 P-2
Marietta, GA 30062

OMEGA PSI PHI FRATERNITY SCHOLARSHIP PROGRAMS
2714 Georgia Avenue, N.W.
Washington, D.C. 20001

PHI BETA SIGMA FRATERNITY SCHOLARSHIP PROGRAMS
1327 R Street, N.W.
Washington, D.C. 20011

PHIL LAMBDA SCHOLARSHIP PROGRAM
5313 Halter Lane
Norfolk, VA 23502

REFORMED CHURCH OF AMERICA SCHOLARSHIP PROGRAMS
475 Riverside Drive, Room 1819
New York, NY 10027

RJR NABISCO SCHOLARSHIP PROGRAMS
500 East 62nd Street
New York, NY 10021

ROY WILKINS EDUCATIONAL SCHOLARSHIP PROGRAM
144 West 125th Street
New York, NY 10027

THE SCHOLARSHIP EXCHANGE
P.O. Box 563
Clarkston, GA 30021

SICKLE CELL FOUNDATION OF GEORGIA
2391 Benjamin E. Mays Drive, S.W.
Atlanta, GA 30311-3291

SIGMA GAMMA RHO SORORITY SCHOLARSHIP PROGRAM
840 East Eighth Street
Chicago, IL 60619

UNITED NEGRO COLLEGE FUND SCHOLARSHIPS
500 East 62nd Street
New York, NY 10021

UNITED METHODIST CHURCH SCHOLARSHIP FUND
P.O. Box 871
Nashville, TN 37202

UNITED PRESBYTERIAN CHURCH SCHOLARSHIP PROGRAM
475 Riverside Drive, Room 430
New York, NY 10115

UNIVERSITY OF NOTRE DAME SCHOLARSHIP PROGRAM
Notre Dame, In 46556

The listings in this directory are available as Mailing Labels. See last page for details.

Embassies and Consulates

African Americans have important links to Africa and the nations of the Caribbean. The embassies are listed to facilitate business and cultural contact with these countries.

AFRICAN

EMBASSY OF ALGERIA
2118 Kalorama Road, N.W.
Washington, D.C. 20008
Mr. Haouam, Information Officer

EMBASSY OF BENIN
2737 Cathedral Avenue, N.W.
Washington, D.C. 20008
Osseni Dagloria, Information Officer

EMBASSY OF BOTSWANA
3400 International Drive, N.W.,
Suite 7-M
Washington, D.C. 20008
Masego Moagi, Information Officer
(202) 244-4990

EMBASSY OF BURUNDI
2233 Wisconsin Avenue, N.W.
Suite 212
Washington, D.C. 20007
Ms. Anthanase Budigi, Info. Officer
(202) 342-2575

EMBASSY OF CAMEROON
2349 Massachusetts Avenue, N.W.
Washington, D.C. 20008
Mr. Jean Missoup, Information Officer
(202) 265-8790

EMBASSY OF CAPE VERDE
3415 Massachusetts Avenue, N.W.
Washington, D.C. 20007
Mr. Jose Monteiro, Information Officer
(202) 965-6820

EMBASSY OF THE CENTRAL AFRICAN REPUBLIC
1618 22nd Street, N.W.
Washington, D.C. 20008
Mr. Gaba, Information Officer
(202) 483-7800

EMBASSY OF CHAD
2002 R Street, N.W.
Washington, D.C. 20008
Ms. Louise Mashi, Information Officer
(202) 462-4009

EMBASSY OF THE PEOPLE'S REPUBLIC OF THE CONGO
4891 Colorado Avenue, N.W.
Washington, D.C. 20011
Mr. Guillaume Owassa, Info. Officer

EMBASSY OF DJIBOUTI
1430 K Street, N.W., Suite 600
Washington, D.C. 20006
Mr. Idriss Chirwa, Information Officer
(202) 331-0270

EMBASSY OF EGYPT
2310 Decatur Place, N.W.
Washington, D.C. 20008
Ahmed Maher El-Sayed, Ambassador
(202) 232-5400

EMBASSY OF EQUATORIAL GUINEA
2112 Leroy Place, N.W.
Washington, D.C. 20008
El Hadj Boubacar Barry, Ambassador
(202) 483-9420

Embassies and Consulates

EMBASSY OF ETHIOPIA
2134 Kalorama Road, N.W.
Washington, D.C. 20008
Tamene Eshette, Chard'D'Affaires

EMBASSY OF GABON
2034 - 20th Street, N.W.
Washington, D.C. 20009
Ms. Alison Meares, Information Officer
(202) 797-1000

EMBASSY OF GHANA
3512 International Drive, N.W.
Washington, D.C. 20008
Horace Dei, Information Officer
(202) 686-4520

EMBASSY OF GUINEA
2112 Leroy Place, N.W.
Washington, D.C. 20008
Mr. Aviz Bah, Information Officer
(202) 483-9420

EMBASSY OF GUINEA-BISSAU
918 Sixteenth Street, N.W.
Washington, D.C. 20006
Ms. Ligia Garcia, Information Officer
(202) 872-4222

EMBASSY OF THE IVORY COAST
2424 Massachusetts Avenue, N.W.
Washington, D.C. 20008
Rene Amany, Ambassador
(202) 483-2400

EMBASSY OF KENYA
2249 R Street, N.W.
Washington, D.C. 20008
William Meda, Information Officer
(202) 387-6101

EMBASSY OF LESOTHO
2511 Massachusetts Avenue, N.W.
Washington, D.C. 20008
Ms. K. Thabane, Information Officer
(202) 797-5533

EMBASSY OF THE REPUBLIC OF LIBERIA
5201 - 16th Street, N.W.
Washington, D.C. 20011
Paul Yerl, Information Officer
(202) 291-0761

EMBASSY OF MADAGASCAR
2374 Massachusetts Avenue, N.W.
Washington, D.C. 20008
Mr. Rasdinarivo, Information Officer
(202) 265-5525

EMBASSY OF MALAWI
2408 Massachusetts Avenue, N.W.
Washington, D.C. 20008
Robert Mbaya, Ambassador
(202) 797-1007

EMBASSY OF MALI
2130 R Street, N.W.
Washington, D.C. 20008
Sekouba Cisse, Information Officer
(202) 332-2249

EMBASSY OF MAURITANIA
2129 Leroy Place, N.W.
Washington, D.C. 20008
Turkia Ould Daddah, Cultural Attache
(202) 232-5700

EMBASSY OF MOROCCO
1601 - 21st Street, N.W.
Washington, D.C. 20009
Mr. Tourougui, Information Officer
(202) 462-7979

Embassies and Consulates

EMBASSY OF MOZAMBIQUE
1990 M Street, N.W., Suite 570
Washington, D.C. 20036
Antonio Matonce, Information Officer
(202) 293-7146

EMBASY OF THE NIGER REPUBLIC
2204 R Street, N.W.
Washington, D.C. 20008
Mrs. Illo, Information Officer
(202) 483-4224

EMBASSY OF NIGERIA
2201 M Street, N.W.
Washington, D.C. 20037
Mr. Jibrella, Information Officer
(202) 822-1500

EMBASSY OF RWANDA
1714 New Hampshire Avenue, N.W.
Washington, D.C. 20009
Christopher Habimani, Information Officer
(202) 232-2882

EMBASSY OF SENEGAL
2112 Wyoming Avenue, N.W.
Washington, D.C. 20008
Amadou Gaye, Information Officer
(202) 234-0540

EMBASSY OF SEYCHELLES
820 Second Avenue, Suite 900F
New York, NY 10017
Mr. Marengo, Information Officer
(212) 687-9766

EMBASSY OF SIERRA LEONE
1701 19th Street, N.W.
Washington, D.C. 20009
Dr. Phillip Cecay, Information Officer
(202) 939-9261

EMBASSY OF SUDAN
2210 Massachusetts Avenue, N.W.
Washington, D.C. 20008
Hassan Abdelwalaab, Information Officer
(202) 338-8565

EMBASSY OF TANZANIA
2139 R Street, N.W.
Washington, D.C. 20008
Mr. Ally Mjenga, Information Officer
(202) 939-6125

EMBASSY OF TOGO
2208 Massachusetts Avenue, N.W.
Washington, D.C. 20008
Mr. Seddoh, Information Officer
(202) 234-4212

EMBASSY OF TUNISIA
1515 Massachusetts Avenue, N.W.
Washington, D.C. 20005
Mr. Tekaya, Information Officer
(202) 862-1850

EMBASSY OF UGANDA
5906 - 16th Street, N.W.
Washington, D.C. 20011
Albert Mutebi, Information Officer
(202) 726-7100

EMBASSY OF UPPER VOLTA
2340 Massachusetts Avenue, N.W.
Washington, D.C. 20008
Traore Melegue, Chard D'Affaires
(202) 332-5577

EMBASSY OF ZAIRE
1800 New Hampshire Avenue, N.W.
Washington, D.C. 20009
Mr. Nzuzi, Information Officer
(202) 234-7690

Embassies and Consulates

EMBASSY OF ZAMBIA
2419 Massachusetts Avenue, N.W.
Washington, D.C. 20008
L. Kapambwe Charge D'Affaires
(202) 265-9717

EMBASSY OF ZIMBABWE
2852 McGill Terrace, N.W.
Washington, D.C. 20008
Thomas Bvuma, Information Officer
(202) 332-7100

CARIBBEAN EMBASSIES

EMBASSY OF THE BAHAMAS
2220 Massachusetts Avenue, N.W.
Washington, D.C. 20008
Dr. Paulette Bethel, Charge D'Affaires
(202) 319-2660

EMBASSY OF BARBADOS
2144 Wyoming Avenue, N.W.
Washington, D.C. 20008
Dr. Rudi Webster, Ambassador
(202) 939-9200

EMBASSY OF BELIZE
2535 Massachusetts Avenue, N.W.
Washington, D.C. 20008
James Hyde, Ambassador
(202) 332-9636

CUBAN INTEREST SECTION
2630 - 16th Street, N.W.
Washington, D.C. 20009
Mr. Ariel Ricardo, Information Officer
(202) 797-8518

EMBASSY OF THE DOMINICAN REPUBLIC
1715 - 22nd Street, N.W.
Washington, D.C. 20008
Jose Del-Carmen Ariza, Ambassador
(202) 332-6280

EMBASSY OF GRENADA
1701 New Hampshire Avenue, N.W.
Washington, D.C. 20009
Denneth Modeste, Ambassador
(202) 265-2561

EMBASSY OF THE REPUBLIC OF GUYANA
2490 Tracy Place, N.W.
Washington, D.C. 20008
Cedric H. Grant, Ambassador
(202) 265-6900

EMBASSY OF HAITI
2311 Massachusetts Avenue, N.W.
Washington, D.C. 20008
Jean Casimir, Ambassador
(202) 332-4090

EMBASSY OF JAMAICA
1850 K Street, N.W., Suite 355
Washington, D.C. 20006
Dr. Richard L. Bernal, Ambassador
(202) 452-0660

EMBASSY OF SAINT LUCIA
2100 M Street, N.W., Suite 309
Washington, D.C. 20037
Ms. Undine George, Counselor
(202) 463-7378

EMBASSY OF TRINIDAD & TOBAGO
1708 Massachusetts Avenue, N.W.
Washington, D.C. 20036
Shas Tri Ali, Contact
(202) 467-6490

The listings in this directory are available as Mailing Labels. See last page for details.

Embassies and Consulates

LIBERATION MOVEMENTS

ANC OF SOUTH AFRICA
801 Second Avenue, Suite 405
New York, NY 10017
J. M. Makatina
(212) 490-3487

PAN AFRICANIST CONGRESS OF AMERICA
211 East 43rd Street, Suite 703
New York, NY 10017
Henry Isaacs

SUPPORT ORGANIZATIONS

AFRICARE
440 R Street, N.W.
Washington, D.C. 20001
C. Payne Lucas, Executive Director
(202) 462-3614

AFRICAN AMERICAN INSTITUTE
833 United Nations Plaza
New York, NY 10017
Vivian Lowery Derryck, Contact
(212) 949-5666

AMERICAN COMMITTEE ON AFRICA
198 Broadway
New York, NY 10038
Jennifer Davis, Executive Director
(212) 962-1210

ARTISTS AND ATHLETES AGAINST APARTHEID
545 Eighth Street, S.E., Suite 200
Washington, D.C. 20003
Arthur Ashe, Chairperson
(202) 547-2550

BLACK AMERICAN RESPONSE TO THE AFRICAN COMMUNITY
127 North Madison Avenue
Suite 400
Pasadena, CA 91102
Frank E. Wilson, President
(818) 584-0303

CARIBBEAN ACTION LOBBY
322 Est Compton Boulevard
Suite 103
Compton, CA 90220
Mervyn Dymally, Chairman
(213) 639-3640

CARIBBEAN-AMERICAN CHAMBER OF COMMERCE AND INDUSTRY
Brooklyn Navy Yard, Building 5
Mezzanine A
Brooklyn, NY 11205
Roy A. Hastick, Sr., President
(718) 834-4544

CONSTITUENCY FOR AFRICA
c/o Africare
440 R Street, N.W.
Washington, D.C. 20001
Melvin Foote, Coordinator
(202) 462-3614

PHELPS-STOKES FUND
10 East 87th Street
New York, NY 10128
(212) 427-8100

ORGANIZATION OF AFRICAN UNITY
346 East 50th Street
New York, NY 10022
Imbrahim Sy, Ambassador
(212) 319-5490

Embassies and Consulates

TRANSAFRICA
545 Eighth Street, S.E.
Washington, D.C. 20003
Randall Robinson, Executive Director
(202) 546-2550

WASHINGTON OFFICE ON AFRICA
110 Maryland Avenue, N.E.
Suite 112
Washington, D.C. 20002
Imani Countess, Executive Director
(202) 546-7961

THE NIGERIAN AMERICAN FRIENDSHIP SOCIETY
10 East 87th Street
New York, NY 10028
Thomas A. Johnson, President
(212) 427-8100

UNITED NATIONS CENTER AGAINST APARTHEID
United Nations Secretariat
Room 2775
New York, NY 10017
(212) 754-6674

Engineering Firms

The African-American companies represented in this section are involved in engineering nationwide.

ARIZONA

BILLY C. MILLS ENGINEERING, INC.
816 North Sixth Avenue
Phoenix, AZ 85003
Bill C. Mills, President
(602) 252-0416

CALIFORNIA

ACKLAND INTERNATIONAL, INC.
333 Hegenberger Road, Suite 304
Oakland, CA 94621
Ekundayo Sowunmi, Contact
(415) 633-1797

ANDEL ENGINEERING COMPANY
24707 San Fernando Road
Box 428
Newhall, CA 91322
E.L. Bolden, Jr., President
(805) 259-1920

ENERGY RECOVERY ENGINEERING, INC.
30 North Raymond Avenue, Suite 801
Pasadena, CA 91103
Greg Coxson, President
(818) 792-5091

JORDAN ASSOCIATES, INC.
90 New Montgomery Avenue
Suite 410
San Francisco, CA 94105
Fredrick E. Jordan, President
(415) 989-1025

KERCHEVAL ENGINEERS
4740 Mercury Canyon Road
Suite 310
San Diego, CA 92123
Jacqueline Herman, Marketing
   Director
(619) 571-0520

SUPERIOR ENGINEERING & ELECTRONICS COMPANY, INC.
360 North Sepulveda Boulevard
Suite 2020
El Segundo, CA 90245
Ralph Williams, President
(213) 640-0047

JOHN T. WARREN & ASSOCIATES, INC.
1330 Broadway
Suite 1511
Oakland, CA 94612
John Warren PE, President
(415) 465-0980

DELAWARE

ENDECON, INC.
P.O. Box 9543
Wilmington, DE 19802
Owen A. Dixon, Vice President
(302) 764-1991

DISTRICT OF COLUMBIA

ADVANCED ENGINEERING, P.C.
1120 Connecticut Avenue, N.W.
Suite 461
Washington, D.C. 20036
Dr. Eugene M. Bentley, III, P.E., DEE,
    President
(202) 223-4303

DELON HAMPTON &
ASSOCIATES
111 Massachusetts Avenue, N.W.,
    Suite 400
Washington, D.C. 20001
John M. Zimmer, Vice President
(202) 898-1999

INTERNATIONAL SCIENCE &
TECHNOLOGY INSTITUTE
1129 Twentieth Street, N.W.
    Suite 800
Washington, D.C. 20036
Nihal Goonewardene, President
(202) 785-0381

JACKSON AND TULL, CHAR-
TERED ENGINEERS
2705 Bladensburg Road, N.E.
Washington, D.C. 20018
Knox W. Tull, Jr., P.E.
(202) 333-9100

R. M. JONES & ASSOCIATES
6406 Georgia Avenue, N.W.
Washington, D.C. 20012
Raymond M. Jones, Owner
(202) 723-2110

LEGION DESIGN/CAMPBELL &
ASSOCIATES, CHARTERED
1025 Connecticut Ave., N.W.
 Suite 615
Washington, D.C. 20036
Knolly F. Campbell, President
(202) 833-4444

GEORGE IRA WORSLEY, JR. &
ASSOCIATES
7705 Georgia Avenue, N.W.
Washington, D.C. 20012
G. I. Worsley, President
(202) 291-1666

FLORIDA

CHARLES MITCHELL, P.E.
1871 North East 167th Street
North Miami Beach, FL 33162
(305) 945-0202

GEORGIA

A & E ENVIRONMENTAL
SERVICES, INC.
1430 West. Peachtree Street., N.W.
    Suite 617
Atlanta, GA 30309
Algenard Herring, President
(404) 872-1832

HARRINGTON, GEORGE & DUNN,
CONSULTING ENGINEERS
1401 Peachtree St. , N.E., Suite 120
Atlanta, GA 30309
William A. Dunn, III, President
(404) 885-1555

Engineering Firms

JC2N, INCORPORATED
1252 West Peachtree Street, N.W.,
Suite 308
Atlanta, GA 30309
Michael Ndukuba, President
(404) 873-6954

JOSH ASSOCIATED, INC.
1430 West Peachtree Street
Suite 615
Atlanta, GA 30309
Steve Collins, Vice President
(404) 892-3049

KHAFRA ENGINEERING CONSULTANTS
84 Peachtree Street, Suite 1000
Atlanta, GA 30303
Valentino T. Bates, President
(404) 525-2120

PRAD GROUP, INC.
1132 West Peachtree Street
Suite 225
Atlanta, GA 30309
Fred Reynolds, Vice President
(404) 876-1880

R&D TESTING & DRILLING, INC.
2739 Waters Road, S.W.
Atlanta, GA 30354
S. J. Rowe, President
(404) 768-1580

ILLINOIS

W. B. DOLPHIN & ASSOCIATES
Six North Michigan Avenue
Chicago, IL 60602
W. E. Dolphin, Partner
(312) 332-6910

GLOBETROTTERS ENGINEERING CORPORATION
300 South Wacker Drive
Suite 580
Chicago, IL 60606
N. S. Shah, Chairman
(312) 922-6400

KANSAS

TALIAFERRO & BROWNE, INC.
710 Minnesota Avenue
Kansas City, KS 66101
Hagos E. Andebrhan, P.E., Chief
Executive
(913) 342-3456

LOUISIANA

MEL, INC.
1979 Beaumont Drive
Baton Rouge, LA 70806
Morgan M. Watson, President
(504) 927-7240

MARYLAND

AMERICAN HERITAGE, LTD.
943 Brightseat Road
Landover, MD 20785
Roger Evans
(301) 656-7600

DESIGN THREE, INC.
6188 Oxon Hill Road
Suite 602
Oxon Hill, MD 20745
Gino Ward, President
(301) 567-7177

DIVERSIFIED ENGINEERING, INC.
914 Silver Spring Avenue
Silver Spring, MD 20910
Marion Thomas, President
(301) 565-2000

MASSACHUSETTS

ASEC CORPORATION
383 Dorchester Avenue
Boston, MA 02127
John Monteiro, Executive Vice
  President
(617) 268-1560

B & M TECHNOLOGICAL SERVICES, INC.
60 Hamilton Street
Cambridge, MA 02139
Denzil D. McKenzie, Vice President
(617) 491-0233

BRYANT ASSOCIATES, INC.
648 Beacon Street
Boston, MA 02215
Jack D. Bryant, President
(617) 247-1800

DMC ENGINEERING, INC.
1 Kendall Street
Framingham, MA 01701
Daniel M. Carson, President
(508) 872-8030

MICHIGAN

LAND S.E.A. CORPORATION
62 West Seven Mile Road
Detroit, MI 48203
Elias Kattovah, President
(313) 368-3730

ELON H. MICKLES & ASSOCIATES
10641 West McNichols
Detroit, MI 48221
Elon Mickles, President
(313) 864-9100

SCALES & ASSOCIATES, INC.
1553 Woodward Avenue
Whitney Building, Suite 1025
Detroit, MI 48226
Robin M. Scales, Marketing Director

MINNESOTA

GLANTON ENGINEERING COMPANY, INC.
15 North Sixteenth Street
Minneapolis, MN 55403
John Glanton, President
(612) 332-8867

NEW JERSEY

ROBERT L. BOWSER, ASSOCIATES
586 Central Avenue
East Orange, NJ 07018
Robert L. Bowser, Owner

ENVIROTRAN, INC.
115 Evergreen Place
East Orange, NJ 07018
Louis Ripa
(201) 672-5100

CALVIN H. GIBSON GROUP
86 Washington Street
East Orange, NJ 07017
Calvin Gibson, Owner
(201) 673-1851

Engineering Firms

NEW YORK

LEROY CALLENDER, P.C.
236 West 26th Street
New York, NY 10001
LeRoy Callender, President
(212) 989-2900

FIELD ASSOCIATES, P.C.
379 Nassau Road
Roosevelt, NY 11575
Leo Fields, President
(516) 378-2794

EWELL W. FINLEY, P.C.
34-18 Northern Boulevard
Long Island, NY 11101
Macio Jackson, P.E.
(212) 686-8161

**ROBERT W. JONES &
ASSOCIATES, INC.**
80 Fifth Avenue
Suite 401
New York, NY 10011
Robert W. Jones, President
(212) 929-5318

**EUGENE S. RICHARDS ENGI-
NEERING AND LAND SURVEY**
1325 North Forest Road
Suite 342
Williamsville, NY 14221
Eugene S. Richards, President
(716) 688-2838

NORTH CAROLINA

SURTI & ASSOCIATES
217 Henderson Drive
Jacksonville, NC 28540
M. L. Surti, Owner
(919) 455-3564

OHIO

**CROSS, CURRY DE WEAVER,
RANDALL & ASSOCIATES,
INC.**
3605 Lancashire Drive
Dayton, OH 45408
Milton B. Curry, Treasurer
(513) 263-3431

**JOHN E. FOSTER &
ASSOCIATES, INC.**
555 Buttles Avenue
Columbus, OH 43215
John E. Foster, President
(614) 461-9466

POLYTECH, INC.
1744 Payne Avenue
Cleveland, OH 44114
Babu K. Patel, Vice President
(216) 696-3141

**L. THOMPSON CONSULTANTS,
INC.**
929 Harrison Avenue, Suite 301
Columbus, OH 43215
Leslie Thompson, President
(614) 299-1117

**UNITED CONSULTANTS &
ASSOCIATES**
1187 East Broad Street
Columbus, OH 43205
Banwo Longe, P.E., President

OREGON

NERO & ASSOCIATES, INC.
520 S.W. 6th Avenue, Suite 1250
Portland, OR 97204
David M. Nero, Jr., CEO
(503) 223-4150

PENNSYLVANIA

DURANT ENTERPRISES, INC.
P.O. Box 4422
Allentown, PA 18105
Bernie Durant, President
(215) 437-1760

JALORDS, INC.
1080 North Delaware Avenue
Philadelphia, PA 19125
James A. Davis, P.E., President
(215) 427-1970

HARRY E. PURNELL
3341 West Hunting Park Avenue
Philadelphia, PA 19132
Harry E. Purnell, Owner
(215) 225-3535

TENNESSEE

CINKA, INC.
83 Madison Avenue
Memphis, TN 38103
Clair Jones, President
(901) 527-7507

TEXAS

CONDE, INC.
1970 Lee Trevino Drive, Suite 400
El Paso, TX 79936
Tony Conde, President
(915) 592-0283

CURTIS NEAL & ASSOCIATES, INC.
1167 East Comemrce
San Antonio, TX 78205
Curtis E. Neal, Jr., P.E., President
(512) 226-2772

VIRGINIA

TECHNOLOGY APPLICATIONS, INC.
6101 Stevenson Avenue
Alexandria, VA 22304
James Chatman, President
(703) 461-2000

WISCONSIN

DIKITA ENTERPRISES, LIMITED/ DIKITA ENGINEERING
3500 North 26th Street
Second Floor
Milwaukee, WI 53206
George Garland, Jr., Vice President
(414) 445-4663

The listings in this directory are available as Mailing Labels. See last page for details.

Executive Recruiters

The entries in this section represent a partial listing of Black executive recruiters.

ARIZONA

HAMCO, INC.
1820 North Central
Phoenix, AZ 85004
C. C. Hamilton, President
(602) 257-1626

CALIFORNIA

EDWARD K. BURBRIDGE ASSOCIATES, INC.
624 South Grand Avenue
29th Floor
Los Angeles, CA 90017
Edward Burbridge, President
(213) 489-6870

EXECUTIVE OPPORTUNITIES AGENCY
P.O. Drawer EE-PMC
Frazier Park, CA 93225
Moody Staten, President
(805) 242-0123

GREAT 400 GROUP INTERNATONAL
500 East Carson Street, Suite 105
Carson, CA 90745
Jules Howard, Executive Director
(213) 775-8729

CHERYL S. WEBB & ASSOCIATES
2200 Powell Street, Suite 110
Emeryville, CA 94608
Cheryl S. Webb-Davis, President
(415) 547-5588

CONNECTICUT

DEROCHER ASSOCIATES, LIMITED
2320 Main Street
Bridgeport, CT 06606
Frank Davis, President
(203) 579-0878

WENDELL L. JOHNSON ASSOCIATES, INC.
12 Grandview Drive
Danbury, CT 06811
Wendell L. Johnson, President
(203) 743-4112

DISTRICT OF COLUMBIA

PROGRESSIVE PERSONNEL
2349 Ashmeade Place, N.W.
Third Floor
Washington, D.C. 20009
J. Bobby Gregg, Jr.

FLORIDA

BURDELL WILLIAMS AGENCY
406 Reo Street
Suite, 227
Tampa, FL 33609
Kay Shine Williams, Recruiter
(813) 654-4304

GEORGIA

CONTINENTAL TECHNICAL SERVICES, INC.
100 Crescent Centre Pkwy. Suite 250
Tucker, GA 30084
W. H. Dunlap, President
(404) 491-8157

Executive Recruiters

EXECU-SEARCH
1819 Peachtree Road, N.E.
Atlanta, GA 30309
Kevin Smith, Director/Manager
(404) 352-1666

**ROBERT L. LIVINGSTON
  CONSULTANTS**
P. O. Box 568
Lilburn , GA 30226
Robert L. Livingston, Owner
(404) 925-8687

ILLINOIS

ASI PERSONNEL SERVICE, INC.
111 East Wacker Drive
Suite 2824
Chicago, IL 60601
Ellen Lawrence, Administrative Office
  Manager
(312) 819-4690

KENTUCKY

**CITY PLAZA PERSONNEL
  CONSULTANTS**
332 West Broadway
Louisville, KY 40202
Juanita Burks, President
(502) 581-1871

MARYLAND

DEROCHER ASSOCIATES, LTD.
P.O. Box 3714
Silver Spring, MD 20901
Frank D. Davis, President
(301) 384-6625

MASSACHUSETTS

ISAACSON, MILLER, INC.
334 Boylston Street
Boston, MA 02116
(617) 262-6500

MICHIGAN

B.P.A. ENTERPRISES, INC.
19971 James Couzens Highway
Detroit, MI 48235
Will E. Atkins, President
(313) 345-5700

MISSISSIPPI

ALPHA
P.O. Box 1493
Prentiss, MS 39474
Paul G. Polk, Owner
(601) 792-2893

MISSOURI

EBONY EMPLOYMENT, INC.
15 West Tenth
Kansas City, MO 64105
Dr. Samuel Watson, President
(816) 221-2090

**JACKSON EMPLOYMENT
  AGENCY**
3450 Prospect Avenue
Kansas City, MO 64128
Mr. Jackson, Owner
(816) 921-0181

Executive Recruiters

FRANK LOCKETT ASSOCIATES
1009 Glenside Street
St. Louis, MO 63130
Frank Lockett, Owner
(314) 231-9336

NEW JERSEY

**ACES EMPLOYMENT
CONSULTANTS**
P.O. Box 2582
Secaucus, NJ 07096
Anita Ervin, President
(201) 866-1448

**SUBSCRIPTION PERSONNEL
SERVICES, INC.**
Renaissance Towers, Inc.
111 Mulberry Street, Suite 1H
Newark, NJ 07102
Barbara Daniels, President
(201) 623-6700

NEW YORK

**RICHARD CLARKE
ASSOCIATES, INC.**
P. O. Box 20275, Cathedral Station
New York, NY 10025-1512
Richard Clarke, President
(212) 222-5600

INTERSPACE PERSONNEL, INC.
521 Fifth Avenue
New York, NY 10017
William Ellis, President
(212) 867-6660

**PEARL STREET PERSONNEL,
INC., (PSO)**
175 Remsen Street
Brooklyn, NY 11201
A. Harvey, Account Executive
(212) 732-0999

OHIO

**GENESIS PERSONNEL
SERVICES, INC.**
10921 Reed Hartman Highway
Suite 324
Cincinnati, OH 45242
Delora Bennett, President
(513) 891-4433

PENNSYLVANIA

B. P. PERSONNEL ASSOCIATES
P. O. Box 5258
Pittsburgh, PA 15206
William Pendleton, Owner
(412) 661-5601

HOWARD CLARK ASSOCIATES
P.O. Box 58846
Philadelphia, PA 19102
Howard L. Clark, President
(609) 467-3725

**JOHNSON WALKER &
ASSOCIATES, INC.**
21 S. 12th Ave., Suite 1306
Philadelphia, PA 19107
Bernard Johnson, President
(215) 561-1450

**LAMONTE OWENS &
COMPANY, INC.**
P.O. Box 5894
Philadelphia, PA 19128
LaMonte S. Owens, President
(215) 248-0500

TEXAS

MINORITY SEARCH, INC.
777 S.R.L. Thornton Freeway
Suite 105
Dallas, TX 75203
Billy R. Allen, President
(214) 948-6116

**THE URBAN PLACEMENT
SERVICE**
2211 Norfolk
Suite 816
Houston, TX 77098
Willie S. Bright, Owner/Manager
(713) 524-3994

VIRGINIA

ADIA PERSONNEL SERVICES
1525 Wilson Blvd., North, Suite 140
Arlington, VA 22209
J. Robby Gregg, Jr.
(703) 276-8100

WASHINGTON

B & M UNLIMITED ASSOCIATES
1331 Third Ave., Suite 420
Seattle, WA 98101
Lonnie Moore, President
(206) 223-1687

**BRANCH, RICHARDS,
ANDERSON & COMPANY**
441 First Avenue South
Suite 300, Merrill Place
Seattle, WA 98104
Andrew Branch, Senior Manager
(206) 624-4723

Financial Institutions

The nation's black financial institutions play a crucial role in black communities throughout America. Their expertise in money matters are of immense value to individuals and businesses alike.

Banks

ALABAMA

CITIZENS FEDERAL SAVINGS BANK
1728 Third Avenue, North
Birmingham, AL 35203
Dr. A.G. Gaston, President & Chairman of the Board
(205) 328-2041

COMMONWEALTH NATIONAL BANK
2214 St. Stephens Road
Mobile, AL 36601
Alpha Johnson, President & CEO
(205) 476-5938

CALIFORNIA

FOUNDERS NATIONAL BANK OF LOS ANGELES
3910 W. Martin Luther King Blvd.
Los Angeles, CA 90008
Carlton J. Jenkins, Managing Director
(213) 295-3161

DISTRICT OF COLUMBIA

DEVELOPMENT BANK OF WASHINGTON
2000 L Street, N.W.
Suite 702
Washington, D.C. 20036
Jerry Apodaca, President
(202) 332-9333

INDUSTRIAL BANK OF WASHINGTON
4812 Georgia Avenue, N.W.
Washington, D.C. 20011
B. Doyle Mitchell,
Chairman/President
(202) 722-2014

UNITED NATIONAL BANK OF WASHINGTON
3940 Minnesota Avenue, N.E.
Washington, D.C. 20006
Samuel Foggie Sr., President
(202) 828-4300

FLORIDA

METRO SAVINGS BANK
715 Goldwin Avenue
Orlando, FL 32805
William L. Young, President

PEOPLES NATIONAL BANK OF COMMERCE
3275 N.W. 79th Street
Miami, FL 33147
Frances Tyler, Sr., Vice President
(305) 686-0700

Banks (cont.)

GEORGIA

THE CARVER STATE BANK
701 Martin Luther King, Jr., Boulevard
Savannah, GA 31401
Mr. Robert E. James, President
(912) 233-9971

CITIZENS TRUST BANK
P.O. Box 4485
Atlanta, GA 30302
I. Owen Funderburg, President
(404) 659-5959

FIRST SOUTHERN BANK
P.O. Box 1019
Lithonia, GA 30058
Herbert K. Orise, President
(404) 987-3511

ILLINOIS

COMMUNITY BANK OF LAWNDALE
1111 South Homan Avenue
Chicago, IL 60624
Joyce Wade, Chief Executive Officer
(312) 533-6900

DREXEL NATIONAL BANK
3401 South King Drive
Chicago, IL 60616
James Shirley, President
(312) 225-9200

HIGHLAND COMMUNITY BANK
1701 West 87th Street
Chicago, IL 60620
George H. Brokemond, President
(312) 881-6800

INDEPENDENCE BANK OF CHICAGO
7936 South Cottage Grove
Chicago, IL 60619
Edgrick C. Johnson, President
(312) 487-4700

SEAWAY NATIONAL BANK OF CHICAGO
645 East 87th Street
Chicago, IL 60619
Walter E. Grady, President
(312) 487-4800

KANSAS

THE DOUGLASS BANK
1314 North Fifth Street
Kansas City, KS 66101
Sarah Swaters, Vice President
(913) 321-7200

LOUISIANA

LIBERTY BANK & TRUST COMPANY
3939 Tulane Avenue
New Orleans, LA 70160
Alden J. McDonald, Jr., President
(504) 483-6601

Financial Institutions

Banks (cont.)

UNITED BANK & TRUST COMPANY
2714 Canal Street
New Orleans, LA 70119
Marvin D. Beaulieu, President
(504) 827-0060

MARYLAND

HARBOR BANK OF MARYLAND
21 West Fayette Street
Baltimore, MD 21201
Joseph Haskins, Jr., President
(410) 528-1800

MASSACHUSETTS

BOSTON BANK OF COMMERCE
133 Federal Street
Boston, MA 02110
Ronald A. Homer, Chairman
(617) 457-4400

MICHIGAN

FIRST INDEPENDENCE NATIONAL BANK
44 Michigan Avenue
Detroit, MI 48226
Don Davis, Chairman
(313) 256-8250

OMNIBANK
10474 West Jefferson Avenue
River Rouge, MI 48218
Norman Gawlik, President
(313) 843-8856

MISSOURI

GATEWAY NATIONAL BANK
3412 Union Boulevard, North
St. Louis, MO 63115
William X. Smith, President
(314) 389-3000

NEW JERSEY

CITY NATIONAL BANK OF NEW JERSEY
900 Broad Street
Newark, NJ 07102
Louis E. Prezeau, President
(201) 624-0865

NEW YORK

FREEDOM NATIONAL BANK
275 West 125th Street
New York, NY 10027
George A. Russell, President
(212) 678-8408

NORTH CAROLINA

GREENSBORO NATIONAL BANK
P.O. Box 22046
Greensboro, NC 27420
Robert S. Chiles, Sr., President
(919) 373-8500

MECHANICS & FARMERS BANK
P.O. Box 1932
Durham, NC 27702
Ms. J.W. Taylor, President & CEO
(919) 683-1521

Banks (cont.)

UNITED NATIONAL BANK
P.O. Box 1450
137 Gillespie Street
Fayetteville, NC 28302
Leonard Hedgepeth, President & CEO
(919) 483-1131

OKLAHOMA

AMERICAN STATE BANK
Post Office Box 6389
Tulsa, OK 74148
Leon Evans, Jr., Executive Vice
   President
(918) 428-2211

OREGON

AMERICAN STATE BANK
Post Office Box 12348
Portland, OR 97212
Venerable F. Booker, Chairman
(503) 282-2216

PENNSYLVANIA

HERITAGE NATIONAL BANK
205 East Liberty Station
6393 Penn Avenue
Pittsburgh, PA 15206
Deidre Sledge, Operations Manager

SOUTH CAROLINA

VICTORY SAVINGS BANK
1545 Sumter Street
Columbia, SC 29201
James A. Bennett, President
(803) 733-8100

TENNESSEE

CITIZENS BANK
401 Charolette
Nashville, TN 37219
Rick Davidson, Jr., President
(615) 256-6193

TRI-STATE BANK OF MEMPHIS
180 South Main Street
Memphis, TN 38101
Jesse Turner, President
(901) 525-0384

TEXAS

FIRST TEXAS BANK
P.O. Box 29775
Dallas, TX 75229
William E. Stahnke, President
(214) 243-2400

UNITY NATIONAL BANK
2602 Blodgett
Houston, TX 77004
Larry Hawkins, President & CEO
(713) 526-3971

Financial Institutions

Banks (cont.)

VIRGINIA

NEW ATLANTIC BANK
415 St. Paul's Boulevard
Norfolk, VA 23510
Hiliary Holloway, Chairman & CEO
(804) 623-6155

FIRST STATE BANK
P.O. Box 640
Danville, VA 24543
Sylvester L. Jennings, President
(804) 793-4611

WASHINGTON

EMERALD CITY BANK
2320 East Union
Seattle, WA 98122
Leon Smith, President
(206) 329-3434

WISCONSIN

NORTH MILWAUKEE STATE BANK
5630 West Fond Du Lac Avenue
Milwaukee, WI 53216
Snow Mitchell, Jr., Chairman
(414) 466-2344

Savings & Loan Associations

ALABAMA

CITIZENS FEDERAL SAVINGS BANK
300 North Eighteenth Street
Birmingham, AL 35201
Bunny Stokes, Jr., President

GULF FEDERAL SAVINGS AND LOAN ASSOCIATION
901 Springhill Avenue
P.O. Box 42017
Mobile, AL 36646-0217

TUSKEGEE FEDERAL SAVINGS & LOAN ASSOCIATION
301 North Elm Street
Tuskegee, AL 36088
Richard R. Harvey, Managing Officer
(205) 727-2560

CALIFORNIA

BROADWAY FEDERAL SAVINGS & LOAN ASSOCIATION
4501 South Broadway
Los Angeles, CA 90037
Elbert T. Hudson, Chairman
(213) 232-4271

ENTERPRISE SAVINGS & LOAN ASSOCIATION
1219 East Rosecrans Avenue
Compton, CA 90282
Cornell R. Kirkland, Preident
(213) 591-5641

FAMILY SAVINGS & LOAN ASSOCIATION
3683 Crenshaw Boulevard
Los Angeles, CA 90016
Wayne Kent Bradshaw, President
(213) 295-3381

FOUNDERS SAVINGS & LOAN ASSOCIATION
3910 West Santa Barbara Avenue
Los Angeles, CA 90008
Ronald Thigpenn, President
(213) 295-3161

GOLDEN COIN SAVINGS & LOAN ASSOCIATION
170 Columbus Avenue, Room 210
San Francisco, CA 94133
Winfred Tom, President

CONNECTICUT

COMMUNITY FEDERAL SAVINGS & LOAN ASSOCIATION
4490 Main Street
Bridgeport, CT 06606
Donald Finch, Managing Officer

DISTRICT OF COLUMBIA

INDEPENDENCE FEDERAL SAVINGS & LOAN ASSOCIATION
1229 Connecticut Avenue, N.W.
Washington, D.C. 20036
William Fitzgerald, President

Financial Institutions

Savings & Loan Associations (cont.)

FLORIDA

WASHINGTON SHORES FEDERAL SAVINGS & LOAN ASSOCIATION
715 Goldwin Avenue
Orlando, FL 32805
John Hamilton, President
(305) 293-7320

GEORGIA

MUTUAL FEDERAL SAVINGS & LOAN ASSOCIATION
205 Auburn Avenue, N.E.
Atlanta, GA 30303
Hamilton Glover, President
(404) 659-0701

LOUISIANA

LIFE SAVINGS BANK
7990 Scenic Highway
P.O. Box 74108
Baton Rouge, LA 70874
Ernest Johnson, President

FIRST FEDERAL SAVINGS & LOAN
7990 Scenic Highway
Baton Rouge, LA 70874
Henry Stamper, Executive Vice
   President
(504) 775-6133

MARYLAND

ADVANCE FEDERAL SAVINGS & LOAN ASSOCIATION
1405 East Cold Spring Lane
Baltimore, MD 21239
John Hamilton, President
(301) 323-9570

IDEAL FEDERAL SAVINGS BANK
1629 Druid Hill Avenue
Baltimore, MD 21217
Dr. W. O. Bryson, Jr., Chairman
(301) 669-1629

MICHIGAN

HOME FEDERAL SAVINGS BANK
9108 Woodward Avenue
Detroit, MI 48202
Wilburn R. Phillips, President
(313) 873-3310

MISSISSIPPI

FIRST COMMERCE SAVINGS BANK
P.O. Box 3199
Jackson, MS

MISSOURI

NEW AGE FEDERAL SAVINGS & LOAN ASSOCIATION
1401 North Kings Highway Boulevard
St. Louis, MO 63113
David Harper, President
(314) 361-4100

Savings & Loan Associations

NEW YORK

CARVER FEDERAL SAVINGS & LOAN ASSOCIATION
75 West 125th Street
New York, NY 10027
Richard T. Greene, President

NORTH CAROLINA

AMERICAN FEDERAL SAVINGS & LOAN ASSOCIATION
701 East Market Street
Greensboro, NC 20071
J. Kenneth Lee, President
(919) 273-9753

MUTUAL SAVINGS & LOAN ASSOCIATION
112 West Parrish Street
Durham, NC 27701
F.V. Allison, Jr., President
(919) 688-1308

PENNSYLVANIA

BEREAN SAVING ASSOCIATION
5228 Chestnut Street
Philadelphia, PA 19139
Ron Green, President
(215) 472-4545

DWELLING HOUSE SAVINGS & LOAN ASSOCIATION
501 Herron Avenue
Pittsburgh, PA 15219
Robert R. Lavelle, CEO
(412) 683-5116

TEXAS

STANDARD SAVINGS & LOAN ASSOCIATION
P.O. Box 8806
Houston, TX 77288
Gloria R. Hall, Exec. Vice President
(713) 529-9133

VIRGINIA

IMPERIAL SAVINGS & LOAN ASSOCIATION
211 Fayette Street
Martinsville, VA 24114
William B. Muse, Jr., President
(703) 638-7545

PEOPLE'S SAVINGS & LOAN ASSOCIATION
101 North Armistead Avenue
Hampton, VA 23669
John E. Coles, President
(804) 722-2575

WASHINGTON

SOUND SAVINGS AND LOAN ASSOCIATION
1006 Second Avenue
Seattle, WA 98114
Cathy Boydston, President

WISCONSIN

COLUMBIA SAVINGS & LOAN ASSOCIATION
2000 W. Fond du Lac Avenue
Milwaukee, WI 52302
Thalia B. Winfield, President
(414) 374-0480

Fraternal Organizations

The fraternal organizations represented on these pages are involved in philanthropic and charitable work throughout the world. Among other things, they build housing, fund medical research and provide scholarships to needy students.

Fraternities

ALPHA PHI ALPHA FRATERNITY, INC.
National Headquarters
2313 St. Paul Street
Baltimore, MD 21218
James B. Blanton, III, Executive Director
(410) 554-0040

GROOVE PHI GROOVE SOCIAL FELLOWSHIP, INC.
P.O. Box 8337
Silver Spring, MD 20907
Ronald White, President
(202) 994-4466

IOTA PHI THETA FRATERNITY, INC.
P.O. Box 7628
Baltimore, MD 21207
Theodore N. Stephens, II, Grand Polaris
(301) 792-2192

KAPPA ALPHA PSI FRATERNITY, INC.
National Headquarters
2320 North Broad Street
Philadelphia, PA 19132
W. Ted Smith, Ph.D., Executive Secretary
(215) 228-7184

OMEGA PSI PHI FRATERNITY, INC.
National Headquarters
2714 Georgia Avenue, N.W.
Washington, D.C. 20001
Dr. John S. Epps, Executive Secretary
(202) 667-7158

PHI BETA SIGMA FRATERNITY, INC.
National Headquarters
145 Kennedy Street, N.W.
Washington, D.C. 20011
Dr. Lawrence E. Miller, National Executive Director
(202) 726-5434

SIGMA PI PHI FRATERNITY
("The Boule")
920 Broadway
Suite 703
New York, NY 10010
Butler T. Henderson, Executive Secretary
(212) 529-1779

Fraternal Organizations

Sororities

ALPHA KAPPA ALPHA SORORITY, INC.
National Headquarters
5656 South Stony Island Avenue
Chicago, IL 60637
Alison H. Harris, Executive Director
(312) 684-1282

ALPHA PI CHI SORORITY, INC.
1328 Nicholson Street
Hyattsville, MD 20782
Magoline R. Comey, President
(301) 559-4330

CHI ETA PHI SORORITY, INC.
18250 Fairfield
Detroit, MI 48221
Mary Hellen Morris, Supreme Basileus
(313) 861-2832

CHI ETA PHI SORORITY, INC.
3029 Thirteenth Street, N.W.
Washington, D.C. 20009
Mary H. Morris, Supreme Basileus
(202) 723-3384

DELTA SIGMA THETA SORORITY, INC.
National Headquarters
1707 New Hampshire Avenue, N.W.
Washington, D.C. 20009
Dr. Yvonne Kennedy, President
(202) 986-2400

ETA PHI BETA SORORITY, INC.
16815 James Couzens
Detroit, MI 48235
Mildred Harpole, National President
(918) 425-7717

GAMMA PHI DELTA SORORITY, INC.
Alpha Omicron Chapter
1900 Campbell Drive
Suitland, MD 20746
Elsie Conway, Basileus

IOTA PHI LAMBDA SORORITY, INC.
P.O. Box 11609
Montgomery, AL 36111
Dorethea N. Hornbuckle, Preisent
(205) 284-0203

LAMBDA KAPPA MU SORORITY, INC.
9706 Southall Road
Randallstown, MD 21133
Ovella D. Queen, Grand Basileus
(301) 655-8778

PHI DELTA KAPPA, INC.
8233 South Martin Luther King Drive
Chicago, IL 60619
Marguerite McClelland, President
(312) 783-7379

SIGMA GAMMA RHO SORORITY, INC.
8800 South Stony Island Avenue
Chicago, IL 60617
Kattie Kinnard White, Ph.D., Grand Basileus
(312) 873-9000

TAU GAMMA DELTA SORORITY, INC.
2528 West 74th Street
Los Angeles, CA 90043
Annette I. Welford, President
(213) 751-7084

Fraternal Organizations

ZETA DELTA PHI SORORITY, INC.
P.O. Box 157
Bronx, NY 10469
Sonnie Humphrey, Preident

ZETA PHI BETA SORORITY, INC.
1734 New Hampshire Avenue, N.W.
Washington, D.C. 20009
Mrs. Linda Thompson,
   National President
(202) 387-3103

Hospitals

The entries in this section represent a partial listing of black hospitals in America.

BETHANY HOSPITAL
5025 North Paulina Street
Chicago, IL 60640
(312) 271-9040

CHARITY HOSPITAL OF LOUISIANA
'1532 Tulane Avenue
New Orleans, LA 70140
(504) 568-2311

FAIRVIEW MEDICAL CENTER
2048 West Fairview Avenue
Montgomery, AL 36108
(205) 265-7011

GEORGE HUBBARD HOSPITAL OF MEHARRY MEDICAL COLLEGE
1005 Eighteenth Avenue, North
Nashville, TN 37208
(615) 327-6218

HOWARD UNIVERSITY HOSPITAL
2041 Georgia Avenue, N.W.
Washington, D.C. 20060
Haynes Rice, Hospital Director
(202) 865-6660

L. RICHARDSON MEMORIAL HOSPITAL, INC.
Drawer 16167
Greensboro, NC 27406
(919) 275-9741

MOUND BAYOU COMMUNITY HOSPITAL
Drawer R
Mound Bayou, MS 38762
(601) 741-2113

PROVIDENT MEDICAL CENTER
500 East 51st Street
Chicago, IL 60615
Orlando Jones, Chief Administrator
(312) 538-9700

RIVERSIDE GENERAL HOSPITAL
P.O. Box 8128
Houston, TX 77288
(713) 526-2441

ROSELAND COMMUNITY HOSPITAL
45 West 111th Street
Chicago, IL 60628
(312) 995-3000

ST. BERNARD HOSPITAL
326 West 64th Street
Chicago, IL 60621
(312) 962-4100

SOUTHWEST HOSPITAL AND MEDICAL CENTER, INC.
501 Fairburn Road, S.W.
Atlanta, GA 30311
Herbert H. Weldon, Jr.,
    Administrator/CEO
(404) 669-1111

The listings in this directory are available as Mailing Labels. See last page for details.

Information Processing Companies

Many of the companies in this section are national in scope and provide many valuable services to clients nationwide.

CALIFORNIA

ADELPHI, INCORPORATED
P.O. Box 28831
Oakland, CA 94604-8831
Conway B. Jones, Jr., President
(415) 530-3411

ADVANCED SYSTEMS CONCEPTS, INC.
2333 North Lake Avenue
Altadena, CA 91001
Johnetta MacCalla, CEO
(818) 791-0983

COMPUTER SERVICES OF SACRAMENTO
9827 Libra Avenue
Sacramento, CA 95827
Marilyn Levels, Owner
(916) 363-0524

NUMERITRONIX, INC.
2580 Azurite Circle
Newbury Park, CA 91320
James M. Dodds, President
(805) 499-2643

PYRAMID BUSINESS SYSTEMS, INC.
484 Lake Park Avenue, Suite 98
Oakland, CA 94610
Jim Kennedy, President
(415) 527-1733

WESTERN COMPUTER GROUP
858 Burway Road
Burlingame, CA 94010
Peter Schneidermeyer,
  Sales Manager

CONNECTICUT

FAIRFAX COMMUNICATIONS COMPANY
124 Unity Drive, Suite E
Milford, CT 06460
Guy C. Louis-Julie, President
(203) 877-9771

SPECTRUM MANUFACTURING, INC.
25 Science Park
New Haven, CT 06511
Clinton Rogers, President
(203) 786-5200

DISTRICT OF COLUMBIA

AUTOMATED DATA MANAGEMENT, INC.
1920 Bladensburg Road, N.E.
Washington, D.C. 20002
Michele Ashton, President
(202) 526-0440

MARYLAND

MICRO COMPUTER SYSTEMS, INC.
8401 Colesville Road, Suite 305
Silver Spring, MD 20910
Shireen Kahn, Marketing Rep.
(301) 495-4444

Information Processing Companies

MASSACHUSETTS

IOCS, INC.
400 Totten Pond Road
Waltham MA 02254
Isaac Crawford, Marketing Manager
(617) 890-2299

MICHIGAN

MICRO-TIME MANAGEMENT SYSTEMS, INC.
17023 West Ten Mile Road
Southfield, MI 48075
Otis Kirkland, Jr., President
(313) 557-6637

PACE COMMUNICATIONS, INC.
4936 Delemere
Royal Oak, MI 48073
Cortesa Pruner, President
(313) 280-1148

NEW YORK

BEAMON DATA SYSTEMS
5639 Netherland Avenue
Riverdale, NY 10471
Randolph Beamon, President
(212) 796-0375

LOGICAL TECHNICAL SERVICES CORPORATION
71 West 23rd Street
New York, NY 10010
E. A. Greenlee, President
(212) 741-8340

The listings in this directory are available as Mailing Labels. See last page for details.

OHIO

CENTURIAN SYSTEMS, INC.
3030 Euclid Avenue
Cleveland, OH 44115
Chris Eliley, Vice President
(216) 881-3939

DELTA PRODUCTS COMPANY
26250 Euclid Avenue
Cleveland, OH 44132
Thomas A. Cargill, President
(216) 731-3537

ERIE SHORES COMPUTER
401 Broad Street, Suite 300
Elyria, OH 44035
Larry Jones, President
(216) 323-7757

TRACOM SYSTEMS, INC.
230 Northland Boulevard, Suite 215
Cincinnati, OH 45246
Theodore Addison, President
(513) 772-2111

RHODE ISLAND

SYSTEMS DIAGNOSIS, INC.
3 Richmond Square
Providence, RI 02906
Richardson Ogidan, President
(401) 331-8980

TENNESSEE

ADVANCED INTEGRATED TECHNOLOGY, INC.
P.O. Box 612
Columbia, TN 38402-0612
Gene Cheatham, President
(615) 381-4388

Information Processing Companies

TEXAS

INTERNATIONAL BUSINESS CONSUMABLES COMPANY
777 Post Oak Blvd., Suite 509
Houston, TX 77056
Ben Wiley, President
(713) 552-9611

LIB ELECTO-OPTICS CORPORATION
3417 Halifax Street
Dallas, TX 75247-3417
Dennis Warren, Owner
(214) 630-3202

VIRGINIA

FEDERAL MICRO-SYSTEMS, INC.
7420 Fullerton Road, Suite 104
Springfield, VA 22153
William Tutman, President
(703) 569-6569

SYSTEMS MANAGEMENT AMERICAN CORPORATION
254 Monticello Avenue
Norfolk, VA 23510
Herman E. Valentine, President
(804) 627-9331

WISCONSIN

FRONTIER TECHNOLOGIES CORPORATION
10201 North Port Washington Road
MeQuon, WI 53092

PM COMPUTER SYSTEMS, INC.
2821 North Fourth Street
Milwaukee, WI 53212
Ronald A. Pemberton, President
(414) 372-7627

Insurance Companies

This section contains a partial listing of African-American insurance companies.

ATLANTA LIFE INSURANCE COMPANY
P.O. Box 897
Atlanta, GA 30301
Jesse Hill, President

BENEVOLENT LIFE INSURANCE COMPANY
1624 Milam Street
Shreveport, LA 71103
Granville Smith, President

BOOKER T. WASHINGTON INSURANCE COMPANY
P.O. Box 697
Birmingham, AL 35201
A.G. Gaston, President
(205) 328-5454

CENTRAL LIFE INSURANCE COMPANY OF FLORIDA
P.O. Box 3286
Tampa, FL 33607
L. Phillip Butler, II, President
(813) 251-1897

CHICAGO METROPOLITAN ASSURANCE COMPANY
4455 Martin Luther King Drive
Chicago, IL 60653
Anderson Schweich, President
(312) 285-3030

GEORGE F. CARTER INSURANCE AGENCY, INC.
P.O. Box 12337
Jacksonville, FL 32209
George F. Carter, President
(904) 764-0025

GERTRUDES GEDDES WILLIS LIFE INSURANCE COMPANY
2128 Jackson Avenue
P.O. Box 53272
New Orleans, LA 70153
Joseph O. Misshore, President
(504) 522-2525

GOLDEN CIRCLE LIFE INSURANCE COMPANY
P.O. Box 293
39 Jackson Avenue
Bronsville, TN 38012
C. A. Rawls, President

GOLDEN STATE MUTUAL LIFE INSURANCE COMPANY
P.O. Box 2332, Terminal Annex
Los Angeles, CA 90018
Ivan Houston, President

GOODRICH JOHNSON BROKERAGE
271 West 125th Street, Suite 208
New York, NY 10027
Thelma E. Goodrich, President
(212) 865-5606

LIGHTHOUSE LIFE INSURANCE COMPANY
1544 Milam Street
Shreveport, LA 71103
Bunyan Jacobs, President

Insurance Companies

LOVETT'S LIFE AND BURIAL INSURANCE COMPANY
P.O. Box 364
Mobile, AL 36603
L.M. Lovett

MAJESTIC LIFE INSURANCE COMPANY
1833 Dryades Street
New Orleans, LA 70113
James V. Haydel, President

MAMMOTH LIFE & ACCIDENT INSURANCE COMPANY
P.O. Box 2099
Louisville, KY 40201
Julius Price, President

MCAP BONDING & INSURANCE AGENCY, INC.
89-50 164th Street, Suite 2B
Jamaica, NY 11432
Sherman Brown, President
(718) 657-6444

NATIONAL SERVICE INDUSTRIAL LIFE INSURANCE COMPANY
1716 North Claiborne Avenue
New Orleans, LA 70116
Duplain Rhodes, President

NORTH CAROLINA MUTUAL LIFE INSURANCE COMPANY
Mutual Plaza
Durham, NC 27701
W.J. Kennedy, President
(919) 682-9201

PEOPLES PROGRESSIVE INSURANCE COMPANY
109 Harrison Street
Rayville, LA 71269
Marion Hill, President

THE PILGRIM HEALTH & LIFE INSURANCE COMPANY
P.O. Box 1897
Augusta, GA 30901
W.S. Homsby, President

PROTECTIVE INDUSTRIAL INSURANCE COMPANY OF ALABAMA, INC.
P.O. Box 2744
Birmingham, AL 35204
Virgil Harris, President

PURPLE SHIELD LIFE INSURANCE COMPANY
Post Office Box 3157
Baton Rouge, LA 70802
Homer Sheeler, Sr., President

RELIABLE LIFE INSURANCE COMPANY
Post Office Box 1157
108 North 23rd Street
Monroe, LA 71201
Joseph Miller, President

SECURITY LIFE INSURANCE OF THE SOUTH
P.O. Box 159
Jackson, MS 39203
F.D. Boston, President

SOUTHERN AID LIFE INSURANCE COMPANY
P.O. Box 12024
Richmond, VA 23241
E.L. Simon, President

SUPREME LIFE INSURANCE COMPANY OF AMERICA
3501 Martin Luther King Drive
Chicago, IL 60653
John H. Johnson, Chairman
(312) 538-5100

Insurance Companies

**UNITED MUTUAL LIFE
INSURANCE COMPANY**
310 Lenox Avenue
New York, NY 10027
James L. Howard, President
(212) 369-4200

**UNIVERSAL LIFE INSURANCE
COMPANY**
P.O. Box 241
Memphis, TN 38101
A.M. Walker, President

**WINSTON MUTUAL LIFE INSUR-
ANCE COMPANY**
P.O. Box 998
Winston-Salem, NC 27102
George Hill, President

**WRIGHT MUTUAL INSURANCE
COMPANY**
2995 East Grand Boulevard
Detroit, MI 48202
Wardell Croft, President

Judiciary

The names on the following pages represent a partial listing of the nation's African American judges.

United States Supreme Court

CLARENCE THOMAS
Justice, U.S. Supreme Court
Supreme Court of the United States
One First Street, N.E.
Washington, D.C. 20543

United States Court of Appeals

HARRY T. EDWARDS
Judge, U.S. Court of Appeals
D.C. Circuit
Third and Constitution Avenue, N.W.
Washington, D.C. 20001

RICHARD C. ERWIN
Judge, U.S. Circuit Court of Appeals
North Carolina Middle District
251 North Main Street, Suite 223-A
Winston Salem, NC 27101

J. JEROME FARRIS
Judge, U.S. Court of Appeals
Ninth Circuit
1908 - 34th Avenue South
Seattle, WA 98104

A. LEON HIGGINBOTHAM, JR.
Chief Judge, U.S. Court of Appeals
Third Circuit
601 Market Street, Room 22613
Philadelphia, PA 19106

AMALYA L. KEARSE
Judge, U.S. Court of Appeals
Second Circuit
U.S. Courthouse - Foley Square
New York, NY 10007

DAMON KEITH
Judge, U.S. Court of Appeals
Sixth Circuit
240 Federal Building
Detroit, MI 48226

CECIL POOLE
Judge, U.S. Court of Appeals
Ninth Circuit
Post Office Box 547
San Francisco, CA 94101

SPOTTSWOOD ROBINSON, III
Judge (Senior Status)
U.S. Court of Appeals
D.C. Circuit
Third and Constitution Avenue, N.W.
Washington, D.C. 20001

THEODORE MCMILLAN
Judge, U.S. Court of Appeals
1114 Market Street
Room 526
St. Louis, MO 63101
(314) 539-3601

United States District Court

SAUNDRA BROWN-ARMSTRONG
Judge, U.S. District Court
Northern District of California
450 Golden Gate Avenue
San Francisco, CA 94102

U.W. CLEMON
Judge, U.S. District Court
Northern District of Alabama
305 Federal Courthouse
Birmingham, AL 35203

ROBERT F. COLLINS
Judge, U.S. District Court
Eastern District of Louisiana
500 Camp Street, Suite 465
New Orleans, LA 70130

JULIAN ABELE COOK, JR.
Judge, U.S. District Court
Eastern District of Michigan
231 Lafayette Boulevard
Detroit, MI 48226

BENJAMIN F. GIBSON
Chief Judge, U.S. District Court
Western District of Michigan
110 Michigan Avenue, N.W.
Room 601
Grand Rapids, MI 49503

CLIFFORD S. GREEN
Judge, U.S. District Court
Eastern District of Pennsylvania
601 Market Street
Suite 15613
Philadelphia, PA 19106

JOHN HARGROVE
Judge, U.S. District Court
District of Maryland
101 West Lombard Street
Room 520
Baltimore, MD 21201

TERRY HATTER
Judge, U.S. District Court
Central District of California
312 North Spring Street
Los Angeles, CA 90012

THELTON E. HENDERSON
Chief Judge, U.S. District Court
Northern District of California
450 Golden Gate Avenue
Room 19042
San Francisco, CA 94102

ODELL HORTON
Judge, U.S. District Court
Western District of Tennessee
Federal Court
957 Federal Building
Memphis, TN 38103

GEORGE HOWARD, JR.
Judge. U.S. District Court
Eastern District of Arkansas
Post Office Box 349
Little Rock, AR 72203

JOSEPH C. HOWARD
Judge, U.S. District Court
District of Maryland
101 West Lombard Street
Room 340
Baltimore, MD 21201

HERBERT J. HUTTON
Judge, U.S. District Court
Eastern District of Pennsylvania
601 Market Street, Suite 5118
Philadelphia, PA 19106

STERLING JOHNSON, JR.
Judge, U.S. District Court
Eastern District of New York
225 Cadman Plaza
Brooklyn, NY 11201

TIMOTHY K. LEWIS
Judge, U.S. District Court
Western District of Pennsylvania
Seventh Avenue and Grant Street
Pittsburgh, PA 15219

Judiciary

CONSUELO MARSHALL
Judge, U.S. District Court
Central District of California
312 North Spring Street
Los Angeles, CA 90012

CONSTANCE B. MOTLEY
Chief Judge, U.S. District Court
Southern District of New York
U.S. Courthouse
Foley Square
New York, NY 10007

DAVID S. NELSON
Judge, U.S. District Court
District of Massachusetts
McCormack Post Office
Boston, MA 02109

JAMES B. PARSONS
Senior Judge
U.S. District Court, Northern
District of Illinois, Eastern Division
219 South Dearborn
Room 2286
Chicago, IL 60604

MATTHEW J. PERRY
Judge, U.S. District Court
District of South Carolina
Post Office Box 867
Columbia, SC 29202

JAMES R. SPENCER
Judge, U.S. District Court
Eastern District of Virginia
Post Office Box 2-AD
Richmond, VA 23205

JACK E. TANNER
Senior Judge, U.S. District Court
Western District of Washington
Post Office Box 2015
Tacoma, WA 98401

ANNE E. THOMPSON
Judge, U.S. District Court
District of New Jersey
402 East State Street
Trenton, NJ 08608

MYRON H. THOMPSON
Judge, U.S. District Court
Middle District of Alabama
Post Office Box 235
Montgomery, AL 36101

HORACE T. WARD
Judge, U.S. District Court
Northern District of Georgia
2388 U.S. Court House
75 Spring Street
Atlanta, GA 30303

JAMES WARE
Judge, U.S. District Court
Northern District of California
280 South First Street
San Jose, CA 95113

GEORGE W. WHITE
Judge, U.S. District Court
Northern District of Ohio
201 Superior
Room 135
Cleveland, OH 44114

ANNE CLAIRE WILLIAMS
Judge, U.S. District Court
Northern District of Illinois
Eastern Division
219 South Dearborn
Room 1956
Chicago, IL 60604
(312) 435-5532

United States Bankruptcy Court

RANDOLPH BAXTER
Judge, U.S. Bankruptcy Court
Northern District
412 U.S. Courthouse
Cleveland, OH 44114

CHARLES N. CLEVERT
Judge, U.S. Bankruptcy Court
517 East Wisconsin Avenue
Milwaukee, WI 53203

R. GUY COLE
Judge, U.S. Bankruptcy Court
Southern District
85 Marconi Boulevard
Columbus, OH 43215

BERNICE DONALD
Judge, U.S. Bankruptcy Court
First Memphis Place Building
200 Jefferson
Memphis, TN 38103

JAMES R. DOOLEY
Judge, U.S. Bankruptcy Court
312 North Spring Street
Los Angeles, CA 90012

BENJAMIN E. FRANKLIN
Chief Judge, U.S. Bankruptcy Court
812 North Seventh Street
Kansas City, MO 66101

RAY R. GRAVES
Judge, U.S. Bankruptcy Court
Eastern District
231 West LaFayette Boulevard
Room 1063
Detroit, MI 48226

ALBERT A. SHEEN
Judge, U.S. Bankruptcy Court
Post Office Box 720
St. Thomas, VI 00801

United States Magistrates

JOYCE LONDON ALEXANDER
U.S. Magistrate
932 Post Office and Courthouse
Boston, MA 02109

CALVIN BOTLEY
U.S. Magistrate
Southern District of Texas
Post Office Box 61205
Houston, TX 77208

FRANKLIN BURGESS
U.S. Magistrate
Western District
Post Office Box 2214
Tacoma, WA 98401

ZACHERY W. CARTER
U.S. Magistrate
Eastern District
225 Cadman Plaza
Brooklyn, NY 11201

WILLIAM F. HALL, JR.
U.S. Magistrate
Pennsylvania Eastern District
601 Market Street, Room 4613
Philadelphia, PA 19106

WILLIAM J. HAYNES, JR.
U.S. Magistrate
649 U.S. Court House
Nashville, TN 37203

Judiciary

LYNN V. HOOE, JR.
U.S. Magistrate
Eastern District
231 W. Lafayette Blvd., Room 1027
Detroit, MI 48226

HENRY L. JONES, JR.
U.S. Magistrate
Post Office Box 3393
Little Rock, AR 72203

IVAN L.R. LEMELLE
U.S. Magistrate
Louisiana Eastern District
500 Camp Street
New Orleans, LA 70130

LOUIS MOORE, JR.
U.S. Magistrate
Louisiana Eastern Division
500 Camp Street
New Orleans, LA 70130

W. THOMAS ROSEMOND
U.S. Magistrate
219 South Dearborn, Room 2422
Chicago, IL 60604

JACK SHERMAN, JR.
U.S. Magistrate
Southern District
Fifth and Walnut Street, Room 823
Cincinnati, OH 45202

ALABAMA

Supreme Court

OSCAR W. ADAMS, JR.
Associate Justice
State Supreme Court
Post Office Box 218
Montgomery, AL 36101

Circuit Court

RALPH D. COOKE
Judge, Circuit Court
Tenth Judicial Circuit
613 Courthouse Annex
Bessemer, AL 35020

CAIN J. KENNEDY
Judge, Circuit Court
Thirteenth Judicial District
Mobile, AL 36602

J. RICHMOND PEARSON
Judge, Circuit Court
Tenth Judicial District
Courthouse, Room 504
Birmingham, AL 35263

CHARLES PRICE
Judge, Circuit Court
Fifteenth Judicial Court
134 North Haardt Drive
Montgomery, AL 36105

District Court

AUBREY FORD
Judge, District Court
Macon County
Post Office Box 703
Tuskegee, AL 36083

EDDIE HARDAWAY, JR.
Judge, District Court
Sumter County
Post Office Box 9
Livingston, AL 34570

RICHARD L. OSBORNE
Judge, District Court
Greene County
Post Office Box 310
Eutaw, AL 35462

JO CELESTE PETTWAY
Judge, District Court
Wilcox County
Post Office Box 549
Camden, AL 36726

HERMAN THOMAS
Judge, District Court
Thirteenth Judicial Circuit
Post Office Box 829
Mobile, AL 36601

NATHANIEL WALKER
Judge, District Court
Fourth Judicial Circuit
Post Office Box 23
Selma, AL 36701

Municipal Court

ERIC FANCHER
Judge, Municipal Court
Brighton County
Post Office Box 8250
Birmingham, AL 35218

THOMAS FIGURES
Presiding Judge, Municipal Court
City of Prichard
Post Office Box 10427
Prichard, AL 36610

H. LEWIS GILLIS
Judge, Municipal Court
Post Office Box 1111
Montgomery, AL 36101

CECIL MONROE
Judge, Municipal Court
Post Office Box 2446
Mobile, AL 36601

MALCOLM R. NEWMAN
Judge, Municipal Court
Gordon County
219 Crawford Street
Dothan, AL 36302

CAROLE C. SMITHERMAN
Judge, Municipal Court
710 20th Street, North
Birmingham, AL 35203

EUGENE R. VERIN
Judge, Municipal Court
1813 Second Avenue, North
Bessemer, AL 35020

ARIZONA

Superior Court

THOMAS DUNEVANT, III
Judge, Superior Court
201 West Jefferson, Suite 9D
Phoenix, AZ 85003

MAURICE PORTLEY
Judge, Superior Court
222 East Jaulina, Suite 4B
Phoenix, AZ 85210

Municipal Court

JEAN F. WILLIAMS
Judge, Municipal Court
Division 21
455 North Fifth Street
Phoenix, AZ 85004

Judiciary

ARKANSAS

Municipal Court

MARION A. HUMPHREY
Judge, Municipal Court
Pulaski County
600 West Markham Street
Little Rock, AR 72201

EDWIN KEATON
Judge, Municipal Court
Camden-Quachita County
Post Office Box 524
Camden, NJ 71701

Circuit Court

JOYCE WARREN WILLIAMS
Judge, Circuit-Chancery Court
Pulaski County
3201 West Roosevelt
Little Rock, AR 72204

CALIFORNIA

Supreme Court

ALLEN BROUSSARD
Associate Justice
State Supreme Court
455 Golden Gate Avenue
San Francisco, CA 94102

The listings in this book are available as Mailing Labels. See last page for details.

Court of Appeals

VAINO SPENCER
Judge, Court of Appeals
Second Appellate District
3580 Wilshire Boulevard
Los Angeles,CA 90010

CLINTON WHITE
Judge, Court of Appeals
First Appellate District
455 Golden Gate Avenue
San Francisco, CA 94102

ARLEIGH WOODS
Judge, Court of Appeals
Second Appellate District
3580 Wilshire Boulevard
Los Angeles, CA 90010

Superior Court

GILBERT ALSTON
Judge, Superior Court
300 East Walnut Street
Pasadena, CA 90001

GORDON BARANCO
Judge, Superior Court
Alameda County, Department 35
24405 Amador Street
Hayward, CA 94544

WILLIAM BEVERLY, JR.
Judge, Superior Court
200 West Compton Boulevard
Compton, CA 90220

CANDACE D. COOPER
Judge, Superior Court
210 West Temple Street
Los Angeles, CA 90012

LA DORIS CORDELL
Judge, Superior Court
Santa Clara County
170 Park Center Plaza
San Jose, CA 95113

JOHN F. CRUIKSHANK, JR.
Judge, Superior Court
San Joaquin County
235 West Euclid Avenue
Stockton, CA 95204

JOHN DEARMAN
Judge, Superior Court
San Francisco County
Room 300, City Hall
San Francisco, CA 94102

ROOSEVELT DORN
Judge, Superior Court
210 West Temple Street
Los Angles, CA 90012

REGINALD DUNN
Judge, Superior Court
210 West Temple Street
Los Angeles, CA 90012

REGINALD DUNN
Judge, Superior Court
210 West Temple Street
Los Angeles, CA 90012

RAYMOND EDWARDS
Judge, Superior Court
San Diego County
220 West Broadway
San Diego, CA 92102

ROBERT B. HUTSON
Judge, Superior Court
Department D
301 City Drive South
Orange, CA 92668

CHARLES E. JONES
Judge, Superior Court
111 North Hill Street
Los Angeles, CA 90012

LAWRENCE JONES
Judge, Superior Court
Fresno County
1100 Van Ness
Room 550
Fresno, CA 93721

NAPOLEAN A. JONES, JR.
Judge, Superior Court
San Diego Judicial District
220 West Broadway
San Diego, CA 92101

JAMES LONG
Judge, Superior Court
Sacramento County
920 Ninth Street
Sacramento, CA 95814

ROBERT MACKEY
Judge, Superior Court
111 North Hill Street
Los Angeles, CA 90012

STANLEY MALONE
Judge, Superior Court
111 North Hill Street
Los Angeles, CA 90012

LOREN MILLER
Judge, Superior Court
111 North Hill Street
Los Angeles, CA 90012

ALPHA MONTGOMERY
Judge, Superior Court
San Diego County
220 West Broadway
San Diego, CA 92101

Judiciary

RUDOLPH MOORE
Judge, Superior Court
7625 South Central Avenue
Los Angeles, CA 90001

DION MORROW
Judge, Superior Court
111 North Hill Street
Los Angeles, CA 90012

FLORENCE PICARD
Judge, Superior Court
111 North Hill Street
Los Angeles, CA 90012

DONALD F. PITTS
Judge, Superior Court
200 Compton Boulevard
Compton, CA 90220

RAY RANSOM
Judge, Superior Court
Sacramento County
920 Ninth Street
Sacramento, CA 95814

ROBERT L. ROBERSON
Judge, Superior Court
111 North Hill Street
Los Angeles, CA 90012

CHARLES R. SCARLETT
Judge, Superior Court
110 N. Grand Avenue
Los Angeles, CA 90012

PHRASEL L. SHELTON
Presiding Judge, Superior Court
San Mateo County
Hall of Justice, Suite 3400
Redwood City, CA 94063

SHERMAN SMITH, JR.
Judge, Superior Court
111 North Hill Street
Los Angeles, CA 90012

EMILY STEPHENS
Judge, Superior Court
111 North Hill Street
Los Angeles, CA 90012

WILLIAM STEPHENS
Judge, Superior Court
Marin County
Marin County Hall of Justice
San Rafael, CA 94903

WILMONT SWEENEY
Judge, Superior Court
Alameda County
400 Broadway
Oakland, CA 94607

BENJAMIN TRAVIS
Judge, Superior Court
Alameda County
1225 Fallon Street
Oakland, CA 94612

MARCUS O. TUCKER
Judge, Superior Court
111 North Hill Street
Los Angeles, CA 90012

MARVIN WEEKS
Judge, Superior Court
700 Civic Center Drive W
Santa Ana, CA 92701

Municipal Court

ERNEST L. AUBREY
Judge, Municipal Court
110 North Grand Avenue
Los Angeles, CA 90012

GLENETTE BLACKWELL
Judge, Municipal Court
110 North Grant Avenue
Los Angeles, CA 90012

CHARLES D. BOAGS
Judge, Municipal Court
Beverly Hills Judicial District
9355 Burton Way
Beverly Hills, CA 90210

IRMA BROWN
Judge, Municipal Court
200 West Compton Boulevard
Compton, CA 90220

JOHN CARTWRIGHT
Judge, Municipal Court
661 Washington Street
Oakland, CA 94607

HERBERT CURTIS, III
Judge, Municipal Court
Ventura County Judicial District
Post Office Box 6489
Ventura, CA 93006

G. WILLIAM DUNN
Judge, Municipal Court
415 West Ocean Boulevard
Long Beach, CA 90802

JUDITH FORD
Judge, Municipal Court
Oakland County
661 Washington Street
Oakland, CA 94607

HOLLY GRAHAM
Judge, Municipal Court
13260 Central Avenue
Chino, CA 91710

HUGO HILL
Judge, Municipal Court
200 West Compton Boulevard
Compton, CA 90220

CHARLES JAMES
Judge, Municipal Court
San Francisco County
Room 300, City Hall
San Francisco, CA 94102

MARTIN JENKINS
Judge, Municipal Court
Oakland County
661 Washington street
Oakland, CA 94607

MARION JOHNSON
Judge, Municipal Court
110 North Grand Avenue
Los Angeles, CA 90012

MORRIS BRUCE JONES
Judge, Municipal Court
200 West Compton Boulevard
Compton, CA 90220

XENOPHON F. LANG, JR.
Judge, Municipal Court
200 West Compton Boulevard
Compton, CA 90220

JOE O. LITTLEJOHN
Judge, Municipal Court
220 West Broadway
San Diego, CA 92101

RUDOLPH LONCKE
Judge, Municipal Court
Sacramento County
920 Ninth Street
Sacramento, CA 95814

SHERRILL DAVID LUKE
Judge, Municipal Court
Los Angeles, Judicial District
110 North Grand Avenue
Los Angeles, CA 90012

Judiciary

ALICE LYTLE
Judge, Municipal Court
Sacramento County
920 Ninth Street
Sacramento, CA 95814

VERONICA MCBETH
Judge, Municipal Court
210 West Temple Street
Los Angeles, CA 90012

PERKER MEEKS
Judge, Municipal Court
San Francisco County
Room 300, City Hall
San Francisco, CA 94102

DAVID MILTON
Judge, Municipal Court
110 North Hill Street
Los Angeles, CA 90012

ELVIRA MITCHELL
Judge, Municipal Court
200 North Garfield Avenue
Pasadena, CA 91101

CARL MORRIS
Judge, Municipal Court
661 Washington Street
Oakland, CA 94607

WARDELL MOSS
Judge, Municipal Court
One Regent Street
Inglewood, CA 90301

ALBAN NILES
Judge, Municipal Court
210 West Temple Street
Los Angeles, CA 90012

L. C. NUNLEY
Judge, Municipal Court
110 North Grand Avenue
Los Angeles, CA 90012

WILLIAM M. ORMSBY
Judge, Municipal Court
One Regent Street
Inglewood, CA 90301

RISE PICHON
Judge, Municipal Court
Santa Clara County
200 West Hedding
San Jose, CA 95110

ROOSEVELT ROBINSON
Judge, Municipal Court
One Regent Street
Inglewood, CA 90301

CAREY SCOTT
Judge, Municipal Court
Kern County
1215 Truxtum Avenue
Bakersfield, CA 93301

RENARD SHEPARD
Judge, Municipal Court
Sacramento County
920 Ninth Street
Sacramento, CA 95814

ROSEMARY SHUMSKY
Judge, Municipal Court
110 North Grand Avenue
Los Angeles, CA 90012

CHRISTOPHER SMITH
Judge, State Bar Court
333 South Beaudry Street, Ninth Floor
Los Angeles, CA 90017

SANDRA THOMPSON
Judge, Municipal Court
825 Maple Street
Torrance, CA 90503

HORACE WHEATLEY
Presiding Judge, Municipal Court
Oakland-Piedmont Judicial District
661 Washington Street
Oakland, CA 94607

REGINALD YATES
Judge, Municipal Court
350 W. Mission Boulevard
Pomona, CA 91766

COLORADO

Court of Appeals

RAYMOND DEAN JONES
Judge, Court of Appeals
State Judicial Building
Two East 14th Avenue
Denver, CO 80203

District Court

JAMES C. FLANIGAN
Senior Judge, District Court
Second Judicial District
2400 Monaco Parkway
Denver, CO 80207

JAMES M. FRANKLIN
Judge, District Court
20 East Vermijo
Colorado Springs, CO 80903

R. MICHAEL MULLINS
Judge, District Court
Judicial Building
City and County Building
1437 Bannock Street
Denver, CO 80202

LARRY J. NAVES
Judge, District Court
City County Building
1437 Bannock Street
Denver, CO 80202

Municipal Court

JERRY L. STEVENS
Judge, Municipal Court
15001 East Alameda Drive
Aurora, CO 80011

County Court

ALFRED C. HARRELL
Judge, County Court
City County Building
1437 Bannock Street
Denver, CO 80202

ROBERT PATTERSON
Judge, County Court
City and County Building
1437 Bannock Street
Denver, CO 80202

ROBERT H. RUSSELL, II
Judge, County Court
Judicial Building
15400 East Fourteenth Place
Aurora, CO 80011

Judiciary

CONNECTICUT

Supreme Court

ROBERT D. GLASS
Associate Justice
Supreme Court
231 Capitol Avenue
Hartford, CT 06106

Appeals Court

FLEMMING NORCOTT, JR.
Judge, Appellate Court
95 Washington Street
Hartford, CT 06106

Superior Court

E. CURTISSA R. COFIELD
Judge, Superior Court
231 Capital Avenue
Hartford, CT 06106

CLARENCE JONES
Judge, Superior Court
14 West River Street
Milford, CT 06460

L. SCOTT MELVILLE
Judge, Superior Court
Fairfield Judicial District
1061 Main Street
Post Offfice Box 101
Bridgeport, CT 06604

EUGENE SPEARS
Judge, Superior Court
Fairfield Judicial District
1061 Main Street
Post Offfice Box 101
Bridgeport, CT 06604

DELAWARE

Superior Court

JOSHUA MARTIN, III
Judge, Superior Court
Court House
Eleventh and King Streets
Wilmington, DE 19801

CHARLES H. TOLIVER, IV
Judge, Superior Court
Public Building
Eleventh and King Streets
Wilmington, DE 19801

Municipal Courts

ALEX J. SMALLS
Associate Judge
Municipal Court
Tenth and King Streets
Wilmington, DE 19801

LEONARD L. WILLIAMS
Associate Judge
Municipal Court
1000 King Street
Wilmington, DE 19801

DISTRICT OF COLUMBIA

Court of Appeals

JULIA COOPER MACK
Senior Judge, Court of Appeals
500 Indiana Avenue, N.W.
Washington, D. C. 20001

Judiciary

WILLIAM C. PRYOR
Senior Judge, Court of Appeals
500 Indiana Avenue, N.W.
Washington, D. C. 20001

JUDITH W. ROGERS
Senior Judge, Court of Appeals
500 Indiana Avenue, N.W.
Washington, D. C. 20001

ANNICE MCBRYDE WAGNER
Senior Judge, Court of Appeals
500 Indiana Avenue, N.W.
Washington, D. C. 20001

Superior Court

SHELLIE F. BOWERS
Associate Judge, Superior Court
500 Indiana Avenue, N.W.
Washington, D.C. 20001

ARTHUR L. BURNETT, JR.
Associate Judge, Superior Court
500 Indiana Avenue, N.W.
Washington, D.C. 20001

KAYE F. CHRISTIAN
Associate Judge, Superior Court
500 Indiana Avenue, N.W.
Washington, D.C. 20001

HAROLD L. CUSHENBERRY
Associate Judge, Superior Court
500 Indiana Avenue, N.W.
Washington, D.C. 20001

HERBERT B. DIXON, JR.
Associate Judge, Superior Court
500 Indiana Avenue, N.W.
Washington, D.C. 20001

FREDERICK D. DORSEY
Associate Judge, Superior Court
500 Indiana Avenue, N.W.
Washington, D.C. 20001

WILLIAM C. GARDNER
Associate Judge, Superior Court
500 Indiana Avenue, N.W.
Washington, D.C. 20001

EUGENE N. HAMILTON
Associate Judge, Superior Court
500 Indiana Avenue, N.W.
Washington, D.C. 20001

MARGARET A. HAYWOOD
Associate Judge, Superior Court
500 Indiana Avenue, N.W.
Washington, D.C. 20001

NAN R. HUHN
Associate Judge, Superior Court
500 Indiana Avenue, N.W.
Washington, D.C. 20001

HENRY H. KENNEDY, JR.
Associate Judge, Superior Court
500 Indiana Avenue, N.W.
Washington, D.C. 20001

CHERYL LONG
Associate Judge, Superior Court
500 Indiana Avenue, N.W.
Washington, D.C. 20001

GEORGE W. MITCHELL
Associate Judge, Superior Court
500 Indiana Avenue, N.W.
Washington, D.C. 20001

ZINORA M. MITCHELL-RANKIN
Associate Judge, Superior Court
500 Indiana Avenue, N.W.
Washington, D.C. 20001

Judiciary

EVELYN E. CRAWFORD QUEEN
Associate Judge, Superior Court
500 Indiana Avenue, N.W.
Washington, D.C. 20001

MICHAEL L. RANKIN
Associate Judge, Superior Court
500 Indiana Avenue, N.W.
Washington, D.C. 20001

EMMET G. SULLIVAN
Associate Judge, Superior Court
500 Indiana Avenue, N.W.
Washington, D.C. 20001

WILLIAM S. THOMPSON
Associate Judge, Superior Court
500 Indiana Avenue, N.W.
Washington, D.C. 20001

ROBERT S. TIGNOR
Associate Judge, Superior Court
500 Indiana Avenue, N.W.
Washington, D.C. 20001

PAUL R. WEBBER, III
Associate Judge, Superior Court
500 Indiana Avenue, N.W.
Washington, D.C. 20001

SUSAN R. WINFIELD
Associate Judge, Superior Court
500 Indiana Avenue, N.W.
Washington, D.C. 20001

PATRICIA A. WYNN
Associate Judge, Superior Court
500 Indiana Avenue, N.W.
Washington, D.C. 20001

The listings in this book are available as Mailing Labels. See last page for details.

FLORIDA

Supreme Court

LEANDER H. SHAW, JR.
Chief Justice
State Supreme Court
500 South Duvall Street
Tallahassee, FL 32301

Court of Appeals

WILKIE D. FERGUSON
Judge, Court of Appeals
Third Judicial District
2001 S.W. 117th Avenue
Miami, FL 33175

Circuit Court

HENRY ADAMS
Judge, Circuit Court
Fourth Judicial Circuit
330 East Bay Street
Jacksonville, FL 32202

PHILLIP S. DAVIS
Judge, Circuit Court
Dade County
1351 N.W. Twelth Street
Miami, FL 33125

STEPHAN P. MICKLE
Judge, Circuit Court
Alachua County Courthouse
201 East University Avenue
Gainesville, FL 32601

BELVIN PERRY, JR.
Judge, Circuit Court
Ninth Judicial Circuit
Osceola County Court House
Kissimmee, FL 32741

RALPH N. PERSON
Judge, Circuit Court
Dade County
1351 N.W. Twelth Street
Miami, FL 33125

EDWARD ROGERS
Judge, Circuit Court
15th Judicial District
City Courthouse, Room 309
West Palm Beach, FL 33401

EMERSON R. THOMPSON, JR.
Judge, Circuit Court
Ninth Judicial Circuit
65 East Central Avenue, Room 713
Orlando, FL 32801

FRANK WHITE
Judge, Circuit Court
Sixth Judicial Circuit
545 First Avenue, North
St. Petersburg, FL 33701

County Court

A. LEO ADDERLY
Judge, County Court
301 Dade County Courthouse
73 West Flagler Street
Miami, FL 33130

ISAAC ANDERSON
Judge, County Court
Lee County
1700 Monroe Street
Fort Myers, FL 33901

MARVA L. CRENSHAW
Judge, County Court
County Office Building
302 North Michigan Avenue
Room 9
Plant City, FL 33566

GEORGE E. EDGECOMBE
Judge, County Court
Hillsborough County
1710 Tampa Street
Tampa, FL 33610

EVELYN GOLDEN
Judge, County Court
Orange County, Ninth Circuit
150 North Orange Avenue
Orlando, FL 32801

MELVIA B. GREEN
Judge, Circuit Court
Dade County
1351 N.W. 12th Street
Room 212
Miami, FL 33125

HUBERT L. GRIMES
Judge, County Court
Volusia County
Post Office Box 2712
Daytona Beach, FL 32017

PERRY A. LITTLE
Judge, County Court
Hillsborough County
3515 River Grove Drive
Tampa, FL 33610

CALVIN R. MAPP
Judge, County Court
Dade County
1351 N.W. 12th Street
Miami, FL 33125

Judiciary

I. C. SMITH
Judge, County Court
15th Judicial Circuit
300 North Dixie Highway, Room 419
West Palm Beach, FL 33401

THOMAS E. STRINGER, SR.
Judge, County Court
Hillsborough County
801 East Twiggs Street, Room 253
Tampa, FL 33602

FREDDIE J. WORTHEN
Judge, County Court
Volusia County
125 East Orange Avenue, #101
Daytona Beach, FL 32114

ZEBEDEE WRIGHT
Judge, County Court
17th Judicial Circuit
Broward County
3020 N.W. Sixth Court
Fort Lauderdale, FL 33311

GEORGIA

Supreme Court

ROBERT BENHAM
Associate Justice
State Supreme Court
State Judicial Building
Atlanta, GA 30334

Court of Appeals

CLARENCE COOPER
Judge, Court of Appeals
403 State Judicial Building
Atlanta, GA 30334

Superior Court

WILLIAM H. ALEXANDER
Judge, Superior Court
Atlanta Judicial Circuit
405 Fulton County Courthouse
136 Pryor Street, S.W.
Atlanta, GA 30303

MICHAEL HANCOCK
Judge, Superior Court
Stone Mountain Judicial Circuit
556 North McDonough Street
Decatur, GA 30030

EUGENE H. GADSDEN
Judge, Superior Court
Eastern Judicial Circuit
203 Chatham County Courthouse
133 Montgomery Street
Savannah, GA 31499

LINDA HUNTER
Judge, Superior Court
Stone Mountain Judicial Circuit
556 N. McDonough Street
Decatur, GA 30030

ISSAC JENRETTE
Judge, Superior Court
Atlanta Judicial Circuit
Fulton County Courthouse
136 Pryor Street, S.W.
Atlanta, GA 30303

JOHN H. RUFFIN, JR.
Judge, Superior Court
Augusta Judicial Circuit
320 City-County Building
Augusta, GA 30911

Judiciary

W. LOUIS SANDS
Judge, Superior Court
Macon Judicial Circuit
310 Bibb County Courthouse
Macon, GA 31201

LEAH SEARS-COLLINS
Judge, Superior Court
Fulton County
136 Pryor Street, S.W.
Atlanta, GA 30303

State Court

JOHN D. ALLEN
Judge, State Court
Muscogee County
Post Office Box 1340
Columbus, GA 31993

THELMA WYATT CUMMINGS
Judge, State Court
Fulton County
160 Pryor Street, S.W.
Room 204
Atlanta, GA 30303

WILLIAM B. HILL, JR.
Judge, State Court
Fulton County
State Court Building
160 Pryor Street, S.W.
Atlanta, GA 30303

ALBERT L. THOMPSON
Judge, State Court
Fulton County
212 State Court Building
160 Pryor Street, S.W.
Atlanta, GA 30303

Municipal Court

JACQUELINE BENNETT
Pro-Hac Vice Judge
Municipal Court
165 Decatur Street, S.E.
Atlanta, GA 30303

CARL BROWN
Judge, Municipal Court
401 Walton Way
Augusta, GA 30901

ELAINE CARLISLE
Judge, Municipal Court
165 Decatur Street, S.E.
Atlanta, GA 30335

JAMES COUNCIL
Judge, Municipal Court
500 North Toombs Street
Valdosta, GA 31601-4675

CLINTON DEVEAUX
Chief Judge, Municipal Court
1l65 Decatur Street, S.E.
Atlanta, GA 30335

MYRA DICKSON
Pro Hac Vice Judge
Municipal Court
165 Decatur Street, S.E.
Atlanta, GA 30335

BARBARA HARRIS
Judge, Municipal Court
165 Decatur Street, S.E.
Atlanta, GA 30335

HOWARD JOHNSON
Judge, Municipal Court
165 Decatur Street, S.E.
Atlanta, GA 30335

Judiciary

WESLEY M. MATHEWS
Pro Hac Vice Judge
Municipal Court
165 Decatur Street, S.E.
Atlanta, GA 30035

JANISE MILLER
Pro Hac Vice Judge
Municipal Court
165 Decatur Street, S.E.
Atlanta, GA 30335

AKIL KEN SECRET
Pro Hac Vice Judge
Municipal Court
165 Decatur Street, S.E.
Atlanta, GA 30335

BENJAMIN SPAULDING
Pro Hac Vice Judge
Municipal Court
165 Decatur Street, S.E.
Atlanta, GA 30335

City Court

EDWARD BAETY
Judge, Circuit Court
104 Trinity Avenue, S.W.
Atlanta, GA 30335

DONALD DOTSON
Pro Hac Vice Judge, City Court
104 Trinity Avenue, S.W.
Atlanta, GA 30335

ORION DOUGLAS
Judge, City Court
Post Office Box 901
Brunswick, GA 31521

FRED EADY
Judge, City Court
2727 East Point
East Point, 30344

ANDREW HAIRSTON
Judge, City Court
104 Trinity Avenue, S.W.
Atlanta, GA 30335

JEAN HOLLIS
Pro Hac Vice Judge, City Court
104 Trinity Avenue, S.W.
Atlanta, GA 30335

GAIL T. JOYNER
Judge, City Court
104 Trinity Avenue, S.W.
Atlanta, GA 30335

BENSONETTA LANE
Pro Hac Vice Judge, City Court
104 Trinity Avenue, S.W.
Atlanta, GA 30335

GEORGE LAWSON
Pro Hac Vice Judge, City Court
104 Trinity Avenue, S.W.
Atlanta, GA 30335

ILLINOIS

Appellate Court

CALVIN CAMPBELL
Justice, Appellate Court
1st Judicial District
2800 Richard J. Daley Center
Chicago, IL 60602

Judiciary

CHARLES FREEMAN
Justice, Appellate Court
2506 Richard J. Daley Center
Chicago, IL 60602

GLENN T. JOHNSON
Justice, Appellate Court
1st Judicial District
3000 Richard J. Daley Center
Chicago, IL 60602

BLANCHE M. MANNING
Justice, Appellate Court
1st Judicial District
3000 Richard J. Daley Center
Chicago, IL 60602

SYLVESTER W. WHITE
Justice, Appellate Court
1st Judicial District
3000 Richard J. Daley Center
Chicago, IL 60602

WILLIAM S. WHITE
Justice, Appellate Court
1st Judicial District
2830 Richard J. Daley Center
Chicago, IL 60602

Circuit Court

EVERETTE A. BRADEN
Associate Judge, Circuit Court
8948 South Jeffrey Boulevard
Chicago, IL 60617

CLARENCE BRYANT
Judge, Circuit Court
Cook County
10416 South King Drive
Chicago, IL 60628

LAWRENCE CARROLL
Judge, Circuit Court
9651 South Michigan
Chicago, Il 60628

WILLIAM COUSINS, JR.
Judge, Circuit Court
Cook County
1745 East 83rd Place
Chicago, IL 60617

ELLAR DUFF-WILLIAMS
Associate Judge, Circuit Court
3rd Judicial Court
Madison County Court House
Edwardville, IL 62025

CHARLES J. DURHAM
Judge, Circuit Court
9142 South Indiana Avenue
Chicago, IL 60602

MARION W. GARNETT
Supervising Judge, Circuit Court
Cook County
2301 Richard J. Daley Center
Chicago, IL 60602

MARVIN E. GARVIN
Associate Judge, Circuit Court
20643 South Western
Fort Heights, IL 60411

CALVIN H. HALL
Associate Judge, Circuit Court
1735 East 91st Street
Chicago, Il 60617

SOPHIA H. HALL
Judge, Circuit Court
Cook County
1301 East Madison Park
Chicago, IL 60615

Judiciary

ARTHUR HAMILTON
Judge, Circuit Court
Cook County
7724 South Michigan Avenue
Chicago, IL 60619

JAMES L. HARRIS
Associate Judge, Circuit Court
8640 South Rhodes
Chicago, IL 60619

EDDIE C. JOHNSON
Judge, Circuit Court
Cook County
2307 Richard J. Daley Center
Chicago, IL 60602

EVELYN F. JOHNSON
Associate Judge, Circuit Court
6133 South Evans
Chicago, IL 60637

SIDNEY A. JONES, III
Judge, Circuit Court
Cook County
1104 Richard J. Daley Center
Chicago, IL 60602

BERTINA LAMPKIN
Associate Judge, Circuit Court
First Municipal District of Cook County
321 North LaSalle Street, Room 6
Chicago, IL 60610

WENDELL P. MARBLY
Associate Judge, Circuit Court
11531 South Eggleston
Chicago, IL 60628

EARLE MCCASKILL
Associate Judge, Circuit Court
20th Judicial Circuit
10 Public Square
Belleville, IL 62220

CARL MCCORMICK
Judge, Circuit Court
First Municipal District
1303 Richard J. Daley Center
Chicago, IL 60602

HOWARD M. MILLER
Judge, Circuit Court
Cook County
11431 South Parnell Avenue
Chicago, IL 60623

ODAS NICHOLSON
Judge, Circuit Court
Cook County
4940 East End Avenue
Chicago, IL 60615

ALBERT S. PORTER
Judge, Circuit Court
Cook County
2506 Richard J. Daley Center
Chicago, IL 60602

ADOLPHUS D. RIVERS
Associate Judge, Circuit Court
6947 South Cregier Street
Chicago, IL 60649

JOHN W. ROGERS
Judge, Circuit Court
Cook County
4800 South Chicago Beach Drive
Number 1407N
Chicago, IL 60615

HOWARD T. SAVAGE
Associate Judge, Circuit Court
2731 South Michigan Avenue
Chicago, IL 60616

EARL E. STRAYHORN
Judge, Circuit Court
Cook County
2650 South California Avenue
Room 706
Chicago, IL 60608

LUCIA T. THOMAS
Judge, Circuit Court
Cook County
1407 Richard J. Daley Center
Chicago, IL 60602

MILTON S. WHARTON
Associate Judge, Circuit Court
20th Judicial Circuit
10 Public Square
Belleville, IL 62220

CLAUDE E. WHITAKER
Judge, Circuit Court
Cook County
4800 South Chicago Beach Drive,
   Room 407
Chicago, IL 60615

WILLIE WHITING
Judge, Circuit Court
Cook County
601 East 32nd Street
Chicago, IL 60616

JAMES WILLIAMS
Associate Judge, Circuit Court
First Municipal Court of Cook County
321 North LaSalle Street, Room 6
Chicago, IL 60610

WILLIAM S. WOOD
Associate Judge, Circuit Court
4800 Chicago Beach Drive
Room 1301N
Chicago, IL 60615

ROBERT R. WOOLDRIDGE
Associate Judge, Circuit Court
8059 South Wabash
Chicago, IL 60619

INDIANA

Court of Appeals

ROBERT D. RUCKER, JR.
Judge, Court of Appeals
Merchants Plaza, South Tower
115 West Washington Street
Room 1270
Indianapolis, In 46204

Superior Court

CYNTHIA J. AYERS
Judge, Superior Court
Marion County - Civil Division 4
200 East Washington Street
Indianapolis, IN 46204

WEBSTER L. BREWER
Judge, Superior Court
Marion County - Criminal
Division 2
1619 Thomas Woods Trail
Indianapolis, In 46260

Municipal Court

TAYLOR L. BAKER
Judge, Municipal Court
Marion County
Municipal Court, Room 12
TI 4402 City County Building
Indianapolis, IN 46204

Judiciary

CLARENCE D. BOLDEN
Judge, Municipal Court
Marion County, Municipal Court
3627 East Raymond Street
Indianapolis, IN 46225

CARR L. DARDEN
Judge, Municipal Court
Marion County
3627 East Raymond Street
Indianapolis, IN 46225

City Court

CHARLES GRADDIC
Judge, City Court
910 North Vermillion Street
Gary, IN 46403

KANSAS

District Court

DEXTER BURDETTE
Judge, District Court
710 North Seventh Street
Kansas City, KS 66101

CORDELL D. MEEKS, JR.
Judge, District Court
29th Judicial District - Division Six
7915 Walker
Kansas City, KS 66112

ROBERT WATSON
Judge, District Court
Sedgewick County, Division 19
525 North Main Street
Wichita, KS 67203

KENTUCKY

CIRCUIT COURT

BENJAMIN F. SCHOBE
Judge, Circuit Court
Jefferson County, Division 15
Louisville, KY 49203

District Court

GARY PAYNE
Judge, District Court
Fayette County, Division One
Lexington, KY 40507

LOUISIANA

Court of Appeals

CARL STEWART
Judge Second Circuit Court of Appeals
Post Office Box 1528
Shreveport, LA 71665-1528

District Court

MADELINE JASMINE
Judge, District Court
23rd Judicial District
St. John the Baptist Parish
Post Office Box 277
Edgard, LA 70049

BERNETTE JOSHUA JOHNSON
Judge, Civil District Court
Orleans Parish
421 Loyola Avenue, Third Floor
New Orleans, LA 70112

CALVIN JOHNSON
Judge, Criminal District Court
Orleans Parish
2700 Tulane Avenue
New Orleans, LA 70119

OKLA JONES, II
Judge, Civil District Court
Orleans Parish 421 Loyola Avenue
New Orleans, LA 70112

YADA T. MAGEE
Judge, Civil District Court
Louisiana District Court
421 Loyola Avenue
New Orleans, LA 70112

REVIUS O. ORTIQUE, JR.
Judge, Civil District Court
Orleans Parish
421 Loyola Avenue
New Orleans, LA 70112

FREDDIE PITCHER, JR.
Judge, District Court
East Baton Rouge Parish - Division 8
222 Saint Louis Street, Suite 679
Baton Rouge, LA 70801

RONALD J. SHOLES
Judge, Civil District Court
Orleans Parish
421 Loyola Avenue
New Orleans, LA 70112

JAMES STEWART
Judge, District Court
First Judicial District
Caddo Parish
501 Texas Street
Shreveport, LA 71101

FELICIA WILLIAMS
Judge, District Court
Sixth Judicial District
Madison Parish
Post Office Box 111
Tallulah, LA 71284-0111

Criminal District Court

ARTHUR L. HARRIS, SR.
Magistrate, Criminal District Court
Orleans Parish
2700 Tulane Avenue
New Orleans, LA 70119

Municipal Court

BRYCE J. MCCONDUIT
Judge, Municipal Court, Section B
727 South Broad Street
New Orleans, LA 70119

City Court

CURTIS CALLOWAY
Judge, City Court
Post Office Box 3438
Baton Rouge, LA 70821

LARRY D. JEFFERSON
Judge, City Court
Post Office Box 277
Monroe, LA 71201

RALPH TYSON
Judge, City Court of Baton Rouge
Post Office Box 3438
Baton Rouge, LA 70821

Judiciary

MARYLAND

Court of Appeals

ROBERT BELL
Associate Justice, Court of Appeals
634 Courthouse East
111 North Calvert Street
Baltimore, MD 21202

Court of Special Appeals

ARRIE W. DAVIS
Judge, Court of Special Appeals
Court House East, Room 630
111 North Calvert Street
Baltimore, MD 21202

Circuit Court

DELAWRENCE BEARD
Associate Judge, Circuit Court
Montgomery County, District 6
50 Courthouse Square
Rockville, MD 20851

ROGER BROWN
Judge, Circuit Court
Mitchell Court House, Room 130
110 North Calvert Street
Baltimore, MD 21202

ANDRE DAVIS
Judge, Circuit Court
Mitchell Court House, Room 636
110 North Calvert Street
Baltimore, MD 21202

CLIFTON GORDY
Judge, Circuit Court
111 North Calvert Street
Court House East, Room 330
Baltimore, MD 21202

MABLE HOUZE HUBBARD
Judge, Circuit Court
C. Mitchell Court House, Room 426
Baltimore, MD 21202

G. R. HOVEY JOHNSON
Judge, Circuit Court
Prince George's County Courthouse
Upper Marlboro, MD 20772

KENNETH JOHNSON
Judge, Circuit Court
111 North Calvert Street
Baltimore, MD 21202

LARNZELL D. MARTIN
Judge, Circuit Court
Prince George's County Courthouse
Upper Marlboro, MD 20772

WILLIAM D. MISSOURI
Judge, Circuit Court
Prince George's County Courthouse
Upper Marlboro, MD 20772

DAVID B. MITCHELL
Judge, Circuit Court
111 North Calvert Street
Baltimore, MD 21202

THOMAS E. NOEL
Judge, Circuit Court
Court House East
110 North Calvert Street, Room 505A
Baltimore, MD 21202

Judiciary

PAUL SMITH
Judge, Circuit Court
Mitchell Court House, Suite 251
110 North Calvert Street
Baltimore, MD 21202

JAMES H. TAYLOR
Judge, Circuit Court
Seventh Judicial Circuit
Post Office Box 240
Upper Marlboro, MD 20772

District Court

ASKEW GATEWOOD
Judge, District Court
5800 Wabash Avenue
Baltimore, MD 21215

CLAYTON GREENE, JR.
Judge, District Court
Anne Arundel Court
124 Amesbury Court
Severna Park, MD 21146

C. YVONNE HOLT-STONE
Judge, District Court
5800 Wabash Avenue
Baltimore, MD 21215

KEITH MATTHEWS
Judge, District Court
5800 Wabash Avenue
Baltimore, MD 21215

MICHAEL MCCAMPBELL
Judge, District Court
Baltimore County
111 Allegheny Avenue
Towson, MD 21204

THURMAN H. RHODES
Judge, District Court
14757 Main Street
Upper Marlboro, MD 20772

DAVID YOUNG
Judge, District Court
5800 Wabash Avenue
Baltimore, MD 21215

MASSACHUSETTS

Court of Appeals

FREDERICK L. BROWN
Associate Judge, Court of Appeals
New Court House
Boston, MA 02108

RODERICK IRELAND
Associate Justice, Court of Appeals
1500 New Court House
Boston, MA 02108

Superior Court

BARBARA A. DORTCH
Associate Justice, Superior Court
1110 North Court House
Boston, MA 02108

HARRY J. ELAM
Associate Justice, Superior Court
New Court House and Pemberton
  Square
Boston, MA 02108

Judiciary

MALCOLM GRAHAM
Associate Justice, Superior Court
State of Massachusetts
New Court House and Pemberton
  Square
Boston, MA 02108

JAMES MCDANIEL, JR.
Associate Justice, Superior Court
New Court House and Pemberton
  Square
Boston, MA 02108

JOSEPH S. MITCHELL
Associate Justice, Superior Court
New Court House and Pemberton
  Square
Boston, MA 02108

District Court

RICHARD L. BANKS
Presiding Justice, District Court
Roxbury Division
85 Warren Street
Roxbury, MA 02119

JULIAN T. HOUSTON
Justice, District Court
Suffolk County
85 Warren Street
Roxbury, MA 02119

MARIE JACKSON
Judge, District Court
Cambridge, Arlington and Belm
40 Thorndike Street
Cambridge, MA 02141

BARON H. MARTIN
Associate Justice, District Court
Wareham
Junction Route 2B and 5B
West Wareham, MA 02576

DARRELL L. OUTLAW
Judge, District Court
Dorchester and Suffolk Counties
510 Washington Street
Dorchester, MA 02124

GEORGE A. SHEEHY
Associate Justice, District Court
Springfield, Agawam and Longmead
50 State Street
Springfield, MA 01103

Municipal Court

CHARLES RAY JOHNSON
Associate Judge
Municipal Court
380 Old Courthouse
Boston, MA 02108

MICHIGAN

DENNIS W. ARCHER
Associate Justice
State Supreme Court
211 West Fort Street
Detroit, MI 48226

CONRAD MALLETT, JR.
Associate Justice
State Supreme Court
1200 Comerica Building
Detroit, MI 48226

Court of Appeals

HAROLD HOOD
Judge, Court of Appeals
900 First Federal Building
Detroit, MI 48226

MYRON H. WAHLS
Judge, Court of Appeals
First Federal Building, Room 900
Detroit, MI 48226

Circuit Court

RICHARD D. KUHN
Chief Judge, Circuit Court
Oakland County
1200 North Telegraph
Pontiac, MI 48053

CLAUDIA H. MORCOM
Judge, Circuit Court
City County Building, Room 1607
Detroit, MI 48226

JOHN MURPHY
Judge, Circuit Court
Third Judicial District
1611 City County Building
Detroit, MI 48226

LOUIS F. SIMMONS, JR.
Judge, Circuit Court
36th Judicial Court
1907 City County Building
Detroit, MI 48826

SAMUEL A. TURNER
Judge, Circuit Court
Third Judicial District
Two Woodward Avenue, Room 910
Detroit, MI 48226

VALDEMAR L. WASHINGTON
Judge, Circuit Court
County Court House
900 South Saginaw, Room 107
Flint, MI 48502

LUCILE WATTS
Judge, Circuit Court
Wayne County
1921 City County Building
Detroit, MI 48226

District Court

ALEX J. ALLEN, JR.
Chief Judge, District Court
36th Judicial District
1943 Hyde Park Drive
Detroit, MI 48207

TRUDY DUMCOMBE ARCHER
Judge, District Court
36th Judicial District
421 Madison, Room 3074
Detroit, MI 48226

WENDY M. BAXTER
Judge, District Court
Criminal Court
1441 St. Antoine Street
Detroit, MI 48226

NANCY BLOUNT
Judge, District Court
36th Judicial District
421 Madison, Room 4070
Detroit, MI 48226

GERALD BROCK
Judge, District Court
36th Judicial District
421 Madison
Detroit, MI 48226

CHRISTOPHER C. BROWN
Judge, District Court
50th Judicial District
70 North Saginaw Street
Pontiac, MI 48058

Judiciary

FREDERICK E. BYRD
Judge, District Court
36th District Court
421 Madison
Detroit, MI 48226

WENDY COOLEY
Judge, District Court
36th Judicial District
421 Madison, Suite 5067
Detroit, MI 48226

JOHN COZART
Judge, District Court
36th Judicial District
421 Madison, Suite 5670
Detroit, MI 48226

DAPHNE MEANS CURTIS
Judge, District Court
36th Judicial District
1441 St. Antoine, Courtroom G-1
Detroit, MI 48226

JOHN W. DAVIS
Judge, District Court
Judicial District 54-A
City Hall - Sixth Floor
Lansing, MI 48933

THERESA DOSS
Judge, District Court
Wayne County
36th Judicial District
421 Madison, Room 4067
Detroit, Mi 48226

NORMA Y. DOTSON
Judge, District Court
36th Judicial District
421 Madison, Room 4075
Detroit, MI 48226

PRENTIS EDWARDS
Judge, District Court
36th Judicial District
Frank Murphy Hall of Justice
1441 St. Antoine Street
Detroit, MI 48226

JIMMYLEE GRAY
Magistrate, District Court
36th Judicial District
421 Madison
Detroit, MI 48226

RUFUS GRIFFIN
Judge, District Court
36th Judicial Court
421 Madison
Detroit, MI 48226

L. KEMP HOAGLAND
Judge, District Court
30th Judicial District
28 Gerald Avenue
Highland Park, MI 48203

SYLVIA A. JAMES
Judge, District Court
22nd Judicial District
27331 South River Park Drive
Inkster, MI 48141

WILLIE LIPSCOMB
Judge, District Court
36th District Court
421 Madison, Room 3075
Detroit, MI 48226

MARION MOORE
Judge, District Court
36th Judicial District
421 Madison
Detroit, MI 48226

Judiciary

ELBERT E. NANCE, JR.
Judge, District Court
36th Judicial District
421 Madison, Room 3066
Detroit, MI 48226

BEVERLY NETTLES NICKERSON
Judge, 54A District Court
City Hall
220 West Michigan Avenue
Lansing, MI 48933

NATHANIEL PERRY
Judge, District Court
68th Judicial District
120 East Fifth Street
Flint, MI 49502

LONGWORTH QUINN, JR.
Chief Judge Pro Tem, District Court
36th Judicial District
421 Madison
Detroit, MI 48226

CYNTHIA DIANE STEPHENS
Judge, District Court
3rd Judicial District
Wayne County
1801 City County Building
Detroit, MI 48226

CHRIS E. STITH
Judge, District Court
36th Judicial District
Madison Center, Room 3067
Detroit, MI 48226

ANNA DIGGS TAYLOR
Judge, District Court
Eastern District
231 West Lafayette
Detroit, MI 48226

CLAUDE R. THOMAS
Judge, District Court
Judicial District 54-A
Lansing City Hall
Lansing, MI 48933

MINNESOTA

State Trial Court

PAMELA ALEXANDER
Judge, State Trial Court
Fourth Judicial District
Hennepin County Government Center
Minneapolis, MN 55487

HARRY SEYMOUR CRUMP
Judge, State Trial Court
Fourth Judicial District
Hennepin County Government Center
Minneapolis, MN 55487

MICHAEL J. DAVIS
Judge, State Trial Court
Fourth Judicial District
Hennepin County Government Center
Minneapolis, MN 55487

LAJUNE THOMAS LANGE
Judge, State Trial Court
Fourth Judicial District
Hennepin County Government Center
Minneapolis, MN 55487

WILLIAM S. POSTEN
Judge, State Trial Court
Fourth Judicial District
Hennepin County Government Center
Minneapolis, MN 55487

Judiciary

District Court

EDWARD WILSON
Judge, District Court
Second Judicial District
1608 Ramsey County Courthouse
St. Paul, MN 55102

MISSISSIPPI

Supreme Court

Fred L. Banks, Jr.
Justice, State Supreme Court
Post Office Box 117
Jackson, MS 39205

Circuit Court

ROBERT GIBBS
Judge, Circuit Court
Seventh Judicial Circuit
Post Office Box 327
Jackson, MS 39205

JAMES GRAVES
Judge, Circuit Court
Seventh Judicial Circuit
Post Office Box 327
Jackson, MS 39205

ISADORE W. PATRICK
Judge, Circuit Court
Ninth Judicial Circuit
Post Office Box 351
Vicksburg, MS 39180

The listings in this directory are available as Mailing Labels. See last page for details.

Municipal Court

BARRY W. FORD
Judge, Municipal Court
Pontotoc County
Post Office Box 1661
Tupelo, MS 38802

WILLIE GRIFFIN
Judge, Municipal Court
Post Office Box 189
Greenville, MS 38702

VERNITA JOHNSON
Judge, Municipal Court
Goyer Shopping Center
Greenville, MS 38701

ORAN PAIGE
Judge, Municipal Court
Post Office Box 17
Jackson, MS 39205

VICKI ROACH-BARNES
Judge, Municipal Court
Post Office Box 1495
Vicksburg, MS 39180

LILLIE BLACKMAN SANDERS
Judge, Municipal Court
Fayette County
Post Office Box 555
Natchez, MS 39120

GWENDOLYN J. THOMAS
Judge, Municipal Court
Post Office Box 932
Rosedale, MS 38769

KENNETH L. THOMAS
Judge, Municipal Court
Gunnison-Shaw
Post Office Box 66
Rosedale, MS 38769

CLELL WARD
Judge, Municipal Court
Leland County
Post Office Box 575
Greenville, MS 38701

HAROLD L. WARE, JR.
Judge, Municipal Court
Post Office Box 680
Mound Bayou, MS 38762

Justice Court

JOHNNY L. COLLINS
Judge, Justice Court
LeFlore County, District 3
Post Office Box 1468
Greenwood, MS 38930

ARCHIE COOK
Judge, Justice Court
Quitman County, District 1
Post Office Box 131
Darling, MS 38623

BERNARD CRUMP
Judge, Justice Court
Oktibbeha County, District 2
110 Grand Ridge Road
Starkville, MS 39759

EARNEST CUNNINGHAM
Judge, Justice Court
Marshall County, District 1
Post Office Box 867
Holly Spring, MS 38635

JERRY FISHER
Judge, Justice Court
Holmes County, District 2
Route 3, Box 216
Lexington, MS 39095

DEBBIE GAMBRELL
Judge, Justice Court
713 Ronie Street
Hattiesburg, MS 39401

JAMES GRIFFIN
Judge, Justice Court
Benton County, Post 1
Route 1, Box 4AA
Lamar, MS 38642

LEROY GUICE
Judge, Justice Court
Jefferson County, District 1
Route 2, Box 35
Fayette, MS 39069

JOHNNY HARTZOG
Judge, Justice Court
Jefferson Davis County
District 2
Post Office Box 198
Prentiss, MS 39474

ERMA INGE
Judge, Justice Court
Bolivar County, District 3
Post Office Box 48
Mound Bayou, MS 38762

PAUL S. JOHNSON
Judge, Justice Court
Coahoma County, District 4
Post Office Box 393
Clarksdale, MS 38614

DANIEL LUCAS
Judge, Justice Court
Claiborne County, Eastern District
Post Office Box 497
Port Gibson, MS 39150

Judiciary

SPENCER M. NASH
Judge, Justice Court
Pike County, Central District 2
Post Office Box 509
Magnolia, MS 39652

LARRY NEAL
Judge, Justice Court
Leflore County
120 McGee Street
Greenwood, MS 38930

SHIRLEY NEAL
Judge, Justice Court
Holmes County, Beat 4
Post Office Box D
Lexington, MS 39095

MARY TOLES
Judge, Justice Court
Adams County
200 Bluebird Drive
Natchez, MS 39120

ROBERT WARD
Judge, Justice Court
Wilkinson County, West District
Route 1, Box 1750
Woodville, MS 39669

LEON WILLIAMSON
Judge, Justice Court
Grenada County, District 1
866 South Street
Grenada, MS 38901

County Court

HOUSTON J. PATTON
Judge, County Court
Hinds County
Post Office Box 327
Jackson, MS 39205

KENNETH L. THOMAS
Judge, County and Youth Court
Bolivar County
Post Office Box 188
Cleveland, MS 38732

MISSOURI

Court of Appeals

FERNANDO J. GAITAN, JR.
Judge, State Court of Appeals
1330 Oak Street
Kansas City, MO 64106

Circuit Court

HENRY AUTREY
Associate Judge, Circuit Court
Civil Court Building
10 North 12th Street
St. Louis, MO 63101

EVELYN MARIE BAKER
Judge, Circuit Court
22nd Judicial Circuit
Division 3
Municipal Court Building
St. Louis, MO 63103

CLYDE S. CAHILL, JR.
Judge, Circuit Court
1114 Market Street, Room 541
St. Louis, MO 63101

JON GRAY
Judge, Circuit Court
16th Judicial Circuit
Division 18
415 East 12th Street
Kansas City, MO 64106

LEONARD HUGHES, III
Associate Judge Circuit Court
Jackson County District 8
415 East 12th Street
Kansas City, MO 64106

CHARLES A. SHAW
Judge, Circuit Court
22nd Judicial Circuit, Division 21
Municipal Court Building
St. Louis, MO 63103

DANIEL T. TILLMAN
Judge, Circuit Court
22nd Judicial Circuit
Division 17
Municipal Court Building
St. Louis, MO 63103

Circuit Court - Municipal Division

ANDREW MOSBY
Police Judge
108 West Francis Street
Howardville, MO 63839

CHRISTOPHER M. SMITH
Judge, Municipal Court
Municipal Division
Kiel Auditorium, Room 317
St. Louis, MO 63103

NEVADA

District Court

ADDELIAR D. GUY
Judge, District Court
Clark County, 8th Judicial District
5 Third Street
Las Vegas, NV 89101

LIZZIE R. HATCHER
Referee, District Court
8th Judicial District
302 E. Carson, Suite 930
Las Vegas, NV 89101

NEW JERSEY

Superior Court

IRVIN B. BOOKER
Judge, Superior Court
50 West Market Street, Room 614A
Newark, NJ 07102

DENNIS BRAITHWAITE
Judge, Superior Court
1201 Bacharach Boulevard
Atlantic City, NJ 08401

JAMES H. COLEMAN, JR.
Judge, Superior Court
Appellate Division
155 Morris Avenue
Springfield, NJ 07081

THEODORE Z. DAVIS
Judge, Superior Court
Hall of Justice
Nickel Boulevard
Camden, NJ 08103

RUDOLPH HAWKINS
Judge, Superior Court
2 Broad Street
Elizabeth, NJ 07207

RENEE JONES-WEEKS
Judge, Superior Court
Union County Courthouse
2 Broad Street, 10 Tower
Elizabeth, NJ 07207

Judiciary

DONALD KING
Judge, Superior Court
Essex County
Essex County Courthouse
Newark, NJ 07102

LAWRENCE M. LAWSON
Judge, Superior Court
Monmouth County Courthouse
Post Office Box 1266
Freehold, NJ 07728

BETTY LESTER
Judge, Superior Court
470 Dr. Martin Luther King Blvd.
Newark, NJ 07102

SHIRLEY TOLENTINO
Judge, Superior Court
41 Gifford Avenue
Jersey City, NJ 07304

WILLIAM WALLS
Judge, Superior Court
Essex County Hall of Records
Newark, NJ 07102

Municipal Court

JOSEPH M. CLARK
Judge, Municipal Court
73 South Van Brunt Street
Englewood, NJ 07631

GOLDEN E. JOHNSON-BURNS
Presiding Judge, Municipal Court
Montclair
647 Broomfield Avenue
Montclair, NJ 07042

ALISON BROWN JONES
Judge, Municipal Court
31 Greene Street, Room 301
Newark, NJ 07102

**FRANCES ANTONIN
LAWRENCE**
Judge, Municipal Court
769 Montgomery Street
Jersey City, NJ 07306

CLIFFORD J. MINOR
Presiding Judge, Municipal Court
31 Green Street
Room 301
Newark, NJ 07102

CHESTER A. MORRISON
Judge, Municipal Court
31 Green Street
Room 301
Newark, NJ 07102

CAROL P. NEWTON
Judge, Municipal Court
111 Broadway
Paterson, NJ 07505

FREDDIE POLHILL
Judge, Municipal Court
593 LIncoln Avenue
Orange, NJ 07050

JOAN ROBINSON-GROSS
Judge, Municipal Court
325 Watchung Avenue
Plainfield, NJ 07060

PAULETTE SAPP
Judge, Municipal Court
225 North Clinton Avenue
Trenton, NJ 08609

J. CLIFTON WILKERSON
Acting Judge, Municipal Court
31 Green Street
Room 301
Newark, NJ 07102

NEW MEXICO

Metropolitan Court

KEESHA M. CALDWELL
Judge, Metropolitan Court
Dvision 6
Post Office Box 133
Albuquerque, NM 87103

TOMMY JEWELL
Judge, Metropolitan Court
401 Roma, N.W.
Albuquerque, NM 87107

NEW YORK

Court of Appeals

FRITZ W. ALEXANDER, II
Justice Court of Appeals
100 Centre Street
New York, NY 10032

Supreme Court, Appellate Division

SAMUEL L. GREEN
Associate Justice, Appellate Division
Fourth Department
50 Delaware Avenue
Buffalo, NY 14202

CHARLES B. LAWRENCE
Associate Justice, State Supreme
  Court
Appellate Division
2nd Department
45 Monroe Place
Brooklyn, NY 11201

GEORGE BUNDY SMITH
Justice, State Supreme Court
First Judicial District, Appellate
  Division
60 Centre Street
New York, NY 10007

WILLIAM C. THOMPSON
Justice, State Supreme Court
Second Judicial District, Appellate
  Division
54 Pierrepont Street
Brooklyn, NY 11201

Supreme Court

HOWARD E. BELL
Justice State Supreme Court
1st Judicial District
100 Centre Street
New York, NY 10013

KENNETH N. BROWNE
Judge, State Supreme Court
11th Judicial District
125-01 Queens Boulevard
Kew Gardens, NY 11415

GEORGE D. COVINGTON
Justice State Supreme Court
851 Grand Concourse
Room 531
Bronx, NY 10451

WILLIAM DAVIS
Acting Justice, State Supreme Court
100 Centre Street
New York, NY 10013

LELAND DEGRASSE
Justice State Supreme Court
60 Centre Street
New York, NY 10007

Judiciary

LEWIS DOUGLASS
Acting Justice State Supreme Court
360 Adams Street
Brooklyn, NY 11201

DAVID H. EDWARDS, JR.
Justice State Supreme Court
1st Judicial District
60 Centre Street
New York, NY 10007

ELBERT C. HINKSON
Justice State Supreme Court
Criminal Branch
851 Grand Concourse
Bronx, NY 10451

CAROL E. HUFF
Justice State Supreme Court
1st Judicial District
100 Centre Street
New York, NY 10013

JAMES W. HUTCHERSON
Justice State Supreme Court
2nd Judicial District
Hall of Justice
Rochester, NY 14614

RANDOLPH JACKSON
Justice State Supreme Court
Kings County
360 Adams Street
Brooklyn, NY 11201

THEODORE T. JONES, JR.
Justice, State Supreme Court
2nd Judicial District
Hall of Justice
Rochester, NY 14614

DANIEL W. JOY
Justice State Supreme Court
11th Judicial District
125-01 Queens Boulevard
Kew Gardens, NY 11415

RICHARD LOWE
Justice State Supreme Court
100 Centre Street
New York, nY 10013

HANSEL MCGEE
Acting Justice State Supreme Court
Civil Division
851 Grand Concourse
Bronx, NY 10451

EDITH MILLER
Justice State Supreme Court
1st Judicial District
165 West End Street
New York, NY 10023

SONDRA MILLER
Justice State Supreme Court
Westchester County
111 Grove Street
White Plains, NY 10601

THADDEOUS E. OWENS
Justice, State Supreme Court
2nd Judicial District
360 Adams Street
Brooklyn, NY 11201

MICHELE WESTON PATTERSON
Justice, State Supreme Court
2nd Judicial District
Hall of Justice
Rochester, NY 14614

ALFRED S. ROBBINS
Justice, State Supreme Court
10th Judicial District
28 Eldridge Avenue
Hempstead, NY 11550

W. EUGENE SHARPE
Justice, State Supreme Court
11th Judicial District
125-01 Queens Boulevard
Kew Gardens, NY 11415

JAMES H. SHAW, JR.
Justice, State Supreme Court
360 Adams Street
Brooklyn, NY 11201

KENNETH L. SHORTER
Justice, State Supreme Court
1st Judicial District
60 Centre Street
New York, NY 10007

GEORGE B. SMITH
Justice, State Supreme Court
1st Judicial District
60 Centre Street
New York, NY 10007

GEORGE E. WADE
Justice, State Supreme Court
141 Livingston Street
Brooklyn, NY 11201

IVAN WARNER
Justice, State Supreme Court
12th Judicial District
851 Grand Concourse
Bronx, NY 10451

ALBERT P. WILLIAMS
Justice, State Supreme Court
First Judicial District
100 Centre Street, Room 1727
New York, NY 10013

JOSEPH B. WILLIAMS
Justice, State Supreme Court
Second Judicial District
360 Adams Street
Brooklyn, NY 11201

CHARLES L. WILLIS
Justice, State Supreme Court
Monroe County
Hall of Justice, Room 36
Rochester, NY 14614

HAROLD L. WOOD
Justice, State Supreme Court
9th Judicial District
111 Grove Street
White Plains, NY 10601

County Court

JOSEPH K. WEST
Judge, County Court
Westchester County Courthouse
  Building
111 Grove Street
White Plains, NY 10601

Criminal Court

ALEXANDER W. HUNTER, JR.
Judge, Criminal Court
263 East 16th Stret
Bronx, NY 10451

WENDEL LEVISTER
Judge, Criminal Court
100 Centre Street
New York, NY 10013

Judiciary

District Court

MARQUETTE L. FLOYD
Judge, Suffolk District Court
Dennison Building, Vets Highway
Hauppauge, NY 11718

City Court

TERESA JOHNSON
Judge, City Court
Hall of Justice
99 Exchange Street
Rochester, NY 14614

REGINALD S. MATTHEWS
Supervising Judge, City Court
900 Sheridan Avenue
Bronx, NY 10475

LANGSTON MCKINNEY
Judge, City Court
Public Safety Building
511 South State Street
Syracuse, NY 13202

ROSE H. SCONIERS
Judge, City Court
Buffalo City Court
50 Delaware Avenue
Buffalo, NY 14202

Civil Court

ANTONIO BRANDVEEN
Judge Civil Court
215 East 16th Street
Bronx, NY 10451

GEORGE M. FLEARY
Judge Civil Court
141 Livingston Street
Brooklyn, NY 11201

YVONNE LEWIS
Judge Civil Court
141 Livingston Street
Brooklyn, NY 11201

WILFRED R. O'CONNOR
Judge Civil Court
111 Centre Street
New York, NY 10013

RICHMOND B. RUTLEDGE
Judge Civil Court
120-55 Queens Boulevard
Kew Gardens, NY 11424

JOSCELYN SMITH
Judge Civil Court
City of New York
138-46 225th Street
Laurelton, NY 11413

WILLIAM H. WALLACE, III
Judge Civil Court
City of New York
111 Centre Street
New York, NY 10013

NORTH CAROLINA

Supreme Court

HENRY E. FRYE
Associate Justice, State Supreme
 Court
Post Office Box 1841
Raleigh, NC 27602

Court of Appeals

CLIFTON E. JOHNSON
Judge, Court of Appeals
Ruffin Building
Post Office Box 888
Raleigh, NC 27602

JAMES E. WYNN
Judge, Court of Appeals
Jones County
Post Office Box 1
Pollocksville, NC 28573

Superior Court

W. STEVEN ALLEN
Judge, Superior Court
District 18
Post Office Box T-5
Greensboro, NC 27402

JAMES A. BEATY, JR.
Judge, Superior Court
District 21
325 Mayfair Drive
Winston-Salem, NC 27105

G. K. BUTTERFIELD
Judge, Superior Court
District 7
615 East Nash Street
Wilson, NC 27893

ERNEST B. FULLWOOD
Judge, Superior Court
Senior Resident
5th Judicial District
Post Office Box 1388
Wilmington, NC 28402

SHIRLEY L. FULTON
Judge, Superior Court
26th Judicial District
608 Walnut Avenue
Charlotte, NC 28208

CY GRANT
Judge, Superior Court
Senior Resident, District 6
Post Office Box 129
Ahaskie, NC 27910

GEORGE R. GREENE
Judge, Superior Court
2101 Lyndhurst Drive
Raleigh, NC 27610

ORLANDO F. HUDSON
Judge, Superior Court
14th Judicial District
Sandstone Drive
Ridge, NC 27713

W. TERRY SHERRILL
Judge, Superior Court
26th Judicial District
800 East Fourth Street
Charlotte, NC 28202

ALBERT LEON STANBACK, JR.
Judge, State Superior Court
8 Melstone Turn
Durham, NC 27707

QUINTON SUMNER
Judge, Superior Court
Seventh Judicial District
Post Office Box 1215
Rocky Mount, NC 27802

GREGORY WEEKS
Judge, Superior Court
District 12
2631 Torcross Drive
Fayetteville, NC 28304

Judiciary

District Court

LORETTA C. BIGGS
Judge, District Court
457 Windsor Park Road
Kernersville, NC 27824

STAFFORD G. BULLOCK
Judge, District Court
Wake County, District 10
Wake County Courthouse
Raleigh, NC 27611

ROLAND HAYES
Judge, District Court
21st Judicial District
Post Office Box 1411
Winston-Salem, NC 27102

CAROLYN D. JOHNSON
Judge, District Court
Office of the District Judges
Post Office Box 1772
Durham, NC 27702

FLOYD B. MCKISSICK, SR.
Judge, District Court
Post Office Box 931
Oxford, NC 27565

LAWRENCE C. MCSWAIN
Judge, District Court
Guilford County, District 18
Post Office Drawer T-5
Greensboro, NC 27402

**JACQUELINE MORRIS-
GOODSON**
Judge, District Court
Fifth Judicial District
316 Princess Street, Room 519
Wilmington, NC 28401

HERBERT RICHARDSON
Judge, District Court
16th Judicial District
Post Office Box 1084
Lumberton, NC 28359

PATRICIA TIMMONS-GOODSON
Judge, District Court
12th Judicial District
Post Office Box 363
Fayetteville, NC 28302

OHIO

Court of Appeals

PATRICIA ANN BLACKMON
Judge, Court of Appeals
8th Appellate District
1 Lakeside Avenue
Cleveland, OH 44113

SARA J. HARPER
Judge, Court of Appeals
8th Appellate District
1 Lakeside Avenue
Cleveland, OH 44113

Court of Common Pleas

CARL CHARACTER
Judge, Court of Common Pleas
Cuyahoga County
1200 Ontario Avenue
Cleveland, OH 44113

CHARLES J. DONEGHY
Judge, Court of Common Pleas
Lucas County
Lucas County Courthouse
Toledo, OH 43624

Judiciary

ARTHUR O. FISHER
Judge, Court of Common Pleas
Montgomery County
303 West Second Street
Dayton, OH 45402

LILLIAN GREENE
Judge, Court of Common Pleas
Justice Center
1200 Ontario Street
Cleveland, OH 44113

JAMES R. WILLIAMS
Judge, Court of Common Pleas
Justice Center
Summit County
209 South High Street
Akron, OH 44308

Municipal Court

RONALD B. ADRINE
Judge, Municipal Court
Justice Center
1200 Ontario Street
Cleveland, OH 44113

NADINE ALLEN
Judge, Municipal Court
Hamilton County
222 East Central Avenue
Cincinnati, OH 45202

JAMES CANNON
Judge, Municipal Court
Safety Building
335 West Third Street, Room 306
Dayton, OH 45402

C. ELLEN CONNALLY
Judge, Municipal Court
Justice Center, Room 15C
1200 Ontario Street
Cleveland, OH 44113

CHARLES W. FLEMING
Presiding Judge, Municipal Court
3058 Becket Road
Cleveland, OH 44120

DEBORAH GAINES
Judge, Domestic Relations Court
Hamilton County Courthouse
1000 Main Street, Room 404
Cincinnati, OH 45202

JANET JACKSON
Judge, Municipal Court
Franklin County Courthouse
375 South High Street
Columbus, OH 43215

MABLE M. JASPER
Judge, Municipal Court
Justice Center
1200 Ontario Street
Cleveland, OH 44113

LARRY A. JONES
Judge, Municipal Court
Justice Center
1200 Ontario Street
Cleveland, OH 44113

UNA H. R. KEENON
Judge, Municipal Court
14340 Euclid Avenue
East Cleveland, OH 44112

MELBA D. MARSH
Judge, Municipal Court
Hamilton County
222 E. Central Avenue
Cincinnati, OH 45202

ALICE O. MCCOLLUM
Judge, Municipal Court
Safety Building
335 West Third Street
Dayton, OH 45402

Judiciary

CARLA D. MOORE
Judge, Municipal Court
217 South High Street, Room 917
Akron, OH 44308

JAMES A. PEARSON
Judge, Municipal Court
Franklin County Court House
375 South High Street, Room 14-D
Columbus, OH 43215

ROBERT PENN
Judge, Municipal Court
4034 Marlaine
Toledo, OH 43666

GUY L. REESE, II
Judge, Municipal Court
Franklin County
375 South HIgh
Columbus, OH 43215

CARL B. STOKES
Presiding Judge, Municipal Court
Justice Center
1200 Ontario Street
Cleveland, OH 44113

SHIRLEY E. STRICKLAND
Judge, Municipal Court
Justice Center
1200 Ontario Street
Cleveland, OH 44113

GEORGE W. TRUMBO
Judge, Municipal Court
Justice Center, Room 15A
1200 Ontario Street
Cleveland, OH 44113

The listings in this directory are available as Mailing Labels. See last page for details.

OKLAHOMA

District Court

SUSAN W. BRAGG
Judge, District Court
Seventh Judicial District
321 West Park Road, Court House
Oklahoma City, OK 73102

JESSE HARRIS
Special Judge, District Court
Tulsa County Courthouse
500 South Denver
Tulsa, OK 74103

CHARLES L. OWENS
Judge, District Court
Oklahoma County
321 Park Avenue, Room 811
Oklahoma City, OK 73102

MAJOR R. WILSON
Special Judge, District Court
Seventh Western District
5905 North Classen
Oklahoma City, OK 73118

OREGON

Circuit Court

MERCEDES F. DEIZ
Judge, Circuit Court
1021 S.W. Fourth Avenue
Portland, OR 97204

ANCER HAGGERTY
Judge, Circuit Court
1021 S.W. Fourth Avenue
Portland, OR 97204

District Court

AARON BROWN, JR.
Judge, District Court
Multnomah County Courthouse
1021 S.W. Fourth Avenue
Portland, OR 97204

ROOSEVELT ROBINSON
Judge, District Court
1021 S.W. Fourth Avenue
Portland, OR 97204

PENNSYLVANIA

Supreme Court

ROBERT C. NIX, JR.
Chief Justice
State Supreme Court
3 Penn Center, Room 515
Philadelphia, PA 19107

Superior Court

JUSTIN M. JOHNSON
Judge, Superior Court
2702 Grant Building
330 Grant Street
Pittsburgh, PA 15219

Court of Common Pleas

JOHN L. BRAXTON
Judge, Court of Common Pleas
First Judicial District
1 East Pennsylvania Square
Room 203
Philadelphia, PA 19107

CURTIS C. CARSON, JR.
Judge, Court of Common Pleas
First Judicial District
1 East Pennsylvania Square
Room 203
Philadelphia, PA 19107

TAMA MYERS CLARK
Judge, Court of Common Pleas
First Judicial District
1 East Pennsylvania Squar
Room 1503
Philadelphia, PA 19107

EUGENE H. CLARKE, JR.
Judge, Court of Common Pleas
First Judicial District
1 East Pennsylvania Square
Room 1902
Philadelphia, PA 19107

HORACE A. DAVENPORT
Judge, Court of Common Pleas
38th Judicial District
Montgomery County Courthouse
Norristown, PA 19404

LEGROME DAVIS
Judge, Court of Common Pleas
1 East Pennsylvania Square
Room 1408
Philadelphia, PA 19107

LEVAN GORDON
Judge, Court of Common Pleas
1 East Pennsylvania Square
Room 1041
Philadelphia, PA 19107

THOMAS A. HARPER
Judge, Court of Common Pleas
Fifth Judicial District
5260 Centre Avenue, Room 506
Pittsburgh, PA 15232

Judiciary

DORIS M. HARRIS
Judge, Court of Common Pleas
First Judicial District
City Hall, Room 229
Philadelphia, PA 19107

KENNETH S. HARRIS
Judge, Court of Common Pleas
First Judicial District
1 East Pennsylvania Square
Room 1016
Philadelphia, PA 19107

RICARDO C. JACKSON
Judge, Court of Common Pleas
692 City Hall
Philadelphia, PA 19107

NORMAN A. JENKINS
Judge, Court of Common Pleas
First Judicial District
City Hall, Room 229
Philadelphia, PA 19107

LIVINGSTONE JOHNSON
Judge, Court of Common Pleas
Fifth Judicial District
705 City County Building
Pittsburg, PA 15219

DARNELL C. JONES, III
Judge, Court of Common Pleas
1 East Pennsylvania Square
Room 1401
Philadelphia, PA 19107

J. CURTIS JOYNER
Judge, Court of Common Pleas
Court House
Westchester, PA 19380

JULIAN F. KING
Judge, Court of Common Pleas
First Judicial District
50 Hamilton Circle
Philadelphia, PA 19103

KATHRYN S. LEWIS
Judge, Court of Common Pleas
1 East Pennsylvania Square
Room 1407
Philadelphia, PA 19107

WALTER R. LITTLE
Judge, Court of Common Pleas
Fifth Judicial District
528 Courthouse
Pittsburgh, PA 15219

FREDERICA A. MASSIAH-JACKSON
Judge, Court of Common Pleas
First Judicial District
1 East Pennsylvania Square
Room 1002
Philadelphia, PA 19107

THEODORA A. MCKEE
Judge, Court of Common Pleas
First Judicial District
1 East Pennsylvania Square
Room 1516
Philadelphia, PA 19107

LAWRENCE PRATTIS
Judge, Court of Common Pleas
City Hall, Room 344
Philadelphia, PA 19107

FRANK ABRAM REYNOLDS
Judge, Court of Common Pleas
1 East Pennsylvania Square
Room 1503
Philadelphia, PA 19107

PETRESE BROWN TUCKER
Judge, Court of Common Pleas
1 East Pennsylvania Square
Room 1004
Philadelphia, PA 19107

J. WARREN WATSON
Judge, Court of Common Pleas
Fifth Judicial District
1700 Frick Building
Pittsburgh, PA 15219

CALVIN T. WILSON, SR.
Judge, Court of Common Pleas
1st Judicial District
City Hall, Room 236
Philadelphia, PA 19107

CHARLES WRIGHT
Judge, Court of Common Pleas
First Judicial District
8C 5 Penn Center
Philadelphia, PA 19103

ROBERT A. WRIGHT
Judge, Court of Common Pleas
32nd Judicial District
Delaware County Courthouse
Media, PA 19063

Municipal Court

LYNWOOD F. BLOUNT
Judge, Municipal Court
1 East Pennsylvania Square
Room 106
Philadelphia, PA 19107

JAMES M. DELEON
Judge, Municipal Couurt
1 East Pennsylvania Square
Room 1417
Philadelphia, PA 19107

LYDIA Y. KIRKLAND
Judge, Municipal Court
1 East Pennsylvania Square
Room 2003
Philadelphia, PA 19107

RONALD MERRIWEATHER
Judge, Municipal Court
First Judicial District
1 East Pennsylvania Square
Room 2004
Philadelphia, PA 19107

District Justice Court

WILLIAM L. BROWN, JR.
District Justice
Chester Regional Court
418 Avenue of the States
Chester, PA 19013

KEVIN E. COOPER
District Justice
Ward 13
566 Brushton Avenue
Pittsburgh, PA 15208

PAUL JOHNSON
District Justice
Chester County, District 15-103
514 Elm Street
Coatesville, PA 19320

EDWARD A. TIBBS
District Justice
Allegheny County
7243 Somerset Street
Pittsburgh, PA 15235

JACOB H. WILLIAMS
District Justice
Wards 1, 2, 3 & 5
14 Wood Street
West Penn Building
Pittsburgh, PA 15222

Judiciary

LOUISE B. WILLIAMS
District Justice - Ward 7
331 South Franklin Street
Lancaster, PA 17602

District Court

A. KENNETH MANN
Judge, District Court
2342 Orlanda Place
Pittsburgh, PA 15235

RHODE ISLAND

Superior Court

ALTON WILEY
Judge, Superior Court
Frank Licht Judicial Complex
250 Benefit Street
Providence, RI 02903

District Court

O. ROGERIEE THOMPSON
Associate Judge, District Court
1 Dorrance Plaza
Providence, RI 02903

SOUTH CAROLINA

Supreme Court

ERNEST A. FINNEY, SR.
Associate Justice, Supreme Court
Post Office Box Drawer 1309
Sumter, SC 29151

Court of Appeals

JASPER MARSHALL CURETON
Judge, Court of Appeals
Post Office Box 11629
Columbia, SC 29211

Circuit Court

RICHARD E. FIELDS
Judge, Circuit Court
Ninth Judicial Circuit
2144 Melbourne Drive
North Charleston, SC 29402

JOSEPH A. WILSON, II
Judge, Circuit Court
Richland County
Fifth Judicial Circuit
Post Office Box 192, Room 314
Columbia, SC 29202

Municipal Court

CARTRELLE A. BROWN
Judge, Municipal Court
Marion County
Post Office Box 1190
Marion, SC 29571

MERL F. CODE
Judge, Municipal Court
Greenville County
22 West Board Street
Greenville, SC 29601

LINCOLN C. JENKINS, III
Judge, Municipal Court
Post Office Box 644
Columbia, SC 29202

ARTHUR C. MCFARLAND
Judge, Municipal Court
Charleston County
205 King Street, Suite 409
Charleston, SC 29401

VERONICA G. SMALL
Judge, Municipal Court
Charleston County
Post Office Box 1116
Charleston, SC 29402

JOSEPH THOMAS
Judge, Municipal Court
Lee County
Post Office Box 147
Lynchburgh, SC 29080

TENNESSEE

Criminal Appeals Court

A. A. BIRCH
Judge, Middle Division
Court of Criminal Appeals
Supreme Court Building
Middle Division
Nashville, TN 37243-0610

Circuit Court

D'ARMY BAILEY
Judge, Circuit Court
Division Eight
140 Adams Avenue
Memphis, TN 38105

GEORGE H. BROWN, JR.
Judge, Circuit Court
Shelby County
140 Adams Avenue
Memphis, TN 38105

JAMES E. SWEARENGEN
Judge, Circuit Court
Shelby County, Division 4
140 Adams Avenue
Memphis, TN 38105

SHEPPERSON A. WILBUN, SR.
Judge, Circuit Court
15th Judicial Circuit
1548 Gold Street
Memphis, Tn 38106

Criminal Court

ARTHUR T. BENNETT
Judge, Criminal Court
Shelby County
201 Poplar Avenue
Memphis, TN 38103

JOSEPH B. BROWN, JR.
Judge, Criminal Court
Division 9
201 Poplar Avenue
Memphis, TN 38103

ANTHONY JOHNSON
Judge, Criminal Court
General Sessions Criminal Court
201 Poplar Avenue
Memphis, TN 38103

H. T. LOCKARD
Judge, Criminal Court
Shelby County
201 Poplar Avenue
Memphis, TN 38103

The listings in this directory are available as Mailing Labels. See last page for details.

Judiciary

Civil Court

RUSSELL SUGARMON
Judge, Civil Court
General Sessions Civil Court
140 Adams Avenue
Memphis, TN 38104

General Sessions Court

C. ANTHONY JOHNSON
Judge, General Sessions
201 Poplar Avenue
Memphis, TN 38103

IRA H. MURPHY
Judge, General Sessions
Post Office Box 901079
Memphis, TN 38109

City Court

ERNESTINE HUNT
Judge, City Court
201 Poplar Avenue
Memphis, TN 38103

TEXAS

Criminal Appeals Court

MORRIS OVERSTREET
Justice, Texas Court of Criminal
  Appeals
Austin, TX 78768

Court of Appeals

KEN HOYT
Judge, Court of Appeals
Harris County
3715 Rosedale Street
Houston, TX 77004

Criminal District Court

LARRY W. BARAKA
Judge, Criminal District Court
Dallas County, District 2
600 Commerce Street
Dallas, TX 75202

BERLAIND L. BRASHEAR
Judge, Criminal District Court
Dallas County Government Center
600 Commerce, 3rd Floor
Dallas, TX 75020

L. CLIFFORD DAVIS
Judge, Criminal District
Court 2
Criminal Courts Building
300 West Belknap Street
Fort Worth, TX 76196

District Court

WELDON H. BERRY
Judge, District Court
Harris County, District 80
723 Main Street, Room 620
Houston, TX 77002

Judiciary

DONALD J. FLOYD
Judge, District Court
Jefferson County, District 172
1001 Pearl Street
Beaumont, TX 77701

MARYELLEN HICKS
Judge, District Court
Tarrant Count, District 231
400 Civil Court Building
Fort Worth, TX 76196

FAITH JOHNSON
Judge, District Court
Dallas County
363rd Judicial District
133 North Industrial Street
Dallas, TX 75207

JOHN W. PEAVY, JR.
Judge, District Court
Harris County, District 246
1115 Congress
Houston, TX 77002

FRED TINSLEY
Judge, District Court
195th Judicial District
600 Commerce Street
Government Center
Dallas, TX 75202

CARL WALKER
Judge, District Court
185th Judicial District
301 San Jacinto
Houston, TX 77002

CAROLYN WRIGHT
Judge, District Court
Old Red Courthouse
100 South Houston, Fourth Floor
Dallas, TX 75202

County Court

WILFORD FLOWERS
Judge, County Court at Law
Travis County, Court 6
Post Office Box 1748
Austin, TX 78767

CAROLYN D. HOBSON
Judge, County Court at Law
Harris County, Post 3
301 Fannin, Room 512
Houston, TX 77002

BRENDA KENNEDY
County Court at Law Number 7
Post Office Box 1748
Austin, TX 78767

Municipal Court

ROBERT ANDERSON
Judge, Municipal Court
Post Office Box 1562
Houston, TX 77251

HOWARD O. BANKS
Judge, Municipal Court
2014 Main Street
Suite 210
Dallas, TX 75201

GLADYS BRANSFORD
Associate Judge, Municipal Court
1400 Lubbock Street
Houston, TX 77002

SHIRLEY HUNTER
Associate Judge, Municipal Court
Post Office Box 1562
Houston, TX 77251

Judiciary

HARRIET MOORE MURPHY
Judge, Municipal Court
Post Office Box 2135
Austin, TX 78768

WILLIAM J. RICE, JR.
Associate Judge, Municipal Court
1400 Lubbock Street
Houston, TX 77002

FRANCELIA E. TOTTY
Judge, Municipal Court
1400 Lubbock Street
Houston, TX 77002

FAD WILSON, JR.
Judge, Municipal Court
1400 Lubbock Street
Houston, TX 77002

UTAH

Circuit Court

TYRONE MIDLEY
Judge, Circuit Court
Third Judicial Circuit
3600 South 2700 West
West Valley, UT 84119

VIRGINIA

Supreme Court

LEROY R. HASSELL
Justice, State Supreme Court
Post Office Box 1315
Richmond, VA 23210

Court of Appeals

JAMES W. BENTON, JR.
Judge, Court of Appeals
101 North Eighth Street
Richmond, VA 23219

Circuit Court

MELVIN R. HUGHES, JR.
Judge, Circuit Court
13th Judicial Circuit
800 East Marshall Street
Richmond, VA 23219

JEROME JAMES
Chief Judge, Circuit Court
Fourth Judicial Circuit
100 St. Paul Boulevard
Norfolk, VA 23510

RANDALL G. JOHNSON
Judge, Circuit Court
13th Judicial District
800 East Marshall Street
Richmond, VA 23219

THOMAS R. MONROE
Judge, Circuit Court
17th Judicial Circuit Arlington
1400 North Courthouse Road
Room 602
Arlington, TX 22201

JOHNNY E. MORRISON
Judge, Circuit Court
Drawer 1217
Portsmouth, VA 23705

MARCUS D. WILLIAMS
Judge, Circuit Court
Fairfax County
4110 Chain Bridge Road
Fairfax, VA 22030

General District Court

LUTHER C. EDMONDS
Judge, General District Court
811 East City Hall Avenue
Norfolk, VA 23510

LUTHER C. EDWARDS
Judge, Civic Court
Norfolk General District Court
811 East City Hall Avenue
Norfolk, VA 23510

GWEN JONES JACKSON
Judge, General District Court
811 East City Hall Avenue
Norfolk, VA 23510

LEONARD W. LAMBERT
Substitute Judge, General District
Court
Post Office Box 7999
Richmond, VA 23223

HAROLD M. MARSH
Substitute Judge, General District
Court
509 North Third Street
Richmond, VA 23219

DAVID F. PUGH
Judge, General District Court
2501 Huntington Avenue
Newport News, VA 23607

JOHN W. SCOTT
Judge, General District Court
15th Judicial District
Post Office Box 69
Stafford, VA 22554

WILLIAM THOMAS STONE
Substitute Judge, General District
Court
Ninth Judicial Circuit
7345 Pocahontas Trail
Williamsburg, VA 23185

IRVIN D. SUGG
Judge, General District Court
Tenth Judicial District
Post Office Box 458
Halifax, VA 24558

WILFORD TAYLOR, JR.
Judge, General District Court
Post Office Box 70
Hampton, VA 23669

District Court

GEORGE W. HARRIS, JR.
Judge, District Court
23rd Judicial District
Roanoke County Court
Main Street
Salem, VA 24153

JAMES E. HUME
Judge, District Court
Juvenile and Domestic Relations
27 Tabb Street
Petersburg, VA 23803

WASHINGTON

Superior Court

DONALD HALEY
Judge, Superior Court
King County Courthouse
Seattle, WA 98125

Judiciary

CHARLES V. JOHNSON
Chief Judge, Superior Court
King County Courthouse
415 Randolph
Seattle, WA 98122

LEROY MCCULLOUGH
Chief Judge, Superior Court
King County Courthouse
415 Randolph
Seattle, WA 98122

NORMA SMITH HUGGINS
Chief Judge, Superior Court
King County Courthouse
415 Randolph
Seattle, WA 98122

Municipal Court

GEORGE HOLLIFIELD
Judge, Municipal Court
610 Third Avenue
Seattle, WA 98104

WEST VIRGINIA

Circuit Court

HERMAN CANADY, JR.
Judge, Circuit Court
Kanawha County Courthouse
Judicial Annex, Fourth Floor
Charleston, WV 25310

BOOKER T. STEPHENS
Chief Judge, Circuit Court
8th Judicial Circuit
Post Office Box 310
Welch, WV 24801

WISCONSIN

Circuit Court

CLARENCE R. PARRISH
Judge, Circuit Court
Branch 21
901 West 9th Street
Milwaukee, WI 53233

RUSSELL STAMPER
Judge, Circuit Court
Milwaukee County
821 West State Street
Milwaukee, WI 53233

Municipal Court

STANLEY MILLER
Judge, Municipal Court
851 North Seventh Street
Milwaukee, WI 53233

VIRGIN ISLANDS

Territorial Court

ALPHONSO A. CHRISTIAN
Judge, Territorial Court
Post Office Box 70
St. Thomas, VI 00801

RAYMOND L. FINCH
Associate Judge, Territorial Court
RFD 2
Post Office Box 9000
St. Croix, VI 00850

VERNE A. HODGE
Presiding Judge, Territorial Court
Post Office Box 70
St. Thomas, VI 00801

ISHMAEL A. MEYERS
Judge, Territorial Court
Post Office Box 70
St. Thomas, VI 00801

EILEEN R. PETERSEN
Judge, Territorial Court
RFD 2, Box 9000
Kingshill
St. Croix, VI 00850

The listings in this directory are available as Mailing Labels. See last page for details.

Media

The African American media has grown considerably over the past decade. The entries listed in this section play a vital role in disseminating information to black communities throughout the United States.

Black Owned Cable Companies

BARDON CABLEVISION
26380 Michigan Avenue
Inkster, MI 48141
Don Bardon, President
(313) 561-7883

COLLIER CITY CABLEVISION
2114 N.W. Fifth Street
Pompano Beach, FL 33060
Sid Jones, President

**CONNECTION COMMUNICA-
TIONS CORPORATION**
360 Central Avenue
Newark, NJ 07103
J. Barry Washington, President
(201) 622-6150

**DELTA DEVELOPMENT &
MANAGEMENT CORPORA-
TION**
P.O. Box 588
819 Main Street
Greenville, MS 38701
Charles Bannerman, Contact
(601) 335-5291

KBLE OHIO, INC.
124 South Washington Street
Columbus, OH 43215
William T. Johnson, President
(614) 221-0692

**PYRAMID COMMUNICATIONS
INTERNATIONAL**
800 Third Street, N.E.
Washington, D.C. 20002
Derrick Gibbs Johnson, Executive
Director
(202) 675-4169

**QUEENS INNER CITY UNITY
CABLE SYSTEM**
801 Second Avenue
New York, NY 10017
Percy Sutton, Chairman
(212) 682-5955

Broadcast Groups

These entries represent the giants in the black broadcasting industry. Each of them are involved in many facets of the electronic media.

ABF INCORPORATED
Produceers of Americas Black Forum
Television Program
2016 O Street, N.W.
Washington, D.C. 20036
Byron Lewis, Producer
(202) 833-3915

Media

AMERICAN URBAN RADIO NETWORKS
463 Seventh Avenue
New York, NY 10018
Ronald Davenport, Chairman
(212) 714-1000

INNER-CITY BROADCASTING CORPORATION
801 Second Street
New York, NY 10017
Percy Sutton, Chairperson
(212) 661-3344

NBN BROADCASTING INCORPORATED
463 Seventh Avenue
Sixth Floor
New York, Ny 10018
Sydney Small, Chairman
(212) 714-1000

SHERIDAN BROADCASTING CORPORATION
411 Seventh Avenue, Suite 1500
Pittsburgh, PA 15219
Ronald Davenport, President
Jerry Lopes, News Director
(412) 281-6747

WILLIS BROADCASTING CORPORATION
I645 Church Street, Suite 400
Norfolk, VA 23510
Bishop L.E. Willis, CEO
(804) 622-4600

The listings in this directory are available as Mailing Labels. See last page for details.

Magazines

The entries in this section represent magazines serving black America. Collectively, they have millions of subscribers and play a crucial role by providing many well written articles on critical issues facing America.

AFRICAN ARTS
African Studies Center
U.C.L.A.
Los Angeles, CA 90024-1310
Donald F. Cosentino, Editor
(213) 825-1218

AFRICA REPORT MAGAZINE
833 United Nations Plaza
New York, NY 10017
Margaret A. Novicki, Editor
(212) 949-5728

AFRICAN STUDIES REVIEW
Credit Union Building
Emory University
Atlanta, GA 30322
Carol Thompson, Editor
(404) 329-6410

AMERICAN VISIONS MAGAZAINE
The Visions Foundation
National Museum of America History
Smithsonian Institute, Room A1040
Washington, D.C. 20560
Gary Puckrein, Publisher
(202) 357-1946

Media

BLACK BOOKS BULLETIN
7525 South Cottage Grove
Chicago, IL 60619
Haki R. Mahubuti, Editor
(312) 651-0700

BLACK COLLEGIAN MAGAZINE
1240 South Broad Street
New Orleans, LA 70125
Preston J. Edwards, Publisher
(504) 821-5694

BLACK ENTERPRISE MAGAZAINE
130 Fifth Avenue, 10th Floor
New York, NY 10011
Earl G. Graves, Editor & Publisher
(212) 242-8000

BLACK ISSUES IN HIGHER EDUCATION
10520 Warwick Avenue, Suite B8
Fairfax, VA 20230
Frank L. Matthews, Esquire, Publisher
(703) 385-2981

BLACK SCHOLAR MAGAZINE
Post Office Box 2869
Oakland, CA 94609
Robert Chrisman, Editor
(415) 547-6633

NAACP CRISIS MAGAZINE
4805 Mount Hope Drive
Baltimore, MD 21215
Fred Beauford, Editor
(410) 358-8900

DAWN MAGAZINE
2002 Eleventh Street, N.W.
Washington, D.C. 20001
Linda Harris, Editor
(202) 332-0080

DOLLARS & SENSE MAGAZINE
1610 East 79th Street
Chicago, IL 60649
Donald C. Walker, Editor & Publisher
(312) 375-6800

EBONY MAGAZINE
820 South Michigan Avenue
Chicago, IL 60605
John H. Johnson, Publisher
(312) 322-9200

EBONY MAN
820 South Michigan Avenue
Chicago, IL 60605
John H. Johnson, Publisher
(312) 322-9200

ESSENCE MAGAZINE
1500 Broadway, Twelfth Floor
New York, NY 10036
Susan L. Taylor, Editor-In-Chief
(212) 642-0600

THE FINAL CALL
734 West 79th Street
Chicago, IL 60620
James G. Muhammad, Editor-In-Chief
(312) 602-1230

FREEDOMWAYS QUARTERLY
799 Broadway Street
New York, NY 10003
Esther Jackson, Jean Carey Bond;
   Editors
(212) 477-3895

JET MAGAZINE
820 South Michigan Avenue
Chicago, IL 60605
Robert Johnson, Associate Publisher
(312) 322-9200

Media

JOURNAL OF AFRICAN CIVILIZATONS
347 Feldon Avenue
Highland Park, NJ 08904
Ivan Van Sertima, Editor
(201) 828-4667

THE JOURNAL OF NEGRO HISTORY
Box 20
Morehouse College
Atlanta, GA 30314
Dr. Alton Hornsby, Jr., Editor
(404) 215-2620

NATIONAL BLACK MONITOR
410 Central Park West
New York, NY 10025
Jeanne Jason, Editor-In-Chief
(212) 222-3555

NSBE JOURNAL
National Society of Black Engineers
Journal
1240 South Broad Street
New Orleans, LA 70125
Bill Bowers, Publisher
(504) 822-3533

U.S. BLACK ENGINEERS
729 East Pratt Street
Suite 504
Baltimore, MD 21201
Tyrone D. Taborn, Publisher
(410) 244-7101

WASHINGTON VIEW MAGAZINE
1101 Fourteenth Street, N.W.
Suite 1050
Washington, D.C. 20005
Malcolm E. Beech, Sr., Publisher/
Editor
(202) 371-1313

National Media Organizations

The organizations highlighted in this section play a significant role on behalf of the black media. They are the primary advocates for increasing black participation and ownership of media outlets. Without them, Black Americans would be deprived of representation in most areas of the media.

BLACK FILMMAKER FOUNDATION
375 Greenwich Street, Suite 600
New York, NY 10013
Warrington Hudlin, President
(212) 941-3944

BLACK WOMEN IN PUBLISHING
Post Office Box 6275, F.D.R. Station
New York, NY 10150
Anna Muskelly, President
(212) 572-2445

NATIONAL ALLIANCE OF THIRD WORLD JOURNALISTS
Post Office Box 43208
Washington, D.C. 20010
Leila McDowell-Head, Contact
(202) 387-1662

NATIONAL ASSOCIATION OF BLACK JOURNALISTS
Post Office Box 17212
Washington, D.C. 20041
DeWayne Wickham, President
(703) 648-1270

Media

NATIONAL ASSOCIATION OF BLACK OWNED BROADCASTERS
1730 M Street, N.W., Suite 708
Washington, D.C. 20036
James L. Winston, Executive Director
(202) 463-8970

NATIONAL ASSOCIATION OF MEDIA WOMEN
157 West 126th Street
New York, NY 10027
Alyce M. Ware, President
(212) 666-1320

NATIONAL BLACK MEDIA COALITION
38 New York Avenue, N.E.
Washington, D.C. 20002
Pluria Marshall, Chairman
(202) 387-8155

NATIONAL BLACK PROGRAM- MING CONSORTIUM, INC.
1266 East Broad Street
Columbus, OH 43205
Mable Haddock, Executive Director

Networks

BLACK ENTERTAINMENT TELEVISION (CABLE)
1232 - 31st Street, N.W.
Washington, D.C. 20007
Robert L. Johnson, President
(202) 337-5260

NATIONAL BLACK NETWORK
10 Columbus Circle, 10th Floor
New York, NY 10019
Eugene D. Jackson, Chairman
(212) 586-0610

SHERIDAN BROADCASTING NETWORK
411 Seventh Avenue, Suite 1500
Pittsburgh, PA 15219
Ronald Davenport, President
(412) 281-6747

The listings in this directory are available as Mailing Labels. See last page for details.

Newspapers

Since the founding of Freedom's Journal in 1827, the black press has performed a valuable service on behalf of African Americans. Numbering Approximately 170 newspapers, they talk to their readers ... not about them.

ALABAMA

BIRMINGHAM TIMES
115 Third Avenue, West
Birmingham, AL 32504
James E. Lewis, Publisher
(205) 251-5158

BIRMINGHAM WORLD
Post Office Box 2285
Birmingham, AL 35201
Joe N. Dickson, Publisher
(205) 251-6523

GREENE COUNTY DEMOCRAT
214 Boligee Street
Post Office Box 598
Eutaw, AL 35462
John Zippert, Publisher
(205) 372-3373

INNER CITY NEWS
Post Office Box 1545
Mobile, AL 36633
Charles W. Porter, Publisher
(205) 473-2767

MOBILE BEACON AND ALABAMA CITIZEN
Post Office Box 1407
Mobile, AL 36633
Mrs. Cleretta Blackmon, Publisher

MONTGOMERY-TUSKEGEE TIMES
3900 Birmingham Highway
Montgomery, AL 36108
Rev. Al Dixon, Editor
(205) 264-7149

SHOALS NEWS-LEADER
Post Office Box 427
Florence, AL 35630
William Liner, Publisher
(205) 766-5542

SPEAKIN' OUT NEWS
2006 Poole Avenue
Suite A
Huntsville, AL 35810
William Smothers, Publisher/Editor

THE NEW TIMES
156 South Broad Street
Mobile, AL 36602
Vivian D. Figures, Managing Editor
(205) 432-0356

THE TUSKEGEE NEWS
1 Court Square
Tuskegee, AL 36083
Paul R. Davis, Publisher

ARIZONA

ARIZONA INFORMANT
1746 East Madison Street
Suite 2
Phoenix, AZ 85034
Clovis C. Campbell, Sr., Publisher
(602) 257-9300

PHOENIX PRESS WEEKLY
623 East Euclid Avenue
Phoenix, AZ 85040
Lee Norman, Editor

Media

Newspapers (cont.)

ARKANSAS

ARKANSAS STATE PRESS
1517 South Broadway
Little Rock, AR 72202
Janis Kearney, Publisher
(501) 371-9991

CALIFORNIA

CALIFORNIA VOICE
2956 Sacramento Street, Suite C
Berkeley, CA 94703
Dr. Ruth B. Love, Publisher
(415) 644-2446

CARSON BULLETIN
Post Office Box 4248
Compton, CA 90224
Betty Wilson, Editor
(213) 774-0018

COMPTON BULLETIN
Post Office Box 4248
Compton, CA 90224
O. Ray Watkins, President
(213) 774-0018

INGLEWOOD TRIBUNE
Post Office Box 4248
Compton, CA 90224
Betty Wilson, Editor
(213) 774-0018

LYNWOOD JOURNAL
Post Office Box 4248
Compton, CA 90224
Betty Wilson, Editor
(213) 774-0018

WILMINGTON BEACON
Post Office Box 4248
Compton, CA 90224
Betty Wilson, Editor
(213) 774-0018

CALIFORNIA ADVOCATE
Post Office Box 11826
Fresno CA 93775
Lesley H. Kimber, Publisher
(209) 268-0941

NATIONAL RECORD
5617 Hollywood Boulevard
Suite 3
Hollywood, CA 90028
Jim Goodson, Publisher
(213) 461-4196

OBSERVER GROUP
NEWSPAPERS
Post Office Box 3624
Bakersfield, CA 93385
Joseph Coley, President/Publisher
(805) 324-9466

CENTRAL STAR JOURNAL
WAVE
2621 West 54th Street
Los Angeles, CA 90043
Alice Marshall, Editor
(213) 290-3000

COMPTON CARSON WAVE
2621 West 54th Street
Los Angeles, CA 90043
Alice Marshall, Editor
(213) 290-3000

Newspapers (cont.)

CULVER CITY WESTCHESTER WAVE
2621 West 54th Street
Los Angeles, CA 90043
Alice Marshall, Editor
(213) 291-0219

FIRESTONE PARK NEWS
3860 Crenshaw Boulevard
Los Angeles, CA 90008
Lela Ward, Editor
(213) 295-6323

HERALD DISPATCH
4053 Marlton Avenue
Los Angeles, CA 90008
John H. Holoman, President
(213) 291-9486

INGLEWOOD HAWTHORNE WAVE
2621 West 54th Street
Los Angeles, CA 90043
Alice Marshall, Editor
(213) 291-0219

LOS ANGELES SENTINEL
1112 East 43rd Street
Los Angeles, CA 90011
Kenneth R. Thomas, Chief Executive
(213) 232-3261

LYNWOOD WAVE
2621 West 54th Street
Los Angeles, CA 90043
Alice Marshall, Editor
(213) 290-3000

MESA TRIBUNE WAVE
2621 West 54th Street
Los Angeles, CA 90043
Alice Marshall, Editor
(213) 290-3000

SOUTHWEST TOPICS SUN WAVE
2621 West 54th Street
Los Angeles, CA 90043
Alice Marshall, Editor
(213) 290-3000

SOUTHWEST WAVE
2621 West 54th Street
Los Angeles, CA 90043
Alice Marshall, Editor
(213) 290-3000

WATTS STAR REVIEW
3860 Crenshaw Boulevard
Los Angeles, CA 90008
Lela Ward, Editor
(213) 295-6323

BERKELEY TRI CITY POST
630 20th Street
Oakland, CA 94612
Thomas Berkley, Publisher
(415) 763-1120

METROPOLITAN GAZETTE
Post Office Box 93275
Pasadena, CA 91109-3275
Mrs. Beverly Hamm, Publisher
(818) 791-7239

PASADENA GAZETTE
Post Office Box 93275
Pasadena, CA 91109-3275
Mrs. Beverly Hamm, Publisher
(818) 791-7239

OAKLAND POST
630 - 20th Street
Oakland, CA 94612
Thomas L. Berkley, Publisher
(415) 763-1120

Media

Newspapers (cont.)

RICHMOND POST
630 - 20th Street
Oakland, CA 94612

SAN FRANCISCO POST
630 - 20th Street
Oakland, CA 94612
Thomas Berkley, Publisher

BLACK VOICE NEWS
3585 Main Street, Suite 201
Riverside, CA 92501
Mrs. Cheryl Brown, Co-Publisher
(714) 682-6070

THE OBSERVER NEWSPAPER
3540 Fourth Avenue
Sacramento, CA 95817
Dr. William H. Lee, Publisher

PRECINCT REPORTER
1677 West Baseline Street
San Bernardino, CA 92411
Art Townsend, Publisher
(714) 889-0597

SAN BERNARDINO AMERICAN
1583 West Baseline Street
San Bernardino, CA 92411-0010
Mrs. Willie Mae Martin, Publisher
(714) 889-7677

SAN DIEGO VOICE & VIEWPOINT
1729 Euclid Avenue
San Diego, CA 92105
John Warren, Publisher
(619) 266-2233

BERKELEY METRO REPORTER
1366 Turk Street
San Francisco, CA 94115
Amelia Ward, Managing Editor
(415) 931-5778

CALIFORNIA VOICE
1336 Turk Street
San Francisco, CA 94115
Amelia Ward, Managing Editor
(415) 931-5778

SAN FRANCISCO NEW BAYVIEW
1624 Oakdale Avenue
San Francisco, CA 94124
Muhammad Al-Kareem, Publisher
(415) 282-7984

OAKLAND METRO REPORTER
1366 Turk Street
San Francisco, Ca 94115
Amelia Ward, Managing Editor
(415) 931-5778

RICHMOND METRO REPORTER
1366 Turk Street
San Francisco, CA 94115
Amelia Ward, Managing Editor
(415) 931-5778

SAN FRANCISCO METRO REPORTER
1366 Turk Street
San Francisco, CA 94115
Dr. Carlton B. Goodlett, Publisher
(415) 931-5778

SAN JOSE / PENINSULA REPORTER
1366 Turk Street
San Francisco, CA 94115
Amelia Ward, Managing Editor
(415) 931-5778

SAN FRANCISCO SUN REPORTER
1366 Turk Street
San Francisco, CA 94115
Dr. Calton B. Goodlett, Publisher
(415) 931-5778

Newspapers (cont.)

VALLEJO METRO REPORTER
1366 Turk Street
San Francisco, CA 94115
Dr. Carlton B. Goodlett, Publisher
(415) 931-5778

**SEASIDE POST NEWS-
SENTINEL**
1244 Broadway Avenue, Suite A
Seaside, CA 93955
Juley Harvey, Editor
(408) 899-5648

COLORADO

DENVER WEEKLY NEWS
Post Office Box 732
Denver, CO 80201
Freeman C. Harris, Publisher/Editor
(303) 839-5800

CONNECTICUT

BRIDGEPORT INQUIRER
3281 Main Street
Hartford, CT 06143
William R. Hales, Publisher
(203) 522-1462

HARTFORD INQUIRER
Post Office Box 1260
Hartfort, CT 06143
William R. Hales, Publisher
(203) 522-1462

NEW HAVEN INQUIRER
3281 Main Street
Hartford, CT 06143
William R. Hales, Publisher

HARTFORD STAR
Post Office Box 606
Hartford, CT 06101
Henry Morris, Publisher

SPRINGFIELD INQUIRER
3281 Main Street
Hartford, CT 06143
William R. Hales, Publisher
(203) 522-1462

WATERBURY INQUIRER
3281 Main Street
Hartford, CT 06143
William R. Hales, Publisher
(203) 522-1462

NORTH END AGENT'S
680 Blue Hills Avenue
Hartford, CT 06112
John Allen, Publisher
(203) 522-1888

DELAWARE

DELAWARE DEFENDER
Post Office Box 828
1702 Locust Street
Wilmington, DE 19899
C. Charles Carmichael, President
(302) 656-3252

DISTRICT OF COLUMBIA

CAPITAL SPOTLIGHT
1266 National Press Building
Washington, D.C. 20045
Robert E. Kendrick, Publisher
(202) 628-0700

Media

Newspapers (cont.)

THE NATIONAL CHRONICLE
1134 Eleventh Street, N.W.
Washington, D.C. 20001
Mrs. LaVerne Gill, Publisher
(202) 408-0808

THE WASHINGTON AFRO-AMERICAN
2001 Eleventh Street, N.W.
Washington, D.C. 20001
Mrs. Frances L. Murphy, Editor
(202) 332-0080

WASHINGTON INFORMER
3117 Martin L. King, Jr., Ave., S.E.
Washington, D.C. 20032
Dr. Calvin W. Rolark, Publisher
(202) 561-4100

THE WASHINGTON NEW OBSERVER
811 Florida Avenue, N.W.
Washington, D.C. 20001-3089
Robert B. Newton, Editor
(202) 232-3060

FLORIDA

DAYTONA TIMES
429 S. Martin Luther King Boulevard
Daytona Beach, FL 32115
Charles W. Cherry, Publisher
(904) 253-0321

WESTSIDE GAZETTE
545 N.W. Seven Terrace
Fort Lauderdale, FL 33311
Levi Henry, Jr., Publisher
(305) 523-5115

FORT PIERCE CHRONICLE
1527 Avenue D
Fort Pierce, FL 34950
C.E. Bolen, Publisher/Editor
(305) 416-7093

HAVANNA HERALD
103 West Seventh Avenue
Havanna, FL 32333
John Bert, Publisher/Editor
(904) 539-6586

FLORIDA STAR NEWS
Post Office Box 40629
Jacksonville, FL 32203
Eric O. Simpson, Publisher/Editor
(904) 354-8880

THE COMMUNITY VOICE
3046 Lafayette Street
Fort Myers, FL 33916
Charles P. Weaver, Publisher/Editor
(813) 337-4444

PALM BEACH GAZETTE
70 West 21st Street
Riviera Beach, FL 33404
Mrs. Gwen Ivory, Publisher
(407) 844-5501

THE MIAMI TIMES
900 N.W. 54th Street
Miami, FL 33127
Garth C. Reeves, Publisher
(305) 757-1147

THE FLORIDA SUN
1115 Henton Lane
Orlando, FL 32805
James W. Macon, Publisher/Editor
(407) 295-1636

Newspapers (cont.)

ORLANDO SUN REVIEW
702 Eighteenth Street
Orlando, FL 32802
James W. Macon, Publisher/Editor
(407) 423-8146

ORLANDO TIMES
4403 Vineland Road, Suite B-5
Orlando, FL 32811
Calvin Collins, Jr., Publisher
(407) 841-3052

PENSACOLA VOICE
213 East Yonge Street
Pensacola, FL 32503
Les Humphrey, Publisher/Editor
(904) 434-6963

WEEKLY CHALLENGER
2500 Ninth Street, South, Suite F
St. Petersburg, FL 33705
Cleveland Johnson, Publisher
(813) 896-2922

JACKSONVILLE ADVOCATE
6172 Pettiford Drive West
Jacksonville, FL 32209
Isiah J. Williams, III Publisher/Editor
(904) 764-4740

JACKSONVILLE FREE PRESS
Post Office Box 43580
Jacksonville, FL 32202
Ms. Rita Perry, Publisher/Editor
(904) 634-1993

THE NEW AMERICAN PRESS
402 West Cervants Street
Pensacola, FL 32501
Ms. Angelena LeRoy, Editor
(904) 432-8410

FLORIDA SENTINEL-BULLETIN
Post Office Box 3363
Tampa, FL 33601
C. Blythe Andrews, Jr., Publisher
(813) 248-1921

NEWS REPORTER
1610 North Howard Avenue
Tampa, FL 33602
James A. Jackson, Publisher/Editor
(813) 254-2608

FLORIDA PHOTO NEWS
Post Office Box 1583-46
West Palm Beach, FL 33402
Ms. Yasmin Cooper, Publisher
(407) 833-4511

THE BULLETIN
Post Office 2560
Sarasota, FL 34230-2560
Fred L. Bacon, Publisher
(813) 953-3990

CAPITAL OUTLOOK
Post Office Box 11335
Tallahassee, FL 32302
Roosevelt Wilson, Publisher
(904) 878-3895

DOLLAR STRETCHER
Post Office Box 8205
Tampa, FL 33674
Nathaniel G. Hannah, Publisher
(813) 247-4313

GEORGIA

ALBANY-SOUTHWEST GEORGIAN
Post Office Box 1943
Albany, GA 31702
A. C. Searles, Publisher
(912) 436-2156

Media

Newspapers (cont.)

ATLANTA DAILY WORLD
145 Auburn Avenue, N.E.
Atlanta, GA 30335-1201
C. A. Scott, Editor/General Manager
(404) 659-1110

THE ATLANTA INQUIRER
947 Martin L. King, Jr., Drive, N.W.
Atlanta, GA 30314-2367
John B. Smith, Publisher/CEO
(404) 523-6086

ATLANTA VOICE
633 Pryor Street, S.W.
Atlanta, GA 30312
Ms. Janice Ware, Publisher/Editor
(404) 524-6426

GEORGIA NEWS WEEKLY
Post Office Box 4596
Atlanta, GA 30302
C. T. Taylor, Publisher/Editor
(404) 344-7414

FORT VALLEY HERALD
315 North Camellia Boulevard
Post Office Box 899
Fort Valley, GA 31030
Bob James, Publisher
(912) 825-7000

PEOPLE'S CRUSADER
1959 Boulevard Drive, S.E.
Atlanta, GA 30317
Rev. Hosea Williams, Editor
(404) 373-5751

AUGUSTA FOCUS
Post Office Box 10112
Augusta, GA 30901
Charles Walker, Publisher
(404) 724-7867

METRO COURIER
Post Office Box 2385
Augusta, GA 30903
Barbara A. Gorden, Publisher
(404) 724-6556

COLUMBUS TIMES
2230 Buena Vista Road
Columbus, G 31906
Ophelia DeVore-Mitchell, Publisher
(404) 324-2404

SOUTHEASTERN NEWS
302 West 16th Avenue
Cordele, GA 31015
Lovie Jackson, Editor
(912) 273-6714

MACON COURIER
Post Office Box 4423
Macon, GA 31208
Melvin Williams, Publisher
(912) 742-4508

THE GEORGIA POST
341 & D.E. Agency
Roberta, GA 31078-0860
Walter B. Geiger, Editor
(912) 836-3195

THE HERALD
Post Office Box 486
Savannah, GA 31402
Floyd Adams, Jr., Publisher
(912) 232-4505

THE MACON METRO TIMES
1691 Forsyth Street
Macon, GA 31201
Charles Richardson,
   Acting Publisher
(912) 746-2405

Newspapers (cont.)

GEORGIA SENTINEL BULLETIN
250 Auburn Avenue, N.E.
Atlanta, GA 30303
Andre M. White, Publisher
(404) 577-4091

THE SAVANNAH TRIBUNE
Post Office Box 2066
Savannah, GA 31402
Mrs. Shirley B. James, Publisher
(912) 233-6128

ILLINOIS

ARGUS
105 South Main Street
Abingdon, IL 61410
Joe Acklin, Publisher/Editor
(309) 462-3221

CHATAM SOUTHEAST CITIZEN
412 East 87th Street
Chicago, IL 60619
William Garth, Publisher/President
(312) 487-7700

THE CHICAGO CRUSADER
6429 South Martin Luther King Drive
Chicago, IL 60637
Dorothy Leavell, Publisher/Editor
(312) 752-2500

CHICAGO DEFENDER
2400 South Michigan Avenue
Chicago, IL 60616
John H. Sengstacke, Publisher
(312) 225-2400

CHICAGO METRO NEWS
2600 S. Michigan Ave., Suite 308
Chicago, IL 60616
Nat Clay, Editor

CHICAGO SHORELAND NEWS
11740 South Elizabeth
Chicago, IL 60643
Al Johnson, Publisher/Editor
(312) 568-7091

CHICAGO SHORELAND NEWS
11740 South Elizabeth
Chicago, IL 60643
Al Johnson, Publisher/Editor
(312) 568-7091

CHICAGO SOUTH SHORE SCENE
7426 South Constance
Chicago, IL 60649
Claudette McFarland, Publisher/Editor
(312) 363-0441

CHICAGO SUN TIMES
401 North Wabash
Chicago, IL 60611
Kenneth D. Tower, Executive Editor
(312) 321-3000

CHICAGO WEEKEND
412 East 87th Street
Chicago, IL 60619
William Garth, Publisher
(312) 487-7700

HYDE PARK CITIZEN
412 East 87th Street
Chicago, IL 60619
William Garth, Publisher
(312) 487-7700

CHICAGO INDEPENDENT BULLETIN
2037 West 95th Street
Chicago, IL 60643
Hurley Green, Sr., Publisher
(312) 783-1040

Media

Newspapers (cont.)

SOUTH END CITIZEN
412 East 87th Street
Chicago, IL 60619
William Garth, Publisher
(312) 487-7700

CHICAGO TRI-CITY JOURNAL
8 South Michigan Avenue, Suite 1111
Chicago, IL 60603
Ibn Sharrieff, Publisher
(312) 346-8123

MUSLIM JOURNAL
910 West VanBuren Avenue, Suite 10
Chicago, IL 60607
Ayesha K. Mustafaa
(312) 243-7600

OBSERVER PUBLICATIONS
6040 South Harper Street
Chicago, IL 60637
Leon D. Finney, Publisher
(312) 651-7665

SOUTH SUBURBAN CITIZEN
15341 South Center Avenue
Harvey, IL 60426
William Garth, Publisher/President
(708) 596-6225

CHICAGO STANDARD NEWS
615 South Halsted
Chicago Heights, IL 60411
Lorenzo E. Martin, Publisher
(312) 755-5021

SOUTH SUBURBAN STANDARD
615 South Halsted
Chicago Heights, IL 60411
Patricia Martin, Publisher
(708) 755-5021

VOICE OF BLACK COMMUNITY
625 East Wood Street
Decatur, IL 62523
Horace Livingston, Publisher/Editor
(217) 423-2231

EAST SAINT LOUIS MONITOR
1501 State Street
East Saint Louis, IL 62205
Anne E. Jordan, Publisher
(618) 271-0468

MARKET/JOURNAL VII
101 Center Street
Grayslake, IL 60030
Don Baumgart, Publisher
(312) 223-3200

CHICAGO WESTSIDE JOURNAL
16618 South Hermitage
Markham, IL 60426
Don McIlvaine, Publisher/Editor
(312) 333-2210

THE FINAL CALL
734 West 79th Street
Chicago, IL 60620
James G. Muhammad, Editor
(312) 602-1230

INDIANA

FROST ILLUSTRATED
3121 South Calhoun Street
Fort Wayne, IN 46807-1901
Edward N. Smith, Publisher
(219) 745-0552

GARY AMERICAN
2268 Broaday
Gary, IN 46407
Fred Harris, Jr., Publisher/Editor
(219) 883-4903

Newspapers (cont.)

THE GARY CRUSADER
1549 Broadway
Gary, IN 46407
Dorothy Leavell, Publisher/Editor
(219) 885-4357

GARY INFO
1953 Broadway
Gary, IN 46407
Imogene Harris, Publisher
(219) 882-5591

INDIANA HERALD
2170 North Illinois Avenue
Indianapolis, IN 46402
Mary B. Tandy, Publisher
(317) 923-8291

INDIANAPOLIS RECORDER
2901 North Tacoma Avenue
Indianapolis, IN 46218
William G. Mays, Publisher/Editor
Charles M. Blair, Vice president
(317) 924-5143

KENTUCKY

LOUISVILLE DEFENDER
1720 Dixie Highway
Louisville, KY 40210
Clarence Leslie, Executive Vice
  President
(502) 772-2591

LOUISIANA

ALEXANDRIA NEWS WEEKLY
1746 Mason Street
Alexandria, LA 71301
Leon Coleman, Publisher
(318) 443-7664

DATA NEWS WEEKLY
Post Office Box 51933
New Orleans, LA 70153
Terry B. Jones, Publisher
(504) 522-1419

THE MONROE DISPATCH
2301 DeSiard Street
Monroe, LA 71201
Irma Detieque, Editor
(318) 387-3001

LOUISIANA WEEKLY
616 Baronne Street
New Orleans, LA 70150
C. C. Dejoie, Jr., Publisher/Editor
(504) 524-5563

SHREVEPORT SUN
Post Office Box 9328
Shreveport, LA 71139
Sonya C. Landry Publisher/Editor
(318) 631-6222

MARYLAND

**THE BALTIMORE AFRO-
  AMERICAN**
628 North Eutaw Street
Baltimore, MD 21201
John J. Oliver, Jr., Publisher
(301) 383-3219

THE BALTIMORE TIMES
12 East 25th Street
Baltimore, MD 21218
Ms. Joy Bramble, Publisher
(301) 225-3600

Media

Newspapers (cont.)

MASSACHUSETTS

BAY STATE BANNER
925 Washington Street
Dorchester, MS 02124
Brian O'Connor, Editor
(617) 288-4900

BOSTON GREATER NEWS
2377 Washington Street
Roxbury, MA 02119
Fred J. Clark, Publisher/Editor
(617) 445-7063

ROXBURY COMMUNITY NEWS
26 Highland Avenue
Roxbury, MA 02119
M.A.O. Crayton, Publisher/Editor
(617) 445-7315

MICHIGAN

MICHIGAN CHRONICLE
479 Ledyard Street
Detroit, MI 48201
Samuel Logan, General Manager
(313) 963-5522

ECORSE TELEGRAM
4122 Tenth street
Ecorse, MI 48229
J.C. Wall, Editor & Publisher
(313) 928-2955

GRAND RAPIDS TIMES
1300 Madison Street, S.E.
Grand Rapids, MI 49507
Yergan & Patricia Pulliam, Publisher
(616) 245-8737

MICHIGAN CITIZEN
12541 Second Street
Highland park, MI 48203
Charles Kelly, Publisher
(313) 869-0033

THE BLAZER NEWS
Post Office Box 806
Jackson, MI 49204
Ben Wade, Publisher
(517) 787-0450

MINNESOTA

MINNEAPOLIS SPOKESMAN
3744 Fourth Avenue South
Minneapolis, MN 55409
Launa Q. Newman, Pubisher/Editor
(612) 827-4021

INSIGHT NEWS, INC.
422 University Avenue, Suite 8
St. Paul, MN 55103
Al McFarlane, Jr., Publisher/Editor
(612) 227-8968

SAINT PAUL RECORDER
3744 Fourth Avenue, South
Minneapois, MN 55409
Sumner Jones, Editor
(612) 224-4886

MISSISSIPPI

JEFFERSON COUNTY
   CHRONICLE
512 Main Street
Fayette, MS 39069
Kennie E. Middleton, Publisher/Editor
(601) 786-6397

Newspapers (cont.)

JACKSON ADVOCATE
300 North Farish Street
Jackson, MS 39202
Charles W. Tisdale, Publisher/Editor
(601) 948-4122

MISSISSIPPI MEMO DIGEST
2511 Fifth Street
Meridian, MS 39301
Robert E. Williams, Publisher/Editor
(601) 693-2372

MISSOURI

THE CALL
1715-17 East 18th Street
Kansas City, MO 64141
Lucile Bluford, Editor
(816) 842-3804

KANSAS CITY GLOBE
615 East 29th Street
Kansas City, MO 64109
Marion Jordan, Publisher/Editor
(816) 531-5253

EVENING WHIRL
1449 McLaran Street
St. Louis, MO 63147
Benjamin Thomas, Publisher/Editor

SAINT LOUIS AMERICAN
4144 Lindell Boulevard, Suite B5
St. Louis, MO 63108
Dr. Donald M. Suggs, Publisher
(314) 533-8000

SAINT LOUIS ARGUS
4595 Martin Luther King Drive
St. Louis, MO 63113
Zelma Harris, Editorial Director
(314) 531-1323

SAINT LOUIS CRUSADER
4371 Finney Avenue
St. Louis, MO 63113
William P. Russell, President
(314) 531-5860

SAINT LOUIS SENTINEL
2900 North Market Street
St. Louis, MO 63106
Jane E. Woods, President/Publisher
(314) 531-2101

NEBRASKA

OMAHA STAR
2216 North 24th Street
Omaha, NE 68110
Marguerita L. Washington, Publisher
(402) 346-4041

NEVADA

LAS VEGAS SENTINEL-VOICE
1201 South Eastern Avenue
Las Vegas, NV 89104
Lee Brown, Publisher
(702) 383-4030

NEW JERSEY

THE CONNECTION
Post Office Box 2122
Teaneck, NJ 07666
Ralph F. Johnson, Managing Editor
(201) 692-1512

CITY NEWS
Post Office Box 22889
Newark, NJ 07101
Henry C. Johnson, Publisher
(908) 754-3400

Media

Newspapers (cont.)

THE NEW JERSEY AFRO-AMERICAN
Post Office Box 22162
Newark, NJ 07012
Frances Draper, Publisher

GREATER NEWS/NEW JERSEY
Post Office Box 173
1188 Raymond Boulevard
Newark, NJ 07012
Jean Jasons, Publisher
(201) 643-3364

NEW YORK

AFRO-AMERICAN TIMES
Post Office Box 4295
Brooklyn, NY 11247
Keri Watkins, Publisher
(718) 636-9500

BIG RED NEWS
155 Water Street, Fourth Floor
Brooklyn, NY 11201
Walter Smith, Jr., Publisher
(718) 852-6001

THE CITY SUN
GPO 560
Brooklyn, NY 11202
Andrew Cooper, Publisher
(718) 624-5959

NEW YORK DAILY CHALLENGE
1360 Fulton Street
Brooklyn, NY 11216
Thomas H. Watkins, Publisher
(718) 636-9500

NEW YORK RECORDER
86 Bainbridge
Brooklyn, NY 11233
Glenora Watkins, Editor
(718) 493-4616

THE CHALLENGER
1303 Fillmore Avenue
Buffalo, NY 14211
Barbara Banks, Publisher/Editor
(716) 897-0422

BUFFALO CRITERION
623-625 William Street
Buffalo, NY 14206
Frank E. Merriweather, Editor
(716) 882-9570

FINE PRINT NEWS
806 Fillmore Avenue
Buffalo, NY 14205
Ronald H. Fleming, Publisher/Editor
(716) 855-3810

THE HEMPSTEAD BEACON
1 Jonathan Avenue
Hicksville, NY 11801
Sheila Noeth, Editor
(516) 931-1400

THE UNIONDALE BEACON
1 Jonathan Avenue
Hicksville, NY 11801
Sheila Noeth, Editor
(516) 931-1400

AMSTERDAM NEWS
2340 Frederick Douglass Boulevard
New York, NY 10027
Wilbert A. Tatum, Publisher
(212) 932-7400

Newspapers (cont.)

THE BLACK AMERICAN
310 Lenox Avenue, Suite 304
New York City, NY 10027
Thomas Watkins, Jr., Publisher
(212) 427-3880

NEW YORK VOICE
75-43 Parsons Boulevard
Suite 311
Flushing, NY 11366
Kenneth Drew, Chairman
(718) 591-6600

NEW YORK CARIB NEWS
15 West 39th Street, 13th Floor
New York, NY 10018
Karl B. Rodney, Co-Publisher
(212) 944-1991

NATIONAL BLACK MONITOR
231 West 29th Street, Suit 1205
New York, NY 10001
Dr. Calvin W. Rolark, Chairman

THE MILITANT
410 West Street
New York, NY 10014
Greg McCartan, Editor
(212) 243-6392

HUDSON VALLEY BLACK PRESS
Post Office Box 2160
Newburgh, NY 12550
Chuck Stewart, Publisher/Editor
(914) 562-1313

COMMUNICADE
Post Office Box 60739
Rochester, NY 14606
Frank B. Willis, Managing Editor
(716) 235-6695

WESTCHESTER COUNTY PRESS
1 Prospect Avenue
Second Floor
White Plains, NY 10602
M. Paul Redd, Publisher
(914) 684-0006

NORTH CAROLINA

CHARLOTTE POST
Post Office Box 30144
Charlotte, NC 28230
Gerald O. Johnson, Publisher
(704) 376-0496

STAR OF ZION
401 East Second Street
Post Office Box 31005
Charlotte, NC 22831
Dr. Morgan W. Tann, Editor
(704) 377-4239

THE CAROLINA TIMES
923 Old Fayetteville Street
Durham, NC 27701
Mrs. V.A. Edmonds,
    Publisher/Editor
(919) 682-2913

THE FAYETTEVILLE BLACK TIMES
Post Office Box 863
Fayetteville, NC 28302
Miles B. Austin, President
(919) 484-4840

THE CHALLENGER
2215 Murchison Road., Suite 4
Fayetteville, NC 28301
Tony Grear, Editor
(919) 483-8688

Media

Newspapers (cont.)

METRO TIMES
Post Office Box 1935
Goldsboro, NC 27533
Jimmy Swinson, Publisher
(919) 734-0302

CAROLINA PEACEMAKER
Post Office Box 20853
Greensboro, NC 27420
John M. Kilimanjaro, Publisher
(919) 274-6210

THE PUBLIC POST
Post Office Box 1093
Raeford, NC
Roosevelt McPherson
(919) 875-8938

THE CAROLINIAN
Post Office Box 25308
Raleigh, NC 27611
Prentice J. Monroe, Publisher
(919) 834-5558

IREDELL COUNTY PRESS
Post Office Box 407
Statesville, NC 28766
Mason McCullough, President
(919) 873-1054

WILMINGTON JOURNAL
412 South Seventh Street
Wilmington, NC 28401
Thomas Jervey, Publisher/Editor

WINSTON-SALEM CHRONICLE
617 North Liberty Street
Winston-Salem, NC 27102
Ernest Pitt, Publisher
(919) 722-8624

OHIO

REPORTER
Post Office Box 2042
Akron, OH 44309
William R. Ellis, Publisher/Editor
(216) 253-0007

BEDFORD TIMES-REGISTER
711 Broadway
Bedford, OH 44146-0059
Lois A. Bowers, Editor
(216) 232-4055

CINCINNATI HERALD
863 Lincoln Avenue
Cincinnati, OH 45206
Marjorie Parham, Publisher
(513) 221-5440

CALL AND POST
Cleveland Edition
Post Office Box 6237
Cleveland, OH 44101
John H. Bustamente, Publisher
(216) 791-7600

CALL AND POST
Five Star Edition
Post Office Box 6237
Cleveland, OH 44104
Wilhelmina Ingram, Editor
(216) 791-7600

CALL AND POST
Columbus Edition
Post Office Box 2606
Columbus, OH 43216
Amos H. Lynch, Sr.,
  Managing Editor
(614) 224-8123

Newspapers (cont.)

TOLEDO JOURNAL
3021 Douglas Road
Toledo, OH 43606
Sandra S. Stewart, Publisher
(419) 472-4521

BUCKEYE REVIEW
620 Belmont Avenue
Youngstown, OH 44502
Crystal Ann Williams-Jackson,
Editor
(216) 743-2250

THE COMMUNICATOR NEWS
510 East Mound Street
Columbus, OH 43215
Jack Harris, Publisher
(614) 464-0020

OKLAHOMA

BLACK CHRONICLE
Post Office Box 17498
Oklahoma City, OK 73136
Russell M. Perry, Publisher
(405) 424-4695

THE OKLAHOMA EAGLE
Post Office Box 3267
Tulsa, OK 74101
James O. Goodwin,
Co-Publisher
(918) 582-7124

OKLAHOMA EBONY TRIBUNE
800 N.E. 36th Street
Oklahoma City, OK 73105
(405) 525-9885

OREGON

PORTLAND OBSERVER
Post Office Box 3137
Portland, OR 97208
Alfred L. Henderson, Publisher

THE SKANNER
Post Office Box 5455
Portland, OR 97228
Bobby Foster, Editor
(503) 287-3562

PENNSYLVANIA

PHILADELPHIA NITE OWL
2806 West Girard Avenue
Philadelphia, PA 19142
Bernice Williams, Publisher
(215) 232-2414

PHILADELPHIA NEW OB-SERVER
1930 Chestnut Street, Suite 900
Post Office Box 30092
Philadelphia, PA 19103
J. Hugo Warren, III, Publisher
(215) 665-8400

THE NEW INFORMER
805 North Homewood Avenue
Pittsburgh, PA 15208
Carl Murbury, Publisher
(412) 243-4114

PITTSBURGH RENAISSANCE NEWS
1517 Fifth Avenue
Pittsburgh, PA 15219
Connie Portiss, Publisher/Editor
(412) 391-8208

Media

Newspapers (cont.)

PHILADELPHIA TRIBUNE
520 South 16th Street
Philadelphia, PA 19146
Robert W. Bogle, President
(215) 893-4050

SCOOP U.S.A.
1220 North Broad Street
Philadelphia, PA 19121
R. Sonny Drive, Publisher/Editor
(215) 232-5974

NEW PITTSBURGH COURIER
315 East Carson Street
Pittsburgh, PA 15219
Rod Ross, Vice President, General
  Manager
(412) 481-8302

SOUTH CAROLINA

THE CHARLESTON CHRONICLE
534 King Street
Charleston, SC 29403
J. John French, Publisher/Editor
(803) 723-2785

THE COASTAL TIMES
701 East Bay Street
BTC Box 1407
Charleston, SC 29403
James E. Clyburn, Publisher

CHARLESTON BLACK TIMES
1310 Harden Street
Columbia, SC 29204
Zack Weston, Editor
(803) 799-5252

COLUMBIA BLACK NEWS
1310 Harden Street
Columbia, SC 29204
Gail Moore, Editor
(803) 799-5252

FLORENCE BLACK SUN
1310 Harden Street
Columbia, SC 29204
Gail Moore, Editor
(803) 799-5252

GREENVILLE BLACK STAR
1310 Harden Street
Columbia, SC 29204
Gail Moore, Editor
(803) 799-5252

ORANGEBURG BLACK VOICE
1310 Harden Street
Columbia, SC 29204
Gail Moore, Editor
(803) 799-5252

ROCK HILL BLACK VIEWS
1310 Harden Street
Columbia, SC 29204
Gail Moore, Editor
(803) 799-5252

SUMTER BLACK POST
1310 Harden Street
Columbia, SC 29204
Gail Moore, Editor
(803) 799-5252

THE PEE DEE TIMES
1457 West Evans Street
Florence, SC 29501
Larry D. Smith, Publisher
(803) 667-1018

Newspapers (cont.)

VIEW SOUTH NEWS
Post Office Box 1849
Orangeburg, SC 29116
Cecil J. Williams, Publisher
(803) 531-1662

TENNESSEE

TRI-STATE DEFENDER
124 East Calhoun Avenue
Memphis, TN 38103
Audrey McGhee, General Manager
(901) 523-1818

THE CHRISTIAN RECORDER
500 Eighth Avenue, South
Nashville, TN 37202
R. H. Reid, Jr., Editor
(615) 256-8458

THE METRO FORUM
Post Office Box 326
Jackson, TN 38302
Bobby Lee, Publisher
(901) 427-3477

MEMPHIS SILVER STAR NEWS
3144 Park Avenue
Memphis, TN 38111
J. Delnoah Williams, Publisher
(901) 272-3986

NASHVILLE PRIDE
1215 Ninth Avenue, North
Suite 200
Nashville, TN 37208-2552
Larry Davis, Publisher
(615) 329-0360

TEXAS

THE VILLAGER
1223 A-Rosewood Avenue
Austin, TX 78702
T. L. Wyatt, Publisher
(512) 476-0082

DALLAS EXAMINER
424 Centre Street
Dallas, TX 75208
Charles O'Neal, Co-Publisher
(214) 948-9175

DALLAS POST TRIBUNE
Post Office Box 763939
Dallas, TX 753676-3939
George Fuller, Editor
(214) 946-7679

THE DALLAS WEEKLY
3101 Martin Luther King Blvd.
Dallas, TX 75215
James A. Washington, Publisher
(214) 428-8958

LA VIDA NEWS
1621 Miller Avenue
Fort Worth, TX 76105
Audrey Pruitt, Publisher/Editor
(817) 531-3879

TEXAS TIMES
2830 Evans Avenue
Fort Worth, TX 76104
Mary Webber, Editor
(817) 926-4666

HOUSTON FORWARD TIMES
Post Office Box 2962
Houston, TX 77252
Lenora Carter, Publisher
(713) 526-4727

Media

Newspapers (cont.)

HOUSTON DEFENDER
Post Office Box 8005
Houston, TX 77288
Sonceria Messiah-Jiles, Publisher
(713) 663-7716

HOUSTON SUN
2322 Blodgett
Houston, TX 77004
Dorris Ellis, Publisher/Editor
(713) 524-4474

THE INFORMER
Post Office Box 3086
Houston, TX 77253
George McElroy, Publisher/Editor
(713) 527-8261

CAPITAL CITY ARGUS
Post Office Box 140471
Austin, TX 78714
Charles Miles, Publisher/Editor
(512) 451-6600

THE OBSERVER
Post Office Box 1131
Austin, TX 78767
Akwasi Evans, Publisher/Editor
(512) 499-8713

HOUSTON NEWSPAGES
4997 Martin Luther King, Jr., Blvd.
Houston, TX 77221
Francis Page, Sr., Publisher
(713) 645-6386

SOUTHWEST DIGEST
510 East 23rd Street
Lubbock, TX 79404
Eddie P. Richardson, Managing Editor
(806) 762-3612

SAN ANTONIO REGISTER
235 Saint Charles Street
San Antonio, TX 78202
Edwin Glosson, Publisher/Editor
(512) 222-1721

THE COLONY LEADER
4916 Main Street
Suite 150
The Colony, TX 75056
Jeff Ball, Managing Editor
(214) 370-6397

WACO MESSENGER
504 Clifton Street
Waco, TX 76703
M.P. Harvey, Pubisher/Editor
(817) 799-6911

VIRGINIA

CHARLOTTESVILLE-
ABERMARLE TRIBUNE
1055 Grady Avenue
Charlottesville, VA 22903
R. L. White, Publisher/Editor
(804) 979-0373

JOURNAL & GUIDE
3535-F Tidewater Drive
Norfolk, VA 23509
Brenda Andrews, Publisher
(804) 625-3686

THE RICHMOND AFRO-
AMERICAN
301 East Clay Street
Richmond, VA 23219
Jerry Harewood, Editor
(804) 648-8478

Newspapers (cont.)

ROANOKE TRIBUNE
2318 Melrose Avenue, N.W.
Roanoke, VA 24017
Claudia A. Whitworth, Publisher/Editor
(703) 343-0326

THE VOICE
214 East Clay Street, Suite 202
Richmond, VA 23219
Jack Green, Publisher
(804) 644-9060

VIRGIN ISLANDS

VIRGIN ISLANDS DAILY NEWS
Post Office Box 7760
St. Thomas, U.S., VI 00801
Ariel Melchoir, Jr., Publisher/Editor
(809) 774-8772

WASHINGTON

FACTS
Post Office Box 22015
Seattle, WA 98122
F. Beaver, Publisher

SEATTLE MEDIUM
2600 South Jackson
Seattle, WA 98144
Christopher H. Bennett, Publisher
(206) 323-3070

THE NORTHWEST DISPATCH
1108 South 11th Street
Tacoma, WA 98405
Virginia Taylor, Publisher/Editor
(206) 272-7587

TACOMA TRUE CITIZEN
1206 East Eleventh Street
Building 11
Tacoma, WA 98405
Connie Cameron, Editor
(206) 627-1103

THE METRO HOME MAKER
2600 South Jackson Street
Seattle, WA 98144
Christopher Bennett, Publisher
(206) 323-3070

SEATTLE SKANNER
1326 Fifth Avenue
Seattle, WA 98101
Ted Banks, Publisher
(206) 233-9888

SOUL TOWN REVIEW
2600 South Jackson
Seattle, WA 98144
Christopher Bennett, Publisher
(206) 323-3070

THURSON COUNTY DISPATCH
1108 South Eleventh Street
Post Office Box 5637
Tacoma, WA 98405
Virginia Taylor, Publishr
(206) 272-7587

WEST VIRGINIA

WVA BEACON DIGEST
5510 Shenandoah Drive
Charleston, WV 25313
Deborah S. Starks, Editor
(304) 342-4600

Media

Newspapers (cont.)

WISCONSIN

THE COMMUNICATOR NEWS
2183 North Sherman
Milwaukee, WI 53208-0489
Nathan Conyers, Publisher/Editor
(414) 444-8611

MILWAUKEE COMMUNITY JOURNAL
3612 North Martin Luther King Drive
Milwaukee, WI 53212
Patricia Thomas, Publisher
(414) 265-5300

MILWAUKEE COURIER
2431 West Hopkins Street
Milwaukee, WI 53206
Crol Geary, Publisher
(414) 449-4864

MILWAUKEE STAR
3815 North Teutonia Avenue
Milwaukee, WI 53206
Matthew Stelly, Editor
(414) 449-4860

THE MILWAUKEE TIMES
Post Office Box 16489
Milwaukee, WI 53216
Nathan Conyers, Publisher
(414) 444-8611

RACINE COURIER
3815 North Teutonia Avenue
Milwaukee, WI 53206
Matthew Stelly, Editor
(414) 449-4860

Black Formatted Radio Stations

The radio stations listed on these pages have direct contact with millions of African Americans nationwide. They collectively provide ready access to the 160 billion dollar black consumer market.

ALABAMA

WAGG-AM
Post Office Box 697
Birmingham, AL 35201
Kirkwood Balton, General Manager
(205) 254-1820

WATV-AM
3025 Ensley Avenue
Birmingham, AL 35208
Erskine R. Faush, General Manager
(205) 780-4034

WAYE-AM
1408 Third Avenue, West
Birmingham, AL 35208
Bishop L.E. Willis, President
(205) 786-9293

WENN-FM
Post Office Box 697
Birmingham, AL 35201
Kirkwood Balton, General Manager
(205) 254-1820

WJLD-AM
1449 Spaulding Ishkooda Road
Birmingham, AL 35211
Gary Richardson, General Manager

WCOX-AM
Post Office Box 820
Camden, AL 36726
Rev. Leroy T. Griffith,
   General Manager
(205) 682-9048

WYVC-FM
Post Office Box 820
Camden, AL 36726
Rev. Leroy T. Griffith,
   General Manager
(205) 682-9048

WMGJ-AM
815 Tuscaloosa Avenue
Gadsden, AL 35901
Floyd L. Donald, General Manager
(205) 546-4434

WEUP-AM
2609 Jordan Lane
Huntsville, AL 35806
Huntley Batts, President
(205) 837-9387

WBLX-AM/FM
Post Office Box 1967
Mobile, AL 36633
Harry Williams, General Manager
(205) 432-7609

WGOK-AM
800 Gum Street
Mobile, AL 36601
Irene Ware, General Manager
(205) 432-8661

Media

Radio Station (cont.)

WVAS-FM
Alabama State University
915 South Jackson Street
Montgomery, AL 36195
John F. Knight, General Manager
(205) 293-4287

WXVI-AM
Post Office Box 4280
Montgomery, AL 36195
Robert Burns, General Manager
(205) 263-3459

WZMG-AM
Post Office Box 2329
Opelika, AL 36803
Gary Fuller, President
(205) 745-4656

WQIM-FM
Post Office Box 604
Prattville, AL 36067
Walter Huntsbery, General Manager
(205) 365-0393

WTQX-AM
1 Valley Creek Circle
Selma, AL 36701
Bob Carl Bailey, President
(205) 872-1570

WTSK-AM
142 Skyland Boulevard
Tscaloosa, AL 35405
(205) 345-7200

WZZA-AM
1570 Woodmont Drive
Tuscumbia AL 35674
Bob Carl Bailey, President
(205) 381-1862

WBIL-AM/FM
Post Office Box 666
Tuskegee, AL 36083
George H. Clay, President
(205) 727-2100

WSFU-FM
108 East Conecuh Street
Union Springs, AL 36089
Tony Calhoun, President
(205) 738-3375

WAPZ-AM
Route 6, Box 43, Highway 231 North
Wetumpka, AL 36092
Johnny Roland, President
(205) 567-2251

WSLY-FM
Route 1, Box 400-B
York, AL 36925
William B. Grant, General Manager
(205) 392-5234

ARKANSAS

KSWH-FM
Henderson State University
Post Office Box 7536
Arkadelphia, AR 71923
Dr. Martha Anderson, Advisor
(501) 246-5511

KAYZ-FM
2525 North West Avenue
El Dorado, AR 71730
Bob Parks, General Manager
(501) 862-1031

KELD-AM
2525 North West Avenue
El Dorado, AR 71730
Bob Park, General Manager
(501) 863-6126

Radio Stations (cont.)

KXAR-FM
Post Office Box 320
Hope, AR 71801
Bill Hoglund, General Manager
(501) 777-3601

KFTH-FM
Route 1, Box 6C
Marion, AR 72364
Bishop Levi E. Willis, President
(501) 739-3887

KSNE-FM
Highway 95
Marshall, AR 72650
Bishop Levi E. Willis, President
(501) 739-3887

KCAT-AM
Post Office Box 8808
Pine Bluff, AR 71611
Donna Kritchfield, General Manager
(501) 534-5001

KYDE-AM
Post Office Box 5086
Pine Bluff, AR 71611
Jackie Mallard, General Manager
(501) 534-0300

KCLT-FM
307 Highway, 49 By Pass
Post Office Box 2870
West Helena, AR 72390
Milli Mills, Program Director
(501) 572-9506

KJIW-AM
Post Office Box 2501
West Helena, AR 72390
Sylvester Huling, General Manager
(501) 572-1600

KMZX-FM
314 Main Street
North Little Rock, AR 72114
Bishop L.E. Willis, President
(501) 375-1069

CALIFORNIA

KBLX AM/FM
601 Ashby Avenue
Berkeley, CA 94710
Pierre M. Sutton, President
(510) 848-7713

KACE-FM
161 North LaBrea
Inglewood, CA 90301
Willie D. Davis, President
(213) 330-3100

KDAY-AM
1700 North Alvarado Street
Los Angeles, CA 90026
Ed Kerbey, General Manager
(213) 665-1105

KGFJ-AM
1100 South LaBrea
Los Angeles, CA 90019
William Shearer, President
(213) 930-9090

KJLH-FM
3847 Crenshaw Boulevard
Los Angeles, CA 90008
Steveland Morris, President
(213) 299-5960

KJOP-AM
15279 Hanford Armona Road
Lemoore, CA 93245
John Pembroke, President
(209) 582-5567

Media

Radio Station (cont.)

KDIA-AM
100 Swan Way
Oakland, CA 94621
Ragan Henry, President
(510) 633-2548

KMAX-FM
3844 East Foothill Boulevard
Pasadena, CA 91107
N. John Douglas, President
(213) 681-2486

KHTN-FM
980 Pacific Street, Suite B
Placerville, CA 95667
Lee Schlesinger, General Manager
(916) 621-0921

KFOX-FM
123 West Torrance Boulevard
Redondo Beach, CA 90277
B. J. Howell, President
(213) 374-9796

KGGI-FM
Post Office Box 1290
San Bernardino, CA 92402
Steve Virissimo, General Manager
(714) 889-2651

KEST-AM
185 Berry Street, Suite 6500
San Francisco, CA 94107
N. John Douglas, President
(415) 978-5378

KPOO-FM
Post Office Box 425000
San Francisco, CA 94142
Terry Collins, President
(415) 346-5373

KWWN-FM
980 Pacific Street
Suite B
Placerville, CA 95667
N. John Douglas, President
(916) 621-0921

COLORADO

KDHT-FM
9351 Grant Street
Suite 550
Thornton, CO 80229
Willie D. Davis, President
(303) 451-6700

CONNECTICUT

WTIC-AM
1 Financial Plaza
Hartford, CT 06103
Gary Zenobi, Vice President &
    General Manager
(203) 522-1080

WTIC-FM
1 Financial Plaza
Hartford, CT 06103
Gary Zenobi, Vice President &
    General Manager
(203) 522-1080

WKND-AM
Post Office Box 1480
Windsor, CT 06095
Marion Anderson, General Manager
(203) 688-6221

Radio Stations (cont.)

DISTRICT OF COLUMBIA

WDCU-FM
4200 Connecticut Avenue, N.W.
Washington, D.C. 20008
Edith B. Smith, General Manager
(202) 282-7588

WJZE-FM
5321 First Place, N.E.
Washington, D.C. 20011
John Columbus, General Manager
(202) 722-1000

WHUR-FM
529 Bryant Street, N.W.
Washington, D.C. 20059
Millard J. Watkins, III, General
   Manager
(202) 806-3500

WKYS-FM
4001 Nebraska Avenue, N.W.
Washington, D.C. 20016
Skip Finley, President &
   General Manager
(202) 686-9300

WMMJ-FM
400 H Street, N.E.
Washington, D.C. 20002
Catherine Hughes, President
(202) 675-4800

WOL-AM
400 H Street, N.E.
Washington, D.C. 20002
Catherine Hughes, President
(202) 675-4800

WPFW-FM
702 H Street, N.W.
Washington, D.C. 20001-3794
Leon Collins, General Manager
(202) 783-3100

WUST-AM
815 V Street, N.W.
Washington, D.C. 20001
Louis Hankins, General Manager
(202) 462-0011

WYCB-AM
National Press Building
529 - 14th Street, N.W., Suite 228
Washington, D.C. 20045
Karen Jackson, General Manager
(202) 737-6400

FLORIDA

WSWN-AM
Post Office Box 1505
Belle Glade, FL 33430
Phil Haire, General Manager
(407) 996-2063

WYFX-AM
400 Gulfstream Boulevard
Delray Beach, FL 33444
Gary Lewis, President

WRBD-AM
4431 Rock Island Road
Fort Lauderdale, FL 33319
John Ruffin, Jr., President &
   General Manager
(305) 731-4800

WSVE-AM
4343 Springrove Street
Jacksonville, Fl 32209
Darryl Spann, President
(904) 766-1211

Media

Radio Station (cont.)

WZAZ-AM
2611 WERD Radio Drive
Jacksonville, FL 32204
Mark Picus, General Manager
(904) 389-1111

WWAB-AM
Post Office Box 65
Lakeland, FL 33802
Dee Van Pelt, General Manager
(813) 646-2151

WTOT-AM
140 West Lafayette Street
Suite A
Marianna, FL 32446
Lina Parish, General Manager
(904) 482-3046

WEDR-FM
3790 N.W. 167th Street
Miami, FL 33005
Jerry Rushin, General Manager
(305) 623-7711

WMBM-AM
814 First Street
Miami Beach, FL 33139
Edward Margolis, General Manager
(305) 672-1199

WFHT-FM
345 Office Plaza Drive
Tallahassee, FL 32301
Lee Clear, General Manager
(904) 877-1014

WWSD-AM
345 Office Plaza Drive
Tallahassee, FL 32301
Lee A. Clear, General Manager
(904) 877-1014

WRXB-AM
3000 - 34th Street, South
Suite 206-B
St. Petersburg, FL 33711
J. Eugene Danzey, President and
   General Manager
(813) 864-1515

WPUL-AM
2598 South Nova Road
South Daytona, FL 33121
Charles Cherry, Chairman
(904) 767-1131

WAMF-FM
Florida A&M University
314 Tucker Hall
Tallahassee, FL 32307
Phillip Jeter, General Manager
(904) 599-3083

WANM-AM
Post Office Box 10174
Tallahassee, FL 32302
Bob Badger, General Manager
(904) 222-1070

WTMP-AM
5207 Washington Boulevard
Tampa, FL 33619
Paul C. Major, President
(813) 626-4108

GEORGIA

WJIZ-FM
Post Office Box 5226
Albany, GA 31706
Brady Keys, Jr., President
(912) 883-5397

Radio Stations (cont.)

WJYZ-AM
506 West Oglethorpe Street
Albany, GA 31706
(912) 432-7447

WXAG-AM
2145 South Milledge Avenue
Athens, GA 30605
Larry Blount, President
(404) 549-1470

WAOK-AM
120 Ralph McGill Boulevard
Suite 1000
Atlanta, GA 30365
C. B. Rogers, General Manager
(404) 898-8900

WIGO-AM
1532 Howell Mill Road, N.W.
Atlanta, GA 30318
Al Parks, General Manager
(404) 352-3943

WVEE-FM
120 Ralph McGill Boulevard
Suite 1000
Atlanta, GA 30365
C. B. Rogers, General Manager
(404) 898-8900

WYZE-AM
1111 Boulevard, S.E.
Atlanta, GA 30312
J. Leroy Swanger, Sr., General
   Manager
(404) 622-4444

WFXA-AM/FM
Post Office Box 1584
Augusta, GA 30903
Gregory A. Davis, President
(803) 279-2330

WKZK-AM
Post Office Box 1454
Augusta, GA 30903
Walter Robinson, General Manager
(404) 738-9191

WTHB-AM
Post Office Box 1584
Augusta, GA 30903
Bill Jaeger, General Manager
(803) 279-2330

WFXE-FM
Post Office Box 1998
Columbus, GA 31994
Gregory A. Davis, President
(404) 576-3565

WOKS-AM
Post Office Box 1998
Columbus, GA 31994
Gregory A. Davis, President
(404) 576-3575

WFAV-FM
910 - 20th Avenue East
Cordele, GA 31015
Dr. John Robert E. Lee, President
(912) 273-1404

WMJM-AM
910 - 20th Avenue East
Cordele, GA 31015
Dr. John Robert E. Lee, President
(912) 273-1404

WTJH-AM
2146 Dodson Drive
East Point, GA 30344
Bishop L.E. Willis, President
(404) 344-2233

Media

Radio Station (cont.)

WXKO-AM
P.O. Box 1150
Fort Valley, GA 31030
Ken Woodfin, President
(912) 825-5547

WJGA-FM
Brownlee Road
Jackson, GA 30233
Don Earnhart, General Manager
(404) 775-3151

WDDO-AM
544 Mulberry Street, Suite 700
Macon, GA 31201
Walter Jackson, Program Director
(912) 745-3375

WFXM-FM
369 Second Street
Macaon, GA 31208
Ken Woodfin, President
(912) 742-2505

WIBB-AM
369 Second Street
Macaon, GA 31208
Ken Woodfin, President
(912) 742-2505

WSNT-AM
Post Office Box 150
Sandersville, GA 31082
James Whaley, General Manager
(912) 552-5182

WKXK-FM
Post Office Box 1150
Fort Valley, GA 31030
Ken Woodfin, President
(912) 825-5547

WEAS-FM
Post Office Box 3538
Savannah, GA 31414
Williams Moore, General Manager
(912) 234-7264

WHCJ-FM
Post Office Box 20484
Savannah, GA 31404
Carol Gordon, General Manager
(912) 356-2399

WXRS-AM
Post Office Box 1590
Swainsboro, GA 30401
Lamar Studstill, General Manager
(912) 237-1590

WSFT-AM
Post Office Box 689
Thomaston, GA 30286
Claude Thames, General Manager
(404) 647-5421

ILLINOIS

WJPC-AM
820 South Michigan Avenue
Chicago, Il 60605
John H. Johnson, President
(312) 322-9400

WKKC-FM
6800 South Wentworth Avenue
Chicago, IL 60621
Harold Tates, President
(312) 962-4612

WLNR-FM
820 South Michigan Avenue
Chicago, IL 60605
John H. Johnson, President
(312) 322-9400

Radio Stations (cont.)

WVON-AM
3350 South Kedzie Avenue
Chicago, IL 60623
Wesley W. South, Chief Officer &
  General Manager
(312) 247-6200

WBEE-AM
400 East Sibley Boulevard
Harvey, IL 60426
Charles R. Sherrell, President
(708) 210-3230

WBCP-AM
Post Office Box 1023
Champagne, IL 61820
J. W. Pirtle, President
(217) 359-1580

WESL-AM
149 South Eighth Street
East Saint Louis, IL 62201
Bishop L.E. Willis, President
(618) 271-1490

WVAZ-FM
408 South Oak Park Avenue
Oak Park, IL 60302
Barry Mayo, General Manager
(312) 524-3200

INDIANA

WVPE-FM
2424 California Road
Elkhart, IN 46514
Tim Eby, General Manager
(219) 262-5660

WLTH-AM
3669 Broadway Street
Gary, IN 46409
Lorenzo Butler, General Manager
(219) 884-9409

WWCA-AM
487 Broadway, Suite 207
Gary, IN 46402
Bishop L.E. Willis, President
(219) 886-9171

WYCA-FM
6336 Calumet Avenue
Hammond, IN 46324
Taft Harris, General Manager
(312) 734-4455

WPZZ-FM
4475 Ollisonville Road
Suite 525
Indianapolis, IN 46205
Bishop L.E. Willis, President
(317) 542-9690

WTLC-FM
Post Office Box 697
Indianapolis, IN 46206
Al Hobbs, General Manager
(317) 923-1456

WOVR-FM
133 Main Street
Versailles, IN 47042
Maria D. Hankins, General Manager
(812) 689-5595

IOWA

KBBG-FM
527 1/2 Cottage Street
Waterloo, IA 50703
Mrs. L. Porter, President
(319) 234-1441

Media

Radio Station (cont.)

KANSAS

KEYN-FM
2829 Salina Avenue
Wichita, KS 67204
Steve Evans, General Manager
(316) 838-7744

KQAM-AM
2829 Salina Avenue
Wichita, KS 67204
Steve Evans, General Manager
(316) 838-7744

KENTUCKY

WQKS-AM
905 South Main
Hopkinsville, KY 42240
Mike Sadler,General Manager
(502) 886-1480

WLOU-AM
2549 South Third Street
Louisville, KY 40208
John H. Johnson, President
(502) 636-3535

LOUISIANA

KTRY-AM/FM
Post Office Box 1075
Bastrop, LA 71220
Henry Cotton, Station Manager
(318) 381-3656

KQXL-FM
7707 Waco Avenue
Baton Rouge, LA 70806
Peter Moncrieffe, President
(504) 926-1106

WXOK-AM
7707 Waco Avenue
Baton Rouge, LA 70806
Peter Moncrieff, President
(504) 926-1106

KBCE-FM
Post Office Box 69
Boyce, LA 71409
Gus E. Lewis, President
(318) 793-2923

KGRM-FM
Post Office Drawer K
Grambling, LA 71245
Jennifer Sparks Green,
    Station Manager
(318) 274-2345

KJCB-AM
413 Jefferson Street
Lafayette, LA 70501
Horatio Handy, General Manager
(318) 233-4262

WYLD-AM/FM
2228 Gravier Street
New Orleans, LA 70119
Thomas Lewis, Partner
(504) 822-1945

WWOZ-FM
Post Office Box 51840
New Orleans, LA 70151
(504) 568-1239

Radio Stations (cont.)

KXLA-AM
Post Office Box 990
Rayville, LA 71269
Calvin Murray, General Manager
(318) 728-6990

KRUS-AM
500 North Monroe Street
Ruston, LA 71270
Dan Hollingsworth, General Manager
(318) 255-2530

WBOK-AM
1639 Gentilly Boulevard
New Orleans, LA 70119
Bishop L.E. Willis, President
(504) 943-4600

KDKS-FM
1000 Grimmet Drive
Shreveport, LA 71107
Pam Judd-Edwards, General Manager
(318) 221-5357

KOKA-AM
135 Milam Street
Shreveport, LA 71101
Diane Camp, General Manager
(318) 221-9802

MARYLAND

WANN-AM
1081 Bay Ridge Road
Annapolis, MD 21403
Morris H. Blum, General Manager
(301) 269-0700

WBGR-AM
334 North Charles Street
Baltimore, MD 21201
Sam Beasley, General Manager
(410) 727-1177

WEAA-FM
Hillen Road/Coldspring Lane
Baltimore, MD 21239
Alfie Williams, General Manager
(410) 444-3564

WEBB-AM
3000 Druid Park Drive
Baltimore, MD 21215
Dorothy Brunson, General Manager
(410) 367-9322

WWIN-AM/FM
200 South President Street
Suite 600
Baltimore, MD 21202
Alfred Liggins, President
(410) 332-8200

WXTR-FM
5207 Auth Road
Marlow Heights, MD 20746
Bob Woodward, General Manager
(301) 899-3014

WESM-FM
University of Maryland, Eastern Shore
Backbone Road
Princess Anne, MD 21853
Robert A. Franklin, General Manager
(301) 651-2816

WJDY-AM
1633 North Division Street
Salisbury, MD 21801
J.P. Conner, Jr., General Manager
(301) 742-5191

Media

Radio Station (cont.)

MASSACHUSETTS

WEIB-FM
6 Wilken Drive
Longmeadow, MA 01106
Carol Moore Cutting, President
(413) 567-7644

WILD-AM
90 Warren Street
Boston, MA 02119
Kendell Nash, President
(617) 427-2222

MICHIGAN

WLLJ-AM
206 East State Street
Cassopolis, MI 49031-0393
Larry Langford, General Manager
(616) 445-2543

WMTG-AM
15001 Michigan Avenue
Dearborn, MI 48126
Joe Bacarella, Station Manager
(313) 846-8500

WMHG-FM
Post Office Box 4217
Muskegon Heights, MI 49444
Richard Culpepper, President &
   General Manager
(616) 744-2405

WGPR-FM
3146 East Jefferson Avenue
Detroit, MI 48207
George Mathews,President
(313) 259-8862

WJZZ-FM
2994 East Grand Boulevard
Detroit, MI 48202
Mrs. Mary Bell, President
(313) 871-0591

WDZZ-FM
1820 Genesee Towers
Flint, MI 48501
Sam Williams, General Manager
(313) 767-0130

WFLT-AM
317 South Averill
Flint, MI 48506
Neal Mason, General Manager
(313) 239-5733

WCXT-FM
220 Polk Road
Hart, MI 49420
Nancy Waters, President
(616) 873-7129

WCHB-AM
32790 Henry Ruff Road
Inkster, MI 48141
Mrs. Mary Bell, President
(313) 278-1440

WKWM-AM
Post Office Box 828
Kentwood, MI 49518
Richard Culpepper, President
(616) 676-1237

WXCD-FM
850 Stevenson Highway
Suite 405
Troy, MI 48083
Ragan Henry, President
(313) 589-7900

Radio Stations (cont.)

WXLA-AM
101 Northcrest Road, Suite 4
Lansing, MI 48906
Helena DeBose, President & General
    Manager
(517) 484-9600

WLTZ-FM
Post Office Box 107
Saginaw, MI 48606
Jack Lich, General Manager
(517) 754-1071

WQHH-FM
101 Northcrest Road, Suite 4
Lansing, MI 48906
Helena DeBose, President & General
    Manager
(517) 484-9600

MISSISSIPPI

WBAD-FM
7 Oaks Road
Greenville, MS 38701
William D. Jackson, President
(601) 378-9405

WESY-AM
7 Oaks Road
Greenville, MS 38701
William D. Jackson, President
(601) 378-9405

WKXG-AM
Post Office Box 1686
Browning Road
Greenwood, MS 38930
Jim Chick, General Manager
(601) 453-2174

WJMG-FM
1204 Graveline Street
Hattiesburg, MS 39401
Vernon C. Gloyd, President
(601) 544-1941

WORV-AM
1204 Graveline Street
Hattiesburg, MS 39401
Vernon C. Floyd, President
(601) 544-1941

WJMI-FM
1850 Lynch Street
Jackson, MS 39203
Carl Haynes, General Manager
(601) 948-1515

WJSU-FM
Post Office Box 18450
Jackson, MS 39217
Anthony Dean, General Manager
(601) 968-2140

WKXI-AM
222 Beasley Road
Jackson, MS 39206
Bob O'Brien, General Manager
(601) 957-1300

WOAD-AM
Post Office Box 10387
Jackson, MS 39289
John H. Pembroke, President
(601) 948-1515

WLTD-FM
Route 1, Box 288E
Lexington, MS 39095
Phillip Scott, General Manager
(601) 834-1103

Media

Radio Station (cont.)

WHTN-AM
Post Office Drawer M
Lexington, MS 39095
Brad Cothran, General Manager
(601) 834-1254

WPRL-FM
Alcorn State University
Lorman, MS 39096
David Crosby, General Manager
(601) 877-6613

WALT-AM
Highway 45 North
Meridian, MS 39302
Ken Rainey, General Manager
(601) 693-2661

WNBN-AM
1290 Hawkins Crossing Road
Meridian, MS 39301
Frank Rackley, Jr., General Manager
(601) 483-3401

WQIC-FM
2711 Seventh Street
Meridian, MS 39301
Larry Tongerson, General Manager
(601) 693-4851

WMIS-AM
Post Office Box 1248
Natchez, MS 39120
Jame H. Dulaney, Vice President and
  General Manager
(601) 445-2522

WTYJ-FM
Post Office Drawer 1248
Natchez, MS 39121
David Shaw, General Manager
(601) 442-2522

WBFL-AM
1000 Blue Meadow Road
Bay St. Louis, MS 39520
Dan Diamond, President & General
  Manager
(601) 467-5243

WACR-AM/FM
1910 Fourteenth Avenue, North
Columbus, MS 39701
Bennie Turner, President & General
  Manager
(601) 328-1050

WGNL-FM
503 Ione Street
Greenwood, MS 38930
Ruben C. Hughes, President &
  General Manager
(601) 453-1643

MISSOURI

KCXL-AM
810 East 63rd Street
Kansas City, MO 64110
Elbert Anderson, President
(816) 333-2583

KIDZ-AM
10841 East 28th Street
Independence, MO 64052
Ragan Henry, President
(816) 836-5055

KPRS-AM/FM
2440 Pershing Road
Kansas City, MO 64108
Michael L. Carter, President
(816) 763-2040

Radio Stations (cont.)

KPRT-AM
2440 Pershing Road
Kansas City, MO 64108
Michael L. Carter, President
(816) 471-2100

KIRL-AM
3713 Highway 94 North
St. Charles, MO 63301
Johnny Roland, President
(314) 946-6600

KATZ-AM/FM
1139 Olive Street
St. Louis, MO 63101
Thomas P. Lewis, President
(314) 241-6000

NEW JERSEY

WNJR-AM
600 North Union Avenue
Hillside, NJ 07205
Elizabeth Satchell, General Manager
(201) 688-5000

WCMC-AM
3010 New Jersey Avenue
Wildwood, NJ 08260
Ragan Henry, President
(609) 522-1416

WZXL-FM
3010 New Jersey Avenue
Wildwood, NJ 08260
Ragan Henry, President
(609) 522-1416

WUSS-AM
1507 Atlantic Avenue
Atlantic, NJ 08401
Jim Cuffee, President
(609) 345-7134

NEW MEXICO

KANW-FM
2020 Coal Avenue
Albuquerque, NM 87106
Michael Brasher, General Manager
(505) 242-7163

NEW YORK

WUFO-AM
89 LaSalle Avenue
Buffalo, NY 14214
Ronald Davenport, President
(716) 834-1080

WEIF-FM
Post Office Box 86
Clayville, NY 13322
Christopher & Clara Crocco, Owners
(315) 839-5375

WTHE-AM
260 East Second Street
Mineola, NY 11501
Paul Ploener, General Manager
(516) 742-1520

WBLS-FM
801 Second Avenue
New York, NY 10017
Pierre Sutton, President
(212) 661-3344

Media

Radio Station (cont.)

WLIB-AM
801 Second Avenue
New York, NY 10017
Pierre Sutton, President
(212) 661-3344

WRKS-FM
1440 Broadway
New York, NY 10018
Barry Mayo, General Manager
(212) 642-4000

WDKX-FM
683 East Main Street
Rochester, NY 14605
Andrew A. Langston, Chairman
(716) 262-2050

WWRL-AM
41-30 58th Street
Woodside, NY 11377
Vince Sanders, Vice President &
  General Manager
(718) 335-1600

NORTH CAROLINA

WVOE-AM
Route 3, Box 39B
Chadbourne, NC 28431
Willie Walls, President
(919) 654-5621

WSRC-AM
3202 Guess Road
Durham, NC 27705
Bishop L.E. Willis, President
(919) 477-7999

WBXB-FM
Post Office Box 765
Edenton, NC 27932
Bishop L.E. Willis, President
(919) 482-3200

WDKS-FM
Post Office Box 20008
Fayetteville, NC 28302
Vonneva Carter, Station Manager
(919) 484-2107

WIDU-AM
Post Office Drawer 2247
Fayetteville, NC 28802
Charles W. Cookman, General
  Manager
(919) 483-6111

WOKN-FM
Post Office Box 804
Goldsboro, NC 26533
Jimmy Swinson, General Manager
(919) 734-4213

WQMG-AM
14702 - 1060 Gatewood Avenue
Greensboro, NC 27415
Morgan Rees Poag, President
(704) 272-5121

WNAA-FM
North Carolina A&T State University
Price Hall, Suite 200
Greensboro, NC 27411
Lut Williams, News Director
(919) 334-7936

WCLY-AM
647 Maywood Avenue
Raleigh, NC 27603
Benny Moore, General Manager
(919) 821-1550

Radio Stations (cont.)

WLLE-AM
522 East Martin street
Raleigh, NC 27601
Henry & Prentiss Monroe, Owners
(919) 833-3874

WGSP-AM
4209 F Stewart Andrew Boulevard
Charlotte, NC 28217
Bishop L.E. Willis, President
(704) 527-9477

WTNC-AM
Post Office Box 1920
726 Salem Street
Thomasville, NC 27360
Rev. Alvin Rooks, Sr., President
(919) 472-0790

WBMS-AM
812-C Castle Street
Wilmington, NC 28402
Frank McNeil, President
(919) 763-4633

WGTM-AM
Post Office Box 3837
Highway 42 West
Wilson, NC 27893
Celestine Willis, President
(919) 243-2188

WQOK-FM
8601 Six Forks Road
Suite 609
Raleigh, NC 27615
Ragan Henry, President
(919) 848-9736

WAUG-FM
St. Augustine's College
Post Office Box 14815
Raleigh, NC 27620
Jay Holloway, Assistant Vice President

WRSV-FM
Post Office Box 2666
Rocky Mount, NC 27802
Charles O. Johnson, President
(919) 442-9776

WAAA-AM
4950 Indiana Avenue
Post Office Box 11197
Winston-Salem, NC 27116-1197
Mutter D. Evans, President & General
    Manager
(919) 767-0430

WSMX-AM
Post Office Box 16056
Winston-Salem, NC 27115
S. D. Johnson, President
(919) 761-1545

WSNC-FM
Winston Salem State University
Post Office Box 13062
Winston-Salem, NC 27110
Sonja Williams, Faculty Advisor
(919) 750-2304

OHIO

WCIN-AM
106 Glenwood Avenue
Cincinnati, OH 45217
Carl Shye, President
(513) 281-7180

Media

Radio Station (cont.)

WIZF-FM
7030 Redding Road
Cincinnati, OH 45237
Thomas P. Lewis, Chairman
(513) 351-5900

WABQ-AM
8000 Euclid Avenue
Cleveland, OH 44103
Michael J. Gallagher, President
(216) 231-8005

WJMO-AM
11821 Euclid Avenue
Cleveland, OH 44106
Curtis E. Shaw, General Manager
(216) 795-1212

WCKX-FM
510 Mound
Columbus, OH 43215
Jack Harris, President
(614) 464-0020

WAKR-AM
1735 South Hawkins Avenue
Akron, OH 44320
Ragan Henry, President
(216) 869-9800

WONE-FM
1735 South Hawkins Avenue
Akron, OH 44320
Ragan Henry, President
(216) 869-9800

WRZR-FM
1150 Morse Road
Columbus, OH 43229
Ragan Henry, President
(614) 436-1040

WJTB-AM
105 Lake Avenue
Elyria, OH 44035
James Taylor, President
(216) 327-1844

WZAK-FM
1729 Superior Avenue, Suite 401
Cleveland, OH 44114
Xenophon Zapis, President & General
  Manager
(216) 621-9300

WDAO-AM
4309 West Third Street
Dayton, OH 45417
James Johnson, President
(513) 263-9326

WVOI-AM
6695 Jackman Road
Toledo, OH 43613
Ken McDowell, Station Manager
(419) 243-7052

OKLAHOMA

KALU-FM
Langston University
Post Office Box 837
Langston, OK 73050
Byron Marshall, Station Manager
(405) 466-2314

PENNSYLVANIA

WLIU-FM
Lincoln University
Lincoln University, PA 19352
Chijioke U.N. Okoro, General Manager
(215) 923-8300

Radio Stations (cont.)

WDAS-AM/FM
Belmont Avenue & Edgely Drive
Philadelphia PA 19131
Eugene Jackson, Chairperson
(215) 878-2000

WHAT-AM
2471 North 54th St., Suite 220
Philadelphia, PA 19131
W. Cody Anderson, President
(215) 581-5161

WRTI-FM
Temple University
Annenberg Hall
Philadelphia, PA 19122
W. Theodore Eldredge, General
   Manager
(215) 787-8405

WURD-AM
5301 Tacony Street
Building 10
Philadelphia PA 19137
Celestine Willis, General Manager
(215) 533-8900

WAMO-AM/FM
411 Seventh Avenue, Suite 1500
Pittsburgh, PA 15219
Ronald Davenport, President

WIMG-AM
Post Office Box 436
Washington Crossings, PA 18977
Bishop L.E. Willis, President
(215) 321-1300

WCDL-AM
43 Seventh Avenue
Carbondale, PA 18407
Bob VanDerheyden, General Manager
(717) 282-2770

WSGD-FM
1 Montag Mountain Road, Suite B
Moosic, PA 18507
Bob VanDerheyden, General Manager
(717) 341-9494

WRAW-AM
1265 Perkiomen Avenue
Reading, PA 19602
Ragan Henry, President
(215) 376-7173

WRFY-FM
1265 Perkiomen Avenue
Reading, PA 19602
Ragan Henry, President
(215) 376-7173

WPRP-FM
2727 West Albert Drive
Altoona, PA 16602
Gary Guton, President
(814) 944-9456

WVAM-AM
2727 West Albert Drive
Altoona, PA 16602
Gary Guton, President
(814) 944-9456

WCXJ-AM
2001 Wylie Avenue
Pittsburgh, PA 15219
Del King, General Manager
(412) 391-1670

SOUTH CAROLINA

WVGB-AM
806 Monson Street
Beaufort, SC 29902
Vivian M. Galloway, President
(803) 524-4700

Media

Radio Station (cont.)

WTGH-AM
1303 State Street
Cayce, SC 29033
Raleigh Williams, General Manager
(803) 796-9533

WKQB-FM
Post Office Box 10164
Charleston, SC 29411
Steve Judy, Chairman
(803) 744-1779

WPAL-AM
1717 Wappo Road
Charleston, SC 29403
William Saunders, President &
  General Manager
(803) 763-6330

WQIZ-AM
Post Office Box 10164
Charleston, SC 29411
Steve Judy, President
(803) 744-1779

WWWZ-FM
Post Office Box 30669
Charleston, SC 29417
Cliff Fletcher, President
(803) 556-9132

WYNN-AM/FM
Post Office Box F-14
Florence, SC 29501
Jim Maurer, General Manager
(803) 662-6364

WCOS-AM/FM
2440 Millwood Avenue
Columbia, SC 29205
Ragan Henry, President
(803) 256-7348

WHYZ-AM
Post Office Box 4309
Greenville, SC 29608
Steven Brisker, President
(803) 246-1970

WLGI-FM
Route 2
Post Office Box 69
Hemingway, SC 29554
Trewitt White, General Manager

WWKT-FM
Post Office Box 1125
Highway 52 North
Kingstree, SC 29556
Arnie Graham, General Manager
(803) 382-2361

WLBG-AM
Post Office Box 1989
Laurens, SC 29360
Emil Finlay, General Manager
(803) 984-3544

WWPD-FM
American Legion Road
Marion, SC 29571
Bishop L.E. Willis, President
(803) 423-5971

WNCJ-AM
314 Rembert Dennis Boulevard
Moncks Corner, SC 29461
Clay Butler, President
(803) 761-6010

WSSB-FM
Post Office Box 3056
Orangeburg, SC 29117
Gil Harris, Station Manager
(803) 536-8938

Radio Stations (cont.)

WQKI-AM
Post Office Box 777
St. Matthews, SC 29135
Robert Newsham, General Manager
(803) 874-2777

WMNY-AM
Route 1, Box 189
Santee, SC 29142
Bob Frazier, General Manager
(803) 854-2671

WASC-AM
840 Wofford Street
Spartanburg, SC 29304
Joe Sessoms, Station Manager
(803) 585-1530

WSJW-AM
Post Office Box 576
Woodruff, SC 29388
Garry Jarrett, General Manager
(803) 476-8189

TENNESSEE

WBOL-AM
Box 191
Bolivar, TN 38008
Johnny Shaw, President
(901) 658-3690

The listings in this directory are available as Mailing Labels. See last page for details.

WTBG-FM
Post Office Box 198
Brownsville, TN 38012
Carlton Veirs, Station Manager
(901) 772-3700

WDIA-AM
112 Union Avenue
Memphis, TN 38103
Rick Caffey, General Manager
(901) 529-4300

WEVL-FM
Post Office Box 40925
Memphis, TN 38174
Judy Dorsey, General Manager
(901) 278-3845

KFTH-FM
2265 Central Avenue
Memphis, TN 38104
Bishop Levi E. Willis, President
(901) 272-3004

WHRK-FM
112 Union Avenue
Memphis, TN 38103
Rick Caffey, General Manager
(901) 529-4300

WLOK-AM
Post Office Box 69
363 South Second Street
Memphis, TN 38101
Art Gilliam, President
(901) 527-9565

WFSK-FM
1000 17th Avenue North
Nashville, TN 37208
Dennis Whitehead, General Manager
(615) 329-8757

Media

Radio Station (cont.)

WMDB-AM
3051 Stokers Lane
Nashville, TN 37218
Morgan Babb, President & General
    Manager
(615) 255-2876

WQQK-FM
Post Office Box 70085
1320 Brick Church Pike
Nashville, TN 37207
Samuel Howard, President & General
    Manager

WVOL-AM
1320 Brick Church Pke
P.O. Box 70085
Nashville, TN 37207
Samuel Howard, President & General
    Manager
(615) 227-1470

WFKX-FM
425 East Chester
Jackson, TN 38301
James Wolf, President & General
    Manager
(901) 427-9616

WNOO-AM
1108 Hendricks Street
Chattanooga, TN 37406
Bill McKay, General Manager
(615) 698-8617

WFXX-FM
1108 Hendricks Street
Chattanooga, TN 37406
Bill McKay, General Manager
(615) 698-8617

TEXAS

KAZI-FM
4700 Loyola Lane
Suite 014
Austin, TX 78723
Gary Cobs, Chairman
(512) 926-0275

KWWJ-AM
4638 Decker Drive
Baytown, TX 77520
Darrell E. Martin, President
(713) 424-7000

KKDA-AM/FM
Post Office Box 530860
Grand Prairie, TX 75053
Hymen Childs, General Manager
(214) 263-9911

KHRN-FM
219 North Main Street
Suite 600
Bryan, TX 77803
Joe Lee Walker, President & General
    Manager
(409) 779-5476

KCOH-AM
5011 Almeda Street
Houston, TX 77004
Mike Petrizzio, General Manager
(713) 522-1001

KMJQ-FM
24 Greenway Plaza
Houston, TX 77046
Monte Lang, Vice President & General
    Manager
(713) 623-0102

Media

Radio Stations (cont.)

KYOK-AM
24 Greenway Plaza
Suite 1590
Houston, TX 77046
Monte Lang, Vice President & General
   Manager
(713) 621-1590

KBWC-FM
711 Roseborough Springs
Marshall, TX 75670
Melvin C. Jones, Sr., General Manager
(214) 938-8341

KALO-AM
7700 Gulfway Drive
Port Arthur, TX 77642
Dale Matteson, General Manager
(409) 963-1276

KPVU-FM
Prairie View A&M University
Hillard Hall
Prairie View, TX 77446
Lori Gray, Station Manager
(409) 857-4511

KSAQ-FM
217 Alamo Plaza, Suite 200
San Antonio, TX 78205
Charles Andrews, General Manager
(5120 271-9600

KSJL-AM
217 Alamo Plaza, Suite 200
San Antonio, TX 78205
Charles Andrews, General Manager
(512) 271-9600

KJOJ-AM/FM
29801 I-45 North
Spring, TX 77381
Ragan Henry, President
(713) 367-0107

KTER-AM
1412-C West Moore
Terrell, TX 75160
Andy Collins, Station Manager
(214) 563-2646

KZEY-AM
Post Office Box 4248
Tyler, TX 75712
Al Brooks, General Manager
(214) 593-1744

VIRGINIA

WKBY-AM
Route 2, Box 105-A
Chatham, VA 24531
Everett C. Peace, Jr., General
   Manager
(804) 432-8108

WPAK-AM
Post Office Box 494
800 Old Plank Road
Farmville, VA 23901
Rick Darnell, General Manager
(804) 392-8114

WHOV-FM
Hampton University
Hampton, VA 23668
Frank D. Sheffield, General Manager
(804) 727-5670

Media

Radio Station (cont.)

WTJZ-AM
533 Michigan Drive
Hampton, VA 23669
Eric Reynolds, President
(804) 723-3391

WJJS-AM
Post Office Box 6440
1105 Main Street
Madison Heights, VA 24504
Denny Dee Rover, General Manager
(804) 847-1267

WOWI-FM
645 Church Street
Suite 201
Norfolk, VA 23510
Ragan Henry, President
(804) 627-5800

WPCE-AM
645 Church Street
Suite 400
Norfolk, VA 23510
Bishop L.E. Willis, President
(804) 624-9723

WPLZ-AM/FM
Post Office Box 1510
3267 South Crater Road
Petersburg, VA 23805
Charles Giddens, President
(804) 733-4567

WPVA-AM
1011-B Amelia
Petersburg, VA 23803
Paul Moore, Station Manager
(804) 732-3478

WVST-FM
Post Office Box 10
Petersburg, VA 23903
Cathis Hall, Station Manager
(804) 520-6161

WRBN-AM
6001 Wilkinson Road
Richmond, VA 23227
Dr. Charles Cummings, President
(804) 264-1540

WBSK-AM
645 Church Street, Suite 201
Norfolk, VA 23510
Ragan Henry, President
(804) 627-5800

WANT-AM
1101 Front Street
Richmond, VA 23222
John Galloway, President & General
  Manager
(804) 353-9113

WCLM-AM
4719 Nine Mile Road
Richmond, VA 23223
Warren Moon, President
(804) 236-0532

WFTH-AM
5021 Brooks Road, Suite 101
Richmond, VA 23227
J.I. Jack Johnson, Jr., President
(804) 262-8624

WRBN-AM
6001 Wilkinson Road
Richmond, VA 23227
Jon C. King, General Manager
(804) 264-1540

Radio Stations (cont.)

VIRGIN ISLANDS

WTBN-FM
Executive Towers
19 Estate Thomas, Suite 103
St. Thomas, U.S. VI 00801
Kervin Clenance
(809) 776-2610

WSTX-AM/FM
Post Office Box 3279
Christiansted, St. Croix
St. Thomas, U.S., VI 00822
G. Luz A. James, Esquire, President
(809) 773-0490

WASHINGTON

KUJ-AM
Route 5, Box 513
Walla Walla, WA 99362
Patrick Prout, President
(509) 529-8000

WISCONSIN

WLUM-FM
4222 West Capitol Drive
Milwaukee, WI 53216
Willie D. Davis, President
(414) 444-1290

WNOV-AM
3815 North Teutonia Avenue
Milwaukee, WI 53206
Sandra Robinson, General Manager
(414) 449-9668

WMVP-AM
4222 West Capitol Drive
Milwaukee, WI 53216
Willie D. Davis, President
(414) 444-1290

The listings in this directory are available as Mailing Labels. See last page for details.

Media

Television Stations

CALIFORNIA

KNTV-TV
645 Park Avenue
San Jose, CA 95110
W. Don Cornwell, President
(408) 286-1111

DISTRICT OF COLUMBUA

WHMM-TV 32
Howard University
2222 Fourth Street, N.W.
Washington, D. C. 20059
Ed Jones, General Manager
(202) 806-3500

FLORIDA

WBSF-TV 43
4450-L Enterprise Court
Melbourne, FL 32934
John Oxendine, President
(4007) 254-4343

WTVT-TV 13
Post Office Box 31113
Tampa, FL 33631-3113
David Whitaker, President
(813) 876-1313

GEORGIA

WFXL-TV 31
Post Office Box 4050
Albany, GA 31708
Manny Cantu, President
(912) 435-3100

WGXA-TV 24
Post Office Box 340
Macon, GA 31297
Herman J. Russell, President
(912) 745-2424

ILLINOIS

WEEK-TV
2907 Springfield Road
East Peoria, IL 61611
Dennis Upah, General Manager
(309) 698-2525

WJYS-TV 62
18600 Oak Park Avenue
Tinley Park, IL 60477
Joseph Stroud, President
(708) 633-0001

INDIANA

WPTA-TV
3401 Butler Road
Fort Wayne, IN 46808
Barbara Wingham, President
(219) 483-0584

Televison Stations (cont.)

LOUISIANA

WNOL-TV
1661 Canal Street
New Orleans, LA 70112
Quincy Jones, President
(504) 525-3838

MAINE

WVII-TV
371 Target Industrial Circle
Bangor, ME 04401
Dr. James Buckner, President
(207) 945-6457

MICHIGAN

WGPR-TV 62
3146 East Jefferson Street
Detroit, MI 48207
George Matthews, President
(313) 259-8862

MINNESOTA

KBJR-TV
230 East Superior Street
Duluth, MN 55802
W. Don Cornwell, President
(218) 727-8484

MISSISSIPPI

WLBT-TV 3
715 South Jefferson Street
Jackson, MS 39202
Frank E. Melton, President
(601) 948-3333

MISSOURI

WHSL-TV 46
1408 North Kingshighway, Suite 300
St. Louis, MI 63113
Michael Roberts, Chairman
(314) 367-4600

NEW YORK

WKBW-TV
7 Broadcast Plaza
Buffalo, NY 14202
Bruce Llewellyn, Chairman
(716) 845-6100

OREGON

KBST-TV
4923 Indian School Road, N.E.
Salem, OR 97305
Judy Koenig, General Manager
(503) 390-2202

Media

Television Stations (cont.)

PENNSYLVANIA

WGTW-TV 48
642 North Broad Street
Philadelphia, PA 19130
Dorothy E. Brunson, President
(215) 765-4800

SOUTH CAROLINA

WRDW-TV
1301 Georgia Avenue
North Augusta, SC 29841
William Evans, Vice President &
General Manager
(803) 278-1212

VIRGINIA

WJCB-TV
2700 Washington Avenue, Fourth
Floor
Newport News, VA 23607
Bishop Samuel Green, Chairman
(804) 247-0049

WISCONSIN

WJFW-TV
Box 858
South Oneida Avenue
Rhinelander, WI 54501
Dr. James Buckner, Chairman

WJJA-TV
Post Office Box 92
Oakcreek, WI 53154
Joel Kinlow, President
(414) 764-4953

Museums

This section contains a partial listing of black museums in the United States. For those interested in the black experience, valuable data can be found in them.

ALABAMA

TUSKEGEE INSTITUTE NATIONAL HISTORIC SITE

Post Office Drawer 10
Tuskegee, AL 36830
Jerry Belson, Director
(205) 727-6390

CALIFORNIA

AFRICA HOUSE

3463 State Street
Santa Barbara, CA 93105
Magnolia Raine, President
(805) 565-1314

CALIFORNIA AFRO-AMERICAN MUSEUM

600 State Drive, Exposition Park
Los Angeles, CA 90037
Bridget Cullerton, Acting Director
(213) 744-7432

DUNBAR HOTEL CULTURAL AND HISTORICAL MUSEUM

4225 South Central Avenue
Los Angeles, CA 90011
Bernard Johnson, Director
(213) 462-3475

EBONY MUSEUM OF ART, INC.

1034 14th Street
Oakland, CA 94607
Aissatoui A. Vernita,
  Executive Director
(415) 763-0141

MUSEUM OF AFRICAN AMERICAN ART

4005 Crenshaw Boulevard
Third Floor
Los Angeles, CA 90008
Cheryl Dixon, Director
(213) 294-7071

NORTHERN CALIFORNIA CENTER FOR AFRO-AMERICAN HISTORY AND LIFE

5606 San Pablo Avenue
Oakland, CA 94606
Eugene Lasartemay, Director
(415) 658-3158

SAN FRANCISCO AFRICAN-AMERICAN HISTORICAL & CULTURAL SOCIETY

Fort Mason Center, Building C-165
San Francisco, CA 94123
Juliana Haile, Executive Director
(415) 441-0640

COLORADO

BLACK AMERICAN WEST MUSEUM AND HERITAGE CENTER

606 - 26th Street
Denver, CO 80205
Joe Mangrum, Director
(202) 295-1026

Museums

CONNECTICUT

CONNECTICUT AFRO-AMERICAN
Historical Society, Inc.
444 Orchard Street
New Haven, CT 06511
George Bellinger, President
(203) 776-4907

DELAWARE

AFRO-AMERICAN HISTORICAL
SOCIETY OF DELAWARE
512 East Fourth Street
Wilmington, DE 19801
Harmon R. Carey, President
(302) 984-1423

DISTRICT OF COLUMBIA

AFRICAN STUDIES AND
RESEARCH PROGRAM
Howard University
Post Office Box 231
Washington, D.C. 20059
Dr. Sulayman S. Nyang, Director
(202) 636-7115

AFRO-AMERICAN RESOURCE
CENTER
Founders Library
Howard University
Washington, D.C. 20059
Ethelbert Miller, Director

ANACOSTIA NEIGHBORHOOD
MUSEUM
Smithsonian Institution
1904 Fort Place, S.E.
Washingtin, D.C. 20020
(202) 287-3306

BETHUNE MUSEUM-ARCHIVE,
INC.
National Historic Site
1318 Vermont Avenue, N.W.
Washington, D.C. 20005
Dr. Bettye Collier-Thomas, Executive
    Director
(202) 332-1233

EVANS-TIBBS COLLECTION
1910 Vermont Avenue, N.W.
Washington, D.C. 20001
Thurlow E. Tibbs, Jr., Director
(202) 234-8164

FREDERICK DOUGLASS HOME
1411 W Street, S.E.
Washington, D.C. 20020
Carnell Poole, Site Manager
(202) 426-5961

HOWARD UNIVERSITY
GALLERY OF ART
College of Fine Arts
2455 Sixth Street, N.W.
Washington, D.C. 20059
Tritobia H. Benjamin, Director
(202) 636-7070

MOORLAND-SPRINGARN
RESEARCH CENTER
Howard University
Washington, D.C. 20059
Dr. Thomas C. Battle, Director
(202) 636-7240

NATIONAL COUNCIL FOR
EDUCATION & ECONOMIC
DEVELOPMENT
Nat'l. Afro-American Heritage Museum
1875 Eye Street, N.W.
Washington, D.C. 20006
Barbara W.Franklin, Executive Director
(202) 554-5100

Museums

NATIONAL MUSEUM OF AFRICAN ART
Smithsonian Institute
950 Independence Avenue, S.W.,
  MRC 708
Washington, D.C. 20560
Sylvia H. Williams, Director
(202) 357-4600

FLORIDA

BLACK ARCHIVES RESEARCH CENTER AND MUSEUM
Florida A&M University
Post Office Box 809
Tallahassee, FL 32307
James N. Eaton, Director
(904) 599-3020

BLACK HERITAGE MUSEUM
Post Office Box 570327
Miami, FL 33257-0327
Priscilla Stephens Kruize, President

CARL SWISHER LIBRARY - LEARNING RESOURCE CENTER
Bethune Cookman College
640 Second Avenue
Daytona Beach, FL 32015
Bobby Henderson, Director
(904) 255-1401

GALLERY ANTIGUA, INC.
5138 Biscayne Boulevard
Miami, FL 33137
Caleb A. Davis, Director
(305) 759-5355

GEORGIA

AFRICAN AMERICAN FAMILY HISTORY ASSOCIATION, INC.
Post Office Box 115268
Atlanta, GA 30310
Herman "Skip" Mason, Jr., President
(404) 736-1942

THE AFRICAN AMERICAN PANORAMIC EXPERIENCE MUSEUM
135 Auburn Avenue, N.E.
Atlanta, GA 30303
Dan Moore, President
(404) 521-2654

HARRIET TUBMAN HISTORICAL AND CULTURAL MUSEUM
340 Walnut Street
Macon, GA 31208
Dorothy Hardman, Director
(912) 743-8544

HERNDON HOMES
587 University Place, N.W.
Atlanta, GA 30314
Carole Merritt, Director
(404) 581-9813

KING LIBRARY AND ARCHIVES
Martin Luther King, Jr. Center for
  Nonviolent Social Change
671 Beckwith Street, S.W.
Atlanta, GA 30314
Broadus N. Butler, Director
(404) 524-1956

Museums

RUTH HALL HODGES ART GALLERY
Morris Brown College
643 Martin Luther King, Jr., Dr., S.W.
Atlanta, GA 30314
Dr. Lee A. Ransaw, Chairperson
(404) 525-7831

ILLINOIS

DUSABLE MUSEUM OF AFRICAN AMERICAN HISTORY
740 East 56th Place
Chicago, IL 60637
Useni Eugene Perkins, Director
(312) 947-0600

SOUTHSIDE COMMUNITY ART CENTER
3831 South Michigan
Chicago, IL 60653
Gerald Sanders, Managing Director
(312) 373-1028

KANSAS

FIRST NATIONAL BLACK HISTORICAL SOCIETY OF KANSAS
601 North Water
Wichita, KS 67201
Ruby V. Parker, Director
(316) 326-7651

LOUISIANA

AMISTAD RESEARCH CENTER
Tulane University
Tilton Hall
New Orleans, LA 70118
Clifton Johnson, Executive Director
(504) 865-5535

MARYLAND

BALTIMORE'S BLACK AMERICAN MUSEUM/THIRD WORLD MUSEUM
1765-69 Carswell Street
Baltimore, MD 21218
Frank Richardson, Director
(410) 243-9600

EUBIE BLAKE NATIONAL MUSEUM
409 North Charles Street
Baltimore, MD 21201
Norman E. Ross, Coordinator
(301) 396-3181

GALLERY OF ART, MORGAN STATE UNIVERSITY
Carl Murphy Fine Arts Center
Hillen & Coldspring Lane
Baltimore, MD 21239
Professor James Lewis, Director
(410) 444-3030

GREAT BLACKS IN WAX MUSEUM
1601 East North Avenue
Baltimore, MD 21213
Tulani Salahu-din, Director
(410) 563-3404

LILLIE CARROLL JACKSON MUSEUM, INC.
Civil Rights Museum
1320 Eutaw Place
Baltimore, MD 21217
Gail Mitchell, Director
(301) 523-1634

MARYLAND COMMISSION ON AFRO-AMERICAN HISTORY AND CULTURE, BANNEKER-DOUGLASS MUSEUM

84 Franklin Street
Annapolis, MD 21401
Dr. Ronald Sharps, Director
(301) 974-2893

ORCHAD STREET CULTURAL MUSEUM

24 South Abington Avenue
Baltimore, MD 21229
Marguerite Campbell, Director
(410) 669-3100

MASSACHUSETTS

AFRICAN AMERICAN MASTER ARTISTS IN RESIDENCY PROGRAM

Northeastern University
360 Huntington Avenue
Building 590
Boston, MA 02115
Dana Chandler, Director
(617) 437-3139

AFRICAN AMERICAN MUSEUM AND CULTURAL CENTER OF WESTERN MASSACHUSETTS

Post Office Box 4033
Springfield, MA 01101
(413) 737-9209

HARRIET TUBMAN GALLERY AND RESOURCE CENTER

United South End Settlements
566 Columbus Avenue
Boston, MA 02118
Frieda Garcia, Director
(617) 536-8610

MUSEUM OF AFRO AMERICAN HISTORY, AFRICAN MEETING HOUSE

Abiel Smith School
46 Joy Street
Boston, MA 02114
Ruth M. Batson, President
(617) 742-1854

MUSEUM OF THE NATIONAL CENTER OF AFRO-AMERICAN ARTISTS, INC.

300 Walnut Avenue
Boston, MA 02119
Edmund Barry Gaither, Director
(617) 442-8014

PARTING WAYS MUSEUM OF AFRO-AMERICAN ETHNOHISTORY

130 Court Street
Plymouth, MA 02360
Diane Haynes, President
(508) 746-6028

MICHIGAN

GRAYSTONE JAZZ MUSEUM

1521 Broadway
Detroit, MI 48226
Toni Costoni, Co-Director
(313) 963-3813

MUSEUM OF AFRICAN AMERI-CAN HISTORY

301 Frederick Douglass
Detroit, MI 48202
Marion Moore, Executive Director
(313) 833-9800

Museums

YOUR HERITAGE HOUSE
110 East Ferry Street
Detroit, MI 48202
Josephine Herreld Love, Director
(313) 871-1667

MISSISSIPPI

SMITH-ROBERTSON MUSEUM AND CULTURAL CENTER
Post Office Box 3259
Jackson, MS 59207
Jesse Mosley, Director
(601) 960-1424

MISSOURI

BLACK ARCHIVES OF MID-AMERICA, INC.
2033 Vine Street
Kansas City, MO 64108
Horace M. Peterson, III, Director
(816) 483-1300

NEBRASKA

GREAT PLAINS BLACK MUSEUM
2213 Lake Street
Omaha, NE 68110
Bertha Calloway, Director
(402) 345-2212

NEW JERSEY

AFRICAN ARTS MUSEUM - S.M.A. FATHERS
23 Bliss Avenue
Tenafly, NJ 07670
Very Rev. S. John Murray, SMA
(201) 567-0450

AFRO-AMERICAN HISTORICAL & CULTURAL SOCIETY OF JERSEY CITY, INC.
1841 Kennedy Boulevard
Jersey City, NJ 07305
Theodore Brunson, President
(201) 547-5262

CARTER G. WOODSON FOUNDATION
Post Office Box 1025
Newark, NJ 07101
Phillip Thomas, President
(201) 242-0500

MERABASH MUSEUM, INC.
Museum for Education and Research in American Black Art, Science and History
Post Office Box 752
Willingboro, NJ 08046
Mark Henderson, Jr., Executive Director
(609) 877-3177

NEWARK MUSEUM
Newark Museum Association
Post Office Box 540
49 Washington Street
Newark, NJ 07101
Samuel Miller, Curator of Ethnology
(201) 596-6550

NEW YORK

AFRICAN-AMERICAN MUSEUM OF NASSAU COUNTY
110 North Franklin Street
Hempstead, NY 11550
Shirley Darkeh, Director
(516) 485-0470

Museums

AFRO-AMERICAN HISTORICAL SOCIETY OF THE NIAGARA FRONTIER
Post Office Box 1663
Buffalo, NY 14216
Dr. Monroe Fordham, Director
(716) 694-5096

AUNT LEN'S DOLL AND TOY MUSEUM
6 Hamilton Terrace
New York, NY 10031
Lenon H. Hoyte, Director
(212) 281-4143

BLACK FASHION MUSEUM
157 West 126th Street
New York, NY 10027
Jorge Saunders, Director
(212) 666-1320

COMMUNITY FOLK ART GALLERY
2223 East Genesis Street
Syracuse, NY 13210
Herbert Williams, Director
(315) 424-8487

GENESIS II MUSEUM OF INTERNATIONAL BLACK CULTURE
509 Cathedral Parkway
New York, NY 10025
Andi Owens, Director
(212) 666-7222

GRINNELL GALLERY
800 Riverside Drive
New York, NY 10032
Ademola Olugebtoia and Pat Davis, Co-Directors
(212) 927-7941

LANGSTON HUGHES INSTITUTE, INC, KUSH MUSEUM
25 Hugh Street
Buffalo, NY 14203
Keith E. Baird, Director
(716) 881-3266

SCHOMBURG CENTER FOR RESEARCH IN BLACK CULTURE
The New York Public Library
515 Lenox Avenue
New York, NY 10037
Howard Dodson, Director
(212) 862-4000

SOCIETY FOR THE PRESERVATION OF WEEKSVILLE & BEDFORD STUYVESANT HISTORY
Post Office Box 130120
St. John's Station
Brooklyn, NY 11213-0002
Joan Maynard, Director
(718) 765-5250

STORE FRONT MUSEUM
48 Alder Drive
Mastic Beach, NY 11951
Tom Lloyd, Executive Director
(516) 281-7585

THE STUDIO MUSEUM IN HARLEM
144 West 125th Street
New York, NY 10027
Kinshasha Conwill, Director
(212) 864-4500

Museums

WESTCHESTER AFRICAN-AMERICAN HISTORICAL SOCIETY
1126 Howard Street
Peekskill, NY 10566
Kay Amory-Mosier, President

NORTH CAROLINA

AFRO-AMERICAN CULTURAL CENTER
401 North Myers Street
Charlotte, NC 28202
Vanessa Green, Director
(704) 374-1565

MUSEUM OF ART
North Carolina Central University
1805 Fayetteville Street
Durham, NC 27707
Norman E. Pendergraft, Director
(919) 560-6211

SOMERSET PLACE STATE HISTORIC SITE
Post Office Box 215
Creswell, NC 27928
William Edwards, Jr., Site Manager
(919) 797-4560

YMI CULTURAL CENTER
47 Eagle Street
Ashville, NC 28801
Wanda Henry-Coleman, Executive Director
(704) 252-4614

OHIO

AFRICAN-AMERICAN MUSEUM
1765 Crawford Road
Cleveland, OH 44120
Eleanor Engram, Director
(216) 791-1700

AFRO-AMERICAN CULTURAL CENTER
Cleveland State University
Black Studies Program
2121 Euclid Avenue
Cleveland, OH 44115
Professor Curtis Wilson, Director
(216) 687-3655

DUNBAR STATE MEMORIAL
Post Office Box 1872
Dayton, OH 45401
LaVerne Kenon, Director
(513) 224-7061

HARRIET TUBMAN MUSEUM AND CULTURAL ASSOCIATION
Post Office Box 20178
Cleveland, OH 44120-0178
Mr. Hanif Wahab, Director/Curator
(216) 663-1115

KARAMU HOUSE
2355 East 89th Street
Cleveland, OH 44106
Margaret Ford Taylor, Director
(216) 795-7070

NATIONAL AFRO-AMERICAN MUSEUM & CULTURAL CENTER
Post Office Box 578
Wilberforce, OH 45384
John E. Fleming, Ph.D., Director
(513) 376-4944

RESIDENT ART AND HUMANITIES CONSORTIUM
1515 Linn Street
Cincinnati, OH 45214
Ernest O. Britton, Director
(513) 381-0645

WATKINS ACADEMY MUSEUM OF CULTURAL ARTS
724 Mineola Avenue
Akron, OH 44320
James Watkins, Director
(216) 864-0673

OKLAHOMA

SANAMU AFRICAN ART MUSEUM
2100 Northeast 52nd Street
Oklahoma City, OK 73111
Mary Ann Haliburton, Director
(405) 424-7760

PENNSYLVANIA

AFRO-AMERICAN HISTORICAL AND CULTURAL MUSEUM
701 Arch Streets
Philadelphia, PA 19106
Rowena Stewart, Executive Director
(215) 574-0380

RHODE ISLAND

RHODE ISLAND BLACK HERITAGE SOCIETY
1 Hilton Street
Providence, RI 62905
Linda A'Vant-Coleman, Executive Director
(401) 751-3490

SOUTH CAROLINA

AVERY INSTITUTE OF AFRO-AMERICAN HISTORY AND CULTURE
Post Office Box 2262
Charleston, SC 29403
Lucille Whipper, President
(803) 792-5924

AVERY RESEARCH CENTER FOR AFRICAN AMERICAN HISTORY AND CULTURE
College of Charleston
125 Bull Street
Charleston, SC 29424-0001
Myrtle G. Glascoe, Ed.D., Director
(803) 727-2009

I.P. STANBACK MUSEUM AND PLANETARIUM
Post Office Box 1691
South Carolina State College
Orangeburg, SC 29117
Leo F. Twiggs, Executive Director
(803) 536-7174

Museums

MANN-SIMONS COTTAGE
1403 Richland Street
Columbia, SC 29201
Ms. Scott Morris, Director
(803) 252-1450

OLD SLAVE MART MUSEUM
Post Office Box 459
Sullivan's Island, SC 29482
Judith Wragg Chase, Educational
  Director
(803) 883-3797

OYOTUNJI AFRICAN VILLAGE
Post Office Box 51
Sheldon, sC 29941
Oseijeman Adefunmi, Diector
(803) 846-8900

**PENDALTON FOUNDATION FOR
  BLACK HISTORY AND CUL-
  TURE**
116 West Queen Street
Pendleton, SC 29670
Annie Ruth Webb-Morse, Director
(803) 646-3792

PENN CENTER
Fogmore
Post Office Box 126
St. Helena Island, SC 29920
Emory Campbell, Director
(803) 838-2235

TENNESSEE

**BECK CULTURAL EXCHANGE
  CENTER**
1927 Dandridge Avenue
Knoxville, TN 37915
Robert Booker, Director
(615) 524-8461

**CHATTANOOGA AFRICAN
  AMERICAN MUSEUM AND
  RESEARCH CENTER**
200 East Martin Luther King Boulevard
Chattanooga, TN 37402
Vilma Scruggs-Fields, Executive
  Director
(615) 267-1076

**THE NATIONAL CIVIL RIGHTS
  MUSEUM**
450 Mulberry Street
Memphis, TN 28103
Juanita Moore, Executive Director
(901) 521-9699

TEXAS

**AFRICAN AMERICAN CUL-
  TURAL HERITAGE CENTER**
Nolan Estes Educational Plaza
3434 S.R.L. Thornton Freeway
Dallas, TX 75224
Robert Edison, Director
(214) 375-7530

**GEORGE WASHINGTON
  CARVER MUSEUM AND
  CULTURAL CENTR**
1165 Angelina Street
Austin, TX 78702
Bernadette M. Phifer, Director
(512) 472-4809

**JUNIOR BLACK ACADEMY OF
  ARTS AND LETTERS, INC.**
650 Griffin Street
Dallas, TX 75202
Curtis King, President
(214) 720-1964

MUSEUM OF AFRICAN AMERI- CAN LIFE AND CULTURE
Post Office Box 150153
Dallas, TX 75315
Dr. Harry Robinson, Jr., Director
(214) 565-9026

VIRGINIA

HAMPTON UNIVERSITY MUSEUM
Hampton University
Hampton, VA 23668
Dr. William R. Harvey, President
(804) 727-5308

HARRISON MUSEUM AND CULTURAL ASSOCIATION
Post Office Box 194
Roanoke, VA 24002
Melody Stovall, Director
(804) 345-4818

TASK FORCE FOR HISTORIC PRESERVATION AND THE MINORITY COMMUNITY
500 North Third Street
Richmond, VA 23219
Preddy Ray, Executive Director
(804) 788-1709

The listings in this directory are available as Mailing Labels. See last page for details.

Museums

© Robert Sengstacke

National Associations

The associations listed in this section represent a broad spectrum of advocacy in America. They work tirelessly addressing critical issues facing the nation's black community.

A. PHILIP RANDOLPH INSTITUTE
1444 Eye Street, N.W., Suite 300
Washington, D.C. 20005
Norman Hill, President
(202) 289-2774

AFRICAN AMERICAN MUSEUM ASSOCIATION
Post Office Box 548
Wilberforce, OH 45384-0548
Jocelyn Robinson-Hubbuch,
   Executive Director
(513) 376-4611

AFRICAN AMERICAN WOMEN'S ASSOCIATION, INC.
Post Office Box 55122,
   Brightwood Station
Washington, D.C. 20011
Mary P. Dougherty, President
(201) 966-6645

AFRICAN HERITAGE STUDIES ASSOCIATION
P. O. Box 1633, Lincolnton Station
New York, Ny 10037
Charshee McIntyre, President
(212) 795-2096

AMERICAN ASSOCIATION OF BLACK WOMEN ENTREPRENEURS, INC. (AABWE)
Post Office Box 13933
Silver Springs, MD 20911
Brenda Alford, President
(301) 565-0258

AMERICAN ASSOCIATION OF BLACKS IN ENERGY
801 Pennsylvania Avenue, S.E.,
   Suite 250
Washington, D.C. 20003
Robert L. Hill, Chairperson
(202) 547-9378

AMERICAN BRIDGE ASSOCIATION
2798 Lakewood Avenue, S.W.
Atlanta, GA 30315
Anita Troy, President
(404) 768-5517

AMERICAN COUNSELING ASSOCIATION
5999 Stevenson Avenue
Alexandria, VA 22304
Dr. Theodore P. Remley, Jr.,
   Chief Executive Officer
(703) 823-9800

AMERICAN HEALTH & BEAUTY AIDS INSTITUTE (AHBAI)
111 East Wacker Drive
Suite 600
Chicago, IL 60601
Geri Duncan Jones, Executive
   Director
(312) 644-6610

National Associations

AMERICAN LEAGUE OF FINANCIAL INSTITUTIONS
1709 New York Avenue, N.W., Suite 801
Washington, D.C. 20006
John Harshaw, President
(202) 628-5624

ASSOCIATED BLACK CHARITIES
105 East 22nd Street, Suite 915
New York, NY 10010
Livingston S. Francis, Executive Director
(212) 777-6060

ASSOCIATES FOR RENEWAL IN EDUCATION, INC.
The Slater School
45 P Street, N.W.
Washington, D.C. 20001
Brenda Strong Nixon, Executive Director
(202) 483-9424

ASSOCIATION FOR MULTI-CULTURAL COUNSELING AND DEVELOPMENT
5999 Stevenson Avenue
Alexandria, VA 22302
Dr. Patrick J. McDonough, Executive Director
(703) 823-9800

ASSOCIATION FOR THE STUDY OF AFRO-AMERICAN LIFE AND HISTORY
1407 Fourteenth Street, N.W.
Washington, D.C. 20005
Gail A. Hansberry, Executive Director
(202) 667-2822

ASSOCIATION OF BLACK ADMISSIONS AND FINANCIAL AID OFFICERS OF THE IVY LEAGUE AND SISTER SCHOOLS, INC.
Post Office Box 1402
Cambridge, MA 02238-1402
Deborah Pointer, Teran Wittingham, Co-Chairs
(401) 863-2378

ASSOCIATION OF BLACK AMERICAN AMBASSADORS
c/o Africare House
440 R Street, N.W.
Washington, D.C. 20001
Dr. Elliott J. Skinner
(202) 462-3614

ASSOCIATION OF BLACK PSYCHOLOGISTS
Post Office Box 55999
Washington, D.C. 20040
Dr. Les Brinson, President
(202) 722-0808

ASSOCIATION OF BLACK SOCIOLOGISTS
Department of Sociology and Anthropology
Howard University
Washington, D.C. 20059
Mary Joyce Green, President
(202) 806-6853

ASSOCIATION OF BLACK WOMEN IN HIGHER EDUCATION, INC.
Fashion Institute
Office of Academic Affairs
227 West 27th Street, Suite C-913
New York, NY 10001
Lenore R. Gall, Ed.D., President

ASSOCIATION OF CARIBBEAN STUDIES
Post Office Box 22202
Lexington, KY 40522
Dr. O.R. Dathorne, CEO
(606) 257-6966

BLACK CAUCUS OF THE AMERICAN LIBRARY ASSOCIATION
c/o Virginia State
Library and Archives
Eleventh Street at Capitol Square
Richmond, VA 23219

BLACK COACHES ASSOCIATION
Post Office Box J
Des Moines, IA
Rudy Washington, Executive Director
(515) 271-2102

BLACK CREATIVE PROFES- SIONALS ASSOCIATION
Post Office Box 34272
Los Angeles, CA 90034
Carole Wade, President
(213) 964-3550

BLACK PSYCHIATRISTS OF AMERICA
2730 Adeline Street
Oakland, CA 94607
Isaac Slaughter, President
(415) 465-1800

BLACKS IN AGRICULTURE, INC.
817 Fourteenth Street, Suite 300A
Sacramento, CA 95814
Drue P. Brown, President
(916) 444-2924

BLACKS IN GOVERNMENT
1820 Eleventh Street, N.W.
Washington, D.C. 20001
Marion A. Bowdin, President
(202) 667-3280

COALITION OF BLACK TRADE UNIONIST
Post Office Box 73120
Washington, D. C. 20056
William Lucy, President
(202) 429-1203

CONFERENCE OF MINORITY PUBLIC ADMINISTRATORS
COMPA-ASPA
1120 G Street, N.W.
Washington, D.C. 20005
Avon Manning, Chairperson
(202) 393-7878

CONFERENCE OF PRINCE HALL MASONS
4311 Portland Avenue
South Minneapolis, MN 55407
Morris S. Miller, Chairman Steering
  Committee
(612) 825-2474

COUNCIL OF NATIONAL ALUMNI ASSOCIATIONS
c/o Bobbie Jones
Delaware State College
Dover, DE 19901
Thomas Mitchell, President
(904) 561-2408

DRIFTERS, INC.
10 Chelsea Court
Neptune, NJ 07753
Sylvia Thomas, President
(908) 774-2724

National Associations

FRONTIERS INTERNATIONAL, INC.
6301 Crittenden Street
Philadelphia, PA 19138
Floyd W. Alston, President
(215) 549-4550

GIRL FRIENDS, INC,
228 Lansing Avenue
Portsmouth, VA 23704
Rachel N. Smith, President
(804) 397-1339

GOSPEL MUSIC WORKSHOP OF AMERICA
Post Office Box 34635
Detroit, MI 48234
Edward D. Smith, Executive Secretary
(313) 989-2340

INTER AMERICAN TRAVEL AGENTS SOCIETY
2000 Lee Road
Cleveland, OH 44118
James Washington, President
(216) 932-7151

INTERNATIONAL ASSOCIATION OF BLACK PROFESSIONAL FIRE FIGHTERS
1025 Connecticut Avenue, N.W., Suite 610
Washington, D.C. 20036
Romeo O. Spaulding, President
(202) 296-0157

INTERNATIONAL BENEVOLENT SOCIETY, INC.
Post Office Box 1276
837 Fifth Avenue
Columbus, GA 31901
James O. Brown, President
(404) 322-5671

INTERNATIONAL BLACK WOMEN'S CONGRESS
1081 Bergen Street, Suite 200
Newark, NJ 07112
LaFrancis Roger-Rose, President
(201) 926-0570

INTERNATIONAL BLACK WRITERS
Post Office Box 1030
Chicago, IL 60690
Mable J. Terrell, Executive Director
(312) 924-3818

THE LINKS, INC.
1200 Massachusetts Avenue, N.W.
Washington, D.C. 20005
Marion Schmaltz Southerly, President
(202) 842-8696

MINORITY NETWORK OF THE AMERICAN SOCIETY FOR TRAINING AND DEVELOPMENT, INC.
1630 Duke Street, Box 1443
Alexandria, VA 22313
Curtis E. Plott, Executive Vice President
(703) 683-8100

NATIONAL ACTION COUNCIL FOR MINORITIES IN ENGINEERING (NACME)
3 West 35th Street, Third Floor
New York, NY 10001
George Campbell, Jr., Ph.D., President
(212) 279-2626

NATONAL ALLIANCE OF BLACK ORGANIZATIONS
1017 East 11th Street
Austin, TX 78702
M.J. Anderson, President
(512) 577-5380

NATIONAL ALLIANCE OF BLACK SCHOOL EDUCATORS
2816 Georgia Avenue, N.W., Suite 4
Washington, D.C. 20001
Ted Kimbrough, Ph.D., President
(202) 483-8323

NATIONAL ALLIANCE OF POSTAL AND FEDERAL EMPLOYEES
1628 Eleventh Street, N.W.
Washington, D.C. 20001
James M. McGee, President
(202) 939-6325

NATIONAL ASSOCIATION FOR EQUAL OPPORTUNITY IN HIGHER EDUCATION (NAFEO)
Lovejoy Building
400 Twelth Street, N.E., Room 207
Washington, D.C. 20002
Samuel L. Myers, President
(205) 543-9111

NATIONAL ASSOCIATION FOR SICKLE CELL DISEASE, INC.
3345 Wilshire Boulevard, Suite 1106
Los Angeles, CA 90010-1880
Lynda K. Anderson, Executive Director

NATIONAL ASSOCIATION FOR THE ADVANCEMENT OF COLORED PEOPLE
4805 Mt. Hope Road
Baltimore, MD 21215
George Carter, Deputy Director
(410) 358-8900

NATIONAL ASSOCIATION OF BENCH AND BAR SPOUSES, INC.
42 LaSalle Avenue
Piedmont, CA 94611
Bamarese P. Wheatly, President
(510) 652-3256

NATIONAL ASSOCIATION OF BLACK ACCOUNTANTS, INC.
220 I Street, N.E.
Washington, D.C. 20002
Beverly Everson-Jones, CPA,
   Executive Director
(202) 546-6222

NATIONAL ASSOCIATION OF BLACK AND MINORITY CHAMBERS OF COMMERCE
5741 Telegraph
Oakland, CA 94609
Oscar J. Coffey, Jr., Executive Director
(415) 601-5741

NATIONAL ASSOCIATION OF BLACK CATHOLIC ADMINISTRATORS
111 Boulevard of the Allies
Pittsburgh, PA 15222
Dr. Veronica Morgan-Lee, President
(412) 456-3170

NATIONAL ASSOCIATION OF BLACK CONSULTING ENGINEERS
6406 Georgia Avenue, N.W.
Washington, D.C. 20012
Morgan Watson, P.E., President
(202) 291-3550

NATIONAL ASSOCIATION OF BLACK HOSPITALITY PRO-FESSIONALS, INC.
Post Office Box 5443
Plainfield, NJ 07060
Mikoel Turner, President
(908) 354-5117

National Associations

NATIONAL ASSOCIATION OF BLACK JOURNALISTS
Post Office Box 17212
Washington, D.C. 20041
Linda A. Edwards, Executive Director
(703) 648-1270

NATIONAL ASSOCIATION OF BLACK OWNED BROADCASTERS, INC.
1730 M Street, N.W., Suite 412
Washington, D.C. 20036
Jim Winston, Executive Director
(202) 463-8970

NATIONAL ASSOCIATION OF BLACK READING AND LANGUAGE EDUCATORS
Post Office Box 51566
Palo Alto, CA 94303
Mary Rhodes Hoover, Ph.D., President

NATIONAL ASSOCIATION OF BLACK REAL ESTATE PROFESSIONALS
Post Office Box 21421
Alexandria, VA 23320-2421
Sherman L. Ragland, II, President

NATIONAL ASSOCIATION OF BLACK SOCIAL WORKERS, INC.
15231 West McNichols Avenue
Detroit, MI 48235
Gerald K. Smith, President
(313) 836-0210

NATIONAL ASSOCIATION OF BLACK WOMEN ATTORNEYS
3711 Macomb Street, N.W.,
  Second Floor
Washington, D.C. 20016
Mabel D. Haden, President
(202) 966-9691

NATIONAL ASSOCIATION OF BLACKS IN CRIMINAL JUSTICE
Post Office Box 66271
Washington, D.C. 20035
Levan Corgon, Chairman
9301) 681-2361

NATIONAL ASSOCIATION OF COLORED WOMEN'S CLUBS, INC.
5808 Sixteenth Street, N.W.
Washington, D.C. 20011
Dr. Delores M. Harris, President
(202) 726-2044

NATIONAL ASSOCIATION OF HEALTH SERVICES EXECUTIVES
50 F Street, N.W.
Suite 1040
Washington, D.C. 20001
Howard T. Jessamy, President
(202) 628-3953

NATIONAL ASSOCIATION OF INVESTMENT COMPANIES
1111 Fourteenth Street, N.W.,
  Suite 700
Washington, D.C. 20005
JoAnn H. Price, President
(202) 289-4336

NATIONAL ASSOCIATION OF MANAGEMENT CONSULTANTS
3101 Euclid Office Plaza, Suite 501
Cleveland, OH 44115
Hosiah Huggins, Jr., President
(216) 431-0303

National Associations

NATIONAL ASSOCIATION OF MARKET DEVELOPERS, INC.
1422 West Peachtree Street, N.W.,
Suite 500
Atlanta, GA 30309
Bunnie Jackson-Ransom, Executive
Director
(404) 892-0244

NATIONAL ASSOCIATION OF MEDIA WOMEN
123-16 126th Avenue
Laurelton, NY 11413
Eleanor Haynes, President
(718) 712-4544

NATIONAL ASSOCIATION OF MILLINERS, DRESSMAKERS & TAILORS, INC.
157 West 126th Street
New York, NY 10027
Alma Goss, President
(212) 666-1320

NATIONAL ASSOCIATION OF MINORITY CONTRACTORS
1333 F Street, N.W., Suite 500
Washington, D.C. 20004
Ralph C. Thomas, III, Executive
Director
(202) 347-8259

NATIONAL ASSOCIATION OF MINORITY MEDIA EXECU-TIVES
1401 Concord Point Lane
Reston, VA 22091
Albert E. Fitzpatrick, Chairman
(703) 709-5245

NATIONAL ASSOCIATION OF MINORITY POLITICAL WOMEN, USA, INC.
6120 Oregon Avenue, N.W.
Washington, D.C. 20015
Mary E. Ivey, National President
(202) 686-1216

NATIONAL ASSOCIATION OF MINORITY WOMEN IN BUSI-NESS
Post Office Box 26412
Kansas City, MO 64196
Inez Kaiser, President
(816) 421-3335

NATIONAL ASSOCIATION OF NEGRO BUSINESS AND PROFESSIONAL WOMEN'S CLUBS, INC.
1806 New Hampshire Ave., N.W.
Washington, D.C. 20009
Ellen Graves, Executive Director
(202) 483-4206

NATIONAL ASSOCIATION OF NEGRO MUSICIANS, INC.
1952 West 115th Street
Chicago, IL 60643
Ona B. Campbell, Executive Secretary
(312) 779-1325

NATIONAL ASSOCIATION OF RESIDENT MANAGEMENT CORPORATIONS
4524 Douglas Street, N.E.
Washington, D.C. 20019
Ronica L. Houston, Executive Director
(202) 397-7002

National Associations

NATIONAL ASSOCIATION OF SECURITIES PROFESSIONALS
c/o A. G. Edwards
222 South Riverside Plaza
Chicago, IL 60606
Joyce Johnson, President

NATIONAL ASSOCIATION OF UNIVERSITY WOMEN
1501 Eleventh Street, N.W.
Washington, D.C. 20001
Ruth Corbin, President
(202) 232-4844

NATIONAL ASSOCIATION OF URBAN BANKERS (NAUB)
810 First Street, N.E., Suite 530
Washington, D.C. 20002
Adele D. Jackson, Executive Director
(202) 842-1433

NATIONAL BANKERS ASSOCIATION
122 C Street, N.W., Suite 580
Washington, D.C. 20001
Bruce Gamble, Executive Director
(202) 531-1900

NATIONAL BAR ASSOCIATION
1225 Eleventh Street, N.W.
Washington, D.C. 20001
John Crump, Executive Director
(202) 842-3900

NATIONAL BEAUTY CULTURISTS LEAGUE, INC.
25 Logan Circle, N.W.
Washington, D.C. 20005
Cleolis Richardson, President
(202) 332-2695

NATIONAL BLACK ASSOCIATION FOR SPEECH, LANGUAGES AND HEARING
South Carolina State College
Box 1596
Orangeburg, SC 29117
Dr. Harold Powell, Director

NATIONAL BLACK CAUCUS OF LOCAL ELECTED OFFICIALS
c/o Joint Center
1301 Pennsylvania Avenue, N.W.,
Suite 400
Washington, D.C. 20004
Carolyn Long Banks, President
(202) 626-3567

NATIONAL BLACK CAUCUS OF STATE LEGISLATORS
444 North Capitol Street, N.W.,
Suite 206
Washington, D.C. 20001
Regis F. Groff, President
(202) 624-5457

NATIONAL BLACK CHAMBERS OF COMMERCE
5741 Telegraph Avenue
Oakland, CA 94609
Oscar J. Coffey, Jr., President
(510) 601-5741

NATIONAL BLACK CHILD DEVELOPMENT INSTITUTE
1023 Fifteenth Street, N.W., Suite 600
Washington, D. C. 20005
Evelyn K. Moore, Executive Director
(202) 387-1281

NATIONAL BLACK COALITION OF FEDERAL AVIATION EMPLOYEES
9470 Timberleaf
Dallas, TX 75243
Evelyn J. Washington, President
(214) 343-2668

NATIONAL BLACK MBA ASSOCIATION
180 North Michigan Avenue,
   Suite 1820
Chicago, IL 60601
Derryl L. Reed, President
(312) 236-2622

NATIONAL BLACK MEDIA COALITION
38 New York Avenue, N.E.
Washington, D.C. 20002
Pluria W. Marshall, Chairman
(202) 387-8155

NATIONAL BLACK NURSES ASSOCIATION, INC.
Post Office Box 1823
Washington, D.C. 20012-1823
Sadako Soto Holmes, Executive
   Director
(202) 393-6870

NATIONAL BLACK POLICE ASSOCIATION
3251 Mt. Pleasant Street, N.W.
Washington, D.C. 20010
Shelby Lanier, Chairman
(202) 457-0563

NATIONAL BLACK PROGRAM-MING CONSORTIUM
929 Harrison Avenue, Suite 104
Columbus, OH 43215
Mable Haddock, Executive Director
(614) 299-5355

NATIONAL BLACK PUBLIC RELATIONS SOCIETY
6565 Sunset Boulevard, Suite 525
Los Angeles, CA 90028
Pat Tobin, President
(213) 856-0287

NATIONAL BLACK REPUBLI-CAN COUNCIL
440 First Street, N.W., Suite 409
Washington, D.C. 20001
Fred Brown, Chairman
(202) 662-1335

NATIONAL BLACK SISTERS' CONFERENCE
7871 Hillside
Oakland, CA 94605-3242
Sister Marie de Porres Taylor, SNJM,
   Exeuctive Director

NATIONAL BLACK UNITED FRONT
700 East Oakwood Boulevard
Chicago, IL 60653
Dr. Conrad Worrill, National Chairman
(312) 670-1784

NATIONAL BLACK UNITED FUND, INC.
50 Park Place, Suite 1538
Newark, NJ 07102
William T. Merritt, President
(201) 643-5122

NATIONAL BLACK WOMEN'S CONSCIOUSNESS-RAISING ASSOCIATION
1906 North Charles Street
Baltimore, MD 21218
Louis Johnson, Chairman of the Board
(301) 685-8392

National Associations

NATIONAL BOWLING ASSOCIATION, INC.
377 Park Avenue, South,
Seventh Floor
New York, NY 10016
Edward Jones, President
(212) 689-8308

NATIONAL BROTHERHOOD OF SKIERS
2575 Donegal Drive
South San Francisco, CA 94080
Sam Lawler, President
(916) 487-4837

NATIONAL BUSINESS LEAGUE
1629 K Street, N.W., Suite 605
Washington, D.C. 20006-1603
Arthur Teele, Jr., President
(202) 466-5483

NATIONAL CAUCUS AND CENTER ON BLACK AGED, INC.
1424 K Street, N.W., Suite 500
Washington, D.C. 20005
Samuel Simmons, President
(202) 637-8400

NATIONAL COALITION OF BLACK MEETING PLANNERS
50 F Street, N.W., Suite 1040
Washington, D.C. 20001
Howard Mills, President
(202) 628-3952

NATIONAL COALITION OF 100 BLACK WOMEN
300 Park Avenue, Seventeenth Floor
New York, NY 10022
Jewell Jackson McCabe, Chairperson
(212) 974-6140

NATIONAL COALITION ON BLACK VOTER PARTICIPATION
1101 Fourteenth Street, N.W.,
Suite 925
Washington, D.C. 20005
Sonia R. Jarvis, Executive Director
(202) 898-2220

NATIONAL CONFERENCE OF BLACK LAWYERS, INC.
126 West 119th Street
New York, NY 10026
Wilhelm H. Joseph, Esquire,
National Director
(212) 864-4000

NATIONAL CONFERENCE OF BLACK MAYORS, INC.
1430 West Peachtree Street, N.W.,
Suite 700
Atlanta, GA 30309
Michelle D. Kourouma, Executive
Diector
(404) 892-0127

NATIONAL CONFERENCE OF BLACK POLITICAL SCIENTISTS
Department of History and Political
Science
Albany State College
Albany, GA 31705
Dr. Joseph Silver, President
(912) 439-4870

NATIONAL COUNCIL FOR BLACK STUDIES
Ohio State University
1800 Cannon Drive
1030 Lincoln Tower
Columbus, OH 43210
Jacqueline Wade, Ph.D., Director
(614) 291-1035

NATIONAL COUNCIL OF NEGRO WOMEN, INC.
1211 Connecticut Ave., N.W.,
Suite 702
Washington, D.C. 20036
Dorothy Height, President
(202) 659-0006

NATIONAL COUNCIL OF URBAN LEAGUE GUILDS
500 East 62nd Street, Sixth Floor
New York, NY 10021
Mae Cleveland, President
(212) 310-9223

NATIONAL DENTAL ASSOCIATION
5506 Connecticut Avenue, N.W.,
Suite 24-25
Washington, D.C. 20015
Robert Johns, Executive Director
(202) 244-7555

NATIONAL ECONOMIC ASSO-CIATION
Michigan Business School
University of Michigan
Ann Arbor, MI 48109-1234
Alfred L. Edwards, Secretary/Treasurer
(313) 763-0121

NATIONAL FORUM FOR BLACK PUBLIC ADMINISTRATOR
777 N. Capitol St., N.E., Suite 807
Washington, D.C. 20002
Quentin Lawson, Executive Director
(202) 408-9300

NATIONAL FUNERAL DIREC-TORS AND MORTICIANS ASSOCIATON, INC.
102 Mount Vernon Avenue
Mount Vernon, NY 10550
William Russo, President
(914) 668-0422

NATIONAL INSURANCE ASSOCIATION
Post Office Box 53230
Chicago, IL 60653
John W. Mardis, Sr., President
(312) 924-3308

NATIONAL MEDICAL ASSOCIATION
1012 Tenth Street, N.W.
Washington, D.C. 20001
Richard Butcher, M.D., President
(202) 347-1895

NATIONAL MINORITY BUSINESS COUNCIL, INC.
235 East 42nd Street
New York, NY 10017
John F. Robinson, President
(212) 573-2385

NATIONAL MINORITY SUPPLIERS DEVELOPMENT COUNCIL, INC.
15 West 39th Street, Ninth Floor
New York, NY 10018
Harriet R. Mitchell, President
(212) 944-2430

NATIONAL NAVAL OFFICERS ASSOCIATION
Post Office Box 46256
Washington, D.C. 20050
Captain J. Rodger Bailey, President
(800) 772-6662

NATIONAL NEWSPAPER PUB-LISHERS ASSOCIATION
529 Fourteenth Street, N.W.
Suite 948
Washington, D.C. 20045
Robert W. Bogle, President
(202) 662-7323

National Associations

NATIONAL OPTOMETRIC ASSOCIATION
2830 South Indiana Avenue
Chicago, IL 60616
Dr. Terrance Ingraham, president
(312) 791-0186

NATIONAL ORGANIZATION FOR THE PROFESSIONAL ADVANCEMENT OF BLACK CHEMISTS AND CHEMICAL ENGINEERS
c/o Department of Chemistry
Howard Univerity
525 Howard Street
Washington, D.C. 20059
Clarence Tucker, Chairman
(202) 269-4129

NATIONAL ORGANIZATION OF BLACK COUNTY OFFICIALS, INC.
440 First Street, N.W., Suite 500
Washington, D.C. 20001
Crandall O. Jones, Executive Director
(202) 347-6953

NATIONAL ORGANIZATION OF BLACK LAW ENFORCEMENT EXECUTIVES
908 Pennsylvania Avenue, S.E.
Washington, D.C. 20003
Cassandra E. Johnson, Executive
    Director
(202) 546-8811

NATIONAL ORGANIZATION OF MINORITY ARCHITECTS
120 Ralph McGill Boulevard, N.E.
Atlanta, GA 30308
William Stanley, III, President
(404) 876-3055

NATIONAL PAN-HELLENIC COUNCIL
Post Office Box 78044
Nashville, Tn 37307-8044
Dr. Ada Jackson, President
(615) 329-1655

NATIONAL PHARMACEUTICAL ASSOCIATION, INC.
Post Office Box 934
Howard University
Washington, D.C. 20059
James Tyson, Executive Director
(202) 636-6544

NATIONAL POLITICAL CONGRESS OF BLACK WOMEN
Post Office Box 411
Rancocas, NJ 08073
Portia Dempsey, Executive Director
(609) 871-1500

NATIONAL PRESS PHOTOGRAPHERS ASSOCIATION, INC.
3200 Croasdaile Drive, Suite 306
Durham, NC 27705
Charles H. Cooper, Executive Director
(919) 383-7246

NATIONAL RAINBOW COALITION
1700 K Street, N.W., Suite 800
Washington, D.C. 20006
Rev. Jesse L. Jackson, President
(202) 728-1180

NATIONAL SOCIETY OF BLACK ENGINEERS
1454 Duke Street
Alexandria, VA 22314
Flo Morehead, Executive Director
(703) 549-2207

NATIONAL SOCIETY OF CERTIFIED PUBLIC ACCOUNTANTS
1313 East Sibley Boulevard, Suite 107
Dolton, IL 60419
Eugene Varnado, President
(312) 849-0098

NATIONAL STUDENT BUSINESS LEAGUE
7226 Forest Road
Kentland, MD 20785
Amy Green, Executive Director
(202) 895-3926

NATIONAL TECHNICAL ASSOCIATION, INC.
Post Office Box 7045
Washington, D.C. 20032
Carrington Stewart, President
(202) 829-6100

NATIONAL UNITED AFFILIATED BEVERAGE ASSOCIATION
5429 Market Street
Philadelphia, PA 19139
Joseph T. Finn, President
(215) 748-5670

NATIONAL URBAN AFFAIRS COUNCIL
2350 Adam Clayton Powell Boulevard
New York, NY 10030
Sandra Davis Houston, President
(914) 694-4000

NATIONAL URBAN COALITION
8601 Georgia Avenue
Silver Spring, MD 20910
Ramona Edelin, President
(301) 495-4999

NATIONAL URBAN LEAGUE
500 East 62nd Street
New York, NY 10021
John E. Jacobs, President
(212) 310-9212

ORGANIZATIONS OF BLACK AIRLINE PILOTS, INC.
20 North Van Brunt Street, Suite 200
Englewood, NJ 07631
William Norwood, President
(201) 568-8145

PAN-AFRICAN BOOKSELLERS, AUTHORS AND PUBLISHERS ASSOCIATION
51 Court Street
White Plains, NY 10603
Carrie Coard, President
(914) 681-0484

SAMMY DAVIS, JR., NATIONAL LIVER INSTITUTE
Medical Science Building, Room I-506
185 South Orange Avenue
Newark, NJ 07103-2757
Ronald Wellington Brown, Executive
Vice President
(201) 456-4535

STUDENT NATIONAL MEDICAL ASSOCIATION
1012 Tenth Street, N.W.
Washington, D.C. 20001
Annette McLane, Executive Director
(202) 371-1616

UNITED AMERICAN PROGRESS ASSOCIATION
701 East 79th Street
Chicago, IL 60619
Webb Evans, President
(312) 955-8112

National Associations

**369TH VETERANS ASSOCIA-
TION, INC.**
One 369th Plaza
New York, NY 10037
Samuel W. Phillips, President
(212) 281-3308

**WORLD AFRICA CHAMBER OF
COMMERCE**
1725 K Street, N.W., Suite 410
Washington, D.C. 20006
Nana Ohene Darko, President
(202) 223-3244

Political Officeholders and Organizations

The individuals and organizations listed in this section represent the political leadership of millions of Black Americans in both political parties.

Democratic National Committee Black Caucus

WILLIE BAKER
UFCW
1775 K Street N.W.
Washington, D.C. 20006-1598

WILLIE BARROW
920 East 50th Street
Chicago, IL 60615

ODELL BARRY
10858 Roseanna Drive
North Glen, CO 80234

CLARENCE BLOUNT
3410 Copley Road, Second Floor
Baltimore, MD 21215

WILLIAM BOWEN
Statehouse, First Floor
Columbus, OH 43215

RONALD BROWN
430 South Capitol Street, S.E.
Washington, D.C. 20003

WILLIE BROWN
State Capitol, Room 219
Sacramento, CA 95814

JACQUELINE BUTLER
4545 Holly Place
Saint Louis, MO 63115

YOLANDA CARAWAY
65 Hawthrone Court, N.E.
Washington, D.C. 20017

ED COLE
Post Office Box 629
Jackson, MS 39205

CARDISS COLLINS
400 Madison Street, Apartment 1508
Alexandria, VA 22314

VIVIAN COOK
126-44 144th Street
Jamica, NY 11436

SHERMAN COPELIN
107 Harbor Circle
New Orleans, LA 70126

ALICE CORSEY
353 Heather Ridge Apartments
Mantual, NJ 08051

JEANETTE COUNCIL
1844 Cascade Street
Fayetteville, NC 28301

INEZ CRUTCHFIELD
3507 Geneva Court
Nashville, TN 37209

VIVIAN DAVIS FIGURES
2054 Clemente Court
Mobile, AL 36617

PAULA DORSEY
3403 North 44th Street
Milwaukee, WI 53216

ROSETTA DOTSON
888 East 56 Highway, Number 312
Olathe, KS I66061

Political Officeholders and Organizations

AL EDWARDS
3108 South MacGregor
Houston, TX 77021

HERMAN FARRELL
159-00 Riverside Drive
New York, NY 10032

ALEXANDER FARRELLY
Government House
Charlotte Amalie
St. Thomas, VI 00801

JOEL FERGUSON
Post Office Box 26126
Lansing, MI 48909

DEAN FERRIER
3, Route De Chaufour, 78270
Crevent Yvelines, France

GEORGE FLEMING
1100 Lake Washington Boulevard,
    South
Seattle, WA 98144

WILSON FROST
10816 South Parnell Avenue
Chicago, IL 60628

HARVEY GANTT
517 North Poplar Street
Charlotte, NC 28202

DONNA GREEN
Richmond Plot, 102
Christiansted
St. Croix, VI 00820

PAMELA GREEN
Post Office Box 1355
Morningside Station
New York, NY 10026

VERA HALL
2819 Hillsdale Road
Baltimore, MD 21207

ALICE HARDEN
3247 Copperfield Street
Jackson, MS 39209

RUTH HARPER
1427 West Erie Avenue
Philadelphia, PA 19140

PHYLLIS HART
1091 Elsworth Avenue
Columbus, OH 43206

JEAN HERVEY
8211 Geyer Springs Road, Number 8
Little Rock, AR 72209

STANLEY HILL
125 Barclay Street
District Council 37
New York, NY 10007

CATHERINE HUDGINS
11301 Wedge Drive
Reston, VA 22090

K. LEROY IRVIS
205 Tennyson Avenue
Pittsburgh, PA 15213

JESSE JACKSON
930 East 50th Street
Chicago, IL 60615

MAYNARD JACKSON
55 Trinity Avenue, Number 2400
Atlanta, GA 30335

SHARPE JAMES
920 Broad Street
Newark, NJ 07102

Political Officeholders and Organizations

GLORIA JOHNSON
1126 Sixteenth Street, N.W.
Number 601
Washington, D.C. 20036

ANNETTE JONES
5422 Second Street, N.W.
Washington, D.C. 20011

BENJAMIN LAMBERT
904 North First Street
Richmond, VA 23219

MARTHA LOVE
1846 West Cherry Street
Milwaukee, WI 53205

LEON LYNCH
United Steelworkers of America
Five Gateway Center
Pittsburgh, PA 15222

RHINE L. MCLIN
1130 Germantown Street
Dayton, OH 45408
(513) 222-7821

IOLA MCGOWAN
5839 West Midway Park
Chicago, IL 60644

CORA MCGRUDER
11207 South King Drive
Chicago, IL 60628

VICKI MILES LAGRANGE
515 Central Park Drive
Number 400
Oklahoma City, OK 73154

JUANITA MILLER
2965 Sunset Lane
Suitland, MD 20746

RAY MILLER
3040 Elbern Avenue
Columbus, OH 43209

GARRY NORRIS
13 Daybreak Lane
Westport, CT 06880

HAZEL OBEY
Post Office Box 6095
Austin, TX 78762

TERRANCE PITTS
2011 West Capital
Milwaukee, WI 53206

SHARON PRATT KELLY
The District Building
1350 Pennsylvania Avenue, N.W.
Washington, D.C. 20004

HUBERT PRICE
583 Pearsall
Pontiac, MI 48341

JESSIE RATTLEY
529 Ivy Avenue
Newport News, VA 23607

ALZO REDDICK
725 South Goldwyn Avenue
Orlando, FL 32805

EVELYN RICHARDSON
6908 Kedron Street
Pittsburgh, PA 15208

ABDULLAH SALEEM
Post Office Box 3233
Christiansted
St. Croix, VI 00820

LOTTIE SHACKELFORD
1720 Abigail Street
Little Rock, AR 72204

Political Officeholders and Organizations

MARTHA SINGLETON
3029 Gardenia Drive
Fort Worth, TX 76119

CALVIN SMYRE
Post Office Box 181
Columbus, GA 31902

MILDRED STALLINGS
19390 Klinger Street
Detroit, MI 48234

MARYLYN STAPLETON
Veterans Drive Station
Post Office Box 3739
St. Thomas, VI 00803

BEATRICE THOMPSON
1111 Southwood Street
Anderson, SC 39624

JANICE THURMOND
250 Cleveland Road, Number 245
Bogart, GA 30622

BILL THURSTON
437 Southport Way
Vallejo, CA 94591

C. DELORES TUCKER
6700 Lincoln Drive
Philadelphia, PA 19119

BEA UNDERWOOD
218 Seventh Street, S.E.
Washington, D.C. 20003

FRANKYE UNDERWOOD
Post Office Box 2144
Jasper, AL 35501

VENITA VINSON
2685 Fairfax Street
Denver, CO 80207

ROSALEE WALKER
1220 Glacier Avenue, Number 208
Juneau, AK 99801

DORIS WARD
400 Van Ness
City Hall, Room 235
San Francisco, CA 94102

MAXINE WATERS
1207 Longworth House Office Building
Washington, D.C. 20515

VERNON WATKINS
14113 Rippling Brock Drive
Silver Spring, MD 20906

DIANE WATSON
5331 Hartcourt Avenue
Los Angeles, CA 90043

BEA WILLIAMS
1940 West Atherton Road
Flint, MI 48507

JOSLYN WILLIAMS
1311 Delaware Avenue, S.W.
Washington, D.C. 20024

SHERYL WILLIAMS
4616 Crest, S.E.
Albuquerque, NM 87018

JOHN WILSON
1350 Pennsylvania Avenue, N.W.
Washington, D.C. 20004

DARIA WINTER
1355 Underwood Street, N.W.
Washington, D.C. 20012

COLEMAN YOUNG
1126 City-County Building
Detroit, MI 48226

Political Officeholders and Organizations

The following section is a partial listing of Black Mayors representing American cities with Populations of 10,000 people or more.

Mayors

ALABAMA

MAYOR RICHARD ARRINGTON, JR.
City Hall
710 North 20th Street
Birmingham, AL 35203
Population - 280,000

MAYOR JOHNNY FORD
Municipal Complex
101 Fonville Street
Tuskegee, AL 36083
Population - 13,327

MAYOR LARRY LANDFORD
4701 Gary Avenue
Fairfield, AL 35064
Population - 13,040

MAYOR MITCHELL QUITMAN
1800 North Third Avenue
Bessemer, AL 35020
Population- 31,000

ARIZONA

MAYOR COY PAYNE
25 South Arizona Place, Suite 301
Chandler, AZ 85225
Population - 96,865

CALIFORNIA

MAYOR TOM L. BRADLEY
City Hall
200 North Spring Street, Room 305E
Los Angeles, CA 90012
Population - 3,500,000

MAYOR JIM BUSBY
City Hall
14343 Civic Drive
Victorville, CA 92392
Population - 30,000

MAYOR ELIHU HARRIS
1 City Hall Plaza
Oakland, CA 94612

MAYOR GEORGE L. LIVINGSTON
City Hall
Post Office Box 4046
Richmond, CA 94804

MAYOR LANCE MCCLAIR
City Hall
Post Office Box 810
Seaside, CA 93955
Population - 36,567

MAYOR WALTER TUCKER, III
205 South Willowbrook
Compton, CA 90220
Population - 81,286

MAYOR ED VINCENT
1 Mancaster Boulevard
Inglewood, CA 90301
Population - 94,245

MAYOR WILLIAM VINE
2415 University Avenue
East Palo Alto, CA 94303
Population - 20,000

Political Officeholders and Organizations

MAYOR BILLY R. WHITE
1131 Menlo Oaks Drive
Menlo Park, CA 94025
Population - 26,369

COLORADO

MAYOR WELLINGTON E. WEBB
City and County Building, Room 305
Denver, CO 80202

CONNECTICUT

MAYOR JOHN DANIELS
95 Orange Street
New Haven, CT 06510

MAYOR CARRIE S. PERRY
City Hall
550 Main Street
Hartford, CT 06103
Population - 139,000

MAYOR JOSEPH M. SUGGS
City Hall
800 Bloomfield Avenue
Bloomfield, CT 06002
Population - 20,000

DISTRICT OF COLUMBIA

MAYOR SHARON PRATT KELLY
1350 Pennsylvania Avenue, N.W.
Room 520
Washington, D.C. 20004
Population - 638,333

The listings in this directory are available as Mailing Labels. See last page for details.

FLORIDA

MAYOR ROBERT B. INGRAM
777 Sharazad Boulevard
Opa-Locka, FL 33054
Population - 16,000

MAYOR WALTER THOMPKINS
Post Office Box 527
Pierson, FL 32080
Population - 17,000

MAYOR CLARA K. WILLIAMS
Post Office Box 10628
Riviera Beach, FL 33404
Population - 30,000

GEORGIA

MAYOR MAYNARD JACKSON
City Hall, Suite 2400
68 Mitchell Street
Atlanta, GA 30335
Population - 394,017

ILLINOIS

MAYOR CHARLES BOX
City Hall
425 East State Street
Rockford, IL 61104

MAYOR GORDON D. BUSH
City Hall
301 East Broadway
East St. Louis, IL 62201
Population - 43,000

MAYOR BOBBY E. THOMPSON
City of North Chicago
1850 Lewis Avenue
North Chicago, IL 60064
Population - 14,000

Political Officeholders and Organizations

MAYOR DAVID JOHNSON
Harvey Municipal Center
15320 Broadway
Harvey, IL 60426
Population - 30,000

MAYOR EVANS MILLER
16313 Kedzie Avenue
Markham, IL 60426

MAYOR DONALD WILLIAMS
115 South Fifth Avenue
Maywood, IL 60193'

INDIANA

MAYOR THOMAS V. BARNES
Municipal Building
401 Broadway
Gary, IN 46402
Population - 116,646

LOUISIANA

MAYOR SIDNEY BARTHELEMY
City Hall
Civic Center
New Orleans, LA 70112
Population 496,938

MAYOR CLARENCE W. HAWKINS
City Hall
Post Office Box 431
Bastrop, LA 71221
Population - 15,046

MAYOR JOHN W. JOSEPH
Post Office Box 712
Opelousas, LA 70570
Population - 18,151

MAINE

WILLIAM D. BURNEY, JR.
6 Crookey Street
Augusta, ME 04330
Population - 22,000

MASSACHUSETTS

MAYOR KENNETH E. REEVES
795 Massachusetts Avenue
Cambridge, MA 02139
Population - 95,000

MARYLAND

MAYOR KURT SCHMOKE
City Hall
100 North Holliday Street
Baltimore, MD 21202
Population- 736,014

MICHIGAN

MAYOR EDWARD BIVINS, JR.
City Hall
2121 Inkster Road
Inkster, MI 48141
Population - 35,190

MAYOR EMMA HULL
City Hall, 200 Wall Street
Benton Harbor, MI 49022

MAYOR WOODROW STANLEY
1101 South Saginaw Street
Flint, MI 48502

MAYOR HOLLAND E. WALLACE
450 Wide Track Drive, East
Pontiac, MI 48342
Population - 71,166

Political Officeholders and Organizations

MAYOR HENRY NICKLEBERRY
Office of the Mayor
City Hall
1315 South Washington Avenue
Saginaw, MI 48601
Population - 70,000

MAYOR LINSEY PORTER
City Hall
30 Gerald Avenue
Highland Park, MI 48203
Population - 27,000

MAYOR ROBERT WARREN
2724 Peck Street
Muskegon Heights, MI 49442
Population - 14,611

MAYOR COLEMAN YOUNG
1125 City County Building
Detroit, MI 48226
Population - 1,027,974

MAYOR BEVERLY A. MOORE
City Commission
241 West South Street
Kalamazoo, MI 49007-4796

MISSISSIPPI

MAYOR E. S. BISHOP, SR.
Post Office Box 352
Corinth, MS 38834
Population - 15,000

MAYOR HENRY W. ESPY
Post Office Box 940
Clarksdale, MS 38614
Population - 19,526

MAYOR KENNIE MIDDLETON
Post Office Box 370
Fayette, MS 39069

MAYOR ROBERT M. WALKER
City Hall
Post Office Box 150
Vicksburg, MS 39181-0150

MISSOURI

MAYOR EMANUEL CLEAVER, II
City Hall
414 East 12th Street, 29th Floor
Kansas City, MO 64106
Population - 300,000

MAYOR LOTTIE MAE WILLIAMS
2803 Maywood
Velda City, MO 63121

NEW JERSEY

MAYOR ROBERT L. BROWN
29 North Day Street
Orange, NJ 07050
Population - 33,000

MAYOR DOREATHA CAMPBELL
Borough Hall
Salem Road
Willingboro, NJ 08046

MAYOR CARDELL COOPER
City Hall
44 City Hall Plaza
East Orange, NNJ 07019
Population - 77,690

MAYOR SHARPE JAMES
City Hall, Room 200
920 Broad Street
Newark, NJ 07102

Political Officeholders and Organizations

MAYOR SAMUEL T. MC GHEE
Municipal Building
Liberty & Hillside Avenue
Hillside, NJ 07205

MAYOR RALPH N. MILTEER
1548 Maple Avenue
Hillsdale, NJ 07205

MAYOR HAROLD W. MITCHELL
Plainfield City Hall
515 Watchung Avenue
Plainfield, NJ 07061

MAYOR DOUGLAS PALMER
City Hall
319 East State Street
Trenton, NJ 08608

MAYOR AARON THOMPSON
City Hall
Camden, NJ 08101

NEW YORK

MAYOR RONALD A. BLACKWOOD
City Hall
Roosevelt Square
Mt. Vernon, NY 10550
Population - 67,200

MAYOR AUDREY L. CAREY
City Hall
83 Broadway
Newburgh, NY 12550

MAYOR DAVID DINKINS
City Hall
New York, NY 10007
Population - 7,322,564

MAYOR JAMES GARNER
Incorporated Village of Hempstead
999 Nicholas Court
Hempstead, NY 11550
Population - 40,000

NORTH CAROLINA

MAYOR LEANDER MORGAN
Post Office Box 1129
New Bern, NC 28560
Population - 18,000

OHIO

MAYOR WALLCE D. DAVIES
14340 Euclid Avenue
East Cleveland, OH 44112

MAYOR RICHARD C. DIXON
Post Office Box 22
Dayton, OH 45401
Population - 182,044

MAYOR JAMES HUMPHREY
612 Park Street
Sidney, OH 45365
Population 17,657

MAYOR DWIGHT TILLERY
City Hall
801 Plum Street
Cincinnati, OH 45202

MAYOR MICHAEL R. WHITE
Office of the Mayor
601 Lakeside Avenue
Cleveland, OH 44114
Population - 505,616

Political Officeholders and Organizations

PENNSYLVANIA

MAYOR BARBARA B. SHEPPARD
Fifth Welsh Street
Chester, PA 19013
Population - 46,000

MAYOR ROBERT REID
City Hall
60 West Emaus Street
Middletown, PA 17057
Population - 10,122

MAYOR ROBERT L. PITTS
605 Ross Avenue
Wilkinsburg, PA 15221

TENNESSEE

MAYOR W. W. HERENTON
125 North Mid-American Mall
Memphis, TN 38103
Population - 610,337

VIRGINIA

MAYOR LAWRENCE A. DAVIES
Post Office Box 7447
Fredericksburg, VA 22404
Population - 15,322

MAYOR NOEL TAYLOR
215 Church Avenue
Roanoke, VA 24017
Population - 96,397

MAYOR WALTER T. KENNEY
City Hall
900 East Broad Street, Room 201
Richmond, VA 23219
Population - 219,214

WASHINGTON

MAYOR NORMAN B. RICE
1200 Municipal Building
600 Fourth Avenue
Seattle, WA 98104
Population - 497,200

WEST VIRGINIA

MAYOR CHARLENE MARSHALL
417 White Avenue
389 Spruce Street
Morgantown, WV 26505
Population - 26,000

WISCONSIN

MAYOR FRANCES HUNTLEY COOPER
Fitchburg
2377 South Fish Hatchery Road
Madison, WI 53711
Population - 15,648

Political Officeholders and Organizations

Members of Congress

HONORABLE LUCIEN BLACKWELL
1725 Longworth House Office Building
Washington, D.C. 20515
(202) 225-4401

HONORABLE BILL CLAY
2470 Rayburn House Office Building
Washington, D.C. 20515
(202) 225-2406

HONORABLE BARBARA ROSE-COLLINS
1541 Longworth House Office Building
Washington, D.C. 20515
(202) 225-5126

HONORABLE CARDISS COLLINS
2264 Rayburn House Office Building
Washington, D.C. 20515

HONORABLE JOHN CONYERS
2426 Rayburn House Office Building
Washington, D.C. 20515
(202) 225-5126

HONORABLE RONALD L. DELLUMS
2136 Rayburn House Office Building
Washington, D.C. 20515
(202) 225-2661

HONORABLE JULIAN C. DIXON
2400 House Office Building
Washington, D.C. 20515
(202) 225-7084

HONORABLE MERVYN M. DYMALLY
1717 Longworth House Office Building
Washington, D.C. 20515
(202) 225-5425

HONORABLE MIKE ESPY
332 Cannon House Office Building
Washington, D.C. 20515
(202) 225-5876

HONORABLE FLOYD H. FLAKE
1034 Longworth House Office Building
Washington, D.C. 20515
(202) 225-3461

HONORABLE HAROLD E. FORD
2305 Rayburn House Office Building
Washington, D.C. 20515
(202) 225-3256

HONORABLE GARY A. FRANKS
1609 Longworth House Office Building
Washington, D.C. 20515

HONORABLE WILLIAM J. JEFFERSON
506 Cannon House Office Building
Washington, D.C. 20515
(202) 225-6636

HONORABLE JOHN LEWIS
329 Cannon House Office Building
Washington, D.C. 20515
(202) 225-3801

HONORABLE KWEISI MFUME
217 Cannon House Office Building
Washington, D.C. 20515
(202) 225-4741

HONORABLE ELEANOR HOLMES NORTON
1631 Longworth House Office Building
Washington, D.C. 20515

HONORABLE MAJOR R. OWENS
114 Cannon House Office Building
Washington, D.C. 20515
(202) 225-6231

Political Officeholders and Organizations

HONORABLE DONALD M. PAYNE
417 Cannon House Office Building
Washington, D.C. 20515
(202) 225-3436

HONORABLE CHARLES B. RANGLE
2252 Rayburn House Office Building
Washington, D.C. 20515
(202) 225-3436

HONORABLE LOUIS STOKES
2365 Rayburn House Office Building
Washington, D.C. 20515
(202) 225-7032

HONORABLE EDOLPHUS TOWNS
1726 Longworth House Office Building
Washington, D.C. 20515
(202) 225-5936

HONORABLE CRAIG A. WASHINGTON
1711 Longworth House Office Building
Washington, D.C. 20515
(202) 225-3816

HONORABLE MAXINE WATERS
1207 Longworth House Office Building
Washington, D.C. 20515
(202) 225-2201

HONORABLE ALAN WHEAT
1210 Longworth House Office Building
Washington, D.C. 20515
(202) 225-4535

The listings in this directory are available as Mailing Labels. See last page for details.

National Black Republican Leadership

RUBY ABEBE
637 Independence
Waterloo, IA 50703

JUDIS R. ANDREWS
7035 South Central Avenue
Suite 2
Phoenix, AZ 85040

LUTHER BENJAMIN
Post Office Box 1514
St. Thomas, VI 00801

GORHAM L. BLACK
Pennsylvania Department of Aging
231 State Street, Sixth Floor
Harrisburg, PA 17101

ULYSSES W. BOYKIN
17224 Fairfield Street
Detroit, MI 48221

FRED BROWN
10-16 East Richman Plaza
Bronx, NY 10453

PAULA BROWN
6304 Moonglow Drive
Dallas, TX 75241

CARLOS CAMPBELL
Inter-American Development Bank
Department of Treasury
808 Seventeenth Street, N.W.
Washington, D.C. 20577

HONORABLE JOANNE COLLINS
4030 Belle Fontaine
Kansas City, MO 64130

Political Officeholders and Organizations

SAMUEL J. CORNELIUS
Department of Agriculture
12th and Jefferson Drive, S.W.
Washington, D.C. 20250

MRS. LE GREE S. DANIELS
1715 Glenside Drive
Harrisburg, PA 17109

ROY B. DUNN
804 Crest Drive
Charleston, WV 25311

JANET EARL
17525 Tuscan Drive
Granada Hills, CA 91344

WHITTIE ENGLISH
English Enterprises, Inc.
248 Forest Avenue
Englewood, NJ 07631

ROBERT FRANCIS
192 Brookside Avenue
Roosevelt, NY 11575

WENDELL FREELAND, ES-QUIRE
564 Forbes Avenue
Pittsburgh, PA 15219

CLAIRE FREEMAN
Office of the Secretary
Department of Defense
The Pentagon
Washington, D.C. 20301

CHERYL GARRETT
3966 Weaver Road
Memphis, TN 39109

VERA GUNN
6466 Ross Street
Philadelphia, PA 19119

CONNIE MACK HIGGINS
627 East Street, N.W., Suite 300
Washington, D.C. 20004

CLEVELAND JOHNSON
133 Millard Avenue
West Babylon, NY 11704

FRANK PAT MARSHALL
1106 South Nebraska
Marion, IN 46592

RUTH MOSLEY
Post Office Box 20101
Jackson, MS 39209

TOM MOSS
1835 Assembly Street
Columbia, SC

WILLIAM F. PICKARD, PH.D.
2990 West Grand Boulevard, M-15
Dearborn, MI 48202

JACK E. ROBINSON
61 Arborway
Boston, MA 02130

ROOSEVELT O. RIDGWAY
1902 Chelan Street
Flint, MI 48503

MC KINLEY SHEPHARD
Post Office Box 1773
Lubbock, TX 79403

Political Officeholders and Organizations

NILA STOVALL
Executive Assistant to the Deputy
  Undersecretary,
Department of Labor
200 Constitution Avenue, N.W.
Washington, D.C. 20210

WILLIAM STUBBS
559 Centre Street
South Orange, NJ 07079

REV. NORRIS SYDNOR
Booker T. Washington Foundation
1010 Massachusetts Avenue, N.W.
Washington, D.C. 20001

SYLVESTER VAUGHNS
7616 Greenleaf Road
Palmer Park, MD 20785

MILTON WHITE
2924 Handy Drive, N.W.
Atlanta, GA 30318

JOHN L. WILKS
Post Office Box 57153
Washington, D.C. 20037

LUTHER WOODWARD
1723 West Independence Avenue
Tulsa, OK 74127

Political Organizations

**ALABAMA LEGISLATIVE
  BLACK CAUCUS**
Alabama State House
11 Union Street
Montgomery, AL 36130
George Perdue, Chairperson
(205) 242-7778

ALASKA BLACK CAUCUS
Post Office Box 103342
Anchorage, AK 99510
Sterling Taylor, President
(907) 272-5951

**ARKANSAS BLACK LEGISLA-
  TIVE CAUCUS**
State Capitol
Little Rock, AR 72203
Rep. Irma Hunter Brown, Convener
(501) 375-7771

**BLACK AND PUERTO RICAN
  LEGISLATIVE CAUCUS**
Post Office Box 2528
Empire Plaza Station
Albany, NY 12220
Albert Vann, Chairman
(518) 455-5347

**BLACK ELECTED DEMOCRATS
  OF OHIO (BEDO)**
37 West Broad Street, Suite 430
Columbus, OH 43215
Dana Mattison, Executive Director
(614) 341-6912

**CALIFORNIA LEGISLATIVE
  BLACK CAUCUS**
State Capitol
Room 4040
Sacramento, CA 95814
Curtis Tucker, Jr., Chairperson

**CONGRESSIONAL BLACK
  CAUCUS**
House Annex Number 2, Room 344
Third and D Streets, S.W.
Washington, D.C. 20515
Amelia Parker, Executive Director
(202) 226-7790

Political Officeholders and Organizations

CONGRESSIONAL BLACK CAUCUS FOUNDATION, INC.
1004 Pennsylvania Avenue, S.E.
Washington, D.C. 20003
Randalyn Kayne, Acting Director
(202) 543-8767

CONNECTICUT LEGISLATIVE BLACK AND PUERTO RICAN CAUCUS
State Capitol
Hartford, CT 06106
Ernest E. Newton, II, Chairperson
(203) 240-8585

DEMOCRATIC NATIONAL COMMITTEE BLACK CAUCUS
6700 Lincoln Drive
Philadelphia, PA 19119
Dr. C. Delores Tucker, Chairperson
(215) 842-1333

FLORIDA CONFERENCE OF BLACK LEGISLATORS
14251 N.W. 41st Avenue
Opa Locka, FL 33054
Willie Logan, Chairman
(305) 681-0008

GEORGIA LEGISLATIVE BLACK CAUCUS
Georgia State Capitol, Room 401E2
Post Office Box 38028
Atlanta, GA 30334
Representative Charles W. Walker,
   Chairman
(404) 651-5569

GREATER FAIRBANK BLACK CAUCUS
136 Pepperdine Drive
Fairbanks, AK 99709
Darlene Haymon, President
(907) 479-4697

ILLINOIS LEGISLATIVE BLACK CAUCUS
Post Office Box 641255
Chicago, IL 60664-1255
Rep. Robert LeFlore, Chairman
(312) 261-0189

INDIANA BLACK LEGISLATIVE CAUCUS
State House
Indianapolis, IN 46204
Rep. Hurley C. Goodall, Chairperson
(317) 232-9816

IOWA LEGISLATIVE BLACK CAUCUS
2500 Harding Road, Suite 4
Des Moines, IA 50310
Thomas Baker, Chairman
(515) 255-9325

KANSAS BLACK LEGISLATIVE CAUCUS
c/o Representative Sherman Jones
3736 Weaver Drive
Kansas City, KS 66104
Rep. Norman E. Justice, Chairman
(913) 296-2391

LOUISIANA LEGISLATIVE BLACK CAUCUS
Post Office Box 44003
Baton Rouge, LA 70804
Representative Dean Jones,
   Chairperson
(504) 342-7342

MARYLAND LEGISLATIVE BLACK CAUCUS
3518 Everest Drive
Hillcrest Heights, MD 20748
Delegate Christine M. Jones,
   Chairperson
(301) 423-7145

Political Officeholders and Organizations

**MASSACHUSETTS BLACK
LEGISLATIVE CAUCUS**
State House, Room 127
Boston, MA 02133
Bettye Robinson, Executive Director
(617) 722-2680

**MICHIGAN LEGISLATIVE
BLACK CAUCUS**
State Capitol
Lansing, MI 48913
Floyd Clack, Chairperson
(517) 373-7557

**MISSISSIPPI LEGISLATIVE
BLACK CAUCUS**
735 Campbell Street
Jackson, MS 39203
George Flaggs, Chairperson
(601) 359-3330

**MISSOURI LEGISLATIVE
CAUCUS**
House Post Office
State Capitol Building
Jefferson City, MO 65101
Rep. William L. Clay, Jr., Chairperson
(314) 751-2229

**NATIONAL AFRICAN AMERI-
CAN NETWORK**
5113 Georgia Avenue, N.W.
Washington, D.C. 20011
Kathryn Flewellen-Palmer, Executive
Director
(202) 726-0726

**NATIONAL ASSOCIATION OF
MINORITY POLITICAL
WOMEN, USA, INC.**
6120 Oregon Avenue, N.W.
Washington, D.C. 20015
Mary E. Ivey, National President
(202) 686-1216

**NATIONAL BLACK CAUCUS OF
LOCAL ELECTED OFFICIALS**
1301 Pennsylvania Avenue, N.W.,
Suite 400
Washington, D.C. 20004
Carolyn Long Banks, President
(202) 626-3567

**NATIONAL BLACK CAUCUS OF
STATE LEGISLATORS**
444 North Capitol Street, N.W., Suite
206
Washington, D.C. 20001
Representative David P. Richardson,
President
(202) 624-5457

**NATIONAL BLACK INDEPEN-
DENT POLITICAL PARTY**
636 Almeda Avenue
Youngstown, OH 44504
Ron Daniels, Chairperson

**NATIONAL BLACK REPUBLI-
CAN COUNCIL**
440 First Street, N.W., Suite 409
Washington, D.C. 20001
Fred Brown, Chairman
(202) 662-1335

**NATIONAL BLACK WOMEN'S
POLITICAL LEADERSHIP
CAUCUS**
2705 Thirtieth Street, N.E.
Washington, D.C. 20018
Juanita K.Morgan, Contact Person
(202) 529-2806

**NATIONAL BLACK WOMEN'S
POLITICAL CAUCUS**
1628 Eleventh Street, N.W.
Washington, D.C. 20001
Donna Brazile, Executive Director

Political Officeholders and Organizations

NATIONAL CONFERENCE OF BLACK POLITICAL SCIENTISTS
Department of History and Political Science
Albany State College
Albany, GA 31705
Dr. Joseph Silver, President
(912) 439-4870

NATIONAL POLITICAL CON-GRESS OF BLACK WOMEN, INC.
Post Office Box 411
Rancocas, NJ 08073
Portia Perry-Dempsey, Executive Director
(609) 871-1500

NEW ALLIANCE PARTY
2032 Fifth Avenue
New York, NY 10035
Lenora B. Fulani, Ph.D., National Chairperson
(212) 996-4700

NEW JERSEY LEGISLATIVE BLACK CAUCUS
State House
West State Street
Trenton, NJ 08625
Albert A. Harris, Executive Director
(607) 292-7065

NORTH CAROLINA LEGISLA-TIVE BLACK CAUCUS
Room 522
Legislative Office Building
Raleigh, NC 27603
Senator James Richardson, Jr., Chairman
(919) 833-1931

NORTHWEST CONFERENCE OF BLACK PUBLIC OFFICIALS
101 Municipal Building
Seattle, WA 98104
Norwood J. Brooks, President
(206) 684-8383

OKLAHOMA LEGISLATIVE BLACK CAUCUS
417-A State Capitol
Oklahoma City, OK 73105
Senator Vickie Miles-Grange, Chairperson
(405) 521-5531

PARKER COLTRANE PAC
2313 Rayburn House Office Building
Washington, D.C. 20515
Congressman John Conyers, President
(202) 225-5126

PENNSYLVANIA LEGISLATIVE BLACK CAUCUS
Room 308
South Office Building
Harrisburg, PA 17120
Representative Vincent Hughes, Chairman
(717) 772-6955

RHODE ISLAND BLACK CAUCUS OF STATE LEGISLATORS
1453 Broad Street
Providence, RI 02905
Harold Metts, Chairman
(401) 941-937

The listings in this directory are available as Mailing Labels. See last page for details.

Political Officeholders and Organizations

SOUTH CAROLINA LEGISLA-TIVE BLACK CAUCUS
207 Solomon Blatt Building
Columbus, SC 29201
Senator Herbert U. Fielding, Chairperson
(803) 734-3041

TENNESSEE BLACK CAUCUS OF STATE LEGISLATORS
209 War Memorial Building
Nashville, TN 37219
Representative Mary Pruitt, Chairperson
(615) 741-7140

TEXAS LEGISLATIVE BLACK CAUCUS
Post Office Box 2910
Austin, TX 78768
Representative Fred Blair, Chairman
(512) 463-0664

TRANS AFRICA
545 Eighth Street, S.E.
Washington, D.C. 20003
Randall Robinson, Director
(202) 547-2550

VIRGINIA LEGISLATIVE BLACK CAUCUS
256 West Freemason Street
Norfolk, VA 23510
Delegate William P. Robinson, Jr., Chairperson
(804) 622-4770

VOTER EDUCATION PROJECT, INC.
604 Beckwith Street
Atlanta, GA 30314
Ed Brown, Executive Director
(404) 522-7495

Public Administrators

The following entries represent a partial listing of key African-American public administrators in the United States.

JANE ABBOTT-MORRIS
Director, Empl. Compliance/Civil
  Rights Enforcement Agency
10 North Tucker
St. Louis, MO 63101

JUANITA M. ADAMS
Registrar, Director Vital Records
Health Department, City of Cincinnati
1525 Elm Street
Cincinnati, OH 45210

MONA ADKINS-EASLEY
Director, Council on Human Rights
Commonwealth of Virginia
101 North Fourteenth Street,
  Seventeenth Floor
Richmond, VA 23219

ROGER A. AGPAWA
Fire Chief
Markham Fire Department
16313 Kedzie Parkway
Markham, IL 60426

SAMUEL G. AKPAN
Director, Municipal Health Services
Health Department
City of Milwaukee
2770 North Fifth Street
Milwaukee, WI 53212

JAMES C. ALBRITTON
Director of Regional Parks
Chicago Park District
425 E. McFetridge Drive
Chicago, IL 60605

LINDA ALEXANDER
Director, National Urban Fellows, Inc.
55 West 44th Street, Suite 600
New York, NY 10036

DAISY L. ALFORD
Director, Department of Health
City of Cleveland
1700 East Thirteenth Steet,
  Apartment 16T-3
Cleveland, OH 44114

WELDON A. ALLEN
City Planner
Chicago Planning Commission
121 North LaSalle Street,
  Room 1003
Chicago, IL 60602

KEVIN ANDERSON
Director, United Negro College Fund
1212 Broadway, Suite 902
Oakland, CA 94612

SAMUEL P. ANDERSON
Director, Parks and Recreation
City of Knoxville
Post Office Box 1631
Knoxville, TN 37901

JOHN E. ARRADONDO, M.D.
Director, Health and Human Services
City of Houston
8000 North Stadium Drive,
  Eighth Floor
Houston, TX 77054

JOHN ASKEW
Executive Director, Cable TV
  Commission
Prince George's County
9475 Lottsford Road, Suite 130
Landover, MD 20785

Public Administrators

RITA AUGUSTINE
President, Rochester New Futures
  Initiative, Inc.
55 St. Paul Street
Rochester, NY 14604

MARIAN J. AUGUSTUS
Director, Department of Human
  Resources
City of Kansas City
701 North Seventh Street
Kansas City, KS 66101

KENNETH M. AUSTIN
Director, Department of General
  Services
City of Tallahassee
City Hall
300 South Adams Street
Tallahassee, FL 32301

RANDALL C. BACON
General Manager, Department of
  General Services
City of Los Angeles
800 City Hall East
200 North Main Street
Los Angeles, CA 90012

HERBERT J. BAILEY
Assistant City Manager
City of Miami
3500 Pan American Drive
Miami, FL 33133

M. RENEE' BAKER
Director of Personnel
Labor Relations
City of Syracuse
City Hall Commons, Room 712
201 East Washington Street
Syracuse, NY 13202-1476

SHARON BAKER
Director, Employment/Training
  Services
City of Durham
Post Office Box 667
Durham, NC 27702

JUDY D. BANKS
Controller, Department of Personnel
D. C. Government
613 G Street, N.W., Room 310
Washington, D.C. 20001

RONALD L. BARTEE
Chairman, Nebraska Board of Parole
Box 94754, State Capitol
Lincoln, NE 68509

GLORIA J. BATTLE
Director, Human Relations Division
Broward County
115 South Andrews AVenue
Fort Lauderdale, FL 33301

ANNIVORY C. BEARD
Public Works Director
City of Fontana
8353 Sierra Avenue
Fontana, CA 92335

EDWARD BEASLEY
Assistant County Manager
County of Pinal
Post Office Box 727
Florence, AZ 85232

CAROLYN H. BELL
Director, Central Services
City of Savannah
Post Office Box 1027
Savannah, GA 31402

ELDRIN A. BELL
Chief of Police
Atlanta Police Department
175 Decatur Street, S.E.
Atlanta, GA 30335

JOSEPH G. BELL
Director, Department of Social &
   Health Services
12th & Franklin
MS OB-44C
Olympia, WA 98504

NANCY J. BELLARD
Risk Manager
County Administrative Office
1221 Oak Street
Oakland, CA 94612

WILLIAM V. BELLE
Chairman of the Board of County
   Commissioners
Durham County
1003 Huntsman drive
Durham, NC 27713

MONICA G. BENJAMIN
Director, Occupational Health and
   Safety
Bronx Municipal Hospital
Nurses Residence 1358
Pelham Parkway, Eastchester Road
Bronx, NY 10461

KEITH BENNETT
Director of Finance
City of North Chicago
1850 Lewis Avenue
North Chicago, IL 60044

RODNEY B. BENSON
Director of Administration
New York Department of Corrections
138-70 Elder Avenue, Apartment 4W
Flushing, NY 11355

JAMES E. BENTLEY
Fire Chief
City of Pompano Beach
100 West Atlantic Boulevard
Pompano Beach, FL 33060

GREGORY BETHEA
Assistant City Manager
City of Durham
101 City Hall Plaza
Durham, NC 27701

MARVIN F. BILLUPS, JR.
Director, Parks & Recreation
City of Charlotte
600 East Fourth Street
Charlotte, NC 28202

IRVING BIRMINGHAM
Director, Department of Environmental
   Management
County of Fairfax
4050 Legato Road
Fairfax, VA 22030

LARRY J. BLACKWELL
Director, Affirmative Action
   Management
City of Minneapolis
4120 Park Avenue South
Minneapolis, MN 55415

ARTHUR B. BLACKWELL, II
Chairman, Wayne County Commission
600 Randolph, Suite 450
Detroit, MI 48226

JENNIFER BLAKELY
Assistant City Manager
City of Fontana
8353 Sierra Avenue
Fontanta, CA 92335

Public Administrators

JAMES BLEDSOE
Assistant Director, Department of
  Budget
City of Miami
174 East Flagler
Miami, FL 33133

ROBERT C. BOBB
City Manager
City of Richmond
900 East Broad Street, Room 201
Richmond, VA 23219

CORNELIUS L. BOGANEY
City Manager
City of Port Arthur
4148 Forest Drive
Port Arthur, TX 77642

JOYCE BOGLIN
Director, Employee Services
Clerk of the Circuit Court
Hillsborough County
Post Office Box 1110
Tampa, FL 33601

GERALD R. BOUDREQUX
Director, Recreation & Parks
City of Lafayette
Post Office Box 52113
Lafayette, LA 70505

ELAINE BOWEN
Director, Affirmative Action
Office of General Services
Empire Plaza
31 Woodridge Street
Albany, NY 12203

JOHNEL BRACEY
Director of Human Resources &
  Employee Relations
City of Richmond
900 East Broad Street, Suite 201
Richmond, VA 23219

JOSEPH E. BRADSHAW, JR.
Deputy City Manager for Operations
City of Gainesville
Post Office Box 490-7
Gainesville, FL 32602

VALERIE BRANCH
Recycling Coordinator, Sanitation
  Department
City of New Orleans
2400 Canal Street
Room 101
New Orleans, LA 70119

FRANK L. BREEDLOVE
Assistant Director of Aviation
8008 Cedar Springs
Dallas, TX 75235

BEVERLY BREWER
Assistant City Manager
City of Petersburg
Union & Tabb Street
Room 202
Petersburg, VA 23801

DELORES E. BROCK
Contract Administrator
Port Authority
One World Trade Center
New York, NY 10048

NORWARD J. BROOKS
City Comptroller
City of Seattle
600 Fourth Avenue, Room 101
Seattle, WA 98104-1892

RAYMOND BROOKS
Fire Chief
Alhambra Fire Department
301 North Second Street
Alhambra, CA 91801

ALICE E. BROWN
Director, Affirmative Action
New York State Department of Public
  Services
3 Empire State Plaza, 16th Floor
Albany, NY 12223

BUNNIE BROWN
Director, Employhment Services
PG&E
215 Market Street, Room 806
San Francisco, cA 94106

JULIA T. BROWN
Director, Economic Development &
  Employment
City of Oakland
1333 Broadway, 9th Floor
Oakland, CA 94612

LEE ELLIOTT BROWN
Director, Affirmative Action & Contract
  Compliance Division
500 Jefferson Street, Suite 1400
Houston, TX 77002-7333

MARVIN L. BROWN
Executive Director, Greater Detroit
  Alliance of Business
400 River Place, Suite 4214
Detroit, MI 48207

RONALD N. BROWN
Director of Personnel
City of Berkeley
2180 Milvia Street
Berkeley, CA 94704

THOMAS E. BROWN
Fire Chief, Fire Services Department
Decatur County,
4400 Memorial Dr. Compl.
Decatur, GA 30032

J. PAUL BROWNRIDGE
City Treasurer
City of Los Angeles
200 North Spring Street
City Hall, Room 295
Los Angeles, CA 90012

MAE D. BRYANT, DIRECTOR
Department of Human Services
Metro-Dade County
111 N.W. First Street, Suite 2150
Miami, FL 33128

ROBERT BUGGS
Personnel Director
Department of Personnel
City of Topeka
215 S.E. 7th Street, Suite 260
Topeka, KS 66603-3914

I. CONSTANCE BURNETT
Director, Los Angeles County Wide
Interagency Coord. Council
5901 Green Valley Circle
Culver City, CA 90230

VANESSA DALE BURNS
Director, Department of Public Works
City of New Haven
36 Nash Street
New Haven, CT 06513

WILLIAM J. BURNS
Director, Human Resources
Community Economic Development
  Association
Cook County Illinois
224 North Desplaines Street
Chicago, IL 60606

Public Administrators

FRANK C. BURRELL
Administrator, Office of Public Affairs
Minority Business Division
State of Oklahoma
5-A, State Capitol Building
Oklahoma City, OK 73105

DOLLIE B. BURWELL
Register of Deeds, Warren County
   Government
Post Office Box 506
Warrenton, NC 27589

DASCHEL BUTLER
Chief of Police
City of Berkeley
2171 McKinley Avenue
Berkeley, CA 94703

A. C. BYRD
Director of Purchasing
City of Los Angeles
831 Revere Avenue
Montebello, CA 90640

HOWARD CALDWELL
City Manager, City of Compton
205 Willowbrook Avenue
Compton, CA 90220

N. ANTHONY CALHOUN
Comptroller, District of Columbia
415 12th Street, N.W., Suite 412
Washington, D.C. 20004

CHERYL J. CARMICHAEL
Director, Personnel/Human Resources
City of Plainfield
515 Watchung Avenue
Plainfield, NJ 07060

GLENN E. CARR
Commissioner of Personnel
City of Chicago
121 North LaSalle Street
City Hall, Room 1100
Chicago, IL 60602

LAWRENCE R. CARSON, P.E.
Deputy Commissioner
Commissioner of Licenses &
   Inspection
City of Wilmington
3315 Jefferson Street
Wilmington, DE 19802

M. L. CARSTARPHEN
Executive Director, Housing Finance
   Agency
District of Columbia
1275 K Street, N.W., Suite 600
Washington, D.C. 20005

JOSEPH S. CHARLTON
City Manager, City of Muskegon
   Heights
2724 Peck Street
Muskegon Heights, MI 49444

KENNETH T. CHAVIOUS
Finance Director, Orange County
Post Office Box 8181
Hillsborough, NC 27278

RICKEY CHILDERS
Assistant City Manager, City of
   Carrollton
Post Office Box 110535
Carrollton, TX 75011-0535

ALBERT A. CHILDS
Executive Director, Philadelphia
   Municipal Authority
1401 Arch Street, Room 1200
Philadelphial PA 19102

Public Administrators

GERRI COFFEY
Director of Personnel, Office of Pubic
   Affairs
Capitol Building, Room 4-B
Oklahoma City, OK 73105

FRANKIE L. COLEMAN
Executive Director, Private Industry
   Council of Columbus & Franklin
   County
400 East Town Street, Suite 220
Columbus, OH 43215

CECIL A. COLLINS
Director, National Project "Can-do"
Volunteers of America
3813 North Causeway Boulevard
Metairie, LA 70002

TONY COLLINS, DIRECTOR
Economic Development
City of St. Petersburg
Post Office Box 2842
St. Petersburg, FL 33731

ARLENE D. COLVIN
Director, Division of Physical &
   Economic Development
City of Gary, Indiana
401 Broadway
Gary, IN 46402

VALARIA CONERLY
Executive Director, Valley Area
   Agency on Aging
708 Root Street, Room 110
Flint, MI 48503

MARCIA L. CONNER
Budget Director, Arlington County
   Governement
2100 Clarendon Boulevard, Suite 501
Arlington, VA 22201

MARJORIE L. CONNER
Assistant City Manager, City of
   Saginaw
1315 South Washington Avenue
Saginaw, MI 48601

DONALD A. CORLEY
Director, Management/Budget Office
City of Tallahassee
City Hall
300 South Adams Street
Tallahassee, FL 32301

CHARLES E. COUNTEE
Executive Director, Office of Business
   & Economic Development
717 14th Street, N.W.
Washington, D.C. 20005

ARTIS HAMPSHIRE COWAN
General Counsel, D.C. Armory Board
2001 East Capitol Street, S.E.
Washington, D.C. 20001

JERRY CRENSHAW
Superintendent, Aviation Department
City of Houston
Post Office Box 60106
Houston, TX 66205

RUTH CRONE
Executive Director, Metropolitan
   Washington Council of Governments
777 North Capitol Street, N.E.
Washington, D.C. 20002

DELLIE CULPEPPER
Director, City Court of Atlanta
104 Trinity Avenue, S.W.
Atlanta, GA 30335

SUE C. CURRIE
Risk Manager, City of Peoria
5727 Ridgecrest Drive, Room 104
Peoria, IL 61615

Public Administrators

ANNA CURRY
Director, Enoch Pratt Free Library
City of Baltimore
400 Cathedral Street
Baltimore, MD 21202

ERIC V. DABNEY
Director, Parks & Recreation
City of North Las Vegas
Post Office Box 4086
North Las Vegas, NV 89036

CHARLES W. DANIELS
Assistant Director, Office of
Environmental Management
City of San Jose
777 North First Street, Room 450
San Jose, CA 95112

SYLVESTER DAUGHTRY
Chief of Police, City of Greensboro
Police Department
300 West Washington
Greensboro, NC 27401

MICHELLE S. DAVIS, MSPH
Epidemiologist/Research Scientist
Department of Health
149 Jefferson Street, Room 2
Albany, NY 12210

SAMUEL DAVIS, JR.
Diector, Department of Gas Utility
City of Tallahassee
2602 Jackson Bluff Road
Tallahassee, FL 32304

JACKIE DAVISON
Chairma Board of Directors
Jefferson County Transit
Public Transportation
1321 Bush Boulevard
Birmingham, AL 35208

MICHELE K. DESVIGNES
City Planner, Office of Budget and
Management
City of Chicago
121 North LaSalle
Chicago, IL 60602

PATRICIA A. DIXON
Executive Director, Human Rights
Commission
East Chicago
4506 Tod Avenue
Heritage Hall
East Chicago, IL 46312

MEL D. DODD
Supervisor, Contracts
Municipality/Metro. Seattle
821 Second Avenue, M/S 111
Seattle, WA 98104

VERA B. DORSEY
Director, Employment & Training
Services
City of Compton
600 North Alameda Street, Room 191
Compton, CA 90221

PATRICIA DOWELL-CERASOLI
Deputy Commissioner, City of Chicago
Department of Planning
121 North LaSalle Street, Room 1006
Chicago, IL 60602

ALFRETTA F. EARNEST
Finance Director, City of Lynwood
11330 Bullis Road
Lynwood, CA 90262

RALPH W. EMERSON
Director, Parks/Recreation Department
City of Fort Worth
100 North University Drive, Suite 239
Fort Worth, TX 76107

Public Administrators

PRESTON ERVIN, JR.
Risk & Insurance Administrator
Office of Risk Management
City of Houston
Post Office Box 1562
Houston, TX 77251

JAMES ETHEREDGE
Director, Administrative Services
City of Charleston
80 Broad Street
Charleston, SC 29402

WARREN C. EVANS
Diector of Administration
Wayne County Commission
4239 Pasadena
Detroit, MI 48238

PHILIP L. EWELL
Fire Chief, City of Oakland
Fire Department
32 Melvin Court
Oakland, CA 94602

MARVIN H. EXUM
Safety Director, Public Safety
455 Mass Street - Post Office Box 516
Gary, IN 46408

WALTER L. FAGGETT, M.D.
Chief, U.S. Department of Health &
   Human Services
Rockwall 11, Tenth Floor
5600 Fisher Lane
Rockville, MD 20857

BARBARA J. FAUCETT
Director, Personnel Services
University of Wisconsin
Post Office Box 413
Milwaukee, WI 53201

ANITA FAVORS
Deputy City Manager
City Manager's Office
City of Tallahassee
300 South Adams Street
City Hall, Fourth Floor
Tallahassee, FL 32301

PATRICIA FIELDS
Executive Director
Governor's Commitee on Migratory
   and Seasonal Farm Labor
311 West Saratoga Street
Baltimore, MD 21201

TARA L. FIKES
Director, Housing and Community
   Development
Post Office Box 8181
Hillsborough, NC 27278

ULIOUS C. FLUELLEN
Fire Chief, U.S. Army Military Traffic
   Management Command
32 Richard Street
Jersey City, NJ 07035

ALMARIE FORD
Director, Human Resources
Policy and Planning
City of New Orleans
1300 Perdido Street, Number 1W06
New Orleans, LA 70112

ULYSSES G. FORD, III
Director, Public Works Department
City of Houston
601 Sawyer, Fifth Floor
Houston, TX 77007

CHARLES W. FOSTER
Director of Aviation
Port of Oakland
530 Water Street, Sixth Floor
Oakland, Ca 94607

Public Administrators

BETTY HAGER FRANCIS
Director of Public Works
District of Columbia
2000 14th Street, N.W., Sixth Floor
Washington, D.C. 20009

ERNEST FREEMAN
Director, Planning Department
City of Baltimore
417 East Fayette Street, Room 800
Baltimore, MD 21202

KAREN M. FREEMAN
Executive Director, Civil Rights
   Commission
32 East Washington Street, Suite 900
Indianapolis, IN 46204

SANDRA FREEMAN
Executive Director, Housing Authority
   of Elgin
1845 Grandstand Place, Suite 100
Elgin, IL 60123

VERNADETTE FULLER
City Clerk, City of Pompano Beach
2764 West Atlantic Boulevard
Post Office Drawer 1300
Pompano Beach, FL 33060

ISAAC FULWOOD, JR.
Chief of Police, Metropolitan Police
   Department
300 Indiana Avenue, N.W.,
   Room 5080
Washington, D.C. 20001

DONNA R. GAITHER
Executive Director, Commission for
   Women
Baltimore City
111 North Calvert Street
Baltimore, MD 21202

WILLIAM GAMBLE
Director of Purchasing, Cleveland
   Public Schools
1380 East Sixth Street
Cleveland, OH 44114

HENRY GARDNER
City Manager, City of Oakland
One City Hall Plaza
Oakland, CA 94612

CHERYL J. GARRETT
City Treasurer, City of Dayton
101 West Third Street
Dayton, OH 45401

WILLIAM P. GARRETT
Director of Personnel, Montgomery
   County Government
101 Monroe Street
Rockville, MD 20850

CHARLES W. GATES
Director of Aviation
Robert Mueller Municipal Airport
City of Austin
3600 Manor Road
Austin, TX 78723

CHARLES GILLON
Director of Planning, Human Services
City of Elizabeth
County Administration Building
Elizabeth, NJ 07201

C. BERNARD GILPIN
Director, Contract Administrative
   Bureau
Department of Public Works
City of Los Angeles
200 North Spring Street, Room 908
Los Angeles, CA 90012

Public Administrators

ROBERT L. GORDON
Deputy City Manager
City of Colorado Springs
30 West Nevada Avenue, Room 305
Colorado Springs, CO 80903

YVONNE A. GORDON
City Auditor, City of Wilmington
City County Building
800 French Street
Wilmington, DE 19801-3537

GRAHAM GRADY
Zoning Administratior, Department of
    Zoning
City of Chicago
121 North LaSalle, Room 800
Chicago, IL 60602

VINCENT C. GRAY
Director, D.C. Department of
    Human Services
801 North Capitol Street
Washington, D.C. 20002

CARL L. GREEN
Deputy Vice President
New York City Transit
370 Jay Street, Room 1322
Brooklyn, NY 11201

LORRAINE A. GREEN
Director, Personnel Department
District of Columbia
613 G Street, N.W., Room 306
Washington, D.C. 20001

BARBARA A. GRIER
Director, Administration
Metropolitan Transportation Authority
349 Madison Avenue
New York, NY 10017

OSCAR B. GRIFFITH, JR.
Executive Director, Economic
    Opportunity Planning Association
505 Hamilton Street
Toledo, OH 43602

HUBERT GUEST
Assistant City Manager
City of Hartford
73 Canterburn Street
Hartford, CT 06112

WEBSTER J. GUILLORY
Chairman, National Organization of
    Black County Officials
Post Office Box 1169
Santa Ana, CA 92702

GLADYS HALL
Director of Human Services
220 St. Clair Avenue, N.W.
Cleveland, OH 44113

JOSEPH A. HALL
Director, Bureau of Taxicabs
City of Atlanta
818 Washington Street, S.E.
Suite C13, First Floor
Atlanta, GA 30315

ARCHESTER HAMPTON
Director, Metro Area Employment &
    Training
301 North State Street
Jackson, MS 39201

CLAUDE HARRIS
Chief, Seattle Fire Department
301 Second A Street
Seattle, WA 98104

Public Administrators

WILLIAM F. HARRIS
Executive Director, Public Building
  Commission
City of Chicago
Daley Center, Room 705
Chicago, IL 60602

JEROME C. HARRIS, JR.
Assistant State Treasurer
Department of the Treasury
State of New Jersey
125 West State Street, CN002
Trenton, NJ 08625

WILLIE P. HAYWOOD
Superintendent, Public Works
3504 68th Avenue
Oakland, CA 94605

ELLIS HENDERSON
Chief of Administration
City of Richmond
900 East Broad Street, Room 409
Richmond, VA 23219

RAMONA E. HENDERSON
Auditor General, Wayne County
600 Randolph, Room 208
Detroit, MI 48226

WILSON HENDERSON
Director, Equal Opportunity Division
Massachusetts Housing Finance
  Agency
50 Milk Street
Boston, MA 02109

MICHAEL T. HERIOT
City Manager, City of Lynwood
11330 Bullis Road
Lynwood, CA 90262

DEBORAH HESSE
Chairperson, Public Employment
  Relations Board
1031 18th Street
Sacramento, CA 95814

SHIRLEY A. HIBBITTS
Deputy City Manager
City of Oakland
1 City Hall Plaza, Room 318
Oakland, CA 94612

REGINALD HICKS
City Attorney
Legal Department, City of Riviera
  Beach
600 West Blue Heron Boulevard
Riviera Beach, FL 33404

MARY E. HILL
Personnel Director, Metro Action
  Commission
Nashville & Davidson County
1624 Fifth Avenue, North
Nashville, TN 37208

MARY S. HILL
Director, Court Administration
City of Oklahoma City
700 Couth Drive
Oklahoma City, OK 73102

NATHANIEL W. HILL
Director, Human & General Services
City of Little Rock
500 West Markham
West Wing, Room 120
Little Rock, AR 72201

MARILYN HILLIARD
Human Resources Director
Environmental Affairs
100 Cambridge Street, Room 2000
Boston, MA 02202

Public Administrators

CYNTHIA R. HOBSON
Deputy Chief, Adminstrative Services
California Energy Commission
5747 Laguna Park Drive
Elk Grove, CA 95758

RAY H. HODGES
City Manager, City of Forest Park
1201 West Kemper
Forest Park, OH 45240

VIRIA HOLLAND
Deputy Director, Department of
   Revenue
24 East Congress, Second Floor
Chicago, IL 60605

WILLIAM L. HOLLY
Personnel Director, Montgomery
   County Sheriff's Office
41 North Perry Street
Dayton, OH 45422-2427

ADRIENNE HOLMES
Assistant Superintendent
New Jersey Rail
1 Hudson Place
Hoboken, NJ 07030

RICHARD C. JAMES
Director, Bureau/Affirmative Action
Office of Administration
510 Finance Building
Harrisburg, PA 17120

ANDREW JENKINS
Executive Director, Philadelphia
   Redevelopment Authority
1234 Market Street, Eighth Floor
Philadelphia, PA 19107

CHARLES R. JOHNSON
Director, Department of Environmental
   Services
City of Portsmouth
801 Crawford Street
Portsmouth, VA 23704

CRETTA A. JOHNSON
Director of Equal Opportunity
Human Relations Department
Hillsborough County
Post Office Box 1110
Tampa, FL 33601

HAL JOHNSON
Director, GSA Procurement
   Management Division
Metro-Dade County
111 N.W. First Street
Miami, FL 33128-1989

JOSEPH JOHNSON, JR.
City Manager, City of East Point
2777 East Point Street
East Point, GA 30344

TEREE C. JOHNSON
Director, Metro Solid Waste Agency
521 East Locust Street
Des Moines, IA 50309

MINNIE F. JOHNSON, PH.D.
Director of Strategic Planning
Miami Valley Regional Transit
   Authority
600 Longworth Street
Dayton, OH 45402

WALTER L. JOHNSON
Retirement Systems Manager
City of Oakland
One City Hall Plaza, Room 216
Oakland, CA 94612

Public Administrators

CLARENCE JONES
Solid Wast Superintendent
City of Sarasota
1761 12th Street
Sarasota, FL 34236

EMMETT E. JONES
Assistant City Manager
City of Berkeley
2180 Milvia Street
Berkeley, CA 94704

HARRY L. JONES, SR.
Director, Housing Compliance
City of Dallas
1500 Marilla, 4DN
Dallas, TX 75201

ORVILLE W. JONES
Personnel Director
City of Philadelphia
MSB - 15 & JFK Boulevard
Philadelphia, PA 19107

VIRVUS JONES
Comptroller, City of St. Louis
City Hall, Room 212
1200 Market Street
St. Louis, MO 63103

JOSEPH JONES, III
Director or Personnel
Kansas City Area Transportation
   Authority
1350 East 17th Street
Kansas City, MO 64108

OLIVER JORDAN
Executive Director
Commission on Disabilities
City of Philadelphia
143 City Hall
Philadelphia, PA 19107

RITA KERRICK
Director, Office of Adolescent
   Pregnancy Prevention
City of Baltimore
303 East Fayette Street
Baltimore, MD 21202

GEORGE A. KILPATRICK, JR.
Director, Office of Minority Affairs
City of Syracuse
City Hall Commons, Room 605
201 East Washington Street
Syracuse, NY 13202

JACQUELINE S. KNIGHT
Human Resources Director
Department of Human Resources
Durham County Government
200 East Main Street, Third Floor
Durham, NC 27701

JOHN KNIGHT, DIRECTOR
Communication & Public Affairs
Alabama State University
Post Office Box 271
Montgomery, AL 36101-0271

JOHN LABRIE
Director of Solid Waste Management
City of Beaumont
4955 Lafin Road
Beaumont, TX 77705

GAIL L. LATIMORE
Director of Planning, Action for Boston
   Community Development
52 Mt. Pleasant Avenue
Boston, MA 02119

WADE LAWSON
Executive Director, Transportation
   Authority
Atlantic County New Jersey
25 South New York Avenue
Atlantic City, NJ 08401

Public Administrators

ORIN LEHMAN
Commissioner, New York State Office
of Park Recreation and Historic
Preservation
Agency Building One
Empire State Plaza
Albany, NY 12238

VALERIE A. LEMMIE
Director, Arlington County Department
of Environmental Services
#1 Courthouse Plaza, Suite 801
Arlington, VA 22201

EDWARD LEVELL, JR.
Deputy Director, Department of
Aviation
City of New Orleans
Post Office Box 20007
New Orleans, LA 70141

WILLARD C. LEWIS
Assistant Director, Office on Disaster
Preparadness
San Diego County
5201 Q Ruffin Road
San Diego, CA 92123

WALLACE V. LINSEY, SR.
Zoning Administrator
Fulton County Government
141 Pryor Street, S.W., Suite 8071
Atlanta, GA 30303

ALEXANDRE LITTLE
Chief Operating Office
City of Gary
453 Terrace Drive
Benton Harbor, MI 49022

DARRYL LOCKHART
Clerk of Court
Municipal Court, City of Atlanta
104 Trinity Avenue, S.W.
Atlanta, GA 30335

ANDREW LOFTON
Budget Director, Management &
Budget
City of Seattle
Municipal Building
600 Fourth Avenue
Seattle, WA 98116

MICHAEL LOMAX
Chairman of the Board
Fulton County Government
165 Central Avenue, Room 208
Atlanta, GA 30303

MERRITT LONG
Executive Director
Washington State Board/Vocational
Education
Building 17, Airdustrial Park
M/S LS-10
Olympia, WA 98504

WILLIE MAE LONG
Superintendent, Parks & Recreation
City of Fairfield
Post Office Box 412
Fairfield, AL 35064

ADRIENNE M. MACBETH
Director, Minority Women Business
Affairs
City of Miami
300 Biscayne Boulevard Way
400 Dupont Plaza Center
Miami, FL 33131

HOWARD L. MARSHALL
Deputy Director, Equal Opportunity
Department
City of Phoenix
550 West Washington Street
Phoenix, AZ 85003

Public Administrators

DYANNE MASON
Executive Director, Department of
   Human Rights
707 South Houston, Room 303
Tulsa, OK 74127

JACKIE R. MATTISON
Chief of Staff, Mayor's Office
City of Newark
920 Broad Street
Newark, NJ 07102

DARRYL L. MAYFIELD
Assistant City Manager
City of Lufkin
Post Office Drawer 190
300 East Shepherd Street
Lufkin, TX 75901-0190

EDNA LEWIS MAYHAND
Board President, Board of Barber
   Examiners
State of California
1021 O Street, Room A551
Sacramento, CA 95814

WILBERT MCADOO
Director, Public Works Department
Orange County
Post Office Box 8181
Hillsborough, NC 27278

RODERIC MCCALL
Superintendent, Sanitary Engineering
Montgomery County
5624 Westcreek Drive
Dayton, OH 45436

DAVID MCCARY
Superintendent of Administration
Solid Waste Management
City of Houston
601 Sawyer, Room 500
Houston, TX 77007

GWEN MCDONALD
Director, Personnel Relations
   Management
City of Oakland
1417 Clay Street, First Floor
Oakland, Ca 94612

DELOIS MCKINLEY
Executive Director, Metropolitan
   Human Relations Commission
1 Main Street, Room 680
Fort Wayne, IN 46802

CHARLES E. MCNEELY
City Manager, City of Seaside
Post Office Box 810
440 Harcourt Street
Seaside, CA 93955-0810

BERT MCWILLIAMS
Director, Human Resources
City of Lubbock
Post Office Box 2000
1625 13th Street
Lubbock, TX 79457

CHARLES MEADOWS
Director, Community Affairs
City of Dayton
101 West Third Street
Dayton, OH 45401

E. CAROL MILLER
Assistant Investment Manager,
   County of San Diego
1600 Pacific Highway, Room 112
San Diego, CA 92101

MELVIN MILLER
Director, Parks & Recreation
   Department
City of Birmingham
400 Graymont Avenue West
Birmingham, AL 35204

Public Administrators

ISABELL MILLS
Executive Director, New York State
    Dev. Disabilities
12 Tyler Court
Guilderland, NY 12084

ELNORA J. MITCHELL
Director, Equal Opportunity
City of Gainesville
Post Office Box 490, Station 57
Gainesville, FL 32602

ERNEST MITCHELL
Fire Chief
Monrovia Fire Department
141 East Lemon Avenue
Monrovia, CA 91016

MURIEL M. MITCHELL
Director, Deprtment of Housing
City of Atlanta, City Hall
Atlanta, GA 30331

KELLY F. MONTGOMERY
Deputy City Manager
City of Davis
23 Russell Boulevard
Davis, CA 95616

CECIL S. MOORE
Director, Contract Compliance & EEO
Manual J. Maloof Center
1300 Commerce Drive, Sixth Floor
Decatur, GA 30030

JIMMY MOORE
Airport Supervisor, Aviation
    Department
City of Houston
16930 JFK Boulevard
Houston, TX 77032

LAWRENCE M. MOORE
City Manager
City of Richmond
2600 Barrett, Room 301
Richmond, CA 94804

LEMUEL B. MOORE
Director, Culture & Nature Operations
City of Gainesville
Post Office Box 490
Gainesville, FL 32601

ROLAND H. MOORE
Associate Director, Bureau of the
    Census
United States Department of
    Commerce
Washington, D.C. 20233

VIVIAN E. MOORE
Executive Director, Human Rights
    Commission
County of Onondaga
John H. Mulroy Civic Center
421 Montgomery Street
Syracuse, NY 13214

DANA M. MOSS
Director, Water Utilities Department
County Commissioners Board
Palm Beach County
2030 South Congress Avenue
West Plam Beach, FL 33406

THOMAS J. MOYER
Director, Equal Opportunity Contract
    Compliance Office
800 French Street
Wilmington, DE 19801

FRED MURRAY
Director, Community Development
City of North Miami Beach
17011 N.E. 19th Avenue
North Miami Beach, FL 33162

Public Administrators

GEORGE G. MUSGROVE
Director, Department of Human
Services
City of Norfolk
302 City Hall
Norfolk, VA 23510

BOB J. NASH
President, Arkansas Development
Finance Authority
100 Main Street, Room 200
Post Office Box 8023
Little Rock, AR 72203

ROSE S. NEWSOME
Director, Equal Opportunity
Department
City of Phoenix
550 West Washington Street
Phoenix, AZ 85003-2299

FANNIE NICHOLAS
Director, Social Services
Cincinnati Health Department
3101 Burnet Avenue
Cincinnati, OH 45229

SHARON OFUANI
Director, Affirmative Action
City of Tallahassee, City Hall
300 South Adams Street
Tallahassee, Fl 32301

JERRY A. OLIVER
Director, Office of Drug Policy
125 North Mid America Mall
Memphis, TN 38103

CLAYTON H. OSBORNE
Director of Operations
County of Monroe
39 West Main Street, Room 110
Rochester, NY 14614

ROBERT OSBY
Fire Chief
City of San Jose
801 North First Street
San Jose, CA 95110

ALFRED OUTLAW
Revenue Commissioner
City of Philadelphia
1450 Municipal Services Building
Philadelphia, PA 19102

G. JOHN PARKER
Fire Chief
City of Pomona
590 South Park Avenue
Pomona, CA 91766

LAVERNE PARKER-DIGGS
Director of Human Resources
City of San Jose
801 North First Street
San Jose, CA 95110

VIVIAN PEQUES
State Certification Coordinator
Minority Business Programs
Office of Public Affairs
5-A State Capitol Building
Oklahoma City, OK 73105

PAULA M. PHILLIPS
Director, Housing & Community
Development
City of Houston
Post Office Box 1562
Houston, TX 77251

JUDITH T. PIERCE
Chief Administrative Officer
Southeastern PA Transportation
Authority
841 Chestnut Street, Third Floor
Philadelphia, PA 19106

Public Administrators

TINA POITEVIEN
Chief Investment Officer, Board of
  Pensions and Retirement
Two Penn Center, 20th Floor
Philadelphia, PA 19102

DEBORAH POOLE, DIRECTOR
Human Services Department
Fulton County
132 Mitchell Street, Third Floor
Atlanta, GA 30303

ORVILLE POWELL
City Manager, City of Durham
101 City Hall Plaza
Durham, NC 27702

**DORTHULA POWELL-
  WOODSON**
Director, Department of Personnel &
  Training
City of Richmond
101 North Fourteenth Street,
  12th Floor
Richmond, VA 23219

CAROL PRAYLOR
Regional Director, Divison of Human
  Rights
New York State
6317 Church Road
Albany, NY 12203

MARVA L. PRITCHETT
Director, Planning & Development
City of Abilene
Post Office Box 60
555 Walnut Street
Abilene, TX 79604

STERLING R. PRUITT
Assistant City Manager, City of
  Beaumont
Post Office Box 3827
Beaumont, TX 77704

MARTI PRYOR-COOK
Director, Department of Social
  Services
Orange County
Post Office Box 8181
Hillsborough, NC 27278

MICHELE QUANDER-COLLINS
Grants Administrator
City of Saginaw
1315 South Washington Avenue
Saginaw, MI 48601

KEVIN QUINCE
Executive Director
Housing & Mortgage Finance Agency
3625 Quakerbridge Road
Trenton, NJ 08650-2085

BRUCE RANSOM
Executive Director, South Jersey
  Center for Public Affairs
Stockton State College, H-201
Pomona, NJ 08240

NEVA REED
Deputy City Manager
City of Opa-Locka
151 Perviz Avenue
Post Office Box 540371
Opa-Locka, FL 33054

EARL B. REYNOLDS
Assistant City Manager
City of Roanoke
215 Church Avenue, S.W.
Roanoke, VA 24011

DONALD K. RICHMOND
Director, Personnel Administration
City of Richmond
2600 Barrett Avenue, Room 347
Richmond, CA 94804

Public Administrators

EDWIN M. ROBINSON
Executive Director, Council of
  Economic Opportunity
City of Cleveland
668 Euclid, Room 700
Cleveland, OH 44114

PATRICIA MOORE ROGERS
Deputy Director, Personnel
U.S. General Accounting Office
441 G Street, N.W., Room 4747
Washington, D.C. 20548

CLAUDE R. ROGERS
Executive Director
Civil Rights Enforcement Agency
10 North Tucker Road, Room 300
St. Louis, MO 63101

ELRITA ROGERS
Personnel Administrator
Department of Personnel
City of Fort Worth
1000 Throckmorton
Fort Worth, TX 76102

SHIRLEY A. RODGERS
Executive Assistant
City Manager's Office
City of San Jose
801 North First Street
San Jose, CA 95110

LA JUANA JOHNSON ROE
City Manager's Office
City of Stockton
425 North Eldorado Street
Stockton, CA 95202

GEORGE ROWE
Director, Department of Public Works
City of Cincinnati
801 Plum Street, Room 450
Cincinnati, OH 45202

MARJORIE RUSH
Administrator, Teacher Recruitment
New York State Education Department
105 Colonial Avenue
Albany, NY 12205

G. GREGORY RUSSELL
Director of Finance
Maryland Port Administration
World Trade Center
401 East Pratt Street, 20th Floor
Baltimore, MD 21202

LAJUANA JOHNSON-ROE
Office of City Manager
City of Stockton
425 North Eldorado street
Stockton, CA 95202

SAMUEL SAXTON
Director, Department of Corrections
Prince George's Coounty
13400 Dille Drive
Upper Marlboro, MD 20772

MICHAEL W. SCOTT
Director, Department of Special Events
City of Chicago
121 North LaSalle Street
Chicago, IL 60602

GERALD SEALS
City Manager, City of Corvallis
501 S.W. Madison
Post Office Box 1083
Corvallis, OR 97339

JOHNNY F. SESSION
Controller, City of Tallahassee
300 South Adams Street
City Hall
Tallahassee, FL 32301

Public Administrators

PATRICIA SHAW
Director, Health & Human Services
475 Broadway
Gary, IN 46404

LAVONNE M. SHEFFIELD
Chief Administrativ Officer
City of New Haven
City Hall
New Haven, CT 06410

WILLIAM J. SIMMONS
Director, Airport Services
Department of Aviation
Hancock International Airport
Syracuse, NY 13212

GWENDOLYN M. SIMPSON
Director of Personnel
   Metropolitan Transit Authority
Harris County - Post Office Box 61429
Houston, TX 77208

JIM L. SLAUGHTER
Director of Operations
City of Garland
Post Office Box 469002
Garland, TX 75046-9002

DENNISE SMITH
Assistant Regional Commissioner
Social Security Administration
330 Summit Place, Room 3
Point Richmond, CA 94801

MITCHELL SMITH
Executive Director, Governor's Office
   of Minority Affairs
301 West Preston Street,
   Room 1008-E
Baltimore, MD 21201

TONY SMITH
City Manager
City of Riviera Beach
600 West Blue Heron Boulevard
Post Office Box 10682
Riviera Beach, FL 33404

JAMES SMITH, JR.
Personnel Director
City of Spokane
W. 808 Spokane Falls Boulevard
Spokane, WA 99201-3327

KENNETH SPICER
Director of Affirmative Aciton
state Executive Office on Communities
   and Development
100 Cambridge Street, 14th Floor
Boston, MA 02202

FAGAN D. STACKHOUSE
Director of Personnel
City of Virginia Beach
2396 Court Plaza Drive, Suite 200
Virginia Beach, VA 23456

ELLIS M. STANLEY, SR.
Director, Emergency Management
   Agency
Atlanta-Fulton County
130 Peachtree Street, S.W.
Atlanta, GA 30303

C. DON STEGER
Assistant City Manager
City of Charlotte
600 East Trade Street
Charlotte, NC 28202

JAMES L. STEWART
Director, Streets and Sanitation
   Department
City of Birmingham
501 Sixth Avenue, South
Birmingham, AL 35205

Public Administrators

JOHN B. STEWART, JR.
Fire Chief
Hartford Fire Department
275 Pearl Street
Hartford, CT 06103

GOODRICH H. STOKES, JR.
Director, Office of External Affairs
Social Security Administration
6401 Security Boulevard,
   Room 4300 WHR
Baltimore, MD 21235

VERNON E. STONER
Commissioner, Washington State
   Employment Security
212 Maple Park, KS-11
Olympia, WA 98504

E. DOLORES STREET
Director, Commission on Migratory
   Labor
311 West Saratoga Street
Baltimore, MD 21201

EDWARD STRINGFELLOW
Chief of City Marshals
City of Houston
1400 Lubbock
Houston, TX 77002

VERNELL STURNS
Executive Director, Dallas/Fort Worth
   International Airport
Post Office Drawer DFW
Dallas/Fort Worth Airport, TX 75261

FLOYD C. TAYLOR
Director, Kentucky Cabinet for
   Economic Development
Capital Plaza Tower, Floor 22
Frankfort, KY 40601

NORMAN E. TAYLOR
Director, Contract Compliance
Broward County
115 South Andrews Avenue
Fort Lauderdale, FL 33301

SYLVIA J. TAYLOR
Director, Real Estate
City of St. Petersburg
Post Office Box 2842
St. Petersburg, FL 33731

ROBERT "BOB" TERRELL
Assistant City Manager
City of Fort Worth
1000 Throckmorton
Fort Worth, TX 76102

GEORGE D. TERRY
Director, Personnel Management
City of Jackson
Post Office Box 17
Jackson, MS 39205

SAM THOMAS III
Executive Director, Community
   Relations Board
City of Cleveland
601 Lakeside Avenue, Room 11
Cleveland, OH 44114

THEODORE THOMAS
Director, Estate Tax
State of Illinois
300 West Jefferson
Springfield, IL 62706

JEWEL THOMPSON-CHIN
City Administrator, City of Plainfield
515 Watchung Avenue
Plainfield, NJ 07060

Public Administrators

MICHAEL E. THOMPKINS
Director, Planning, Zoning and
  Development
25 West Market Street
Post Office Box 88
Leesburg, VA 22075

ERIC M. TUCKER
Director of Finance
Prince George's County
County Administration Building,
  Room 3200
Upper Marlboro, MD 20772

MARGIE A. UTLEY
Director Human Rights, Minority
  Business Development
D. C. Government
2000 14th Street, N.W.
Washington, D.C. 20001

WILLIAM D. VANCE
Director, Affirmative Action Programs
New York State Labor Department
State Campus Building 12, Room 586
Albany, NY 12240

DAVID L. WALKER
Chief of Police
Jackson Police Department
4950 Willow Creek Drive, A
Jackson, MS 39206

GARY WALKER
Director, Purchasing & Real Estate
City of Atlanta
197 Central Avenue, S.W.
Atlanta, GA 30335

GEORGE E. WALLACE
Assistant City Manager, Community
  Services
City of Hampton
22 Lincoln Street
Hampton, VA 23669

J. W. WALTON
Director, Community Development
  Department
City of Charlotte
600 East Fourth Street
Charlotte, NC 28202

WILLARD WALTON, JR.
Director, Office of Procurement
Montgomery County Government
250 Hungerford Drive, Suite 175
Rockville, MD 20850

ALTON J. WASHINGTON
Director, Human Services Department
City of Phoenix
302 West Washington
Phoenix, AZ 85003

FAYE WASHINGTON
General Manager, Department of
  Aging
City of Los Angeles
600 South Spring Street, Suite 900
Los Angles, CA 90014

PATRICIA C. WASHINGTON
Director of Personnel
City of Hartford
64 Hope Circle
Windsor, CT 06095

WILLIE WASHINGTON
Chief of Staff
City of Los Angeles
City Hall, Room 260
Los Angeles, CA 90012

TOBIAS W. WASHINGTON, JR.
Assistant Director, Department of
  Licensing
State of Washington
405 Black Lake Boulevard
Olympia, WA 98504-8001

Public Administrators

DIANA B. WEBB
Deputy Chief of Operations
Los Angeles Community Redevelop-
    ment Agency
354 South Spring Street, Room 800
Los Angeles, CA 90013

DONALD WESLEY GOREE, JR.
Director of Purchasing
St. Louis Board of Education
City of St. Louis
911 Locust
St. Louis, MO 63101

JO F. WEST
Director and Chief Clerk
Municipal Courts Adminsitration
    Department
City of Houston
1400 Lubbock Street
Houston, TX 77002

DEBORAH WHITE
Director of Administration
Governor's Office on Minorities and
    Women's Business Development
State Capitol, #239
Albany, NY 12224

HERBYE K. WHITE
Director, Parks and Recreation
City of Oakland
1520 Lakeside Drive
Oakland, CA 94612

PAUL WHITE
City Manager, City of Gainesville
200 East University
Post Office Box 490
Gainesville, FL 32602

SALLY WHITED-TAYLOR
Personnel Director
City of Compton
205 S. Willowbrook Avenue
Compton, CA 90220

BEVERLY M. WHITEHEAD
Director, Department of Human
    Resources
Chatham County
124 Bull Street, Suite 310
Savannah, GA 31409

JOHN L. WHITEHEAD,III
Director, Engineering Department
City of Seattle
600 Fourth Avenue, Room 701
Seattle, WA 98104

CHARLES B. WHITEHURST
City Treasurer
801 Crawford Street
Portsmouth, VA 23704

JOSELYN L. WHITSETT BELL
Director of Finance, Department of
    Aviation
City of Chicago
20 North Clark, Suite 3000
Chicago, IL 60602

ANTHONY D. WILLIAMS
Assistant Director
Employee Relations
City of Coral Gables
2327 Salzedo
Coral Gables, FL 33134

CLARENCE E. WILLIAMS
Director of Public Works
City of Dayton
101 West Third Street
Municipal Building
Dayton, OH 45401-0022

JESSIE C. WILLIAMS
Administrator, Minority Business
    Development
Metro-Dade County
111 N.W. First Street
Miami, FL 33128

Public Administrators

OTIS E. WILLIAMS
Director, Administrative Services
 Division
Texas Commission on Alcohol and
 Drug Abuse
720 Brazos, Suite 403
Austin, TX 78701

RICHARD F. WILLIAMS
Director of Finance
Dallas/Fort Worth International Airport
Post Office Drawer DFW
Dallas/Fort Worth Airport, TX 75621

SHIRLEY D. WILLIAMS
Director of Personnel & Employee
 Relations
City of Inglewood
One Manchester Boulevard
Inglewood, CA 90301

JESSE E. WILLIAMS, JR.
Executive Director, Department of
 Human Services
City of Philadelphia
2020 Pennsylvania Avenue
Philadelphia, PA 19130

A. LEROY WILLIS
Director of Operations
Community Redevelopment Agency
City Of Los Angeles
354 South Spring Street
Los Angeles, CA 90013

EDWARD O. WILLIS
Assistant Director, Department of Fish
 & Game
State of California
1416 Ninth Street, Room 1026-22
Sacramento, CA 95814

JIM WILSON
City Administrator
City of Takoma Park
7500 Maple Avenue
Takoma Park, MD 20912

FRANK P. WISE, JR.
Director, Parks & Recreation
City of Dallas
1500 marilla, Suite 6FN
Dallas, TX 75201

PAUL R. WOODIE
Director, Department of Planning
City of Dayton
Post Office Box 22
Dayton, OH 45401

SHARON L. WOODS
Harbor Master
City of Richmond
2600 Barrett Avenue
Richmond, CA 94801

CHARLES J. WORTH
County Manager, Warren County
Post Office Box 619
Warrenton, NC 27589

HARVEY WORTHAM
Airport Superintendent, City of Dayton
Dayton International Airport
Terminal Building
Vandalia, OH 45377

*The listings in this directory
are available as Mailing Labels. See last page for details.*

Recording Studios

The following represents a partial listing of African-American Recording Studios.

CALIFORNIA

APPLE JUICE PRODUCTIONS, INC.
6769 Lexington Avenue
Los Angeles, CA 90038
Robert Brooks, International Director
(213) 464-2482

STAR GLOBE PRODUCTIONS
1901 Avenue of the Stars, Suite 1774
Los Angeles, CA 90067
Wendell Phillips, Marketing Director
(213) 553-5541

MARYLAND

WALL STREET PRODUCTIONS
4700 Auth Place, Suite 300
Marlow Heights, MD 20746
Gregory Johnson, President
(301) 423-0666

MICHIGAN

THE PRODUCTION PEOPLE, LTD.
32231 Schoolcraft, Suite 202
Livonia, MI 48150
W. Jackson Wertz, President
(313) 425-0730

UNITED SOUND SYSTEM, INC.
5840 Second Boulevard
Detroit, MI 48202
(313) 832-3313

OHIO

BODDIE RECORDING & RECORD MANUFACTURING COMPANY
12202 Union Avenue
Cleveland, OH 44105
Thomas Boddie, President
(216) 752-3440

PENNSYLVANIA

PHILADELPHIA INTERNATIONAL RECORDS
309 South Broad Street
Philadelphia, PA 19107
Connie Heigler, President
(215) 985-0900

TENNESSEE

GIL WILLIAMS PRODUCTIONS
315 Tenth Avenue, North
Suite 113
Nashville, TN 37203
(615) 255-4696

The listings in this directory are available as mailing labels. See last page for detail.s.

Resource Organizations

Many of the organizations listed in this section are national in scope and provide many valuable services to the nation.

A BETTER CHANCE
419 Boylston Street
Boston, MA 02116
Edward Dugger, III, Chairman
(617) 421-0950

A. PHILIP RANDOLPH EDUCATIONAL FUND
1444 I Street, N.W., Suite 300
Washington, D.C. 20005
Norman Hill, President
(202) 289-2774

ACTION ALLIANCE OF BLACK MANAGERS
Post Office Box 15636
Columbus, OH 43215
Paul G. Anderson, President
(614) 860-9388

AFFIRMATIVE ACTION GRADUATE FINANCIAL ASSISTANCE PROGRAM
Michigan State University
117 West Owen Hall
East Lansing, MI 48824
Dean Joe T. Darden

AFRICAN AMERICAN BIOGRAPHIES
4045 Kelden Court
College Park, GA 30349
Walter L. Hawkins, Author
(404) 669-9477

AFRICAN AMERICAN COALITION
1100 Sixth Street, S.W.
Washington, D.C. 20024
Wondimu Mersha, President
(202) 488-7830

AFRICAN AMERICAN FAMILY ASSOCIATES, INC.
2913 Bessemer Road
Birmingham, AL 35208
R. Curtis Steele, President
(205) 785-3936

AFRICAN AMERICAN INSTITUTE
833 United Nations Plaza
New York, NY 10017
Donald B. Easum, President
(212) 949-5666

AFRICAN AMERICAN RESOURCE CENTER
Post Office Box 746
Howard University
Washington, D.C. 20059
E. Ethelbert Miller, Director
(202) 806-7242

AFRICAN INFLUENCE
686 West Ventura Street
Altadena, CA 91001
Janet Akousa Edge, Director
(818) 794-7586

AFRICAN NATIONAL REPARA-TIONS ORGANIZATION
Post Office Box 1397
Rockville, MD 20850
Dorothy Lewis, Chairperson
(301) 279-2635

Resource Organizations

AFRICAN SCIENTIFIC INSTITUTE
Post Office Box 29119
Washington, D.C. 20017
Lee Cherry, Executive Director

AFRICANA STUDIES AND RESEARCH CENTER
Cornell University
310 Triphammer Road
Ithaca, NY 14850-2599
Dr. James Turner, Associate Professor

AFRICARE
440 R Street, N.W.
Washington, D.C. 20001
C. Payne Lucas, Executive Director
(202) 462-3614

AFRO-AMERICAN BOOK SOURCE
Post Office Box 851
Boston, MA 02120
Charles Pinderhughes, President
(617) 445-9209

AFRO-AMERICAN COMMUNITY SERVICES
1136 West Montecito Street
Post Office Box 4307
Santa Barbara, CA 93140
Valencia King Nelson, Director
(805) 965-8588

AFRO-AMERICAN HISTORICAL AND GENEALOGICAL SOCIETY
Post Office Box 73086
T Street Station
Washington, D.C. 20056-3086
Faith Davis Ruffins, President
(202) 234-5350

ALCOHOLISM IN THE BLACK COMMUNITY
East Orange General Hospital
300 Central Avenue
East Orange, NJ 07018
Debra Mallory, R.N., M.A., Director

AMERICAN ASSOCIATION FOR AFFIRMATIVE ACTION
Freehafer Hall, Second Floor
Purdue University
401 South Grant Street
West Lafayette, IN 47907
Paul C. Bayless, President
(317) 494-7254

AMERICAN BRIDGE ASSOCIATION, INC.
2798 Lakewood Avenue, S.W.
Atlanta, GA 30315
Thelma Woodson, President
(404) 768-5517

AMERICAN COUNCIL ON EDUCATION, OFFICE OF MINORITIES IN HIGHER EDUCATION
One Dupont Circle, Suite 800
Washington, D.C. 20036
Blandia Cardenas Ramirez
(202) 939-9395

AMERICAN HEALTH AND BEAUTY AIDS INSTITUTE
401 North Michigan Avenue,
24th Floor
Chicago, IL 60611-4267
Geri Duncan Jones, Executive Director
(312) 644-6610

Resource Organizations

AMERICAN SOCIETY FOR TRAINING AND DEVELOPMENT
1640 King Street, Box 1443
Alexandria, VA 22313
Curtis E. Plott, Executive Director
(703) 683-8100

AMISTAD RESEARCH CENTER
Tulane University
New Orleans, LA 70118-5698
Dr. C. H. Johnson, Executive Director
(504) 865-5535

ANCIENT EGYPTIAN ARABIC ORDER NOBLES MYSTIC SHRINE, INC.
1211 Cass Avenue
Detroit, MI 48201
David L. Holiman, Imperial Potentate
(313) 961-9148

ASCENSION POETRY READING SERIES
Post Office Box 441
Howard University
Washington, D.C. 20059
E. Ethelbert Miller, Director
(202) 636-7242

ASSOCIATION OF MINORITY ENTERPRISES OF NEW YORK
250 Fulton Avenue, Suite 505
Hempstead, NY 11550
Lynda Ireland, President
(516) 489-0120

AUDIENCE DEVELOPMENT COMMITTEE, INC.
Post Office Box 30, Manhattanville Station
New York, NY 10027
Louis Alexander, Chairperson
(212) 534-8776

BATON ROUGE MBDC
c/o Wybirk and Associates, Inc.
2036 Wooddale Boulevard
Baton Rouge, LA 70806
Warren Birkett, Jr., President
(504) 924-0186

BETHUNE-DUBOIS FUND
600 New Hampshire Avenue, N.W.
Washington, D.C. 20037
Dr. C. Delores Tucker, President
(202) 625-7048

BEULAH YOUTH DEVELOPMENT COUNCIL
Post Office Box 7243
Columbia, SC 29202
Shirley McClerklin-Motley, Chairperson

BLACK AGENCY EXECUTIVES
115 East 23rd Street
Tenth Floor
New York, NY 10010
(212) 254-2633

BLACK AMERICAN RESPONSE TO THE AFRICAN COMMUNITY
127 North Madison Avenue
Suite 400
Pasadena, CA 91102
Frank Wilson, President
(818) 584-0303

BLACK AWARENESS IN TELEVISION
13217 Livernois Street
Detroit, MI 48238-3162
David Rambeau, Director
(313) 931-3427

Resource Organizations

BLACK CAUCUS OF THE AMERICAN LIBRARY ASSOCIATION
c/o Virginia State
Library and Archives
Eleventh Street at Capital Square
Richmond, VA 23219
Dr. John Tyson, President

BLACK COLLEGIATE SERVICES, INC.
1240 South Broad Street
New Orleans, LA 70125
Reginald Lewis, Contact
(504) 821-5694

BLACK DATA PROCESSING ASSOCIATES
Post Office Box 7466
Philadelphia, PA 19101
Norman Mays, President
(215) 849-0163

BLACK HEALTH ASSOCIATES
206 High Street
Cranford, NJ 07016
D. Gary Robinson, President
(908) 272-2096

BLACK FILMMAKERS FOUNDATION
375 Greenwich Street, Suite 600
New York, NY 10013
Warren Hudlin, President
(212) 941-3944

BLACK PSYCHIATRISTS OF AMERICA
664 Prospect Avenue
Hartford, CT 06105
Dr. Thelissa Harris, President
(203) 236-2320

BLACK RESOURCES, INC.
501 Oneida Place, N.W.
Suite 1153
Washington, D.C. 20011
R. Benjamin Johnson, President
(202) 291-4373

BLACK RETAIL ACTION GROUP, INC.
Post Office Box 1192
Rockefeller Center Station
New York, NY 10185
J.J. Thomas, President
(212) 308-6017

THE BLACK STUDENT FUND
3636 Sixteenth Street, N.W.
Suite AG 23
Washington, D.C. 20010
Barbara Patterson, Executive Director
(202) 387-1414

BLACK UNITED FRONT
700 West Oakwood Boulevard
Chicago, IL 60053
Dr. Conrad Worrill, Chairperson
(312) 268-7500

BLACK WOMEN ACADEMI-CIANS
861 Goldwire Street, S.W.
Birmingham, AL 35211
Dr. Gertrude C. Saunders, President
(205) 252-7901

BLACK WOMEN'S EDUCA-TIONAL ALLIANCE
9200 Bustleton Avenue
Number 2112 Lloyd Building
Philadelphia, PA 19115
Barbara C. Merriweather, President
(215) 698-0836

Resource Organizations

BLACK WOMEN IN PUBLISHING, INC.
Post Office Box 6275, FDR Station
New York, NY 10150
Dolores T. Gordon, President
(212) 772-5951

BLACK WOMEN'S FORUM
3870 Crenshaw Boulevard, Suite 210
Los Angeles, CA 90008
Honorable Maxine Waters, President
(213) 292-3009

BLACK WOMEN'S NETWORK, INC. (MILWAUKEE)
Post Office Box 12072
Milwaukee, WI 53212
Joan M. Price, President
(414) 562-4500

BLACK WOMEN'S NETWORK, INC. (LOS ANGELES)
Post Office Box 56100
Los Angeles, CA 90056
Jessie Coston Reaves, President
(213) 292-6547

BLACKS AND MATHMATICS
Wentworth Institute of Technology
550 Huntington Avenue
Boston, MA 02115
John W. Alexander, Jr., Director
(617) 442-9010

BOOKER T. WASHINGTON FOUNDATION
4324 Georgia Avenue, N.W.
Washington, D.C. 20011
Charles E. Tate, President
(202) 882-7100

BRIMMER & COMPANY, INC.
4400 MacArthur Boulevard, Suite 302
Washington, D.C. 20007
Dr. Andrew F. Brimmer, President
(202) 342-6255

CALIFORNIA ASSOCIATION OF AFFIRMATIVE ACTION OFFICERS
Post Office Box 29146
Oakland, CA 94604-9146
Robert L. Bivens, President
(209) 478-4975

CARATS, INC.
3234 Fairwood Avenue
Columbus, OH 43207
Geri Lynch, President
(614) 491-0457

CAREER EXPO PLANNING COMMITTEE, INC.
31 Milk Street, Suite 205
Boston, MA 02109
Sherron Miller, President
(617) 426-6667

CARIBBEAN ACTION LOBBY
322 West Compton Boulevard
Compton, CA 90220
Honorable Mervyn M. Dymally,
  Chairperson
(213) 639-3641

CARIBBEAN-AMERICAN CHAMBER OF COMMERCE AND INDUSTRY, INC.
Brooklyn Navy Yard
Building 5, Mezzanine A
Brooklyn, NY 11205
Roy A. Hasticks, Sr., President
(718) 834-4544

Resource Organizations

CARROUSELS, INC.
4136 High Summit Drive
Dallas, TX 75244
Deborah Ellison Farris, Esquire
(212) 484-2895

**CARVER RESEARCH
FOUNDATION OF TUSKEGEE
INSTITUTE, INC.**
Tuskegee Institute
Tuskegee, AL 36088
Dr. Margaret E.M. Tolbert, Director
(205) 727-8246

CASY PRODUCTIONS, INC.
1352 South Rimpau
Los Angeles, CA 90019
Yvonne Buchannan, Executive
  Producer
(213) 933-0722

**CENTER FOR AFRO-AMERICAN
STUDIES**
343 High Street
Middletown CT 06457
Professor Marshall Hyatt, Director
(203) 344-7943

**CENTER FOR DEMOCRATIC
RENEWAL**
Post Office Box 50469
Atlanta, GA 30302
Rev. C. T. Vivian, Chairman
(404) 221-0025

**CENTER FOR URBAN ENVIRON-
MENTAL STUDIES, INC.
(NATIONAL)**
516 North Charles Street, Suite 501
Baltimore, MD 21201
Larry Young, President
(301) 727-6212

**CHARLES HAMILTON
HOUSTON LEGAL
EDUCATION INSTITUTE**
Post Office Box 75484
Washington, D.C. 20018
Donald M. Temple, Esquire, President

CHILDREN WORKSHOP
3825 St. Louis Avenue
St. Louis, MO 63107
Edna J. Hanks-Pipes, Author/Consult-
  ant
(314) 535-2872

CHILDREN'S DEFENSE FUND
122 C Street, N.W.
Washington, D.C. 20001
Marion Wright Edelman, President
(202) 628-8787

**CHOCOLATE SINGLES
ENTERPRISES**
Post Office Box 333
Jamaica, NY 11413
(718) 978-4800

CHUMS, INC.
8339 East Beach Drive, N.W.
Washington, D.C. 20012
Lucille J. Gaye, President
(202) 882-0857

**CLARK, MCGILL AND SEAY
PROFESSIONAL CORPORA-
TION**
42 South Fifteenth Street
Suite 1600
Philadelphia, PA 19102
Thomas L. McGill, Attorney-at-Law
(215) 568-6633

Resource Organizations

CLARK, PHIPPS, CLARK & HARRIS, INC.
60 East 86th Street
New York, NY 10028
Dr. Kenneth B. Clark, President
(212) 772-1000

COALITION OF BLACK TRADE UNIONIST
Post Office Box 73120
Washington, D.C. 20056-3120
William Lucy, President
(202) 429-1203

COALITION OF FEDERAL AVIATION EMPLOYEES
2233 West Rosedale Street, South
Fort Worth, TX 76110-1139
(202) 429-1203

COMMITTEE ON BLACK PER-FORMING ARTS
Stanford University
Harmony House, 561 Lomita Drive
Stanford, CA 94305
Dr. Sandra Richards, Director
(415) 723-4402

CONCERNED EDUCATORS OF BLACK STUDENTS
473 Marathon Avenue
Dayton, OH 45406
Maurice Jones, President
(513) 275-9133

CONFERENCE OF PRINCE HALL GRAND MASTERS
50 S Street, N.W.
Washington, D.C. 20001
Morris S. Miller, Chairman
(202) 332-6331

CONGRESSIONAL BLACK ASSOCIATES, INC.
U.S. HOR, Room 1979
Longworth House Office Building
Washington, D.C. 20515
Sam E. Thornton, Director
(202) 225-5865

CONGRESSIONAL BLACK CAUCUS
House Annex Number 2, Room 344
Third and D Streets, S.W.
Washington, D.C. 20515
(202) 226-7790

CONGRESSIONAL BLACK CAUCUS FOUNDATION, INC.
1004 Pennsylvania Avenue, S.E.
Washington, D.C. 20003
(202) 675-6730

CONSORTIUM FOR GRADUATE STUDY IN MANAGEMENT
200 South Hanley, Suite 616
Clayton, MO 63105
Dr. Wally L. Jones, Chief Executive Officer
(314) 935-6364

CONTINENTAL SOCIETIES, INC.
262 Evergreen Avenue
Blackwood, NJ 08012
Evelyn I. Means, President
(609) 227-8228

CORE IMMIGRATION SERVICES
1457 Flatbush Avenue
Brooklyn, NY 11210
(718) 434-2673

Resource Organizations

**CREATIVE CHURCH LEADER-
SHIP DEVELOPMENT, INC.**
3230 South Gessner, Suite 801
Houston, TX 77063
Laurence J. Payne, President
(713) 781-9290

DELTA HEALTH CENTER, INC.
Post Office Drawer 900
Mound Bayou, MS 38762
Dr. L.C. Dorsey, Executive Director
(601) 741-2151

**DELTA RESEARCH & EDUCA-
TIONAL FOUNDATION**
1707 New Hampshire Avenue, N.W.
Washington, D.C. 20009
Louis E. Taylor, Director
(202) 986-2400

DOLL LEAGUE, INC.
150 McLean Blvd.
Patterson, NJ 07506
Carole Brantley, President
(201) 523-4267

DRIFTERS, INC.
10 Chelsea Court
Neptune, NJ 07753
Sylvia Thomas, President
(908) 774-2724

EDGES GROUP
c/o Anmerada Hess Corporation
1 Hess Plaza
Woodbridge, NJ 07095
Walter C. Vertreace, Esquire,
President
(908) 750-6408

**EXECUTIVE LEADERSHIP
COUNCIL**
444 North Capitol Street, Suite 715
Washington, D.C. 20001
Clarence L. James, Jr., Executive
Director
(202) 783-6339

**FEDERATION OF CORPORATE
PROFESSIONALS**
1000 Connecticut Avenue, N.W.
Washington, D.C. 20036
Gregory Matthews, Chairman

**FEDERATION OF MASONS OF
THE WORLD AND FEDERA-
TION OF EASTERN STARS**
1017 East Eleventh Street
Austin, TX 78702
M.J. Anderson, Sr., Chairman
(512) 477-5380

**FEDERATION OF SOUTHERN
COOPERATIVES LAND ASSIS-
TANCE FUND**
100 Edgewood Avenue, N.E.,
Suite 814
Atlanta, GA 30303
Ralph Paige, Executive Director
(404) 524-6882

FLORIDA ENDOWMENT FUND
201 East Kennedy Boulevard,
Suite 1525
Tampa, FL 33602
Dr. Israel Tribble, Jr., President
(813) 272-2772

Resource Organizations

FRONTIERS INTERNATIONAL, INC.
6301 Crittenden Street
Philadelphia, PA 19138
Floyd W. Alston, President
(215) 549-4550

FUTURES' FUND AND FELLOW-SHIP FOUNDATION
2601 South Glebe Road, Suite 2914-4
Arlington, VA 22206
Lee Black, Director
(703) 976-2323

GIRLFRIENDS, INC.
228 Lansing Avenue
Portsmouth, VA 23704
Rachel N. Smith, President
(804) 397-1339

GOSPEL MUSIC WORKSHOP OF AMERICA
Post Office Box 34635
Detroit, MI 48234
Edward D. Smith, Executive Secretary
(313) 989-2340

HARLEM THIRD WORLD TRADE INSTITUTE
163 West 125th Street, 12th Floor
New York, NY 10027
Balozi R. Harvey, Director
(212) 870-4305

HERMAN & ASSOCIATES, INC.
1050 Seventeenth Street, N.W., Suite 560
Washington, D.C. 20036
Alexis Herman, President
(202) 797-7206

HISTORICAL RESEARCH REPOSITORY, INC.
868 Penobsot Building
Detroit, MI 48226-4004
John Green, Executive Director

HOLIDAYS, INC.
12202 Brittany Place
Laurel, MD 20708
Gloria Massie, President
(301) 953-1640

HOWARD UNIVERSITY SMALL BUSINESS DEVELOPMENT CENTER
Howard University, P. O.Box 748
Washington, D.C. 20059
Nancy A. Flake, Director
(202) 636-5150

IDA VAN SMITH FLIGHT CLUB, INC.
Post Office Box 361
Rochdale Village, NY 11434
Ida Van Smith, President
(718) 723-3054

IMPROVED BENOVOLENT PROTECTIVE ORDER OF ELKS OF THE WORLD
Post Office Box 159
Winton, NC 27986
Donald P. Wilson, Grand Exalted Ruler
(919) 358-7661

INDEPENDENT SCHOOL ALLIANCE FOR MINORITY AFFAIRS
110 South LaBrea Avenue, Suite 265
Inglewood, CA 90301
Manasa Hekymara, Executive Director
(213) 672-5544

Resource Organizations

INDIANA BLACK EXPO, INC.
3130 Sutherland Avenue
Indianapolis, IN 46205
Rev. Charles Williams, President
(317) 925-2702

INNER-CITY AIDS NETWORK
1707 Seventh Street, N.W.,
  Second Floor
Washington, D.C. 20001-3508
(202) 387-0800

**INSTITUTE FOR AMERICAN
  BUSINESS**
1275 K Street, N.W., Suite 601
Washington, D.C. 20005
Abraham S. Venable, Chairman
(202) 408-5418

**INSTITUTE FOR THE AD-
  VANCED STUDY OF BLACK
  FAMILY LIFE & CULTURE**
155 Filbert Street, Suite 202
Oakland, CA 94607
Wade Nobles, Ph.D., Executive
  Director
(415) 836-3245

**INSTITUTE FOR INDEPENDENT
  EDUCATION**
1313 North Capitol Street, N.E.
Washington, D.C. 20002
Joan Davis Ratteray, President
(202) 745-0500

**INSTITUTE OF POSITIVE
  EDUCATION**
7524 South Cottage Grove Avenue
Chicago, IL 60619
Haki R. Madhubuti, Director

INTER IMAGE VIDEO
Post Office Box 47501
Los Angeles, CA 90047-0501
J. Bernard Nicolas, President
(213) 756-7789

**INTERNATIONAL BENEVOLENT
  SOCIETY**
Post Office Box 1276
837 Fifth Avenue
Columbus, GA 31901
James O. Brown, President
(404) 322-5671

**INTERNATIONAL BLACK
  WOMEN'S CONGRESS**
1081 Bergen Street, Suite 200
Newark, NJ 07112
Dr. LaFrancis Rodgers-Rose,
  President
(201) 926-0570

**INTERNATIONAL BLACK
  WRITERS CONFERENCE, INC.**
Post Office Box 1030
Chicago, IL 60690
Mable Jean Terrell, President
(312) 924-3818

**INTERNATIONAL CITY MAN-
  AGEMENT ASSOCIATION**
1120 G Street, N.W.
Washington, D.C. 20004
(202) 626-4662

INTERNATIONAL CONSULTANTS
24041 Geneva
Oak Park, MI 48237
Dr. Deborah Livingston-White,
  President
(313) 399-3229

Resource Organizations

INTER-RACIAL COUNCIL FOR BUSINESS OPPORTUNITY
51 Madison Avenue, Suite 2212
New York, NY 10010
William A. Young, III, President
(212) 779-4360

INTERRELIGIOUS FOUNDATION FOR COMMUNITY ORGANIZA-TION, INC.
348 Convent Avenue
New York, NY 10031
Rev. Dr. Lucius Walker, Executive
   Director
(212) 926-5757

JACKIE ROBINSON FOUNDATION
80 Eighth Avenue
New York, NY 10011
Rachel Robinson, Chairperson
(212) 675-1511

JAGME FOUNDATION
5617 Hollywood Boulevard, Suite 103
Hollywood, CA 90028
James A. Goodson, Director
(212) 461-4196

JOB OPPORTUNITIES
Bulletin for Minorities and Women
777 N. Capitol St., N.E., Fifth Floor
Washington, D.C. 20002-4201
Maria Dessenna-Lopes,
   Program Director
(202) 962-3662

JOHN HENRY MEMORIAL FOUNDATION, INC.
Post Office Box 1172
Morgantown, WV 26507
Edward J. Cabbell, Director

JOINT CENTER FOR POLITICAL STUDIES
1301 Pennsylvania Avenue, N.W.,
   Suite 400
Washington, D.C. 20004
Eddie N. Williams, President
(202) 626-3509

JOINT MEMORIAL ASSOCIA-TION OF WASHINGTON
2027 North Captiol Street, N.E.
Washington, D.C. 20002
Rev. Imagene B. Stewart, Chairperson
(202) 797-7460

J.U.G.S., INC.
1965 Thornhill Place
Detroit, MI 48207
Terri L. Bagwell, President

JUNIOR BLACK ACADEMY OF ARTS AND LETTERS, INC.
Dallas Convention Center Theatre
650 South Griffin Street
Dallas, TX 75202
Curtis King, President
(214) 658-7144

LAWYER'S COMMITTEE FOR CIVIL RIGHTS UNDER LAW
1400 Eye Street, N.W.
Washington, D.C. 20005
Barbara R. Arnwine, Executive
   Director
(202) 371-1212

LEADERSHIP CONFERENCE ON CIVIL RIGHTS
2027 Massachusetts Avenue, N.W.
Washington, D.C. 20036
Ralph G. Neas, Executive Director
(202) 667-1780

Resource Organizations

**LENA PARK COMMUNITY DEVEL-
OPMENT CORPORATION**
150 American Legion Highway
Dorchester, MA 02124
Dr. Nathan Allen, President
(617) 436-1900

LEGACIES, INC.
347 Felton Avenue
Highland Park, NJ 08904
Jacqueline L. VanSertima, President
(201) 828-4667

LINKS, INC.
1200 Massachusetts Avenue, N.W.
Washington, D.C. 20005
Marion Schmaltz Southerly, President
(202) 842-8696

**LOW INCOME HOUSING INFOR-
MATION SERVICE**
1012 Fourteenth Street, N.W., Suite
1500
Washington, D.C. 20005
Lydia Tom, President
(202) 662-1530

**MALCOLM X MEMORIAL FOUN-
DATION**
9642 Camden Avenue
Omaha, NE 68134
Wilbur Phillips, Contact
(402) 572-0397

**MARLA GIBBS CROSSROADS
NATIONAL EDUCATION ARTS
CENTER AND THEATRE**
4310 Degnan Boulevard
Los Angeles, CA 90008
Marla Gibbs, President
(213) 291-7321

**MINIATURE PIANO ENTHUSIASTS
CLUB**
5815 North Sheridan Road, Suite 202
Chicago, IL 60660
Janice E. Kelsh, Contact
(312) 271-2970

**MINORITIES FELLOWSHIP
PROGRAM**
Indiana University
Kirkwood Hall, Room 111
Bloomington, IN 47405
Edmond Keller, Director
(812) 335-0822

**MINORITY AGRICULTURAL
RESOURCES CENTER**
817 Fourteenth Street, Suite 300A
Sacramento, CA 95814
Drue P. Brown, President
(916) 444-2924

MINORITY BUSINESS ENTERPRISE
Legal Defense and Education Fund
220 Eye Street, Suite 280
Washington, D.C. 20002
Anthony W. Robinson, President
(202) 543-0040

**MINORITY BUSINESS INFORMA-
TION INSTITUTE, INC.**
130 Fifth Avenue
New York, NY 10011
Earl G. Graves, Executive Director
(212) 242-8000

**MINORITY NETWORK OF THE
AMERICAN SOCIETY FOR
TRAINING AND DEVELOP-
MENT, INC.**
1630 Duke Street, Box 1443
Alexandria, VA 22313
Curtis E. Plott, Executive Vice
President
(703) 683-8100

Resource Organizations

MODERN FREE AND ACCEPTED MASONS OF THE WORLD, INC.
Post Office Box 1072
Columbus, OH 31906
Henry Williams, Supreme Grand Master
(404) 322-3326

MOLES
1418 Floral Drive, N.W.
Washington, D.C. 20012
Margaret T. Nelson, President
(202) 723-1678

MOORLAND-SPRINGARN RESEARCH CENTER
Howard University
Washington, D.C. 20059
Thomas C. Battle, Director
(202) 806-7241

MOST WORSHIPFUL NATIONAL GRAND LODGE FREE AND ACCEPTED ANCIENT YORK MASONS PRINCE HALL ORIGIN NATIONAL COMPACT U.S.A., INC.
26070 Tryon Road
Oakwood Village, OH 44116
Jefferson D. Tufts, Sr., Grand Master
(216) 232-9495

MUHAMMAD UNIVERSITY OF ISLAM
7351 South Stony Island Avenue
Chicago, IL 60649
Sister Shelby X Moody, National Directress

MUSIC RESEARCH INTERNATIONAL
Indiana University
Department of Afro Studies
Bloomington, IN 47405
Dr. P. K. Maultsby, Director

MYPHEDUH FILMS, INC.
48 Q Street, N.E.
Washington, D.C. 20002
Haile Gerima, President
(202) 529-0220

NAACP LEGAL DEFENSE AND EDUCATIONAL FUND, INC.
99 Hudson Street
Suite 1600
New York, NY 10013
Julius L. Chambers, Director-Counsel
(212) 219-1900

NCM CAPITAL MANAGEMENT GROUP, INC.
Two Mutual Plaza
501 Willard Street
Durham, NC 27701-3642
(919) 688-0620

NOBCO AIDS EDUCATION PROJECT
1631 East 120th Street
Building C
Los Angeles, CA 90059
Crandall Jones, Executive Director
(213) 567-7799

NATIONAL ACTION COUNCIL FOR MINORITIES IN ENGINEERING
3 West 35th Street
New York, NY 10001
George Campbell, Jr., Ph.D., President
(212) 279-2626

Resource Organizations

NATIONAL AFRICAN AMERICAN NETWORK
5113 Georgia Avenue, N.W.
Washington, D.C. 20011
Kathryn Flewellen-Palmer, Executive
  Director

NATIONAL ALLIANCE AGAINST RACIST AND POLITICAL REPRESSION
126 West 119th Street, Suite 101
New York, NY 10026
Frank Chapman, Executive Director
(212) 866-8600

NATIONAL ALLIANCE OF BLACK SALESMEN AND SALESWOMEN
Post Office Box 2814
Manhattanville Station
Harlem, NY 10027
Franklyn Bryant, President
(914) 668-1430

NATIONAL ALLIANCE OF BLACK SCHOOL EDUCATORS
2816 Georgia Avenue, Suite 4
Washington, D.C. 20001
Ted Kimbrough, J.D., President
(202) 483-8323

NATIONAL ANTI-KLAN NETWORK
Post Office Box 10500
Atlanta, GA 30310
Rev. C. T. Vivian, Chairman
(404) 221-0025

NATIONAL BLACK ALCOHOLISM COUNCIL, INC.
53 West Jackson Boulevard, Suite 828
Chicago, IL 60604
Frances L. Brisbane, Ph.D.,
  Chairperson
(312) 663-5780

NATIONAL BLACK CHILD DEVELOPMENT INSTITUTE
1023 Fifteenth Street, N.W., Suite 600
Washington, D.C. 20005
Evelyn K. Moore, Executive Director
(202) 387-1281

NATIONAL BLACK MEDIA COALITION
38 New York Avenue, N.E.
Washington, D.C. 20002
Pluria Marshall, Chairman
(202) 387-8155

NATIONAL BLACK UNITED FRONT
700 East Oakwood Boulevard
Chicago, IL 60653
Dr. Conrad Worrill, Chairperson
(312) 268-7500 Extenxion 154

NATIONAL BLACK UNITED FUND, INC.
50 Park Place, Suite 1538
Newark, NJ 07102
William T. Merritt, President
(201) 643-5122

NATIONAL BLACK YOUTH LEADERSHIP COUNCIL, INC.
250 West 54th Street, Suite 811
New York, NY 10019
Dennis Rahim Watson, Executive
  Director
(212) 541-7600

NATIONAL CAUCUS AND CENTER ON BLACK AGED, INC.
1424 K Street, N.W., Suite 500
Washington, D.C. 20005
Samuel J. Simons, President
(202) 637-8400

Resource Organizations

**NATIONAL CENTER FOR NEIGH-
BORHOOD ENTERPRISE**
1367 Connecticut Avenue, N.W.
Washington, D.C. 20036
Robert L. Woodson, President

**NATIONAL CENTER OF AFRO-
AMERICAN ARTISTS, INC.**
Post Office Box 143
Dorchester, MA 02121
Matthew E. Goode, President
(617) 422-2047

**NATIONAL CONFERENCE OF
BLACK MAYORS, INC. (NCBM)**
1430 West Peachtree Street, N.W.,
Suite 700
Atlanta, GA 30309
Michelle D. Kourouma, Executive
Director
(404) 892-0127

**NATIONAL CONFERENCE ON
BLACK STUDENT RETENTION**
Florida Agricultural & Mechanical
University
404 Foote Hilyer Center
Tallahassee, FL 32307
Dr. Clinita A. Ford, Coordinator
(804) 599-3537

**NATIONAL INSTITUTE OF
SCIENCE**
c/o Dr. Arthur C. Washington
Prairie View A&M University
Prairie View, TX 77445
(409) 847-4522

**NATIONAL MINORITY BUSI-
NESS COUNCIL, INC.**
235 East 42nd Street
New York, NY 10017
John F. Robinson, President
(212) 573-2385

**NATIONAL MINORITY SUPPLI-
ERS DEVELOPMENT COUN-
CIL, INC.**
15 West 39th Street, Ninth Floor
New York, NY 10018
Harriet R. Michel, President
(212) 944-2430

**NATIONAL MOVEMENT TO
BOYCOTT CRIME, INC.**
Post Office Box 202
Teaneck, NJ 07666
Julian I. Garfield, President
(201) 836-1838

**NATIONAL ORGANIZATION OF
MINORITY ARCHITECTS**
120 Ralph McGill Boulevard, N.E.
Atlanta, GA 30308
William J. Stanley, III, President
(404) 876-3055

**NATIONAL PAN-HELLENIC
COUNCIL**
IMU Number 30
Bloomington, IN 47405
Daisy Wood, President
(812) 855-8820

**NATIONAL POLITICAL CON-
GRESS OF BLACK WOMEN**
Post Office Box 411
Rancocas, NJ 08073
Portia Dempsey, Executive Director
(609) 871-1500

**NATIONAL SOCIETY OF BLACK
ENGINEERS (NSBE)**
1454 Duke Street
Alexandria, VA 22314
Flo Morehead, Executive Director
(703) 549-2207

Resource Organizations

NATIONAL SOCIETY OF BLACK PHYSICISTS
Department of Physics
Southern University
Baton Rouge, LA 70810
Dr. Eugene Collins, President
(504) 771-4130

NATIONAL SOCIETY OF MINORITY WOMEN IN SCIENCE
c/o American Association for the
   Advancement of Science
1776 Massachusetts Avenue, N.W.
Washington, D.C. 20035
Yolanda George, Chairperson
(202) 467-5433

NATIONAL URBAN AFFAIRS COUNCIL
2350 Adam Clayton Powell Blvd.
New York, NY 10030
Sandra Davis Houston, President
(914) 694-4000

NATIONAL URBAN COALITION
8601 Georgia Avenue, N.W., Suite 500
Silver Spring, MD 20910
Dr. Ramona Edelin, President
(301) 495-4999

NATIONAL URBAN LEAGUE
500 East 62nd Street
New York, NY 10021
John E. Jacob, President
(212) 310-9000

NEW CONCEPT SELF DEVELOPMENT CENTER, INC.
636 West Kneeland Street
Milwaukee, WI 53212
June M Perry, Executive Director
(414) 271-7496

NEW PROFESSIONAL THEATRE
443 West 50 Street
New York, NY 10019
Sheila K. Davis, Executive Producer
(212) 484-9811

NEW YORK AFRICAN AMERICAN FOUNDATION
State University Of New York
State University Plaza, N-502
Albany, NY 12246
Dr. A. J. Williams-Myers, Director
(518) 443-5798

NIGERIAN AMERICAN ALLIANCE
2 Penn Plaza, Suite 1700
New York, NY 10121
James E. Obi, President
(212) 560-5500

NORTHWEST CONFERENCE OF BLACK PUBLIC OFFICIALS
600 Fourth Avenue, Room 1111
Seattle, WA 98104
Sam Smith, Regional Director
(206) 625-2455

OFFICE FOR THE ADVANCEMENT OF PUBLIC BLACK COLLEGES
1 Dupont Circle, Suite 710
Washington, D.C. 20036
Dr. N. Joyce Payne, Director
(202) 778-0818

ONE HUNDRED BLACK MEN
105 East 22nd Street
New York, NY 10010
Dr. Roscoe C. Brown, Jr., President
(212) 777-7070

ONE HUNDRED BLACK MEN OF NEW JERSEY, INC.
141 South Harrison Street
East Orange, NJ 07018
Dr. William Giles, President
(201) 678-6522

OPERA NORTH
Post Office Box 29501
Philadelphia, PA 19144
Sam R. Cosby, Jr., President
(215) 472-3111

OPERATION PUSH
930 East 50th Street
Chicago, IL 60615
Rev. Otis Moss, Chairperson
(312) 373-3366

OPPORTUNITIES INDUSTRIAL- IZATION CENTERS OF AMERICA, INC.
1415 North Broad Street, Suite 111
Philadelphia, PA 19122
Dr. Leon Sullivan, Chairman
(215) 236-4500

OPPORTUNITY FUNDING CORPORATION
2021 K Street, N.W., Suite 303
Washington, D.C. 20006
C. Robert Kemp, President
(202) 833-9580

ORGANIZATION OF BLACK AIRLINE PILOTS, INC.
Post Office Box 86
Laguardia Airport
Flushing, NY 11371
William Norwood, President
(201) 568-8145

PHELPS-STOKES FUND
10 East 87th street
New York, NY 10128
Wilbert J. LeMelle, President
(212) 427-8100

PINOCHLE BUGS SOCIAL AND CIVIC CLUB, INC.
1624 Madison Avenue
Charlotte, NC 28216
Esther Page Hill, President
(704) 334-4802

PRISM DAE CORPORATION
2 Wisconsin Circle, Suite 300
Chevy Chase, MD 20815
Don A. Grigg, Chairman
(301) 907-3300

PROGRESSIVE LIFE CENTER, INC.
1123 Eleventh Street, N.W.
Washington, D.C. 20001
Dr. Frederick B. Phillips, President
(202) 842-4570

PUSH TRADE BUREAU
930 East 50th Street
Chicago, IL 60615
(312) 373-3366

PYRAMID COMMUNICATIONS INTERNATIONAL
800 Third Street, N.E.
Washington, D.C. 20002
Derrick Gibbs-Johnson, Executive Director
(202) 675-4169

Resource Organizations

REMEDIAL READING AND LEARNING CENTER
2239 West Washington Boulevard
Los Angeles, CA 90018
Helen Ramey, Director
(213) 732-1350

RESEARCH FOUNDATION FOR ETHNIC RELATED DISEASES
2231 South Western Avenue
Los Angeles, CA 90018
Randall Maxey, Executive Director
(213) 737-7372

SAMMY DAVIS, JR. NATIONAL LIVER INSTITUTE
Medical Science Building, Room I-506
185 South Orange Avenue
Newark, NJ 07103-2757
Ronald Wellington Brown, Executive Vice President
(201) 456-4535

SAN FRANCISCO AFRICAN AMERICAN HISTORICAL AND CULTURAL SOCIETY
Fort Mason Center, Building C-165
San Francisco, CA 94123
Donneter E. Lane, President
(415) 441-0640

SCHOMBURG CENTER FOR RESEARCH IN BLACK CULTURE
515 Malcolm X Boulevard
New York, NY 10037
Howard Dodson, Director
(212) 862-4000

SCIENCE SKILLS CENTER, INC.
Post Office Box 883, Adelphi Station
Brooklyn, NY 11238
Michael A. Johnson, Executive Director
(718) 636-6215

SOUTHEASTERN ASSOCIATION OF EDUCATIONAL OPPORTUNITY
Program Personnel
Post Office Box 91
Florida A&M University
Tallahassee, FL 32307
Dr. Ben C. McCune, President
(904) 599-3055

SOUTHERN POVERTY LAW CENTER
400 Washington Avenue
Montgomery AL 36104
Morris S. Dees, Jr., Executive Director
(205) 264-0286

SOUTHERN REGIONAL COUNCIL
134 Peachtree Street, N.W., Suite 1900
Atlanta, GA 30303
Lottie Shackleford, President
(404) 522-8764

SOUTHERN RURAL WOMEN'S NETWORK, INC.
Post Office Box 3548
Jackson, MS 39207
Sharon A. Miles, Executive Director
(601) 956-2102

Resource Organizations

STANFORD UNIVERSITY'S BLACK COMMUNITY SERVICES CENTER
418 Santa Teresa
Stanford, CA 94305
Faye McNair Knox, Assistant Dean/
   Director
(415) 723-1587

STUDENT NATIONAL MEDICAL ASSOCIATION, INC
1012 Tenth Street, N.W.
Washington, D.C. 20001
Annette McLane, Executive Director
(202) 371-1616

THE CARTER G. WOODSON FOUNDATION
P. O. Box 1025, G9, Lincoln Park
Newark, NJ 07101
Philip S. Thomas, President
(202) 242-0500

THE COUNCIL OF INDEPEN-DENT BLACK INSTITUTIONS (CIBI)
Post Office Box 50396
East Palo Alto, CA 94303
Dr. Kofi Lomotey, Executive Officer
(415) 327-5848

THE MATHEWS ASSOCIATES
(Africa Commentary)
Post Office Box 53398
Washington, D.C. 20009
Daniel G. Mathews, President
(202) 223-1807

THE NATIONAL ACTION COUNCIL FOR MINORITIES IN ENGINEERING
3 West 35th Street, Third Floor
New York, NY 10001
Lloyd M. Cooke, President
(212) 279-2626

THE WORLD INSTITUTE OF BLACK COMMUNICATIONS, INC.
CEBA Awards
10 Columbus Circle
New York, NY 10019
Adriane T. Gaines & Joan Logue,
   Co-Directors
(212) 586-1771

369TH VETERANS ASSOCIATON, INC.
Post Office Box 91
New York, NY 10037
Sam W. Phillips, President
(212) 281-3308

TOP LADIES OF DISTINCTION, INC.
Post Office Box 1697
Calumet City, IL 60609
Jacquelyn Heath Parker, President
(312) 672-9217

TRANSAFRICA
545 Eighth Street, S.E.
Washington, D.C. 20003
Randall Robinson, Director
(202) 547-2550

TUSKEGEE AIRMEN, INC.
65 Cadillac Square, Suite 3200
Detroit, MI 48226
Elmore M. Kennedy, Jr., President
(313) 965-8858

TWENTY-FIRST CENTURY FOUNDATION
214 Tryon Avenue
Teaneck, NJ 07666
Dr. Robert S. Browne, President
(212) 427-8100

Resource Organizations

THE TRIAD GROUP
1625 K Street, N.W., Suite 1210
Washington, D.C. 20006
Kent B. Amos, Chief Executive
(202) 775-3500

UNITED AMERICAN PROGRESS ASSOCIATION
701 East 79th Street
Chicago, IL 60619
Webb Evans, President
(312) 955-8112

UNITED BLACK CHURCH APPEAL
860 Forrest Avenue
Bronx, NY 10456
Honorable Wendell Foster, President
(212) 992-5315

UNITED BLACK FUND OF AMERICA, INC.
1012 Fourteenth Street, N.W., Suite 300
Washington, D.C. 20005
Dr. Calvin W. Rolark, President
(800) 323-7677

UNITED NEGRO COLLEGE FUND, INC.
500 East 62nd Street
New York, NY 10021
William H. Gray, III, President
(212) 326-1100

URBAN RESEARCH PRESS, INC.
840 East 87th Street
Chicago, IL 60619
Dempsey Travis, President
(312) 994-7200

VOTER EDUCATION PROJECT, INC.
604 Beckwith Street, S.W.
Atlanta, GA 30314
Ed Brown, Executive Director
(404) 522-7495

WORLD INSTITUTE OF BLACK COMMUNICATIONS, INC.
463 Seventh Avenue
New York, NY 10018
Adriane T. Gaines, Executive Director
(212) 714-1508

YOUNG BLACK PROGRAM-MERS COALITION, INC.
Post Office Box 11243
Jackson, MS 39213
Tommy Marshall, President
(601) 995-1300

YOUTH ORGANIZATION USA (YOUSA)
19 Humphrey Street
Englewood, NJ 07631
Julian J. Garfield, Chief Executive
(201) 894-1866

The listings in this directory are available as Mailing Labels. See last page for details.

Sports Agents

The following individuals represent a partial listing of African-American sports agents in America.

ALABAMA

ULLYSSES MCBRIDE
173 Dr. Martin Luther King Boulevard
Atmore, AL 36502
(205) 937-9581

ARIZONA

CLARENCE FOUSE
A.S.F. Agency
6708 West McRae Way
Glendale, AZ 85308
(602) 561-1034

MICHAEL M. SMITH
Smith Financial Services
16006 South 34th Way
Phoenix, AZ 85094
(602) 759-8099

CALIFORNIA

EDWARD D. ABRAM
Morcom Sports Enterprise
1624 Franklin Street, Suite 911
Oakland, CA 94612-2824
(510) 835-4944

RAYMOND E. ANDERSON
A. R. Sports, Inc.
1150 Ballena Boulevard, Suite 211
Alameda, CA 94501
(510) 865-5489

JAMES CASEY
Team Jammin
5621 Chariton Avenue
Los Angeles, CA 90056
(213) 291-8749

HAROLD DANIELS
Professional Stars, Inc.
9807 Haas Avenue
Los Angeles, CA 90047
(213) 777-5046

LOUIS E. DUVERNAY
Attorney at Law
1624 Franklin Street, Suite 911
Oakland, CA 94612-2824
(510) 835-4944

MARVIN FLEMING
909 Howard Street
Marina del Rey, CA 90292
(213) 827-5152

JOHNNIE JOHNSON
Beverly Hills Sports Council
9595 Wilshire Boulevard, Suite 711
Beverly Hills, CA 90212
(213) 858-1935

KENNETH C. LANDPHERE
A. R. Sports, Inc.
1150 Ballena Boulevard, Suite 211
Alameda, CA 94501

RAOL LEE
1038 Magnolia Street, Suite A
Oakland, CA 94607
(415) 444-6474

W. RAY NEWMAN
Attorney at Law
880 West First Street, Suite 302
Los Angeles, CA 90012
(213) 617-8128

Sports Agents

MARVIN POWELL
Rosenfeld, Meyer and Susman
9601 Wilshire Boulevard, Fourth Floor
Beverly Hills, CA 90210
(310) 858-7700

LARRY D. REYNOLDS
A R Sports, Inc.
5055 Canyon Crest Drive, Suite 205
Riverside, CA 92507
(510) 865-5489

RONALD O. SALLY
Crosby, Heafey, Roach & May
700 South Flower Street, Suite 2200
Los Angeles,CA 90017
(213) 896-8000

EDWARD C. SEWELL
Professional Sports Center
1238 Cole Street
San Francisco, CA 94117
(415) 681-1335

KENNETH E. "PETE" SHAW
Career Sports Management
  International
3115 Verde Avenue
Rancho La Costa, CA 92009

JAMES A. SIMS
Attorney-at-Law
1 Park Plaza, Suite 290
Irvine, CA 92714
(714) 263-1514

CHARLES LEE SMITH
Attorney-at-Law
1110 East Green Street, Suite 200
Pasadena, CA 91106
(818) 793-9627

DAVID R. SMITH
Sports Account
Post Office Box 9633
Bakersfield, CA 93389
(805) 324-3283

W. JEROME STANLEY
Attorney at Law
10880 Wilshire Boulevard, Suite 606
Los Angeles, CA 90024
(310) 474-0091

EDWIN R. WATLEY
ERW & Associates
14252 Culver, Suite A-295
Irvine, CA 92714
(714) 262-9468

D'ANDRE C. WELLS
Socrates Sports
Post Office Box 471
Richmond, CA 94808-0471
(510) 232-6783

FREDERICK B. WILLIAMS
Athena Sports Management
10920 Wilshire Bouleveard, Suite 650
Los Angeles, CA 90024-6508
(310) 479-5372

ANTHONY W. WILLOUGHBY
Willoughby & Shorter
8500 Wilshire Boulevard, Suite 903
Beverly Hills, CA 90211
(213) 854-1961

ERNEST H. WRIGHT
E. H. Wright & Associates
2727 Boston Avenue
San Diego, CA 92113
(619) 232-1066

ANGELO WRIGHT
Advantage Sports Management
One Homeplace East, Suite C
Oakland, CA 94610
(510) 273-2457

COLORADO

CHARLES S. JOHNSON
True Sports and Entertainment
1035 Pearl Street, Suite 301
Boulder, CO 80302
(303) 444-3470

LAMONT SMITH
All-Pro Sports Entertainment
1999 Broadway, Suite 3125
Denver, CO 80202
(303) 292-3212

CONNECTICUT

THOMAS DARDEN
Miller Group
545 Longwharf Drive, Suite 700
New Haven, CT 06511
(203) 624-9897

LUBBIE HARPER
The Harper Law Firm
59 Elm Street, Suite 500
New Haven, CT 06510
(203) 624-1918

DISTRICT OF COLUMBIA

DEANNE L. AYERS-HOWARD
Beveridge & Diamond
1350 Eye Street, N.W., Suite 700
Washington, D.C. 20005
(202) 789-6054

DARRYL DENNIS
Post Office Box 41170
Washington, D.C. 20018
(202) 526-6785

ZACHERY M. JONES
Attorney At Law
Post Office Box 29674
Washington, D.C. 20017
(202) 726-8755

BRIGMAN OWENS
Bennett and Owens
3524 K Street, N.W.
Washington, D.C. 20007-3503
(202) 625-3330

GREGORY C. RALEIGH
1301 Fifteenth Street, N.W., Suite 425
Washington, D.C. 20005
(202) 332-5503

STEVEN M. RIGGINS
International Management Group
 (IMG)
601 Thirteenth Street, N.W.,
 Suite 1130-South
Washington, D.C. 20005
(202) 737-9144

WILLIAM STRICKLAND
International Management Group
 (IMG)
601 Thirteenth Street, N.W.,
 Suite 1130-South
Washington, D.C. 20005
(202) 737-9144

BENJAMIN F. WILSON
Beveridge & Diamond
1350 Eye Street, N.W., Suite 700
Washington, D.C. 20005
(202) 789-6023

Sports Agents

SHERRI WYATT
Wyatt and Associates
1413 K Street, N.W., Sixth Floor
Washington, D.C. 20005
(202) 682-1188

FLORIDA

JERRY BELL
Bell and Associates
Post Office Box 270219
Tampa, FL 33688
(813) 961-6579

GRADY C. IRVIN
Margol and Pennington
76 South Laura Street
American Heritage Tower, Suite 1702
Jacksonville, FL 32202
(904) 355-7508

LARRY D. JACOBS
Pentathlon Sports Management
9670 Whittington Drive, West
Jacksonville, FL 32257
(904) 448-5496

RICHARD A. RYLES
Ackerman, Badst, Lauer and Scherer
Post Office Drawer 3948
West Palm Beach, FL 33402
(407) 655-4500

GARY A. SIPLIN
Greenberg, Traurig, Hoffman etal
1221 Brickell Avenue
Miami, FL 33131
(305) 579-0633

HOMER J. THOMAS
Thomas Sports Management
4560 N.W. 49th Court
Coconut Creek, FL 33063
(305) 425-0838

EARL THOMPSON
4411 N.E. 19th Terrace,
    Suite 102
Fort Lauderdale, FL 33308
(305) 491-5165

GEORGIA

VIRGIL LOUIS ADAMS
Mathis, Sands, et.al.
Post Office Box 928
Wachovia Building, Suite 290
Macon, GA 31201
(912) 734-2159

DEBRA R. GADSDEN
Attorney at Law
I70 Fairlie Street, N.W.,
    Suite 410
Atlanta, GA 30303-2100
(404) 524-4746

FREDRICK J. HENLEY
Attorney at Law
4353 Horseshoe Court
Decatur, GA 30034
(404) 808-6066

BRIAN A. RANSOM
T.A.F.T. International
225 Peachtree Street, N.W.,
    Suite 2000
Atlanta, GA 30303
(404) 523-5677

JESSE J. SPIKES
Long, Aldridge & Norman
285 Peachtree Center Avenue,
    Suite 1500
Atlanta, GA 30303-1257
(404) 527-4140

Sports Agents

DAVID R. WARE
Thomas, Kennedy, Sampson et.al.
55 Marietta, Suite 1600
Bank South Building
Atlanta, GA 30303
(404) 688-4503

ILLINOIS

KIM L. HARPER
455 East 88th Place
Chicago, IL 60619
(312) 483-3415

KENNARD MCGUIRE
Coordinated Sports Management
790 Frontage Road
Northfield, IL 60093
(708) 441-4315

WILLIE J. RUCKER
3110 Woodworth Place
Hazelcrest, IL 60429
(708) 335-4966

INDIANA

EUGENE E. PARKER
Burt, Blee, et.al.
200 East Main
1000 Standard Federal Plaza
Fort Wayne, IN 46802
(219) 426-1300

RUBY ANN POWELL
R.A.P. Productions
4116 Grand Boulevard
East Chicago, IN 46312
(219) 397-5442

MARYLAND

ALAN K. ARRINGTON
Mid-Atlantic Sports Management
Post Office Box 4934
Capitol Heights, MD 20791
(301) 369-1231

JAMES H. DAVIS
3629 Childress Terrace
Burtonsville, MD 20866-2037
(301) 890-0871

LEN ELMORE
Precept Sports and Entertainment
10480 Little Paxtuxent Parkway,
   Suite 500
Columbia, MD 21044
(410) 740-5636

KEVIN E. FITZPATRICK
First String Management
15779 Columbia Pike, Suite 470
Burtonsville, MD 20866
(301) 792-3827

JEAN S. FUGETT
Fugett and Associates
4801 Westparkway
Baltimore, MD 21229
(410) 945-7311

WILLIAM T. RILEY, JR., CPA
217 East Redwood Street
Suite 1900
Baltimore, MD 21202-3316
(410) 727-4340

MICHAEL WILCHER
1501 Fairlakes Place
Mitchelville, MD 20716
(301) 499-0131

Sports Agents

KEITH D. WILLIAMS
EnterStar
Box 1549
Columbia, MD 21044
(301) 596-1428

MICHIGAN

EVERETT L. STONE, CPA
600 Renaissance Center, Suite 1400
Detroit, MI 48243
(313) 272-8383

MINNESOTA

JEFFREY C. DURAND
Durand Enterprises, Inc.
Post Office Box 1849
Burnsville, MN 55337
(612) 431-5990

MISSISSIPPI

ROBERT N. DAVIS
University of Mississippi Law School
University, MS 38677
(601) 232-7361

JAMES L. DAVIS, III
Attorney at Law
1904 24th Avenue
Post Office Box 1839
Gulfport, MS 39502
(601) 864-1588

GILBERT T. THOMPSON
Universal Sports
Post Office Box 10529
Jackson, MS 39289-0529
(601) 857-8310

NEW JERSEY

ALBERT E. IRBY
First Round, Inc.
1000 White Horse Road,
    Suite 514
Vorhees, NJ 08043
(609) 782-1113

GERARD K. GILLIAM
Ford & Gilliam
Post Office Box 1392
305 Broadway, Suite 2
Patterson, NJ 07544
(201) 523-6606

JAMES E. WADE
Three Bridge Road
Post Office Box 907
Monroeville, NJ 08343
(609) 358-3536

NEW YORK

PATRICIA ANN BOSWELL
Boswell, Brown & Associates
3128 Grace Avenue
Bronx, NY 10469
(212) 320-1954

ROBERT H. FAYNE
330 East 39th Street, Suite 8F
New York, NY 10017
(212) 661-0076

CRAIG FOSTER
RLR Associates
7 West 51st Street
New York, NY 10019
(212) 541-8641

Sports Agents

CHARLES F. MARTIN
Financial Planning Services
45 John Street, Suite 407
New York, NY 10038
(212) 732-7868

MORRIS MCWILLIAMS
Omni Sports Management, Inc.
44 Edgecombe Avenue
New York, NY 10030
(212) 373-6976

ALTON WALDON
Attorney at Law
115-103 22nd Street
Cambria Heights, NY 11411
(718) 723-6136

NORTH CAROLINA

MASON P. ASHE
Greeson And Grace
102 West Third Street,
   Suite 522
Nationsbank Plaza
Winston-Salem, NC 27101
(919) 725-9428

VARIAN O. BRISTOW
4818 Morgan Street
Charlotte, NC 28208
(704) 394-6778

ERMA L. JOHNSON
Attorney at Law
ELJ Sports
2014 Barnett Avenue
Wilmington, NC 28403
(919) 343-9999

FRED A. WHITFIELD
Attorney at Law
301-F State Street
Post Office Box 21326
Greensboro, NC 27420
(919) 275-4667

OHIO

EVERETT L. GLENN
Attorney at Law
23875 Commerce Park Road,
   Suite 120
Beachwood, OH 44122
(216) 292-3405

NATHANIEL LAMPLEY
Cox Financial Corporation
4199 Crossgate Lane
Cincinnati, OH 45236
(513) 891-1771

STEVEN N. LUKE
U.S. Athletes
733 Lake View Plaza Boulevard
Worthington, OH 43095
(614) 785-0066

PENNSYLVANIA

GREG A. RAY
Sportsray, Inc.
513 Court Place
Pittsburgh, PA 15219
(412) 681-5488

Sports Agents

ALPHONSO R. STEVENSTON
Attorney at Law
1487 Wistar Drive
Wyncote, PA 19095
(215) 887-4866

DWAYNE D. WOODRUFF
Meyer-Darragh
2000 Frick Building
Pittsburgh, PA 15219
(412) 261-6600

SOUTH CAROLINA

JOSEPH RICARDO LEFFT
Nexsen Pruet Jacobs & Pollard
Post Office Drawer 2426
Columbia, SC 29202
(803) 253-8228

JAKE TALLEY
J.T. Sports, Inc.
6752 Ward Avenue
North Charleston, SC 29418
(803) 553-1647

TENNESSEE

EVA MARIE LEMEH
Farris, Warfield, Kanaday
201 Fourth Avenue, Seventeenth Floor
Third National Bank Building
Nashville, TN 37219
(615) 244-5200

TEXAS

GENE BURROUGH
Burrough, Bonner Sports Agency
5615 Kirby Drive, Suite 755
Houston, TX 77005
(713) 520-5611

RONALD W. HARRIS
Pro Am Management Group, Inc.
2626 South Loop West, Suite 330
Houston, TX 77054
(713) 660-8787

ABNER HAYNES
Abner Haynes and Associates
2412 M.L. King Jr. Boulevard
Dallas, TX 75215
(214) 428-0864

CARL C. POSTON
Professional Sports Planning
1300 Main Street, Suite 600
Houston, TX 77002
(713) 659-2255

KEVIN D. POSTON
Professional Sports Planning
1300 Main Street, Suite 600
Houston, TX 77002
(713) 659-2255

THOMAS WILLIAMS
T.W. Rehabilitation & Sports
9630 Clarewood, Suite A1
Houston, TX 77036
(713) 772-5444

VIRGINIA

LOUIS W. CUNNINGHAM
ProServ, Inc.
1101 Wilson Boulevard, Suite 1800
Arlington, VA 22209
(703) 276-3030

RALPH E. STRINGER
Stringer Marketing Group, Inc.
8251 Greensboro Drive, Suite 530
McLean, VA 22102
(703) 506-0900

HARRISON B. WILSON
McGuire, Woods, Battle, and Boothe
One James Center
Richmond, VA 23219
(804) 775-1092

WASHINGTON

R. MILLER ADAMS
Ogden, Murphy & Wallace
1601 Fifth Avenue
2100 Westlaker Tower
Seattle, WA 98101-1686
(206) 447-7000

LARRY JAMES LANDRY
Attorney at Law
2025 First Avenue
Market Place Tower, Suite 730
Seattle, WA 98121
(206) 448-7996

WISCONSIN

RICHARD L. DAVIS
Kidder Peabody and Company
777 East Wisconsin Avenue, Suite 1900
Milwaukee, WI 53202
(414) 277-7500

ULICE PAYNE
Reinhart, Boerner, et.al.
1000 North Water Street, Suite 2100
Milwaukee, WI 53202
(414) 271-1190

The listings in this directory are available as Mailing Labels. See last page for details.

Travel Agencies

The companies highlighted on the following pages represent a partial listing of the nations leading AfricanAmerican travel agencies.

ALABAMA

HENDERSON TRAVEL AGENCY
907 Ethel Drive
Tuskegee Institute, AL 36088
Allan Junier, Contact

CALIFORNIA

A & T TRAVEL, INC
9859 MacArthur Boulevard
Oakland, CA 94606
Alest Coleman, Contact

A-PHI INTERNATIONAL TRAVEL
944 Market Street, Suite 709
San Francisco, CA 94102
William Hunter, Contact

ALL TRAVEL SERVICE
2204 J Street
Sacramento, CA 95816
Ada Hamilton, Contact

COLLEGE AVENUE TRAVEL
5391 College Avenue
Oakland, CA 94618
Patricia Harris, Contact

CONFIDENT TRAVEL, INC.
1499 Bayshore Highway
Burlingame, CA 94010
John Vines, Contact

COSMOS TRAVEL SERVICE
9841 Airport Boulevard, Suite 930A
Los Angeles, CA 90045
Bennie R. Clements, Contact

DE VOE TRAVEL
1629 Bristol Parkway
Culver City, CA 90230
Albert DeVeaux, Contact

FRAN'S TRAVEL SERVICE
806 Tennessee Street
Vallejo, CA 94590
Francena Q. Hodge, Contact

GLENVIEW TRAVEL AGENCY
4200 Park Boulevard
Oakland, CA 94618
Rebekah Fontaine-Sipp, Contact

GLOBAL TRAVEL AGENCY
20 Ashbury Street
San Francisco, CA 94117
Mary Bassett, Contact

HOUSE OF TOURS
1764 Desoto Road
Union City, CA 94587
Loretta Baker, Contact

INTERNATIONAL TRAVEL COMPANY
Post Office Box 5144
Long Beach, CA 90805
Lois Williamson, Contact

KOLA NUT TRAVEL & TOURS
110 South LaBrea, Suite 120
Inglewood, CA 90301
Betty Powell, Contact

L'AMOUR'S TRAVEL & TOURS
2918 Fruitvale Avenue
Oakland, CA 94602
Dorothy L'Amour, Contat

LAND, AIR, SEA TRAVEL, INC.
5820 Rodeo Road
Los Angeles, CA 90016
Bennie Lee Wyatt, Contact

LEIMERT PARK TRAVEL
3411 West 43rd Street
Los Angeles, CA 90008
Guy Holloman, Contact

MORE TRAVEL & TOURS
817 Seabury Drive
San Jose, CA 95136
Muriel Moore, Contact

NEXT TIME TRAVEL
3205 West 84th Street
Inglewood, CA 90305
Bobbie Hodges, Contact

R & K TOURS
6605 Whitney Street
Oakland, CA 94603-1030
Robert & Kathy English, Contact

SFO THE CONCEPT GROUP
690 Market Street
San Francisco, CA 94101-5110
O. Matthew Thomas, Contact

THE TRAVEL COMPANY
3736 Grand Avenue
Oakland, CA 94610
Andre Green, Contact

THOUGHTS OF TRAVEL
2419 Ocean Avenue
San Francisco, CA 94127
Nelda J. Harris, Contact

TRAVEL SHOUP
719 North Fairfax Avenue, Suite C
Los Angeles, CA 90046
Gregg Patterson, Contact

TRIO TRAVEL & TOURS
3000 Manchester Boulevard
Inglewood, CA 90305
Ardelia Wicks, Contact

TYREE ASSOCIATES
1959 Ocean Avenue
San Francisco, CA 94127
Bettie Tyree, Contact

WENTRAVEL & CRUISES
1001 Broadway
Oakland, CA 94607
Wenefrett P. Watson, Contact

WEST COAST TOURS
1749 West 41st Place
Los Angeles, CA 90037

COLORADO

CENTERPOINTE TRAVEL, INC.
950 South Cherry Street
Denver, CO 80222
Johnnie Peters, Contact

CONNECTICUT

BROWNSTONE TRAVEL AGENCY
278 Main Street
Portland, CT 60480
William Evans, Contact

MINGO WORLD TRAVEL SERVICE
1229 Albany Avenue
Hartford, CT 06112
Pauline Hylton-Mingo, Contact

Travel Agencies

NEW EXPERIENCE TRAVEL
45 Allen Road
Bloomfield, CT 06602
Earl Shepard, Contact

DISTRICT OF COLUMBIA

ALLEN TRAVEL SERVICE
231 M Street, N.W.
Washington, D.C. 20037
Brenda Rollins, Contact

EL DORADO TRAVEL SERVICE
1444 Eye Street, N.W.
Washington, D.C. 20002
R. Edward Quick, Contact

GALINDO & FRAZIER TRAVEL
602 Kennedy Street, N.W.
Washington, D.C. 20011

HENDERSON TRAVEL
1522 U Street, N.W.
Washington, D.C. 20009
Gaynelle Henderson, Contact

HORIZON TOURS
1010 Vermont Avenue, N.W.
Washington, D.C. 20005
Ward Morrow, Contact

LINCOLN-DOUGLASS TRAVEL
2817 12th Street, N.E.
Washington, D.C. 20017
John Womack, Contact

ROGERS TRAVEL BUREAU
3903 Georgia Avenue, N.W.
Washington, D.C. 20011
Joanne Russell, Contact

SOUL JOURNEY ENTERPRISES
235 Ben Franklin Station
Washington, D.C. 20044
Bill Cunningham, Contact

FLORIDA

AB & S TRAVEL SERVICE
621 Fercreek Avenue
Orlando, FL 32803
Beulah Monroe, Contact

ACCESS TRAVEL SERVICE
4176 North State Road Seven
Lauderdale Lakes, FL 33319

ACTION TRAVEL
1704 West 45th Street
West Palm Beach, FL 33407

ALPHA TRAVEL
1450 Lake Bradford Road
Tallahassee, FL 32304
Roosevelt Hollman, Contact

BEVERLY'S TRAVEL
10825 1/2 N.W. 27th Avenue
Miami, FL 33167
Beverly McPhee, Contact

BREAKAWAY TRAVEL
Post Office Box 694
Casselberry, FL 32707
Shirley Johnson, Contact

E. C. WORLDWIDE TRAVEL
18327 N.E. Seventh Avenue
Miami, FL 33169
Egbert Christian, Contact

GALA TRAVEL AGENCY
10914 N.W. Seventh Avenue
Miami, FL 33168
Marie Brown, Contact

GET AWAY TRAVEL, INC.
420 U.W. 1 Village Plaza
North Palm Beach, FL 33408
Billie Brooks, Contact

HARBOUR VIEWS TOURS
Post Office Box 470098
Miami, FL 33168
Mary Morgan, Contact

INSPIRED TRAVEL
1312 N.W. 40th Avenue
Lauderhill, FL 33313
Lorenzo Lee, Contact

INTER NET CTD
6001 N.W. Eighth Avenue
Miami, FL 33127
Jimi Lee, Contact

ORION TRAVEL
1320 South Dixie Highway
Coral Gables, FL 33146
Sandra Evans, Contact

SPRINGFIELD TRAVEL
1701 North Main Street
Jacksonville, FL 32206
Sen. Corine Brown, Contact

SOJOURN TOURS
13756 S.W. 84th Street
Miami, FL 33183
Oswald Bartlett, Contact

TIME TO TRAVEL
738 N.W. 199th Street
Miami, FL 33168
Ray Thornton, Contact

TRAVEL 54
136 N.E. 54th Street
Miami, FL 33168
Caludie Adams, Contact

TRINIDAD & TOBAGO TOURS
200 S. E. First Street
Miami, FL 33131
Erica Williams, Contact

GEORGIA

BROWN TRAVEL SERVICE
2286 Cascade Road, S.W., Suite 1
Atlanta, GA 30311
Ernest Brown, Contact

CARIBE WORLD TRAVEL, INC.
41 Marietta Street, N.W.
Atlanta, GA 30303
Ann Marshall, Owner

HENDERSON TRAVEL
1255 Shoreham Drive
College Park, GA 30349
Diane Caviness, Contact

HENDERSON TRAVEL SERVICE, INC.
931 Martin L. King Drive, S.W.
Atlanta, GA 30314
Freddye S. Henderson, Contact

TOUR ATLANTA
3120 Cascade Road, S.W.
Atlanta, GA 30311
Jan Meadows, Contact

TRAVEL AGENTS, INTERNATIONAL
3400 Woodale Drive, N.E.
Atlanta, GA 30326
Janet Tillman-Turner, Contact

The listings in this directory are available as Mailing Labels. See last page for details.

Travel Agencies

ILLINOIS

BURNS & ASSOCIATES TRAVEL
9642 South Peoria Street
Chicago, IL 60634
Doris M. Burns, Contact

CPW GREAT ESCAPE TRAVEL
2059 East 75th Street
Chicago, IL 60649
Elizabeth Cotton, Contact

CASEY'S TRAVEL SERVICE
9300 South Ashland
Chicago, IL 60620
Martha Thornton, Contact

FAIRLEY'S TRAVEL SERVICES
1922 West 170th Street
Hazel Crest, IL 60426
M. Ferguson, Contact

FINESSE TOURS
230 North Michigan Avenue
Chicago, IL 60601
Earl Smith, Contact

HARVEY TRAVEL, INC.
198 East 145th Street
Harvey, IL, 60426
M. Ferguson, Contact

M.J.S.D. TRAVEL
2440 West Lincoln Highway
Olympia Fields, IL 60401
Louise Monegain, Contact

POINTS UNLIMITED TRAVEL
180 West 154 Street
Harvey, IL 60426
Rosa Scott, President

SUN & FUN TRAVEL
400 East 41st Street, Suite 101
Chicago, IL 60653
Deborah T. Polk, Contact

SUNNYSIDE TRAVEL
2100 S. Indiana Avenue
Chicago, IL 60615
Juanita Gilmore, Contact

TRADE WIND TRAVEL
1634 East 53rd Street
Chicago, IL 60615
Olive Blair Waugh, Contact

TRAINS, BOATS & PLANES
8731 South State Street
Chicago, IL 60619

TRAVEL CONNECTIONS, INC.
8 South Michigan Avenue
Chicago, IL 60603

WTMIC TRAVEL SERVICE
1701 East 53rd Street
Chicago, IL 60615
Faye Russell, CTC, Contact

INDIANA

STUDIO FIVE TRAVEL SERVICE, INC.
5252 Hohman Avenue
Hammond, IN 467320
Loretta Jones, Owner

TWILIGHT TRAVEL SERVICE, INC.
4003 Boulevard Place
Indianapolis, IN 46208
Arthur Carter, Owner

KANSAS

C C P TRAVEL & TOURS
751 Minnesota Avenue
Kansas City, KS 66101
Ceolia Belcher

KENTUCKY

TRAVELPLEX HIKES POINT, INC.
4033 Taylorsville Road, Suite 102
Louisville, KY 40220
Rita Y. Phillips, Owner

LOUISIANA

EMERALD REEF HOLIDAYS
1680 Old Spanish Trail
Slidell, LA 74058-5024
Otis Windham, Jr.

ESCAPE WITH TRAVEL, INC.
650 South Pierce Street, Suite 350
New Orleans, LA 70119
Irma M. Dixson, President

FOUR CORNERS TRAVEL
1000 North Broad Street
New Orleans, LA 70119
Leenie Burns, Contact

SUPER TRANSPORTATION BUS COMPANY
7421 Bullard Avenue
New Orleans, LA 70128
Annie Hampton, Contact

MARYLAND

COLUMBIA TRAVEL, INC.
5950 Symphony Woods Road
Columbia, MD 21044
Wokie A. Dick, Contact

FOUR SEAS & SEVEN WINDS TRAVEL
12 West Montgomery
Baltimore, MD 21230
James McLean, President

GALAXY TRAVEL LIMITED
4324 York Road, Suite 103
Baltimore, MD 21212
William Garret, Contact

MONDAWIN TRAVEL CENTER, INC.
108 Metro Plaza
Baltimore, MD 21212
Herb Brown, President

MICHIGAN

DUDLEY TOURS
11000 West Nicholas Avenue
Detroit, MI 48221

IVERY'S PROFESSIONAL TRAVEL PLACE
14500 West Eight Mile Road
Oak Park, MI 48237
Willie Ivery, President

LWS TRAVEL, INC.
14650 West Eight Mile Road
Oak Park, MI 48237
Linda Wilson, Owner

Travel Agencies

MC CER TRAVEL AGENCY
2407 East Seven Mile Road
Detroit, MI 48234

MENDOZA TOURS
Post Office Box 2806
Detroit, MI 48231
Harry Mendoza, Contact

PEOPLE'S TRAVEL
10796 Belleville Road
Belleville, MI 48111
Chuck Covington, President

TRAVEL CENTRE
19360 Livernois Avenue
Detroit, MI 48221
R. B. Williams, President

VISTA TRAVEL
8410 Woodward Avenue
Detroit, MI 48202
Elizabeth Green Doles, Contact

MISSISSIPPI

**GAVIN ROBINSON TRAVEL
AGENCY, INC.**
414 West Pascagoula Street
Jackson, MS 39203
Vern Gavin, President

MISSOURI

ACCENT TRAVEL, INC.
3116 Troost
Kansas City, MO 64109
Frances Hill, President

ALLEN BELL CHARTERS
310 Armour Road
North Kansas City, MO 64116
Allen Bell, Contact

EXPRESS TRAVEL
30 Courthouse Square
Rockville, MO 20850
Carl Fisher, Contact

LIFE STYLES
A National Black Travel Guide
9811 West Florrisant Avenue,
  Suite 207
St. Louis, MO 63136
Charles Gross, Manager

**REGENCY TRAVEL &
  MANAGEMENT, INC.**
104 Main Street
Parkville, MO 64152
Clare Parker, Manager

NEBRASKA

BATES TRAVEL, INC.
6000 South Eastern, Suite 5C
Las Vegas, NV 89119
Sandra Bates, President

**PEOPLE'S TRAVEL AGENCY,
  INC.**
Post Office Box 241037
Omaha, NE 68124
Tom Kamau, President

NEW JERSEY

ARIES TRAVEL, INC.
340 Bloomfield Avenue
Montclair, NJ 07042
Gerry George, Contact

BER MAR SEA & SAND TRAVEL
443 Main Street
East Orange, NJ 07018
Bertha Urquijo, Contact

Travel Agencies

BROOKS TRAVEL SERVICE
302 South Warwick Road
Somerdale, NJ 08083
Ellaine M. Brooks, Contact

EBONY TRAVEL
105 Chandler Avenue
Roselle, NJ 07203
Randolph L. Johnson, Contact

FIVE STAR TRAVEL, INC.
111 North Sixth Street
Camden, NJ 08102
Larry Miles, Contact

FOR TRAVELLERS, INC.
149 White Horse Pike
Lawnside, NJ 08045
Letta Parrott, Contact

LA SALLE TRAVEL SERVICE
134 Evergreen Place, Suite 1A
East Orange, NJ 07018
James Gilliam, Contact

PASSPORT TRAVEL
22 West Belt Plaza
Wayne, NJ 07470
Bill McIntosh, Contact

RELAX-A-TOURS
312 Orange Road
Montclair, NJ 07042
Larry Hubbard, Contact

SALAAM TRAVEL
45 East Main Street, Suite 106
Freehold, NJ 07728
Nancy Malveaux, Contact

SUN TRAVELS
12 William Street
Newark, NJ 07102
Linda D. Fujah, Contact

THE TRAVEL STORE
462 Central Avenue
East Orange, NJ 07018
Clinton Robinson, Contact

THORNWALL TRAVEL AGENCY
411 M. L. King, Jr. Drive
Jersey City, NJ 07304
William Thornton, Contact

TRAVEL LOFT, INC.
Country Garden Center
Sickleville Road
Sickleville, NJ 08081

WHITE KNIGHT TRAVEL
485 Route 1
7 Plainfield Avenue
Edison, NJ 08817
Patricia Sharif, Contact

NEW YORK

ACADIA WORLD OF TRAVEL
3832 White Plains Road
Bronx, NY 10467
Winston Whittingham, Contact

AH WEE WORLD OF TRAVEL
2268 Grand Concourse
Bronx, NY 10457

ALKEN TRAVEL
1661 Nostrand Avenue
Brooklyn, NY 11226
Al Lawrence, Contact

ALOHA TRAVEL
656 Flatbush Avenue
Brooklyn, NY 11213
Lawrence Logan, Contact

Travel Agencies

ANJOY TRAVEL
226-03 Merrick Boulevard
Laurelton, NY 11413
Joyce Haynie, Owner

B & C TRAVEL AGENCY
114-12 Merrick Blvd.
Jamaica, NY 10523
Catherine Smith, Contact

BERMUDA HOME TOURISTS
2 North Stone Avenue
Elmsford, NY 10523
Mary Williams, Contact

BLUE MOUNTAIN TRAVEL
1397 Fulton Street
Brooklyn, NY 11216
Austin Henry, Contact

BONAIR TRAVEL AGENCY
481 Hempstead Turnpike
Elmont, NY 11003
Claire Powell, Contact

BROWN'S NATIONWIDE TRAVEL
89-50 164th Street, Suite 2B
Jamaica, NY 11432
Sherman L. Brown, Contact

BUCCANEER TRAVEL
142-13 Rockaway Boulevard
South Ozone Park, NY 11003
Ollie Beckles, Contact

BUDGET TRAVEL BUREAU
4226 White Plains Road
Bronx, NY 10466
Leonie Young, Contact

CALENDAR TRAVEL AGENCY, LIMITED
227 Utica Avenue
Brooklyn, NY 11213
Ethan C. Smythe, President

CARIBBEAN AMERICAN TRAVEL
1203 Church Avenue
Brooklyn, NY 11218
Francis Readhead, Contact

CARITA TRAVEL
1330 Nostrand Avenue
Brooklyn, NY 11226
H. Christian, Contact

CHARISMA TRAVEL & TOURS
9527 Church Avenue
Brooklyn, NY 11212
G. Harry Lovell, Contact

CLASSIC TRAVEL CONSULTANTS
1270 Broadway, Suite 601
New York, NY 10001
Fred Blackmon, Owner

COCKPIT TRAVEL LIMITED
29 John Street, Suite 702
New York, NY 10038
Pearl Jones, Contact

CONTEMPO TRAVEL 1GT
197-17 Hillside Avenue
Hollis, NY 11423
Carl Bartlett, Contact

CORNERS OF THE WORLD TRAVEL
117-02 New York Blvd.
Jamaica, NY 11434
Irma Holder, Contact

Travel Agencies

COURTESY TRAVEL
122-25A New York Blvd.
Jamaica, NY 11434
James Curtis, Contact

D & D TRAVEL
1107 Nostrand Avenue
Brooklyn, NY 11225

D L & W TRAVEL AGENCY
530 Nostrand Avenue
Brookland, NY 11225
Marion Williams, Contact

EASTERN PARKWAY TRAVEL
293 Troy Avenue
Brooklyn, NY 11213

EMBER TRAVEL SERVICES
157-23 Rockaway Boulevard
Springfield Gardens, NY 11413
Bernice White, Contact

GI GI TRAVEL AGENCY
799 Nostrand Avenue
Brooklyn, NY 11225
Gloria E. Goodwin, Contact

GRACE MOE TRAVEL
223 Fulton Avenue
New York, NY 10035
Grace Moe, Contact

GRACE TRAVEL, LIMITED
223A Fulton Avenue
Hempstead, NY 11550
Grace Moe, President

GRAHAM TRAVEL AGENCY
3992 White Plains Road
Bronx, NY 10466
Ella Graham, Contact

HARLEM RENAISSANCE TOURS
2130 First Avenue, Suite 1601
New York, NY 10025

HARLEM TRAVEL BUREAU
2002 Fifth Avenue
New York, NY 10025
Fred Hewlitt, Contact

HOLLIS TRAVEL BUREAU
111-16 Farmers Boulevard
Hollis, NY 11423
Loretta Rollins, Contact

J.E.M. TRAVEL, INC.
92-38 Brewer Boulevard
Jamaica, NY 11432
Eleanor Willis, Contact

JAY JAY TRAVEL, INC.
149 Grand Street
White Plains, NY 10601
Annie Johnson, Contact

KINGSTON TRAVEL
252 Kingston Avenue
Brooklyn, NY 11213
Goodwin Friday, Contact

LE VOYAGEUR TRAVEL
333 Eastern Parkway
Brooklyn, NY 11213
Roc Volney, Contact

LEWTER-SCOTT TRAVEL
203 Nassau Road
Roosevelt, NY 11575
A. C. Lewter, Contact

MT. VERNON TRAVEL
15 Fourth Avenue
Mt. Vernon, NY 10550
Louis Burnside, Contact

Travel Agencies

NATIONAL PRIDE TRAVEL
1231 Flatbush Avenue
Brooklyn, NY 11226
Nigel O. Pile, Contact

PRISCO TRAVEL
25 Bond Street
Brooklyn, NY 11201
Marion Mitchell, Contact

RAINBOW TRAVEL
377A Nassau Road
Roosevelt, NY 11595
Linda Horton, Contact

S & M TRAVEL AGENCY
548 New York Avenue
Brooklyn, NY 11224
Melvin Martin, Contact

SEALE TRAVEL AGENCY
737 Franklin Avenue
Brooklyn, NY 11238
Laura Seale, Contact

SIENNA TRAVEL AGENCY
726 East 233rd Street
Bronx, NY 10466
Charles Clark, Contact

SKYVIEW TRAVEL
267 Fifth Avenue, Suite 604
New York, NY 10035
Kildane M. Tuku, Contact

TOYOS WORLD TRAVEL
672 Nostrand Avenue
Brooklyn, NY 11216
Carl Parris, Contact

TRANSCONTINENTAL TOURS
192-16 Linden Boulevard
St. Albans, NY 11412
S. Hawley, Contact

TRANSLAND TRAVEL BUREAU
5 East Hartsdale Avenue
Hartsdale, NY 10530
Marion Wiggins, Contact

TRAVEL HUT - HOWARD BEACH
82-17 153rd Street
Howard Beach, NY 11414
Jim Baccus, Contact

TRAVEL INTERNATIONAL
1443 Gunhill Road, Second Floor
Bronx, NY 10469
Eugene Plummer, President

UNIWORLD TRAVEL ASSOCIATES
163 West 23rd Street
New York, NY 10011
Laye Thiam, Contact

DAVE WINTER'S TRAVEL
897A Nostrand Avenue
Brooklyn, NY 11225
Dave Winter, Contact

WHY NOT TRAVEL AGENCY
2230-1 Linden Boulevard
Cambria Heights, NY 08817
Howard Brown, Contact

WINTHROP TRAVEL AGENCY
5924 Glenwood Road
Brooklyn, NY 11234
Winston Wellington, Contact

XAVIER TRAVEL, INC.
50 Main Street
White Plains, NY 10606
Arthur Z. Xavier, Contact

YVONNE-MAYE CAREFREE TRAVEL
2519 Seventh Avenue
New York, NY 10039
Ernie Mayer, Contact

NORTH CAROLINA

HORIZON TOURS
Post Office Box 471172
Charlotte, NC 28247
Dimple Lloyd, Contact

OHIO

BROWN'S TOURS & TRAV EL
Post Office Box 6217
Cincinnati, OH 45206
Mary Brown, Contact

ELITE TRAVEL SERVICES
1601 Madison Road
Cincinnati, OH 45203
Frances Raglin, Contact

LA JEWS TRAVEL SERVICE
1601 Weldon Avenue
Columbus, OH 43224
L'Tanya Lemon, Contact

WORLD TOURS, INC.
2000 Lee Road, Suite 219
Cleveland Heights, OH 44118
James Washington, Contact

PENNSYLVANIA

ARDMORE WORLD TRAVEL
22 Ardmore Avenue
Ardmore, PA 19003

DEPARTURE TRAVEL
Cedarbrook Mall
Wyncollie, PA 19095
John Matthews, Contact

DESIGNER TOURS
225 South Fifteenth Street
Philadelphia, PA 19102
Clarence W. Moore, Contact

**EDMUND TRAVEL
CONSULTANTS**
4415 Fifth Avenue
Pittsburgh, PA 15213
Gladys Edmunds, Contact

EJAY TRAVEL AGENCY
41 South Fiftheenth Street
Philadelphia, PA 19102
Effie Brown, Contact

ESPRI TRAVEL AGENCY
4550 Parkside Avenue
Philadelphia, PA 19131
Becham Davis, Jr., Contact

FOUR SEASONS TRAVEL, INC.
1800 J. F. Kennedy Boulevard
Philadelphia PA 19103
Edith Perry, Contact

FUN TOURS OF PHILADELPHIA
5119 Chestnut Street
Philadelphia, PA 19139
Stephanie Wilson, Contact

PENROSE TRAVEL
7000 Lindbergh Boulevard, Suite 4
Philadelphia PA 19153
Alice Harris, Contact

ROGERS TRAVEL, INC.
5221 Walnut Street
Philadelphia, PA 19139
Norma Pratt, Contact

Travel Agencies

TEXAS

ALLEN STREET TRAVEL
2604 Allen Street
Dallas, TX 75204
Merril Thompson-Hinton, Contact

ALMEDA TRAVEL, INC.
1020 Holcombe, Suite 1306
Houston, TX 77025
Jackye Alton, Contact

BETTER TOURS & TRAVEL
2215 Cleburne Avenue
Houston, TX 77018
Carol Hatcherson, Contact

COLEMAN TOUR & TRAVEL
2600 South Loop West
Houston, TX 77054
Shirley Coleman, Contact

VIRGINIA

AMERICAN WORLD TOURS, INC.
927 Hull Street
Richmond, VA 23224
Jean Williams, President

LAWTON'S TRAVEL
28 West Queens Way
Hampton, VA 23669-4012
Edna J. Lawton, Owner

WASHINGTON

PIZZAZZ TRAVEL, INC.
300 Fourteenth Avenue, South
Seattle, WA 98144
Kent Stevenson, Owner

WORLD TRAVEL CENTER
1127 1/2 Thirty-Fourth Avenue
Seattle, WA 98122
Benjamin Abe-Omara, Contact

WISCONSIN

HAPPY TIME TRAVEL AGENCY
3281 North Fifteenth Street
Milwaukee, WI 53206
Wilhelmina, Manager

BAHAMAS

HAPPY HOURS LIMITED
Post Office Box N1077
Nassau, Bahamas
Albert Brown, Contact

INTERNATIONAL TRAVEL & TOURISM
Post Office Box F580
Freeport, Bahamas
Eulys Strachan, Contract

Travel Agencies

SUN ISLAND TOURS, LIMITED
Post office Box F2585
Freeport, Bahamas
Irma Grant Smith, Contact

SUNSHINE TRAVEL AGENCY
Post Box 14359
Nassau, Bahamas
Clayton Taylor, Contact

TROPICAL TRAVEL & TOURS
Post Office Box N448
Nassau, Bahamas
Harcourt Bastian, Contact

CANADA

SOUL IN CANADA
Black Tourism in Canada
65 Cloverhill Road, Suite 27
Toronto, Ontario
Canada M8Y1T5

The listings in this directory are available as Mailing Labels. See last page for details.

Union Leadership

The following African-Americans are senior members of American labor unions.

WILLIE L. BAKER, JR.
International Vice President
Director, Public Affairs Department
United Food and Commercial Workers
   International Union (UFCW)
1775 K Street, N.W.
Washington, D.C. 20006

CECIL R. BENJAMIN
American Federation of Teachers
   (AFT)
46-47 Company Street
Christiansted, VI 00820
(809) 773-4265

CLAYOLA BROWN
International Vice President
Amalgamated Clothing and Textile
   Workers Union (ACTWU)
99 University Place, Eighth Floor
New York, NY 10003

WILLIAM BURRUS
Executive Vice President
United Paperworkers International
   Union (APWU)
1300 L Street, N.W.
Washington, D.C. 20005

GLORIA C. COBBIN
International Vice President
American Federation of State, County
   and Municipal Employees
   (AFSCME)
2550 West Grand Boulevard
Detroit, MI 48208

DOUG COUTTEE
International Vice President
United Food and Commercial Workers
   International Union (UFCW)
1775 K Street, N.W.
Washington, D.C. 20006

WILLIE J. CULLINS
International Vice President
Bakery Workers
2814 Calloway Circle
Jacksonville, FL 32209

AL DIOP
International Vice President
American Federation of State, County
   and Municipal Employees
   (AFSCME)
Local 1549
125 Barclay Street
New York, NY 10007

JOHN ELLIOTT
Vice President
American Federation of Teachers
   (AFT)
7451 Third Avenue
Detroit, MI 48202-9966
(313) 875-3500

GEORGE FREEMAN
United Automobile, Aerospace &
   Agricultural Implement Workers of
   America International Union (UAW)
1655 W. Market Street
Akron, OH 44313

CAROLE A. GRAVES
Vice President
American Federation of Teachers
   (AFT)
1019 Broad Street
Newark, NJ 07102
(201) 643-8430

Union Leadership

STANLEY HILL
International Vice President
American Federation of State, County
    and Municipal Employees
    (AFSCME)
District Council 37
125 Barclay Street
New York, NY 10007

WILLIAM S. HUDSON, JR.
International Vice President
American Federation of State, County
    and Municipal Employees
    (AFSCME)
7114 Virginia Avenue
Sykesville, MD 21784

CAROLYN J. HOLMES
International Vice President
American Federation of State, County
    and Municipal Employees
    (AFSCME)
3442 Hance Bridge Road
Vineland, NJ 08360

SANDRA C. IRONS
Vice President
American Federation of Teachers
    (AFT)
1301 Virginia Street
 Gary, IN 46407
(219) 886-73209

JAMES JOHNSON
International Vice President
Amalgamated Clothing and Textile
    Workers Union (ACTWU)
13 West Oakland Street
Post Office Box 157
Andrews, SC 29510

LORETTA JOHNSON
Vice President
American Federation of Teachers
    (AFT)
5800 Metro Drive
Baltimore, MD 21215-3209
(410) 358-6600

FREDA JONES
International Vice Preident
Aluminum, Brick and Glassworkers
3362 Hollenberg Drive
Bridgeton, MO 63044

BLONDIE P. JORDAN
International Vice President
American Federation of State, County
    and Municipal Employees (AFCME)
7811 Bay Cedar Drive
Orlando, FL 32811

NATHANIEL LACOUR
Vice President
American Federation of Teachers
    (AFT)
4370 Louisa Drive
New Orleans, LA 70126
(504) 282-1026

SAM LAWRENCE
Chairman of the Board of Trustees
International Union of Electronic,
    Electrical, Salaried, Machine and
    Furniture Workers, AFL-CIO (IUE)
414 West Carter Drive
North Versailles, PA 15137

ERNEST LOFTON
International Vice President
United Automobile, Aerospace &
    Agricultural Implement Workers of
    America International Union (UAW)
8000 East Jefferson
Detroit, MI 48214

Union Leadership

JAMES LUCAS
President, Local Number 888
United Food and Commercial Workers
   International Union (UFCW)
1 Westchester Towers
100 East First Street
Mt. Vernon, NY 10550

WILLIAM LUCY
International Secretary-Treasurer
American Federation of State, County
   and Municipal Employees
   (AFSCME)
1625 L Street, N.W.
Washington, D.C. 20036

LEON LYNCH
International Vice President
United Steelworkers of America
5 Gateway Center
Pittsburgh, PA 15222

OPHELIA MCFADDEN
International Vice President
Service Employees International
   Union, AFL-CIO (SEIU)
1417 South Georgia Street
Los Angeles, CA 90015

CALVIN MOORE
International Vice President
Oil, Chemical and Atomic Workers
   International Union (OCAW)
Post Office Box 2812
Denver, CO 80201

HENRY NICHOLAS
International Vice President
American Federation of State, County
   and Municipal Employees
   (AFSCME)
1417 West Jeff Street
Philadelphia, PA 19121

GERALD OWENS
International Vice President
International Longshoremen's Associa-
   tion AFL-CIO (ILA)
501 Hartford Road
South Orange, NJ 07079

MICHAEL E. RHYNES, SR.
International Vice President
American Federation of State, County
   and Municipal Employees
4802 Oakhurst Court
Indianapolis, IN 46254

HOWARD R. RICHARDSON
International Vice President
Hotel Employees & Restaurant
   Employees International Union
   (HERE)
1219 28th Street, N.W.
Washington, D.C. 20007

EDGAR ROMNEY
International Vice President
International Ladies' Garment Workers
   Union (ILGWU)
1710 Broadway
New York, NY 10019

WILLIE RUDD
President, Furniture Workers Division
International Union of Electronic,
   Electrical, Salaried, Machine and
   Furniture Workers, AFL-CIO (IUE)
1910 Airline Drive
Nashville, TN 37210

ROBERT SIMPSON
International Trustee
Teamsters
300 South Ashland Avenue
Chicago, IL 60607

Union Leadership

BURHMAN D. SMITH
International Vice President
American Federation of State, County
and Municipal Employees
(AFSCME)
303 E. Meehan Avenue
Philadelphia, PA 19119

GEORGE SPRINGER
American Federation of Teachers
(AFT)
1781 Wilbur Cross Parkway
Berlin, CT 06037
(302) 828-1400

WILLIAM STODGHILL
International Vice President
Service Employees International Union
AFL-CIO (SEIU)
4108 Lindell Boulevard
St. Louis, MO 63108

JOHN N. STURDIVANT
International President
American Federation of Government
Employees
80 F Street, N.W.
Washington, D.C. 20001

BROOKS SUNKETT
International Vice President
Communications Workers of America
(CWA)
501 Third Street, N.W.
Washington, D.C. 20001

GENE UPSHAW
President, Federation of Professional
Athletes
2021 L Street, N.W., Sixth Floor
Washington, D.C. 20036

JACQUELINE B. VAUGHN
Vice President
American Federation of Teachers
(AFT)
222 Merchandise Mart Plaza, Suite
400
Chicago, IL 60654-1005
(312) 329-9100

FREDERICK WINTERS
Fireman and Oilers
1243 Central Avenue
St. Petersburg, FL 33705

United Fund Organizations

These fund raising organizations provide financial and technical support to projects that address the critical needs of African American communities throughout the United States. Under their direction, contributions are channeled toward creative and constructive programs that emphasize self-help, volunteerism and mutual aid.

ALASKA

UNITED BLACK FUND OF ALASKA
200 West 34th Avenue
Anchorage, AK 99503

CALIFORNIA

BAY AREA BLACK UNITED FUND, INC.
1440 Broadway, Suite 405
Oakland, CA 94612
Cheryl Garner-Shaw, Executive Director
(510) 763-7270

BROTHERHOOD CRUSADE BLACK UNITED FUND, INC.
200 East Slauson Avenue
Los Angeles, CA 90011

UNITED BLACK FUND OF CALIFORNIA
630 20th Street
Oakland, CA 94612

COLORADO

UNITED BLACK FUND OF COLORADO
8720 East Colfax Street
Denver, CO 80200

CONNECTICUT

UNITED BLACK FUND OF SOUTHERN CONNECTICUT
Post Office Box 594
Norwalk, CT 06856

DELAWARE

UNITED BLACK FUND OF DELAWARE
c/o 1012 Fourteenth Street, N.W., Suite 300
Washington, D.C. 20005

DISTRICT OF COLUMBIA

UNITED BLACK FUND, INC.
1012 Fourteenth Street, N.W.
Washington, D.C. 20005
Dr. Calvin Rolark, President
(202) 783-9300

United Fund Organizations

FLORIDA

UNITED BLACK FUND OF DAYTONA BEACH, FLORIDA
Post Office Box 1873
Daytona Beach, FL 33404

UNITED BLACK FUND OF PALM BEACH COUNTY, FLORIDA
257 East 23rd Street
Riveria Beach, FL 33404

UNITED BLACK FUND OF MIAMI, FLORIDA
14540 Jackson Street
Miami, FL 33176

GEORGIA

ATLANTA BLACK UNITED FUND
106 Ozone Street, S.W.
Atlanta, GA 30318

UNITED BLACK FUND OF ALBANY, GEORGIA
Post Office Box 625
Americus, GA 31709

UNITED BLACK FUND OF ATLANTA, GEORGIA
1640 Loch Lomond Trail, S.W.
Atlanta, GA 30331

ILLINOIS

CHICAGO BLACK UNITED FUND
7800 South Saginaw
Chicago, IL 60649

INDIANA

UNITED BLACK FUND OF INDIANA
2301 Morningside Avenue
Gary, IN 46408

LOUISIANA

UNITED BLACK FUND OF NEW ORLEANS, LOUISIANA
1661 Canal Street
New Orleans, LA 70112

MARYLAND

UNITED BLACK FUND OF GREATER BALTIMORE, MARYLAND
8204 Liberty Road
Baltimore, MD 21208
Shirley Pollard, President
(410) 922-6006

MASSACHUSETTS

BLACK UNITED FUND OF MASSACHUSETTS
Post Office Box 238
Astor Station
Boston, MA 02123

UNITED BLACK FUND OF MASSACHUSETTS
c/o 1012 Fourteenth Street, N.W., Suite 300
Washington, D.C. 20005

United Fund Organizations

MICHIGAN

DETROIT BLACK UNITED FUND, INC.
2187 West Grand Boulevard
Detroit, MI 48208

MISSISSIPPI

UNITED BLACK FUND OF JACKSON, MISSISSIPPI
Post Office Box 23024
Jackson, MS 39225

MISSOURI

BLACK UNITED APPEAL, INC. OF KANSAS CITY
3338 Benton Boulevard
Kansas City, MO 64128

UNITED BLACK COMMUNITY FUND, INC.
1900 Pendleton
St. Louis, MO 63113

UNITED BLACK FUND OF KANSAS CITY, MISSOURI
615-E 29th Street
F.O.B. 5545
Kansas City, MO 64109

UNITED BLACK FUND OF ST. LOUIS, MISSOURI
408 Olive Street
St. Louis, MO 63102

NEBRASKA

UNITED BLACK FUND OF NEBRASKA
c/o 1012 Fourteenth Street, N.W.,
Suite 300
Washington, D.C. 20005

NEW JERSEY

BLACK UNITED FUND OF NEW JERSEY
24 Commerce Street
Suite 417 and 418
Newark, NJ 07102

UNITED BLACK FUND OF NORTHERN NEW JERSEY
29 Warrington Place
Lenox, NJ 07017

NEW YORK

UNITED BLACK FUND OF BUFFALO
1420 Main
Buffalo, NY 17106

UNITED BLACK FUND OF TRI-STATE AREA
507 Fifth Avenue
New York, NY 10017

NORTH CAROLINA

UNITED BLACK FUND OF NORTH CAROLINA
606 Sunset Avenue, Suite 5
Rocky Mount, NC 27804

United Fund Organizations

OHIO

**UNITED BLACK FUND OF
CLEVELAND, OHIO**
1276 West Third
Cleveland, OH 44113

**UNITED BLACK FUND OF
COLUMBUS, OHIO**
1312 East Broad Street, Suite 8A
Columbus, OH 43205

OKLAHOMA

**UNITED BLACK FUND OF
TULSA, OKLAHOMA**
1915 North Main
Tulsa, OK 74106

OREGON

**UNITED BLACK FUND OF
OREGON**
2337 North Williams Avenue
Portland, OR 97227

**BLACK UNITED FUND OF
OREGON**
Post Office Box 12406
Portland, OR 97212

PENNSYLVANIA

**BLACK UNITED FUND OF
PENNSYLVANIA**
1231 North Broad Street
Philadelphia, PA 19122

**UNITED BLACK FUND OF
PHILADELPHIA, PENNSYLVA-
NIA**
6027 Drexal Road
Philadelphia, PA 19131

RHODE ISLAND

**UNITED BLACK AND BROWN
FUND OF RHODE ISLAND**
131 Washington Street
Providence, RI 02903

SOUTH CAROLINA

**UNITED BLACK FUND OF
MIDLAND, SOUTH CAROLINA**
2257 Chappell Street
Columbia, SC 29203

TEXAS

**HOUSTON BLACK UNITED
FUND, INC.**
4375 North MacGregor
Houston, TX 77004

**UNITED BLACK FUND OF
BEXAR COUNTY, TEXAS**
638 Delmar South
San Antonio, TX 78210

**UNITED BLACK FUND OF
LUBBOCK, TEXAS**
510 East 23rd Street
Lubbock, TX 79404

United Fund Organizations

UTAH

UNITED BLACK FUND OF UTAH
5170 South 5170 West
Roy, UT 84067

VIRGIN ISLANDS

UNITED BLACK FUND OF THE VIRGIN ISLANDS
Post Office Box 6385, Sunny Isle
St. Croix, VI 00820

The listings in this directory are available as Mailing Labels. See last page for details.

VIRGINIA

BLACK UNITED FUND OF TIDEWATER, INC.
4021 Springmeadow Crescent
Chesapeake, VA 23321
F. Douglas Johnson, Executive Director
(804) 488-3750

WASHINGTON

UNITED BLACK FUND OF SEATTLE, WASHINGTON
2765 East Cherry Street
Seattle, WA 98122

Urban League Affiliates

The organizations highlighed in this section represent the Urban League in cities thoughout the U.S.

ALABAMA

BIRMINGHAM URBAN LEAGUE
1717 Fourth Avenue, North
P.O. Box 11269
Birmingham, AL 35202-1269
James C. Graham, Jr., President
(205) 326-0162

ARIZONA

PHOENIX URBAN LEAGUE
1402 South Seventh Avenue
Phoenix, AZ 85007
Junious A. Bowman, President
(602) 254-5611

TUCSON URBAN LEAGUE
2305 South Park Avenue
Tucson, AZ 85713
Raymond Clarke, President
(602) 791-9522

ARKANSAS

URBAN LEAGUE OF ARKANSAS
2200 Main Street
P.O. Box 164039
Little Rock, AR 72216
Harold Barrett, Interim Administrator
(501) 372-3037

CALIFORNIA

ORANGE COUNTY URBAN LEAGUE
12391 Lewis Street, Suite 102
Garden Grove, CA 92648
George L. Williams, President
(714) 748-9976

LOS ANGELES URBAN LEAGUE
3450 Mount Vernon Drive
Los Angeles, CA 90008
John W. Mack, President
(213) 299-9660

BAY AREA URBAN LEAGUE
Kaiser Center Mall
344 - 20th Street, Suite 211
Oakland, CA 94612
Jesse J. Payne, President
(415) 839-8011

SAN DIEGO URBAN LEAGUE
4261 Market Street
San Diego, CA 92101
Ibrahim Naeem, Executive Director
(619) 263-3115

GREATER RIVERSIDE AREA URBAN LEAGUE
5225 Canyon Crest Drive
Building 100, Suite 105
Riverside, CA 92507
Rose Oliver, Interim Executive Director
(714) 682-2766

SANTA CLARA VALLEY URBAN LEAGUE, INC.
949 East San Fernando
San Jose, CA 95116-2234
Dian J. Harrison, Executive Director
(408) 971-0117

Urban League Affiliates

COLORADO

URBAN LEAGUE OF METRO-POLITAN DENVER
1525 Josephine Street
Denver, CO 80206
Lawrence H. Borom, President
(303) 388-5861

URBAN LEAGUE OF THE PIKES PEAK REGION
324 North Nevada
Colorado Springs, CO 80903
James E. Miller, President
(719) 634-1525

CONNECTICUT

URBAN LEAGUE OF GREATER BRIDGEPORT
285 Golden Hill Street
Bridgeport, CT 06604
William K. Wolfe, President
(203) 366-2737

URBAN LEAGUE OF GREATER NEW HAVEN
1184 Chapel Street
New Haven, CT 06511
Martha Wright, Interim Director
(203) 624-4168

URBAN LEAGUE OF GREATER HARTFORD
1229 Albany Avenue, Third Floor
Hartford, CT 06112
Esther Bush, President
(203) 527-0147

URBAN LEAGUE OF SOUTH-WESTERN FAIRFIELD COUNTY
1 Atlantic Street, Suite 619
Stamford, CT 06901
Curtiss E. Porter, Ph.D., President
(203) 327-5810

DISTRICT OF COLUMBIA

WASHINGTON URBAN LEAGUE
3501 Fourteenth Street, N.W.
Washington, D.C. 20010
Maudine R. Cooper, President
(202) 265-8200

FLORIDA

URBAN LEAGUE OF BROWARD COUNTY
11 N.W. 36th Avenue
Fort Lauderdale, FL 33311
Willie Myles, Interim Executive Director
(305) 584-0777

URBAN LEAGUE OF GREATER MIAMI
8500 N.W. 25th Avenue
Miami, FL 33132
T. Willard Fair, President
(305) 696-4459

METROPOLITAN ORLANDO URBAN LEAGUE
2512 West Colonial Drive
Orlando, FL 32804
Shirley J. Boykin, President
(407) 841-7654

Urban League Affiliates

PINELLAS COUNTY URBAN LEAGUE
333 - 31st Street, North
St. Petersburg, FL 33713
James O. Simmons, President
(813) 327-2081

JACKSONVILLE URBAN LEAGUE
101 East Union street
Jacksonville, FL 32202
Ronnie A. Ferguson, President
(904) 356-8336

TALLAHASSEE URBAN LEAGUE
923 Old Bainbridge Road
Tallahassee, FL 32301
Reverend Ernest Ferrell, President
(904) 222-6111

GREATER TAMPA URBAN LEAGUE
1405 Tampa Park Plaza
Tampa, FL 33604
Joanna N. Tokley, President
(813) 229-8117

URBAN LEAGUE OF PALM BEACH COUNTY, INC.
1700 Australian Avenue
West Palm Beach, FL 33407
Percy H. Lee, President
(407) 833-1461

GEORGIA

ATLANTA URBAN LEAGUE
100 Edgewood Avenue, N. E.
Sixth Floor, Suite 600
Atlanta, GA 30303
Lyndon A. Wade, President
(404) 659-1150

METRO COLUMBUS URBAN LEAGUE, INC.
802 First Avenue
Columbus, GA 31901
Jessie J. Taylor, Executive Director
(404) 323-3687

ILLINOIS

MADISON COUNTY URBAN LEAGUE
210 Williams Street
Alton, IL 62002
Julia Tibbs, President
(618) 463-1906

CHICAGO URBAN LEAGUE
4510 South Michigan Avenue
Chicago, IL 60653
James W. Compton, President
(312) 285-5800

QUAD COUNTY URBAN LEAGUE
305 East Benton Street
Aurora, IL 60505
Peggy S. Hicks, President
(708) 897-5335

TRI-COUNTY URBAN LEAGUE
317 South MacArthur Highway
Peoria, IL 61605-3892
Frank Campbell
    Executive Director
(309) 673-7474

URBAN LEAGUE OF CHAMPAIGN COUNTY
17 Taylor Street
Champaign, IL 61820
Vernon L. Barkstall, President
(217) 356-1364

Urban League Affiliates

SPRINGFIELD URBAN LEAGUE, INC.
100 North Eleventh Street
P.O. Box 3865
Springfield, IL 62708
Howard R. Veal, President
(217) 789-0830

INDIANA

URBAN LEAGUE OF MADISON COUNTY, INC.
1210 West 10th Street
P.O. Box 271
Anderson, IN 46015
Albert B. Simmons, President
(317) 649-7126

FORT WAYNE URBAN LEAGUE
Foellinger Community Center
227 East Washington Blvd.
Fort Wayne, IN 46802
Rick C. Frazier, President
(219) 424-6326

URBAN LEAGUE OF NORTH-WEST INDIANA, INC.
3101 Broadway
Gary, IN 46408
Eloise Gentry, President
(219) 887-9621

INDIANAPOLIS URBAN LEAGUE
850 Meridian Street
Indianapolis, IN 46204
Sam H. Jones, President
(317) 639-9404

MARION URBAN LEAGUE, INC.
1221 West Twelfth Street
Marion, IN 46953
Arthur N. Banks, III, Executive Director
(317) 664-3933

URBAN LEAGUE OF SOUTH BEND AND ST. JOSEPH COUNTY, INC.
1708 High Street
Post Office Box, 1476
South Bend, IN 46624
(219) 287-7261

KANSAS

URBAN LEAGUE OF WICHITA, INC.
1405 North Minneapolis
Wichita, KS 67214
Otis G. Milton, President
(316) 262-2463

KENTUCKY

URBAN LEAGUE OF LEXING-TON-FAYETTE COUNTY
167 West Main Street, Room 406
Lexington, KY 40507
Porter G. Peeples, Executive Director
(606) 233-1561

LOUISVILLE URBAN LEAGUE
Lyles Mall, Third Level
2600 West Broadway
Louisville, KY 40211
Benjamin K. Richmond, President
(502) 776-4622

LOUISIANA

URBAN LEAGUE OF GREATER NEW ORLEANS
1929 Bienville Street
New Orleans, LA 70112
Clarence L. Barney, President
(504) 524-4667

Urban League Affiliates

MARYLAND

BALTIMORE URBAN LEAGUE
1150 Mondawmin Concourse
Baltimore, MD 21215
Roger I. Lyons, President
(301) 523-8150

MASSACHUSETTS

URBAN LEAGUE OF EASTERN MASSACHUSETTS
88 Warren Street
Roxbury, MA 02119
Joan Wallace Benjamin, Ph.D., President
(617) 442-4519

URBAN LEAGUE OF SPRINGFIELD
756 State Street
Springfield, MA 01109
Henry M. Thomas, III, President
(413) 739-7211

MICHIGAN

URBAN LEAGUE OF FLINT
202 E. Boulevard Dr., Second Floor
Flint, MI 48503
Melvyn S. Brannon, President
(313) 239-5111

GREATER LANSING URBAN LEAGUE, INC.
809 Center Street
Lansing, MI 48906
Marvin Cato, Interim Admin. Director
(517) 487-3608

URBAN LEAGUE OF GREATER MUSKEGON
469 West Webster Avenue
Muskegon, MI 49440
Donald L. Everette, Interim President
(616) 722-3736

PONTIAC AREA URBAN LEAGUE
295 West Huron Street
Pontiac, MI 48053
Jacquelin E. Washington, President
(313) 335-8730

MINNEAPOLIS

MINNEAPOLIS URBAN LEAGUE
2000 Plymouth Avenue, North
Minneapolis, MN 55411
Gleason Glover, President
(612) 521-1099

ST. PAUL URBAN LEAGUE
401 Selby Avenue
St. Paul, MN 55102
Willie Mae Wilson, President
(612) 224-5771

MISSISSIPPI

URBAN LEAGUE OF GREATER JACKSON
3405 Medgar Evers Boulevard
Post Office Box 11249
Jackson, MN 39213
Maggie Tryman, Executive Director
(601) 981-4211

Urban League Affiliates

MISSOURI

URBAN LEAGUE OF KANSAS CITY
1710 Paseo
Kansas City, MO 64108
William H. Clark, President
(816) 471-0550

URBAN LEAGUE OF METRO-POLITAN ST. LOUIS
3701 Grandel Square
St. Louis, MO 63108
James H. Buford, President
(314) 289-0328

NEBRASKA

URBAN LEAGUE OF NEBRASKA
3022-24 North 24th Street
Omaha, NE 68110
George H. Dillard, President
(402) 453-9730

NEW JERSEY

URBAN LEAGUE OF BERGEN COUNTY
106 West Palisade Avenue
Englewood, NJ 07631
William E. Brown, President
(201) 568-4988

URBAN LEAGUE OF UNION COUNTY
272 North Broad Street
Elizabeth, NJ 07207
Ella S. Teal, President
(201) 351-7200

URBAN LEAGUE OF HUDSON COUNTY
779 Bergen Avenue
Jersey City, NJ 07306
Elnora Watson, President
(201) 451-8888

MORRIS COUNTY URBAN LEAGUE
27 Market Street
Morristown, NJ 07960
Janice S. Johnson, President
(201) 539-2121

URBAN LEAGUE OF ESSEX COUNTY
3 Williams Street, Suite 300
Newark, NJ 07102
Lawrence E. Pratt, President
(201) 624-6660

URBAN LEAGUE OF METRO-POLITAN TRENTON
209 Academy Street
Trenton, NJ 08618
Paul P. Pintella, Jr., President
(609) 393-1512

NEW YORK

ALBANY AREA URBAN LEAGUE
95 Livingston Avenue
Albany, NY 12207
Lawrence Burwell, Interim President
(518) 463-3121

URBAN LEAGUE OF LONG ISLAND
221 Broadway, Suite 207
Amityville, NY 11701
Rosemary Durant-Giles, President
(516) 691-7230

Urban League Affiliates

**BROOME COUNTY URBAN
  LEAGUE**
43-45 Carroll Street
Binhamton, NY 13901
Laura C. Keeling, President
(607) 723-5972

**BUFFALO URBAN LEAGUE,
  INC.**
15 East Genesee Street
Buffalo, NY 14203
Leroy R. Coles, Jr., President
(716) 854-7625

NEW YORK URBAN LEAGUE
218 West 40th Street
New York, NY 10018
Dennis M. Walcott, President
(212) 730-5200

URBAN LEAGUE OF ROCHESTER
177 North Clinton avenue
Rochester, NY 14604
William A. Johnson, Jr., President
(716) 325-6530

**URBAN LEAGUE OF
  ONONDAGO COUNTY**
505 East Fayette Street
Syracuse, NY 13202
Leon E. Modeste, President
(315) 472-6955

**URBAN LEAGUE OF
  WESTCHESTER COUNTY**
61 Mitchell Place
White Plains, NY 10601
Ernest S. Prince, President
(914) 428-6300

NORTH CAROLINA

**CHARLOTTE-MECKLENBURG
  URBAN LEAGUE**
A.M.E. Zion Building
401 East Second Street
Charlotte, NC 28202
Madine Hester Fails, President
(704) 376-9834

**WINSTON-SALEM URBAN
  LEAGUE**
201 West Fifth Street
Winston-Salem, NC 27101
Delores Smith, President
(919) 725-5614

OHIO

**AKRON COMMUNITY SERVICE
  CENTER AND URBAN
  LEAGUE**
250 East Market Street
Akron, OH 44308
(216) 434-3101

CANTON URBAN LEAGUE, INC.
Community Center
1400 Sherrick Road, S.E.
Canton, OH 44707-3533
Joseph N. Smith, Executive Director
(216) 456-3479

**URBAN LEAGUE OF GREATER
  CINCINNATI**
2400 Reading Road
Cincinnati, OH 45202
(513) 721-2237

Urban League Affiliates

URBAN LEAGUE OF GREATER CLEVELAND
12001 Shaker Boulevard
Cleveland, OH 44120
Mrs. Jacquelyn Shrosphire, President
(216) 421-0999

COLUMBUS URBAN LEAGUE
700 Bryden Road., Suite 230
Columbus, OH 43215
Samuel Gresham, Jr., President
(614) 221-0544

DAYTON URBAN LEAGUE
United Way Building, Room 200
Dayton, OH 45406
Willie F. Walker, President
(513) 229-6650

LORAINE COUNTY URBAN LEAGUE
401 Broad Street
Robinson Building, Suites 204 & 206
Elyria, OH 44035
Delbert L. Lancaster, President
(216) 323-3364

MASSILLON URBAN LEAGUE, INC.
405 Massillon Building
Massillon, OH 44646
Harold Glen, Interim President
(216) 833-2804

SPRINGFIELD URBAN LEAGUE
521 South Center Street
Springfield, OH 45506
Charles E. Nesbitt, Ph.D., President
(513) 323-4603

WARREN-TRUMBULL URBAN LEAGUE
290 West Market Street
Warren, OH 44481
(216) 394-4316

OKLAHOMA

URBAN LEAGUE OF GREATER OKLAHOMA CITY
3017 Martin Luther King Avenue
Oklahoma City, OK 73111
Leonard D. Benton, President
(405) 424-5243

TULSA URBAN LEAGUE
240 East Apache Street
Tulsa, OK 74106
Laverne Hill, Executive Director
(918) 584-3520

OREGON

URBAN LEAGUE OF PORTLAND
Urban Plaza
10 North Russell
Portland, OR 97277
(503) 280-2600

PENNSYLVANIA

URBAN LEAGUE OF METRO-POLITAN HARRISBURG
25 North Front Street
Harrisburg, PA 17101
Kinneth W. Washington, President
(717) 234-5925

Urban League Affiliates

URBAN LEAGUE OF LANCASTER COUNTY
502 South Duke Street
Lancaster, PA 17602
Milton J. Bondurant, President
(717) 394-1966

URBAN LEAGUE OF PITTSBURGH
200 Ross Street, Second Floor
Pittsburgh, PA 15219
Leon L. Haley, Ph.D., President
(412) 261-1130

URBAN LEAGUE OF PHILADELPHIA
4601 Market Street, Suite 2S
Philadelphia, PA 19139
Robert W. Sorrell, President
(215) 476-4040

URBAN LEAGUE OF SHENANGO VALLEY
39 Chestnut Street
Sharon, PA 16146
Phillip E. Smith, President
(412) 981-5310

RHODE ISLAND

URBAN LEAGUE OF RHODE ISLAND
246 Prairie Avenue
Providence, RI 02905
(401) 351-5000

The listings in this directory are available as Mail Labels. See last page for details.

SOUTH CAROLINA

COLUMBIA URBAN LEAGUE
1400 Barnwell Street
Post Office Drawer J
Columbia, SC 29250
James T. McLawhorn, Jr., President
(803) 799-8150

GREENVILLE URBAN LEAGUE
15 Regency Hill Drive
Post Office Box 10161
Greenville, SC 29603
Myron F. Robinson, President
(803) 244-3862

TENNESSEE

CHATTANOOGA AREA URBAN LEAGUE
P.O. Box 11106
730 Martin Luther King Blvd.
Chattanooga, TN 37401
Jerome W. Page, President
(615) 756-1762

KNOXVILLE AREA URBAN LEAGUE
2416 Magnolia Avenue
P.O. Box 1911
Knoxville, TN 37901
Mark Brown, President
(615) 524-5511

MEMPHIS URBAN LEAGUE
2279 Lamar Avenue
Memphis, TN 38114
Herman C. Ewing, President
(901) 327-3591

Urban League Affiliates

NASHVILLE URBAN LEAGUE
1219 Ninth Avenue
Nashville, TN 37208
Joseph S. Carroll, Executive Director
(615) 254-0525

TEXAS

DALLAS URBAN LEAGUE
2121 Main St., 4th Floor, Suite 410
Dallas, TX 75201
Dr. Beverly Mitchell, Executive Director
(214) 747-4734

**HOUSTON AREA URBAN
LEAGUE**
3215 Fannin
Houston, TX 77004
Sylvia K. Brooks, President
(713) 526-5127

VIRGINIA

**NORTHERN VIRGINIA URBAN
LEAGUE**
901 North Washington Street
Alexandria, VA 22314
George H. Lambert, Interim Director
(703) 836-2858

RICHMOND URBAN LEAGUE
101 East Clay Street
Richmond, VA 23219
Randolph C. Kendall, Jr., President
(804) 649-8407

WASHINGTON

**METROPOLITAN SEATTLE
URBAN LEAGUE**
105 Fourteenth Avenue
Seattle, WA, 98122
Rossalind Y. Woodhouse, Ph.D.,
President
(206) 461-3792

TACOMA URBAN LEAGUE
2550 South Yakima Avenue
Tacoma, WA 98405
Thomas Dixon, President
(206) 383-2006

WISCONSIN

MADISON URBAN LEAGUE
151 East Gorham
Madison, WI 53703
Betty A. Franklin-Hammonds, Executive Director
(608) 251-8550

MILWAUKEE URBAN LEAGUE
2800 West Wright Street
Milwaukee, WI 53210
Jacqueline J. Patterson, President
(414) 374-5850

**URBAN LEAGUE OF RACINE &
KENOSHA, INC.**
718-22 North Memorial Drive
Racine, WI 53404
Rodney Brooks, President
(414) 637-8532

STATISTICAL
CENSUS DATA

The Black Population in the United States

Population Growth

According to the 1990 census the Black population constituted 12.1 percent of the resident population, up from 11.7 percent in 1980. The Black population grew faster than either the total or the White population. Since 1980, the Black population increased by 13.2 percent, compared with 6.0 percent for the white population. The higher growth rate of the Black population was largely the result of higher natural increase-the combined result of a younger population and of age-specific fertility rates somewhat higher than those of Whites.

Social Characteristics

Sex and Age Distribution. There are more females than males in both the Black and White populations, reflecting the longer life expectancy of females.

The Black population had a median age of 27.9 years in 1990, compared to 24.8 years in 1980. In 1990, as in 1980, the Black median age was about 6 years lower that of the White population.

Among both Blacks and Whites, females have a higher median age than males. In 1990, the median age was 29.1 years for Black females compared to 26.4 years for Black males.

The age structures of the Black population and the White population differ. Blacks have a larger proportion under 18 years of age and a smaller proportion ages 65 years and over. In March 1990, 33.1 percent of the Black population was under 18 years of age compared with 24.9 percent of the White population. For the population 65 years old and over, the figures were 8.2 and 12.8 percents respectively.

School Enrollment

In both 1988 and 1980, the percent of Black males 18 to 24 years old who were high school graduates was below that for females. For example, in 1988, about 71.9 percent of Black males compared to 77.9 percent of Black females in this age category had completed high school. However, for both Black males and Black females in 1988, the proportion completing high school represented an increase over the proportion in 1980. The actual numbers of high school graduates in 1988 (1.2 million Black males and 1.5 million Black females) were not different from those in 1980.

The differences between Blacks and Whites in college enrollment of high school graduates were somewhat larger in 1988 than in 1980. Twenty-five percent of Black males compared to 39 percent of White males were enrolled in college in 1988. The pattern was similar for females. In 1988, the percent of Black females (30 percent) was lower than the 37 percent of White female high school graduates enrolled in college. However, unlike the pattern for Black and White males, there was no statistical difference (29 percent versus 30 percent) in the percent of Black and White females in this age group enrolled in college in 1980.

Scholarship Athletes

Blacks make up nearly a quarter of all the scholarship athletes at 245 college and universities in Division I of the National Collegiate Athletic Association. Sixty percent of all the scholarship holders in men's basketball are Black. Yet Blacks constitute only 6 per cent of the full-time undergraduates at those institutions.

At more than 100 of the 245 colleges, at least one of every five full-time, Black male students in academic 1990-91 was an athlete.

Black students on most of the campuses were far more likely to be athletes than were their white counterparts. Fifteen per cent of the black males at Division I colleges-more than one in seven-were scholarship athletes, compared with one in every 43 white males or 2.3 per cent.

Family Type

Since 1980, married-couple families as a proportion of all families in both the Black and White populations declined, although more sharply for Blacks. In 1990, married-couple families accounted for about 4 million or 50.2 percent of all Black families, and 47 million or 83.0 percent of all White families. The corresponding figures for 1980 were 55.5 percent for Blacks and 85.7 percent for Whites.

Black Families maintained by a woman with no spouse present rose from 40.3 percent to 43.8 percent.

Living Arrangements of Children

In 1980, 43.9 percent of all Black children under 18 years of age in families lived with the mother only; by 1990, the proportion had increased to 51.2 percent.

The proportion of children under age 18 living in father-only families also increased between 1980 and 1990. In 1990, 3.5 percent of all Black children under age 18 residing in families lived with the father only, compared with 1.9 percent in 1980

Paralleling the increase in the proportion of children under 18 years of age residing in one-parent families, there was a decrease in the proportion residing with both parents. In 1980, 42.2 percent of all Black children under 18 years old lived with both parents; by 1990, this proportion had declined to 37.7 percent, a 4.5 percentage point change. The corresponding figures for Whites were 82.7 percent in 1980 and 79.0 percent in 1990.

Economic Characteristics

Labor Force

In March 1990, there were 13.5 million Blacks 16 years old and over in the labor force. Of these, 12.0 million were employed and 1.5 million were unemployed. Blacks made up 10.8 percent of the total labor force, 10.1 percent of employed persons and 22.2 percent of unemployed person.

In General, males have higher labor force participation rates than females, and Whites have higher rates than Blacks.

Money Income of Families

Black families had a median income of $20,210 in 1989. This was not statistically different from their 1979 level ($19,770), after adjusting for inflation. The 1989 median income of White families ($35,980) was higher than their 1979 level ($34,910). Black median family income in 1989 represented 56 percent of comparable White median family income - a gap not statistically different from a decade earlier.

Median money income of Black husband-wife families was $30,650 in 1989, a 7 percentage point increase from $28,700 in 1979, after adjusting for inflation, this compared with a 6 percentage point increase amount White husband-wife families ($39,210 versus $37,160). In contrast, neither Black nor White families with a female householder and no spouse represent experienced a significant change in real median family income during this period.

Earnings of Persons

Historically, males have earned more than females and Whites have earned more than Blacks on average. In 1989, the median earnings of Black males and females were $15,320 and $11,520, respectively. The median earnings in 1989 of Black females were about 75 percent of those of Black males. After adjusting for inflation, the median earnings of Black men in 1989 were not statistically different from their 1979 levels. The figures were $15,320 in 1989 and $15,520 in 1979. The median earnings for White men declined between 1979 and 1989, from $23,290 to $22,160.

The median earnings of Black males were about 69 percent of White males' earnings. In contrast, Black females' earnings represented about 98 percent of White females' earnings.

Earnings of Year-round, Full-time Workers

For both male and female year-round, full-time workers, the median earnings ratios of Blacks to Whites were not significantly different from the 1979 ratios. The earnings ratios in 1979 were 0.73 ($21,760 versus $29,770) for males and 0.92 ($16,180 versus $17,500) for females. Hence, there was no narrowing of this earnings differential by race during the decade.

Earnings by Educational Attainment.

In 1989, the median earnings of year-round, full time Black workers 25 years old and over with a high school education was $18,390; over 50 percent (56.5 percent) of them had earnings below $20,000. In contract, the median earnings of year-round, full-time Black workers with 4 years or more of college was $29,480. The median earnings for college educated Black males was $31,380, about 55 percent higher than the median for those with only a high school education ($20,280) while the corresponding median for Black females with a college education ($26,730) was 63 percent higher than those with only a high school education ($16,440)

In general, the median earnings across the educational categories of year-round, full-time workers are higher for males than for females and for Whites than for Blacks. The median earnings of Black females with a high school education ($16,440) was 81 percent of the earnings of their Black male counterparts ($20,280). Black females with four years or more of college had median earnings of $26,730 - 85 percent of their Black male counterparts ($31,380). White females have a lower median earnings ratio to White males than Black females have to Black males. The corresponding figures for Whites were 64 percent ($16,910 versus $26,510) at the high school level and 67 percent at the college level ($27,440 versus $41,090).

Occupational Distribution

In examining differences in earnings between males and females and Blacks and whites, it is important to examine differences by occupation.

The occupational distribution of Black males and females differ, although both Black males and Black females continue to be concentrated in nonprofessional and nonmanagerial occupational groups. One-third (33.4 percent) of Black males compared with over one-tenth (12.0 percent) of Black females were employed as operators, fabricators, and laborers; and 16.3 percent of Black males compared with 2.3 percent of Black females were employed in precision production, craft, and repair type occupations. This reflects the male dominance of these occupations. In contrast, 39.7 percent of Black females compared with 16.6 percent of Black males were employed in technical, sales, and administrative support; and 27.0 percent of Black females compared with 17.5 percent of Black males were employed in service occupations. There was also a larger proportion of Black females (18.8 percent) in the managerial and professional speciality type occupations than Black males (13.4 percent) in 1989.

The occupational distribution of employed Black men in 1990 differed somewhat from that of White men, for example, Black men were more likely to be employed as operator, fabricators, and laborers than in any other occupation group (33.4 percent). White men, however, were more likely to be employed in managerial and professional specialty occupations (27.3 percent).

Both Black and White women were more likely to be employed in technical, sales, and administrative support occupations than in any other occupation group (39.7 percent and 45.7 percent, respectively). Black women were more likely than White women to be employed in service occupations (27.0 percent versus 16.1 percent). Over one-fourth of White women were employed in managerial and professional specialty occupations, compared with about one-fifth of Black women.

Poverty of Persons

Thirty one percent, or 9.3 million, of all Black persons were poor in 1989, unchanged from the 31 percent in 1979 and the 32 percent in 1969. The poverty rate for Black persons reached a high of 36 percent in the first half of the decade. The 1989 poverty rate for Blacks (31 percent) was three times that of Whites (10 percent).

There were twice as many elderly Black females (544,000 or 36.7 percent) as elderly Black males (221,000 or 22.1 percent) below the poverty level in 1989. This in part reflects the larger proportion of Black females 65 years old and over who are widowed, which in turn reflects the longer life expectancy of Black females than Black males.

In 1989, 30.8 percent of all Blacks 65 years of age and over were poor; this was in contrast to 9.6 percent of Whites. Black males 65 years or age and over were four times as likely to be poor as their White male counterparts. Elderly Black females were three times as likely to be poor as elderly White females.

Poor persons, both Black and White, are concentrated in metropolitan areas of this country. In 1989, 79.0 percent of all poor Blacks lived in metropolitan areas compared with 69.4 percent of poor Whites. Within the metropolitan areas, over three-fourths (77.5 percent) of all poor Blacks lived in central cities. Poor Whites were more evenly distributed between the central cities (49.7 percent) and areas outside the central cities (50.3 percent).

Poverty of Families

In 1989, Black families were three and one-half times as likely to be poor as White families. This ratio has not varied much since 1969 when 27.9 percent of all Black families and 7.7 percent of all White families were poor.

The incidence of poverty varies by family type. In 1989, the poverty rate for Black families with female householders with no spouse present was 46.5 percent compared to 11.8 percent for married-couple families, and 24.7 percent for families with male householders with no spouse present.

The proportion of Black families with female householders with no spouse present who were poor in 1989 (46.5 percent) was not statistically different from the 1979 level of 49.4 percent, but was lower than the 1969 level of 53.3 percent. The poverty rate for Black families with female householders with no spouse present has varied widely during the past 20 years, ranging from 61.6 percent in 1978 to 46.5 percent in 1989.

In 1989, 4.3 million or 43.2 percent of all Black related children, and 7.2 million or 14.1 percent of all White related children under 18 years of age in families were poor. Most of the Black children in poverty in 1989 were in families with a female householder with no spouse present.

In 1989, over one-third (35.4 percent) of all Black families with related children under 18 years of age were poor. Over one-half (53.9) of Black children under 18 in families maintained by women were poor in 1989. The corresponding figures for male householders with spouse present and married-couple families were 33.8 percent and 13.3 percent, respectively.

Inmate Population

As of June, 1990, the United States adult inmate population was 403,019. Black inmates made up 47 percent of the 1990 jail population, with 43 percent being Black men and the remaining 4 percent being Black females.

BLACK RESOURCE GUIDE

Business

Black-owned firms increased 37.6 percent from 308,260 in 1982 to 424,165 in 1987. Receipts increased 105 percent from 9.6 billion. At least part of the increase can be attributed to a change in IRS regulations which gave tax advantages to business firms filing as subchapter S corporations. Many firms changed their form of ownership from partnerships and other kinds of corporations to subchapter S corporations for the tax benefits. Because other corporations are not included in the survey universe, this resulted in artificial increases in total Black-owned firms as well as Black-owned subchapter S corporation.

Industry Characteristics

In 1987 the majority of Black-owned firms were concentrated in the service industries. These industries accounted for 49 percent of all Black-owned firms and 31 percent of gross receipts. The next largest concentration of Black-owned firms was in retail trade with 15.6 percent of the firms and 29.8 percent of the receipts.

Geographic Characteristics

California had the largest number of Black-owned firms in 1987 with 47,728 firms whose gross receipts were $2.4 billion. New York was second with 36,289 firms and $1.9 billion in gross receipts. Slightly less than 44 percent of Black-owned firms and 44.7 percent of gross receipts (185,563 firms and $8.8 billion in gross receipts) were concentrated in California, New York, Texas, Florida, Georgia and Illinois.

Legal Form of Organization

The majority of Black-owned firms operated as individual proprietorships in 1987 (400,339 or 94.4 percent, down from 95.0 percent in 1982). This group accounted for 50.9 percent of gross receipts compared to 68.4 percent in 1982. Of the total number of firms, 11,261 or 2.7 percent were partnerships, accounting for 10 percent of gross receipts. Partnerships accounted for 3.3 percent of the Black-owned firms and 13.9 percent of gross receipts in 1982. Subchapter S corporations accounted for only 3 percent of the total number of firms but 39.2 percent of gross receipts. This is up from 1.7 percent of the firms and 17.7 percent of gross receipts in 1982..

Size of Firm

Black-owned firms with paid employees accounted for 16.7 percent of the total number of firms and 71.5 percent of gross receipts. There were 189 firms with 100 employees or more which accounted for $2 billion in gross receipts (14.2 percent of the total receipts of employer firms).

Black-owned firms with gross receipts of $1 million or more accounted for 37 percent of the total gross receipts but only 0.5 percent of the total number of firms. Thirty-five percent of the firms had gross receipts of less than $5 thousand.

Black-Owned Firms Compared To All Firms

Black-owned firms accounted for 3.1 percent of all firms in the United States and 1 percent of gross receipts. The largest portion of firms owned by Blacks is transportation and public utilities with 6.2 percent of all firms and 2.1 percent of gross receipts. Blacks are particularly concentrated in local and interurban passenger transit, where they own 17.1 percent of all firms and account for 6.5 percent of gross receipts.

The District of Columbia has the largest percentage of Black-owned firms with 28.3 percent of the firms and 6.3 percent of gross receipts.

The percentage of all firms owned by Blacks is directly related to the receipts size of the firm. For example, Blacks owned 3.8 percent of the firms with receipts less than $5,000 but only 0.8 percent of the firms with receipts of $1 million or more. The same relationship is true for firms with paid employees, where Blacks owned 1.7 percent of the firms with 1 to 4 employees and 0.9 percent of the firms with 100 employees or more.

1990 Population Totals for Black Persons By State

Rank	State	Total
1	New York	2,859,055
2	California	2,208,801
3	Texas	2,021,632
4	Florida	1,759,534
5	Georgia	1,746,565
6	Illinois	1,694,273
7	North Carolina	1,456,323
8	Louisiana	1,299,281
9	Michigan	1,291,706
10	Maryland	1,189,899
11	Virginia	1,162,994
12	Ohio	1,154,826
13	Pennsylvania	1,089,795
14	South Carolina	1,039,884
15	New Jersey	1,036,825
16	Alabama	1,020,705
17	Mississippi	915,057
18	Tennessee	778,035
19	Missouri	548,208
20	Indiana	432,092
21	District of Columbia	399,604
22	Arkansas	373,912
23	Massachusetts	300,130
24	Connecticut	274,269
25	Kentucky	262,907
26	Wisconsin	244,539
27	Oklahoma	233,801
28	Washington	149,801
29	Kansas	143,076
30	Colorado	133,146
31	Delaware	112,460
32	Arizona	110,524
33	Minnesota	99,944
34	Nevada	78,771
35	Nebraska	57,404
36	West Virginia	56,295
37	Iowa	48,090
38	Oregon	46,178
39	Rhode Island	38,861
40	New Mexico	30,210
41	Hawaii	27,195
42	Alaska	22,451
43	Utah	11,576
44	New Hampshire	7,198
45	Maine	5,138
46	Wyoming	3,606
47	North Dakota	3,524
48	Idaho	3,370
49	South Dakota	3,258
50	Montana	2,381
51	Vermont	1,951
	Total	29,986,060

Source: U.S. Census Bureau

100 Cities with the Largest Black Population, by Rank: 1990

Rank	City	Black Population Number	Percent of Total Population	Total Population
1	New York, NY	2,102,512	28.7	7,322,564
2	Chicago, IL	1,087,711	39.1	2,783,726
3	Detroit, MI	777,916	75.7	1,027,974
4	Philadelphia, PA	631,936	39.9	1,585,577
5	Los Angeles, CA	487,674	14.0	3,485,398
6	Houston, TX	457,990	28.1	1,630,553
7	Baltimore, MD	435,768	59.2	736,014
8	Washington, D.C.	399,604	65.8	606,900
9	Memphis, TN	334,737	54.8	610,337
10	New Orleans, LA	307,728	61.9	496,938
11	Dallas, TX	296,994	29.5	1,006,877
12	Atlanta, GA	264,262	67.1	394,017
13	Cleveland, OH	235,405	46.6	505,616
14	Milwaukee, WI	191,255	30.5	628,088
15	St. Louis, MO	188,408	47.5	396,685
16	Birmingham, AL	168,277	63.3	265,968
17	Indianapolis, IN	165,570	22.6	731,327
18	Oakland, CA	163,335	43.9	372,242
19	Newark, NJ	160,885	58.5	275,221
20	Jacksonville, FL	160,283	25.2	635,230
21	Boston, MA	146,945	25.6	574,283
22	Columbus, OH	142,748	22.6	632,910
23	Cincinnati, OH	138,132	37.9	364,040
24	Kansas City, MO	128,768	29.6	435,146
25	Charlotte, NC	125,827	31.8	395,934
26	Nashville-Davidson, TN	118,627	24.3	488,374
27	Richmond, VA	112,122	55.2	203,056
28	Jackson, MS	109,620	55.7	196,637
29	San Diego, CA	104,261	9.4	1,110,549
30	Norfolk, VA	102,012	39.1	261,229
31	Buffalo, NY	100,579	30.7	328,123
32	Fort Worth, TX	98,532	22.0	447,619
33	Miami, FL	98,207	27.4	358,548
34	Pittsburgh, PA	95,362	25.8	369,879
35	Gary, IN	93,982	80.6	116,646
36	Baton Rouge, LA	93,346	43.9	219,531
37	Shreveport, LA	88,860	44.8	198,525
38	Louisville, KY	79,783	29.7	269,063
39	Montomery, AL	79,217	42.3	187,106
40	San Francisco, CA	79,039	10.9	723,959
41	Mobile, AL	76,407	38.9	196,278
42	Dayton, OH	73,595	40.3	182,044
43	Rochester, NY	73,024	31.5	231,636
44	Oklahoma City, OK	71,064	16.0	444,719
45	Savannah, GA	70,580	51.3	137,560
46	Tampa, FL	70,151	25.0	280,015
47	Columbus, GA	68,157	38.1	178,681
48	Flint, MI	67,485	47.9	140,761
49	Jersey City, NJ	67,864	29.7	228,537
50	East Orange, NJ	66,157	89.9	73,552

100 Cities with the Largest Black Population, by Rank: 1990 *(continued)*

Rank	City	Black Population Number	Percent of Total Population	Total Population
51	San Antonio, TX	65,884	7.0	935,933
52	Toledo, OH	65,598	19.7	332,943
53	Durham, NC	62,449	45.7	136,611
54	Greensboro, NC	62,305	33.9	183,321
55	Denver, CO	60,046	12.8	467,610
56	Little Rock, AR	59,742	34.0	175,795
57	Long Beach, CA	58,761	13.7	429,433
58	Austin, TX	57,868	12.4	465,622
59	Raleigh, NC	57,354	27.6	207,951
60	Newport News, VA	57,077	33.6	170,045
61	Inglewood, CA	56,861	51.9	109,602
62	Sacramento, CA	56,521	15.3	369,365
63	Winston-Salem, NC	56,328	39.3	143,485
64	Macon, GA	55,645	52.2	106,612
65	Akron, OH	54,656	24.5	223,019
66	Hartford, CT	54,338	38.9	139,739
67	Hampton, VA	51,981	38.9	133,793
68	Seattle, WA	51,948	10.1	516,259
69	Chattanooga, TN	51,338	33.7	152,466
70	Phoenix, AZ	51,053	5.2	983,403
71	Paterson, NJ	50,729	36.0	140,891
72	Tulsa, OK	49,825	13.6	367,302
73	Compton, CA	49,598	54.8	90,454
74	Camden, NJ	49,362	56.4	87,492
75	Portsmouth, VA	49,180	47.3	103,907
76	Beaumont, TX	47,164	41.3	114,323
77	New Haven, CT	47,157	36.1	130,474
78	St. Petersburg, FL	46,726	19.6	238,629
79	Orlando, FL	44,303	26.9	164,693
80	Omaha, NE	43,989	13.1	335,795
81	Kansas City, KS	43,834	29.3	149,767
82	Trenton, NJ	43,689	49.3	88,675
83	Albany, GA	42,962	55.0	78,122
84	Columbia, SC	42,837	43.7	98,052
85	Fort Lauderdale, FL	41,995	28.1	149,377
86	Chesapeake, VA	41,662	27.4	151,976
87	East St. Louis, IL	40,161	98.1	40,944
88	Huntsville, AL	39,016	24.4	159,789
89	Richmond, CA	38,260	43.8	87,425
90	Bridgeport, CT	37,684	26.6	141,686
91	Wilmington, DE	37,446	52.4	71,529
92	Mount Vernon, NY	37,138	55.3	67,153
93	San Jose, CA	36,790	4.7	782,248
94	Youngstown, OH	36,487	38.1	95,732
95	Grand Rapids, MI	35,073	18.5	189,126
96	Wichita, KS	34,301	11.3	304,011
97	Charleston, SC	33,439	41.6	80,414
98	East Cleveland, OH	31,009	93.7	33,096
99	Pontiac, MI	30,033	42.2	71,166
100	Prichard, AL	27,249	79.4	34,311

ORDER FORM

Please enter my order for **The Black Resource Guide:**
   10th Edition **$69.95**

> Include $3.50 for 4th class postage & handling
> or $5.00 for 1st class postage & handling.
> **Please add state and local taxes.**

☐   Put me on Standing order for future editions.
☐   Check enclosed - $69.95 plus postage, handling & taxes.

NAME: _____

TITLE: _____

ORGANIZATION: _____

ADDRESS: _____

CITY: _____ STATE: ____ ZIP: _____

– –

Please enter my order for **Black Resource Guide Mailing Labels:**
   Pressure Sensitive Labels ....**$300.00 per set**

> Include $5.00 postage and handling.
> **Please add state and local taxes**

NAME: _____

TITLE: _____

ORGANIZATION: _____

STREET: _____

CITY: _____ STATE: ____ ZIP: _____

SIGNATURE: _____

Payable to: BLACK RESOURCE GUIDE, INC.
                 501 Oneida Place, N.W.
                 Washington, D.C. 20011
                 (202) 291-4373

**Please Note: Purchase order, check or money order must accompany
all orders.**